Unreasonable men

Vic Seidler argues that the identification of masculinity with reason has played a central role in Western concepts of modernity and the forms of social theory and philosophy which have emerged. Reason is defined in opposition to emotions while the mind is set against the body and culture set against nature, as men have learnt to take their reason for granted. This produces an 'unreasonable' form of reason that men learn to use to legislate for others, before learning to speak more personally for themselves. This is part of the power that men can assume in relation to women which is embodied in dominant forms of social theory. Emotions and feelings are discounted as forms of knowledge for they are deemed to be 'personal' and 'subjective' when contrasted with the 'objectivity' and 'impartiality' of reason. The dominant forms of social theory have worked with a universal and impersonal conception of reason which, forming our visions of language, morality and politics, have often discounted experience treating it as an effect of discourses alone.

The book demonstrates how an Enlightenment view of modernity operated to exclude and silence those who it regarded as 'others' for being closer to nature, thereby setting the terms in which 'others' have to prove themselves rational to enter the 'magic circle of humanity'. As reason is set against nature so progress is identified with the control and domination of nature. Traditions of social theory carry both the dreams and demons of a modernity which, blind to the issues of sexism, racism and anti-Semitism, could only recognize 'injustice' and 'oppression' as 'real' and 'objective' within the public world of men.

Victor Jeleniewski Seidler is Reader in Social Theory in the Department of Sociology at Goldsmiths' College, The University of London. He is the editor of *The Achilles Heel Reader*.

Male orders
Edited by Victor J. Seidler
Goldsmiths' College, University of London

MALE ORDERS attempts to understand male forms of identity, practice and association in the modern world. The series explores how dominant forms of masculinity have helped shape prevailing forms of knowledge, culture and experience. Acknowledging the challenges of feminism and gay liberation, the series attempts a broad and critical exploration of men's lives as well as engaging constructively with malestream definitions of modernity and postmodernity.

Also in this series

Recreating Sexual Politics
Men, Feminism and Politics
Victor J. Seidler

The Achilles Heel Reader
Men, Sexual Politics and Socialism
Edited by Victor J. Seidler

Men, Sex and Relationships
Writings from *Achilles Heel*
Edited by Victor J. Seidler

Men's Silences
Predicaments in Masculinity
Jonathan Rutherford

Fathers and Daughters
Sue Sharpe

Dislocating Masculinities
Comparitive Ethnographies
Edited by Andrea Cornwall and Nancy Lindisfarne

Unreasonable men

Masculinity and social theory

Victor J. Seidler

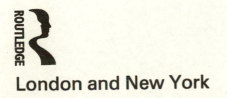

London and New York

First published 1994
by Routledge
11 New Fetter Lane, London EC4P 4EE

Simultaneously published in the USA and Canada
by Routledge
29 West 35th Street, New York, NY 10001

© 1994 Victor J. Seidler

Typeset in Times by Michael Mepham, Frome, Somerset
Printed and bound in Great Britain by
Mackays of Chatham PLC, Chatham, Kent

British Library Cataloguing in Publication Data
A catalogue record for this book is available from the British Library.

Library of Congress Cataloging in Publication Data
Seidler, Victor J., 1945 –
    Unreasonable men/Victor J. Seidler.
    p.   cm. – (Male orders)
    Includes bibliographical references and index.
    1. Masculinity (Psychology) 2. Men – Psychology. 3. Reason.
    4. Power (Social sciences) 5. Social sciences – Philosophy.
    I. Title. II. Series.
    HQ1090. S45   1993
    155.3'32 – dc20   93–3492
                                                            CIP

ISBN 0–415–08293–5 (hbk)
ISBN 0–415–08294–3 (pbk)

With regard to human affairs, not to laugh, not to cry, not to become indignant, but to understand.

Spinoza

Reason has always existed, but not always in reasonable form.

Marx

One needs time to absorb an experience until he understands not only with his head, but with his heart.

Janusz Korczak

In Loving Memory of my stepfather Leo Seidler.

Contents

Preface and acknowledgements

As men have been challenged by the theories and practices of feminism in the ways that we have grown up to think and feel in relationships, so we have also been encouraged to ask new questions of our prevailing traditions of philosophy and social theory. It has taken time to identify the ways our identities as men have been shaped by particular histories, cultures and traditions. We have become so accustomed to being able to talk on behalf of others and to legislate what would be for the best that we have rarely acknowledged how difficult it is for us to talk more personally. If anything, this reflects something 'personal' or 'psychological' rather than revealing anything more significant about the relationship of masculinity to modernity.

But within modernity shaped by the terms of the Enlightenment and the scientific revolutions of the seventeenth century, men have grown accustomed to take their reason and rationality for granted. Unlike our masculinity it is not anything that we have to constantly prove, for reason has been shaped within the image of the dominant form of masculinity. Francis Bacon could talk quite unashamedly about the new sciences as a masculinist philosophy. There was a crucial sense in which masculinity occupied a central space within modernity and in which reason and progress were to be tied with the control and domination of nature. Some of these identifications came to define the dominant forms of reason and rationality, so that to bring their historical and cultural formations into question would set you beyond the pale of reason. But we have gradually learned to listen to the dissident voices of Neitzsche, Freud and Wittgenstein who, each in their own way, have helped to question the terms of modernity. In their different ways they understood that we have to understand ourselves as children of modernity if we are to grasp how we remain trapped – for good and for evil – within its ways.

How we learn to evaluate the project of modernity and whether it has exhausted itself as we have moved into the postmodern that can only be grasped in radically different terms, has become a central question in social theory and philosophy. It crucially affects how we understand and treasure our inherited traditions, or whether we think they have to be put aside if we are to grasp the very different times in which we are living. I am wary of this tendency to ceaselessly search for new ground, since this has long been a central impulse within modernity. It is also characteristic of a particular form of restless masculinity. We are looking for an escape and are unable to detect the crisis of values that has intensified in the post-colonial and post-communist world. Often we confuse pluralism with relativism, as anything seems to go within the postmodern world. Supposedly we are to celebrate our fragmentation and discontinuity, for there is nothing beyond the realm of appearances. What we see is what we get, if we are to believe Baudrillard.

I want to begin by asking different questions, for in crucial respects much of the discussion about postmodernity shares assumptions with the cultures of modernity that it is seeking to break with. In large part it has focused around the supposed crisis in the Cartesian self which is a central figure of modernity, thinking that where there was once unity and self-knowledge there is now fragmentation and displacement. Supposedly we do not have, if we ever did, the coherent identities which allowed us to control and govern our lives through reason alone. But if this resonates with much contemporary experience it also works to undermine any sense of ourselves as gendered, ethnic or class subjects. As identities become dispersed they gain in fluidity what they lose in history. At some level it means that men are off the hook, at the very moment when they were beginning to recognise themselves in their masculinities. Rather, sexual politics, as organised around gendered relationships of power and subordination, become sidelined, as they seem to be organised around pre-existing gendered subjects. But this is crucially to fail to grasp the nature of the challenge which feminism has made to modernity.

If we imagine for a moment two people engaged in a heated discussion within their relationship and all of a sudden one partner turns round to say, 'You're being emotional, and until you are prepared to calm down so that we can have a rational and reasonable discussion, I don't want to talk to you.' If we think about who might respond in this way there is often a smile of recognition from both men and women as they identify men as being more likely to disclaim in this way. This is not simply an incident that reflects upon the individual personalities of the partners involved. It is an insight central to sexual politics to recognise, whatever the issues of sexual orientation, that there is an issue of power. If we say this as men, we have the power to put our partners down and make them feel small. We draw upon a culturally available notion, particularly within the Protestant West, that to be emotional is to be 'irrational' and 'unreasonable'. Emotions and feelings cannot be legitimated as sources of knowledge; rather, they reflect an interference or breakdown in the cool and autonomous logic of pure reason. As men, reason has been shaped in our own image within modernity, for it has been identified with the dominant forms of masculinity.

It is as if the enduring presence of patriarchy is sitting on our shoulders giving force to our words as we put others down and diminish and devalue their experience. This is what legitimates our put-downs and allows us to feel superior as men in relation to women. For it is crucial within modernity that men can take their reason for granted while women are defined by what they lack. It is women who have to prove their reason in the terms that are provided for them by men. Within an Enlightenment vision of modernity, to lack reason is to lack humanity for there is an identification, centrally expressed within Kant's writings, between reason, morality and humanity. So it is that our humanity has been centrally defined by what separates us off from nature, which is supposedly an independent and autonomous faculty of reason. As reason is defined in fundamental opposition to nature within our moral lives, so culture is set up in opposition to nature. This becomes a defining moment of modernity that has shaped the dominant traditions of philosophy and social theory.

Educated as we are to think about the Enlightenment as a moment of reason, science and progress which brings light into the long night of tradition, custom and religious superstition, it becomes difficult to identify its long shadows. We have learned, until quite recently, to separate the history of the Enlightenment and the scientific revolutions from the history of witchburnings and the terrors of slavery. Within the dominant narrative which identified progress with the domination of nature, it became difficult to illuminate how the radical shift from an organic to a mechanistic conception of nature went hand in hand with the devaluation and objectification of those who were deemed to be closer to nature. The magical circle of humanity was tightly drawn. It worked through a system of exclusions. Women and children were deemed to be closer to nature. As far as Kant was concerned, it was only through seeking the guidance of men through marriage that women could learn to steer their lives through reason. So it was that the subordination of women and the devaluation of their experience was written into the terms of modernity. Feminism has been crucially important in questioning the terms of modernity, through challenging the abiding distinction between reason and emotion.

For too long we have learned to think about slavery as a blot on the progress towards a promised freedom and equality. It has been treated as an isolated topic on its own rather than as central to our conceptions of the West. We may need to rethink the ways that the Enlightenment, particularly in Kant's writings, offered us a secularised form of Protestantism. The relationship of Christianity to modernity is far more complex than a movement from faith towards reason and science. The disdain for the body and emotional life was given a new shape in the devaluation of the 'animal' and 'nature'. As people of colour were seen as 'animals' and 'children', so the notion of the white man's burden took shape and colonial exploitation became legitimated as a moral duty. The devaluation of nature was connected to its objectification as matter for nature was no longer recognised as a source of meanings and values. With the disenchantment of nature, as Max Weber calls it, there are no limits in the uses to which we can put nature. We became deaf to the cries of pain, for there was nothing to hear.

I argue that it is crucial to recognise how the distinction between reason and nature has been basic to our conceptions of an Enlightenment modernity. The relationship of masculinity to modernity becomes a crucial point of investigation because of the identification of masculinity with reason. This is not to say that men are 'unreasonable' but that within modernity we learn as men to take for granted a particular concept of reason. This separation of reason from nature both works to divide men from their emotions and feelings which become threatening to our identities as men and so to estrange men from their emotional lives. We learn to disdain emotions and feelings as signs of weakness and so as potentially compromising our sense of male identity. This creates an abiding tension, since masculinity is always something we have to be ready to defend. Unlike our reason, it is not something that we can ever take for granted. Rather it becomes a constant source of anxiety.

While exploring the impact of a dominant form of masculinity which can set the terms through which not only men but also women can feel that they have to evaluate their experience, I have tried not to generalise about the experience of men in general. I have attempted to be clear that I am talking from particular experience of white, middle-class Jewish masculinity while at the same time drawing upon resonances with other masculinities which have grown up under the shadow of an enlightenment masculinity. It would be for others to share differences for I am explicitly questioning a right for men to speak for others before we have learned *how* to speak more personally for ourselves.

Within a Protestant moral culture in its secularised form, men are locked into a struggle with their animal natures. At some level, men are haunted by a sense that they cannot escape their animal natures which are always ready to break through. It is as if there is a central tension between the idea of men as rational selves able to govern their lives through reason alone and an animal sexuality that we have to learn to curb and control. As Freud came to grasp, self-knowledge becomes particularly threatening for men, for we risk discovering that we are 'other' than we present ourselves to be. The disdain for sexuality and bodily life is written into a Cartesian tradition which seeks to identify the self with the mind and reason. We supposedly only have an inner relationship with our reason which is also the source of our freedom and autonomy. Echoing a long Christian tradition, the body is treated as a prison that serves to trap the mind or the soul. We learn to treat the body instrumentally as if it were a machine that has to be trained. But since the body is part of nature it is governed by laws that are external. Similarly, emotions and feelings are supposedly located in our bodies. As Kant develops it they are sources of unfreedom and determination which seek to influence our behaviour externally. We learn to minimise their influence as we identify ourselves with reason alone.

The distinction between culture and nature which would treat the 'natural' as given and so as ahistorical and culture as 'socially and historically constructed' remains crucial to a structuralist tradition. I want to explore the sources of this disdain for nature and emotional life, for it is part of a fragmentation that has been written into modernity. It is partly a refusal to take the coherence and unity of the Cartesian self for granted as has so often been done in working out the relationship between identity and modernity. We have to think more clearly about *how* we have learned to live a Cartesian dualism in our disdain for sexuality and emotional life. This places a concern with the relationship between masculinity and reason at the heart of a renewed social theory which is prepared to integrate the different aspects of our being, recognising that we are more than the rational selves we often take ourselves to be. Foucault's Madness and Civilisation becomes a valuable source, for he traces the history through which we have learned to disdain imagination, dreams and fantasies as forms of 'unreason'.

Within a rationalist intellectual culture we have to learn to control our emotions and feelings, for they can only be recognised as interferences in a life of reason. We learn to fear our emotions and feelings which have no place within the public realm. We embody a notion of self-control as involving the domination and silencing of our emotional lives. We learn to control our experience through managing the meanings that we assign, so that we are often disturbed when others question our feelings. Learning to pride ourselves as men in being independent and self-sufficient, we often reject those who are closest to us. It is as if we do not have emotional needs of our own as men, for needs are a sign of weakness and seem to reflect a lack of self-control. This self-sufficiency can make it difficult in relationships, for it creates its own forms of inequality as women are often left feeling that they alone have emotional needs and demands. Within social theory and philosophy this reflects itself in the poverty of a language of relationships. We are more comfortable with explaining individual actions that can be assessed on rational grounds alone. It becomes difficult to think creatively about how to relate freedom to relationships, assuming in male terms that relationships have to involve a sacrifice of freedom as self-sufficiency.

As ecology has helped us to rethink how the disdain for nature has been written into dominant forms of social theory, it has also helped to introduce notions of balance. For if we are to rework our inherited conceptions of reason and notions of identity in terms of a rational self, we do not simply want to reverse the framework. Rather we seek different notions of self-control that grow out of a familiarity and relationship with our emotional lives. Again it is important to stress that some of these dualities affect women almost as much as men, for they have grown up within the terms of a dominant rationalist culture. This has helped set the terms in which they learn to evaluate their own experience and seek to affirm themselves. Consciousness-raising has helped women explore the workings of these processes within their own lives as they have learned not to internalise blame and responsibility but to grasp the nature of women's oppression. Feminism helped women to create space and time in which they could begin to explore their own meanings and values as they learned to value differences between them as well as different sources of knowledge.

Feminism has also helped illuminate the ways modernity has been shaped by a prevailing distinction between public and private life. It involved a brutal reordering of gender relations as women were excluded from the public sphere and as the public sphere was redefined as a sphere of male reason. Women were confined in the private sphere of emotional life and sexuality. As Rousseau put it, women's sexuality was deemed as a threat to male reason so that women were to be blamed for arousing the sexual feelings of men. So it was that men learned to displace their responsibility on to women and so never learned to take responsibility for their emotional and sexual lives. Women were made to feel responsible for the happiness and well-being of their partners and were despised at the same time for doing the emotional work. The nature of men's emotional dependency on women became hidden. Issues of sexuality and emotional life became invisible within the rationality terms of social theory. They were issues within personal life alone and so were not to be taken seriously. It was to do with women's work in the home and so was barely reflected upon until the 1960s within the terms of social theory. Sexuality, like male violence, was given little recognition within theoretical traditions which could only marginalise it.

The feminist idea that the personal is political was a central challenge to traditions of social theory, including Marx, who had insisted that oppression and injustice were only real within the public realm. Even if Marx helped to question the terms of distributive justice it has taken feminism to remind us that justice has to do with the ways people treat each other. To treat someone as a sexual object alone is to do them an injustice. As Simone Weil has argued, there is a prior sense of justice that has to do with dignity and integrity, so that, in her example if a young girl is dragged into a brothel against her will it is not simply her rights which are being infringed. A liberal language of rights is inadequate to illuminate the moral realities of the situation. There is a violation of the person that cannot be grasped in psychological terms alone. The importance of Weil for social theory is in reminding us of the inescapable connections between power and morality. She offers a way through a crisis of values, despite all the difficulties of her work which a post-structuralist tradition has so often left us with. In learning to treat values as 'subjective' or 'relative', we have found few ways of recognising their centrality for a meaningful social theory.

This resonates with the difficulties of a Protestant inheritance that sees our natures as evil so that we have to look beyond ourselves for the source of our morality. We should not dwell upon emotions and feelings, for they are forms of a self-indulgence that can only lead us astray from the true path. This is part of the arrogance of reason that can set a single path. The issue is then why 'others' have somehow failed to take the path to freedom and modernity. This distrust of nature – of people being able to trust themselves to discover what is meaningful for them – is all too often echoed in the fears around 'essentialism'. Again we fall for a simple duality where the rejection of any conception of 'human nature' goes along with a welcoming of identities as socially and historically constructed. Both sides of this duality need to be rethought as we begin to recognise the deeper structures of a Protestant moral culture. As we learn to distrust our own natures, so we learn that we can only believe in the objective workings of reason. We have to learn to do what is expected of us as we distrust our 'inclinations', for as Durkheim has learned from Kant, left to ourselves we are 'selfish' and 'egoistic'. Society takes the place of reason as providing us with a higher vision of ourselves.

Both Durkheim and Weber draw from a rationalist framework that was prepared by Kant. Weber came to recognise in *The Protestant Ethic and the Spirit of Capitalism* how easy it was for a particular form of reason to become unreasonable, as within the Protestant ethic, work became an end in itself. His text can be helpfully read as an exploration of a particular dominant form of masculinity. It stands as a clear example of how traditions of social theory have unwittingly articulated the experience of dominant masculinities. It has helped to set the new terms of citizenship, presenting them as universal and available to all while at the same time defining 'others' as lacking. The racism and anti-semitism that disfigure so many Enlightenment texts show how much has been hidden from history as traditions have been handed down to us. If people of colour and Jews were to be allowed to join the magic circle of humanity they had to be clear about what it was that they would be prepared to give up to become 'other' than themselves.

The Frankfurt School stressed the dominance of instrumental reason within capitalist societies so that traditions of social theory had lost a capacity to evaluate the ends of action. The scientific rationality that informed the destruction of European Jewry as well as gays, gypsies and the mentally ill in the Holocaust raises fundamental questions about the relationships of reason, science and progress. These issues have long been avoided as fascism has too often been explored as an aberration that marks a breakdown of reason. Horrors have been passed over in silence and our intellectual and philosophical cultures have played their own part in creating the conditions of denial. We have avoided difficult questions of the ways that the Holocaust was deeply implicated with both the conditions of modernity, but also with the relationship between Christianity and modernity. It is salutary to be reminded of the number of professionals holding scientific Ph.Ds who were involved in conceiving and executing the 'final solution' to the 'Jewish question'. When I was a student of philosophy and sociology in the 1960s and 1970s these issues were never raised, for there was little acknowledgement of the ways they challenged the intellectual frameworks that we had inherited within modernity. Even if these issues are not directly addressed, I hopefully begin to ask questions that cast some relevant light.

I worked on an early draft of some of these ideas while on a trip to Brazil in the Summer of 1990. It was a difficult time of family loss that was not made any easier with my absorption in these ideas. It never feels easy to retain a balance between the demands of writing and the demands of family and relationships, especially if you are used to pretending that you can manage it. I want to thank Anna for her love and understanding, though I know it wasn't easy. Daniel and Lily also had to put up with my distractions and I know that they do not look back to it as an easy time. I appreciated their patience and know that we also had some good times. They have both constantly reminded me of what matters in life and why it is so important for men to engage wholeheartedly in a process of change. I would also like to thank my Brazilian family, Marilyn and Sammy Caro with Paulinho and Juliana, for their constant love and support. I also benefited from stimulating conversations with Professor Bruni and other members of the Department of Sociology at the University of Sao Paulo. It was wonderful to talk with people who had also been influenced by Wittgenstein's writings in their social theory.

In the late stages of rewriting I appreciated the support of Chris Rojek who was always enthusiastic about the project as well as comments and support from David

Boadella, Larry Blum, Arthur Brittan, Anna Ichowitz, Sally Inman, Annie and Bob Moore, Caroline Ramazanoglu, Janet Sayers and Tony Seidler. In their different ways they made it clearer.

I also learned a great deal from a trip to Leipzig in December 1991 with my stepfather, Leo Seidler. He was returning a year after unification in the hope that he might be able to receive a doctorate in Law that he had been deprived of over fifty years ago when the Nazis took power in the faculty and he was advised to leave. Somehow he had cherished the hope that justice would be done at long last and we were extremely kindly received by the Dean of the Faculty who did everything that he could on our behalf. It was a trip that helped to heal many wounds as we walked and talked around the city which had changed beyond all recognition, yet was warmly familiar. I cherish those days and Leo's generosity in sharing a painful history and helping me to recover some of my own. Sadly he died before he ever got the degree. This book is dedicated to his memory. I am reminded of how many others were to suffer an even more bitter fate. If we are not to forget them we have to find ways of understanding.

Victor Jeleniewski Seidler

Chapter 1

Introduction

Masculinity, modernity and social theory

ENLIGHTENMENT AND SOCIAL THEORY

Sociology has emerged as a child of the Enlightenment and it seeks its ancestry within the forms of thought and feeling that characterised the Enlightenment. But it is also in part a reaction to the rationalism that supposedly gave birth to the extremes of the French Revolution.[1] It is less common to rethink social theory in terms of the particular Enlightenment identification of masculinity with reason and the notion that society should be made an 'order of reason', with the idea that society should be recast and remade in the 'image of men'. This is to lay bare a particular relationship between masculinity and our inherited forms of social and political theory.

A guiding notion of the Enlightenment that has helped to shape our conceptions of modernity is the idea that through reason alone we can guide and control our lives. It is crucial that reason comes to define our humanity and that our humanity is cast *in opposition* to our 'animal' natures. With both Descartes and Kant, reason is defined as an independent faculty that is set in opposition to our animal natures.

So it is that the relationship of social theory to a masculinity that appropriates reason as its own defining quality is *tied up* with the relationship of social theory to 'nature'. Social theory is to become an aspect of civilisation's attempts to define itself as a feature of modernity and its struggle against nature. So it is that social theory is to be defined in antagonistic relationship to an 'inner nature', with Kant's guiding influence upon the writings of both Durkheim and Weber, and is to be irrevocably connected to an idea that 'progress' and 'civilisation' are to be identified with the domination of the natural world.

The Enlightenment established a sharp distinction between reason and nature and this antagonism to the 'natural' remains central within contemporary social theory that is cast within structuralist terms. It echoes a prevailing distinction between 'culture' and 'nature' that has established itself as part of the common sense of the human sciences.[2] Both Durkheim and Lévi-Strauss rely upon a distinction between nature and culture, with the idea that nature can be identified with the 'given' and 'unchanging'.

Since nature is what we supposedly share, it cannot help to explain the characteristic features of different societies. The idea seems to be that nature is essentially ahistorical and uncreative. It may be of concern to the biologist but it has little to teach the human sciences. In a similar way that our humanity can be supposedly identified with a faculty of reason that separates us off from the animal world, so language as an embodiment of reason is taken to be the defining feature of culture and society. This has placed language as a central concern.

Kant is a central figure in the Enlightenment and he has helped set the terms for both Durkheim and Weber's influence within classical sociology. It was Kant who, following Descartes, established reason as an independent faculty set in opposition to nature. This helped set a fragmented conception of the person at the heart of classical sociology. It established the person as essentially egoistic and selfish if left to his or her own devices. The idea of the individual as infinitely acquisitive and eternally dissatisfied was placed at the core of social theory.

As individuals we could not know fulfilment but only temporary and fleeting satisfaction. We were, in Weber's image of *The Protestant Ethic and the Spirit of Capitalism*, to be continually striving. We were to be continually on edge as we were struggling with a sense of inadequacy to reach beyond ourselves. If this was a feature that Weber identified with capitalism, it was also to be enshrined as a welcome feature of modernity.[3] It was supposedly a strength of modernity when it was compared with traditional societies, which stood accused of not being prepared to develop themselves.

Durkheim had inherited this dualistic vision of human nature from Kant. Its egoism worried him because he sensed that if individuals insisted on pursuing their selfish interests then there would be no sources of social cohesion and solidarity. Durkheim is a theorist of social order in the sense that he accepted the terms set by Comte and Saint-Simon to create the conditions of social solidarity and so avoid the divisions that had marked the French Revolution.[4] He recognised that its idealism had been flawed for it had led to violence and untold misery. This was a price that Durkheim was not willing to pay. He searched for other mechanisms of social transformation which would soften and ameliorate class conflicts and struggles before they broke out into open warfare.

At the same time he recognised the flaws of a utilitarian theory that settled for a calculus of utility. He was dissatisfied with its narrow materialism and its vision of material interests as the guiding theme in people's lives, wanting to conceive of human well-being in broader terms than those of utility. He wanted people to learn to identify in something larger than themselves. It was here that he accepted Kant's challenge to utilitarianism. Kant looked towards duty as something that we could discern through our faculty of reason. It was a higher part of ourselves and so provided a possible escape from selfish interests.

Durkheim adopted this dualistic vision of the person as his own while shifting its terms. He found a way of providing us with a rhetoric of morality while in part undermining a sense of morality through identifying the moral with the 'social'. It was society that was the source of morality for Durkheim. It was to take the place of duty in Kant's moral vision. It is supposedly society that can present us with a higher vision of ourselves, a way of escaping from the demands of a selfish nature. But this is to place morality as essentially *outside* of the individual, somehow provided for by society. Morality becomes externalised as a matter of sanctions and rules as we lose touch with the recognition of interiority that was still part of Kant's Protestant vision.

For Kant, morality was a matter of the moral law and if this remained essentially external, it was through the interiority of reason that we supposedly came to know the duties that it set for us.[5] It was important for Kant's Enlightenment vision that the inner light of reason would often set us in opposition to traditional relationships of power and authority. As we moved away from the darkness of traditional relationships we were to learn to trust the authority of our own reason. We were to learn to think for ourselves and we were to be prepared to argue that traditional authorities of church and aristocracy were to be transformed so that they would accord with reason. It was in this crucial sense that the Enlightenment held that society was to be reorganised according to the demands of reason. It was paradoxically also to prepare the ground for the fateful identification between reason and freedom, as if people could somehow be forced to be free so long as reason was somehow being followed.

For the Enlightenment, reason remained a central notion that brought into question traditional relationships of power and authority. It insisted that authority had to be prepared to justify itself. There was a democratic impulse which insisted that people were equally rational moral agents but equally there was another strain that sought to legitimate the authority of reason. It is this which connects to the authority of a 'rational masculinity', as if men could think of reason as their own and so legitimate the organisation of private and public life in their own image. In part, this resonates with a lack of interiority and inner life that characterises dominant forms of masculinity.

It is as if men learn to use their reason to define what is best both for themselves and for others. As men, we often take it to be our particular task to know what is best. Since we speak with the authority of reason, it is easy for others to be silenced. As men, we learn *to set the terms* within which others can speak. So for Kant it was only in relation to men that women could supposedly escape the hold of their natures and seek the guidance of reason. The authority of reason was clearly tied up with the patriarchal authority of men. Women and children were to exist in relation to men, not as persons in their own right. To the extent that Kant's Enlightenment conception of reason still sustains liberal conceptions of freedom and equality, these visions remain set within men's terms. This partly explains why feminist theory had eventually to challenge liberal conceptions of rights as adequate expressions of freedom and equality.[6] The Women's Movement learned to speak of oppression and liberation as a way of setting their own terms for participation in the public world of men.

Setting a discussion of reason in gendered terms can help to bring into focus the ways that the Enlightenment conception of reason was critical and the ways it fails to be. It taught men to trust in their own reasoning, while at the same time it suggested that answers were to be found in a separate and autonomous realm of their own. In Kant it is clear that it is through reason and a pure will that we can learn to act according to the moral law. Even if this is a law that we supposedly give to ourselves, it still exists independently of our everyday social lives.

This was important for Kant, who was concerned to challenge Hume's empiricism, particularly the notion that morality is relative to the law and customs of a particular society. Kant wants to challenge a relativism that has recently grown into the common sense of the human sciences. For Kant, this is to reduce the powers of reason and make them relative to a particular society or culture. It was crucial for Kant that reason provides an external and independent point from which particular customs and laws can be evaluated. Reason is to be sovereign.

If we have learned to identify modernity with the sovereignty of reason in the recent discussions around features of postmodernity, we have to be careful in discerning the strengths of Kant's challenge to a relativism that has become all too familiar. It we are to escape from the terms of discussion as they were set by the Enlightenment, namely between a rationalist objectivism on the one hand and a pluralistic relativism on the other, then we have to look more carefully at the ways reason was conceptualised. This questions the terms in which the discussions about modernity and post-modernity are usually set.[7]

Rather than focusing upon a distinction between a unified Cartesian conception of reason and a fragmented pluralistic vision of diverse reasons and rationalities, we begin to investigate some of the implications of reason being set in opposition to nature. A sensitivity to issues of gender and ethnicity raises this immediately for it recognises how women, blacks, Jews, gays and lesbians were all in their different ways excluded from the magic circle of humanity. They were deemed to be closer to nature. If they had a voice at all it was not a voice that could be heard within the realms of reason.[8]

But before exploring these issues it is important to recognise the part that sociology, particularly in its positivist expressions, has played in stilling the critical voice of reason. Even if this was a masculine voice it could still be critical, as it was, for instance in Hegel's response to the Enlightenment. Hegel refused to legitimate existing social relationships as 'rational' because they were 'real'. Within a positivist culture we are so used to accusing those who are prepared to imagine a different reality or to live different relationships with others as romantics and dreamers, that it can be hard to listen to what Hegel is saying.

Hegel insists that we do not have to confine our thinking to what exists, so allowing reason to be fixed by existing realities. We have to be prepared to recognise the irrationality in existing relationships so that they have to be *negated* if they are to be made 'rational'. So, for instance, there is no way that slavery can be justified and the fact that it exists as an institution does not make it rational. As Simone Weil thought of it, oppression is a denial of human dignity. It is quite wrong to say that it is relative to the customs and practices of particular societies. This is what draws her to Kant. It is also what makes Aristotle so objectionable to her, because he thought that slavery could be defended.[9]

Hegel tended to assume that people would struggle against conditions of exploitation and oppression. They would challenge institutions and relationships which negated their humanity. This was the source of the historical dialectic for Hegel for it meant that people would negate their conditions until they were eventually transformed into an expression of their humanity. It is this which allows Hegel to think of history as a struggle for freedom and justice.[10] He believed in the historical process as a form of historical subject that sought to bring into existence a regime of reason and freedom as it realised itself.

This helped to form Marx's belief in the proletariat as a historical subject. He shared the Enlightenment belief in reason and progress, as it was transformed by Hegel into a historical vision. In this sense Marxism shared with liberalism a confidence in the progressive nature of the historical process. They shared an Enlightenment inheritance, though it has been hard to discern this influence in Marx's work because he is also opposed to much that it stood for. But he shared its universal aspirations and its dreams of emancipation.

The crisis of modernity is partly characterised by a loss of confidence in this vision of progress as well as the universal terms in which is it expressed. In its different versions this dream seems to have lost much of its grip on us. If we are drawn back to the Enlightenment, it is not to its historical confidence and its belief in progress, but to its scepticism. We have grown suspicious of its grand claims and even of its promises of a transformed life. This feeling has particularly deep roots in Eastern and Central Europe. Vaclav Havel in 'An anatomy of reticence' talks of the

almost mysterious horror of everything overstated, enthusiastic, lyrical, pathetic, or overly serious that is inseparable from our spiritual climate....It seems that in our central European context what is most earnest has a way of blending in a particularly tense manner with what is most comic. It seems that it is precisely the dimension of distance, of rising above oneself and making light of oneself, which lends to our concerns and actions precisely the right amount of shattering seriousness. Is not Franz Kafka, one of the most serious and tragic authors of this century, at the same time a humorist?

(Havel 1987:181)

Havel recognised that 'emotional enthusiasm and rationalistic utopianism are often no more than two sides of the same coin' (1987:181). Simone Weil would have identified with these sentiments though she could also be very earnest and found it difficult to place her concerns in any kind of perspective. But her scepticism about history and progress makes her voice strikingly pertinent even if it is yet to be properly heard. Where she differs from Foucault and post-structuralists is in the intensity of her moral vision.

She refuses moral relativism and any idea that morality is an effect of discourse, which is being continually articulated in different terms. Such relativism makes it impossible to reject fascism in unequivocal terms. She tended to take an absolutist position herself, adopting a religious language and coming increasingly to identify with a realm of moral absolutes. In her later Christian writings it was important that truth, goodness and beauty existed outside of history. She came to distrust a positivistic sociology that would exclude a discussion of values. She helps us to recognise that part of the damage of an Enlightenment inheritance was the way that it separated knowledge from morality, facts from values, science from the humanities. For her this was a weakness within a humanistic tradition. There is much to engage with in her writings if we want to explore ways of reconnecting morality with social theory, even if we reject some of the positions she eventually reached.

Simone Weil came to recognise the tragic consequences of the split between the sciences and the humanities.[11] The Enlightenment was shaped by this guiding opposition. It was integral to the Cartesian inheritance, though its implications for social and political theory still remain to be explored. The natural world was accepted as a world of forces governed by particular laws which could be discovered. The empirical world of science was the world of unfreedom and determination. Within the Cartesian framework nature was no longer conceived in living organic terms but as having died and only existing as matter.

It was through reason that science was able to discern the laws of nature. With Newton this was still conceived as a religious quest, for science was not yet thought of as a secular practice which sought to replace transcendental explanations with explanations from natural causes. But it is also crucial that the scientific revolutions of the seventeenth century conceive of science as a masculinist practice, as part of the development, as Francis Bacon thought of it, of a new masculine philosophy. Science was to be an objective activity that worked with impartial laws. As men in their rationality were to remain unmoved by emotions and feelings, so were the sciences that were created in their image.

With Descartes, we have a mechanistic conception of the universe in which it is only what can be quantified that is real and objective. If Weil is right, there is considerable tension between the vision of science connected to manual skills that Descartes espoused and what came to be viewed as Cartesianism, which tended to reinforce a sharp and unbridgeable gap between mental and physical labour.[12] It embodied the categorical distinction between mind and matter that has done so much to organise our visions of modernity. It left us with a dualistic conception of the person who was caught between the determinations of the physical world, to the extent that we are embodied physical beings, and the mental world in which we could be free and creative.

This was to be reflected in the prevailing split between the sciences and the humanities. It was built upon a particular conception of nature – both our inner natures and the natural world we live in. In large part it set the terms for our traditions of social and political theory which were largely expressions of the tensions of an Enlightenment vision of modernity that was largely taken for granted.

REASON AND NATURE

Descartes set the terms for the opposition between reason and nature. As mind was set in opposition to matter, so was reason set in opposition to nature. It was through reason that we could be free from the determinations of nature. When Descartes says *cogito, ergo sum*, the emphasis is on our thinking as the guarantee of our existence. It is as if we can only exist as individuals to the extent that we learn to think for ourselves.

But our thinking is essentially disembodied and disconnected from our emotional lives that have their grounding in the life of the body. For our bodies are part of nature. We are destined to have an *externalised* relationship to our bodies because they can have no connection to our identity as rational selves. But this vision of the rational self has also been critical in forming modernist conceptions of masculinity. It is men who have learned to claim reason as their own.

Within the Cartesian framework there is little space for the social. It was Kant who worked out that as rational selves we could live as moral agents. He recognised that we live in different worlds and, to the extent that we are empirical selves, our behaviour is unfree and determined. But to the extent that we can abstract ourselves and lift ourselves above our animal natures, so we can be free and self-determining. It is as intelligible beings that we can be moral agents.

This vision of freedom and morality sets the terms for both Durkheim and Weber, though in different ways. Durkheim's early work sets out a positivist vision in which we learn to treat social facts as things and to explore the ways that people's behaviour is governed by social laws. In setting itself in opposition to psychologism it questions the explanations that individuals might otherwise give of their behaviour in terms of intentions and motives. But it sets morality beyond reach of the individual, to be identified with the rights and obligations that are set by society. If our obligations and duties change this is largely because of the division of labour. It is the contractual terms of an organic solidarity that brings the workings of reason into a clearer focus within the social realm.

Durkheim inherits Kant's dismissive attitude towards the natural. If people were left to themselves they would simply follow their egoistic interests. It is society that presents individuals with a higher vision of themselves. Because of this it is important to challenge liberal assumptions that would set individuality against the rules and sanctions of society.

Rather, as Durkheim makes clear, it is society that makes possible a more elaborate and developed form of individuality. As Durkheim responds to M. Brunschwig's attempt to define the progress of civilisation in terms of the individual freedoms which can be exercised 'against the material structure of society':

> These rights and liberties are not inherent in man as such. If you analyse man's constitution you will find no trace of this sacredness with which he is invested and which confers upon him these rights. This character has been added to him by society. Society has consecrated the individual and made him pre-eminently worthy of respect. His progressive emancipation does not imply a weakening

but a transformation of the social bonds. The individual does not tear himself from society but is joined to it in a new manner, and this is because society sees him in a new manner and wishes this change to take place.

(Durkheim 1974:72)

It is through society that individuals can escape from the determinations of nature. For, as Durkheim has it, 'It is to society that we owe the power over matter which is our glory. It is society that has freed us from nature' (Durkheim 1974:13). So it is that society is to be defined in opposition to nature and

Is it not then to be expected that we think of it as a mental being higher than ourselves, from which our mental powers emanate? This explains why it is that when it demands of us those sacrifices, great or small, that make up our moral life, we bow before its demands with deference.

(Durkheim 1974:73)

If it demands different sacrifices from men and women, so be it. We have to learn to be grateful for the particular burdens that we carry. In this context it is difficult to challenge the collective, for its 'moral authority is a psychic reality, a higher and richer conscience than our own, one upon which we feel that our own depends.' (Durkheim 1974:73). This is a secularised version of a particular religious vision which places the source of authority beyond our individual selves in the collective:

The believer bows before his God, because it is from God that he believes that he holds his being, particularly his mental being, his soul. We have the same reasons for experiencing this feeling before the collective.

(Durkheim 1974:73)

This helps to explain why for Durkheim 'the individual submits to society and this submission is the condition of his liberation'. The gendered language carries its own visions of authority, for if freedom is conceived of as wrought from an endless struggle against nature, so, if women are conceived of as closer to nature, then, as with Kant, it is up to women similarly to submit themselves to the authority of men as the condition of their 'liberation'. Durkheim tacitly complies with a masculinist conception of freedom as wrought from a struggle against nature. He looks towards society for a deliverance and protection against the forces of nature. Invoking images forged in the Enlightenment and familiar to Kant, he has it that

for man, freedom consists in deliverance from blind, unthinking, physical forces; this he achieves by opposing against them the great and intelligent force which is society, under whose protection he shelters.

(Durkheim 1974:72)

As these images are externalised, they are easily applied to the threat posed by women to the authority of men. It is part of the great chain of being that man should learn to exercise authority in relation to women who, being closer to nature, are more subject to its 'blind, unthinking physical forces'. As men have to put themselves under the authority of society, so women have to accept the authority of men. Since within this scheme we are supposedly all dependent in our own way, there is little to object to in terms of equality. As Durkheim has it,

> By putting himself under the wing of society, he makes himself also, to a great extent, dependent upon it. But this is a liberating dependence. There is no paradox here.
>
> (Durkheim 1974:72)

It is only if we are blind to the wisdom of the collective that we can supposedly discern anything objectionable here.

Durkheim sets himself against a particular form of liberal individualism. He is confident that society 'is the source and seat of all the intellectual benefits that constitute civilization' (Durkheim 1974:73), and that 'from society derive all the essentials of our mental life' (Durkheim 1974:73). He argues against the view that there is more in the mind of an individual than in the most perfect and complex society by confessing 'that to me it is the exact opposite which has always appeared to be obvious' (Durkheim 1974:67). He is convinced that 'the assembly of moral and intellectual benefits which constitute civilization at each moment of its history has its seat in the collective mind, not in the individual' (Durkheim 1974:67).

This is a crucial insight that has helped form structuralist theory in the diverse hands of Althusser, Lacan and Lévi-Strauss.[13] It awakens us to the significance of structures of language, myth and customs, into which individuals are born and which help to organise their subjectivities. It teaches us a particular humility before these structures as we learn to appreciate the extent to which they help to form and organise our individuality and experience. Durkheim's insights have remained a guiding inspiration for the implicit 'collectivism' that has underpinned a structuralist tradition.

The rationalist tradition of the Enlightenment which sets reason in a categorical way against nature is sustained by a structuralist tradition. It works to define culture in fundamental opposition to nature. For while nature is essentially given and ahistorical, it is culture that is largely conceived of as a linguistic phenomenon. We have learned to think of reason as an autonomous faculty, as the quality that separates us off from animals and so defines our humanity. Within twentieth-century social theory, largely under the influence of Jacobson and Saussure, we have learned to think of language in these autonomous terms.

But language has not simply occupied the space that was defined for reason, for it is also clear that while we learn to think of reason as an individual faculty which allows individuals to define their individuality through learning to think for themselves, we also learn to treat language as a collective resource that helps form and articulate our experience and identities through the categories it provides. Language has moved into a position of priority, as it has been assumed that the signs which language provides for us are the terms in which the social world is classified. As nature is assumed to be given, the ways in which it is ordered are provided for us by language. If this view can be identified with Durkheim and Saussure, it is fundamentally challenged by the later Wittgenstein, who, as we shall go on to explore, suggests a different relationship between language and experience.

Durkheim has been important in shifting the emphasis away from an Enlightenment conception of reason. He makes clear that

> in the sphere of morality, as in other spheres of nature, *individual* reason has no particular prestige as such. The only reason for which one can claim the right of intervention, and of rising above historical moral reality in order to reform it, is not my reason or yours; it is the impersonal human reason, only truly realized in science.
>
> (Durkheim 1974:65)

When Kant talks of a faculty of reason, he is not talking about 'my reason or yours' but a universal conception of reason that stands in contrast to my individual egoistic concerns. But Kant would still want to talk of reason as a moral faculty and this is what Durkheim sets himself against as a form of apriorism. As he explains it,

> If what is meant by the word is a moral faculty which contains, in an immanent state, a moral ideal, the *true* ideal which is able to oppose and should oppose, to that which society follows at each moment of its history, I say that this *a priorism* is an arbitrary affirmation which all known facts contradict.
>
> (Durkheim 1974:66)

In this regard Durkheim sets himself in opposition to the moral philosophy of Kant.[14] He recognises that 'the ambition of moral philosophers has more often been to construct a new morality' (Durkheim 1974:75) and 'they have never set up as their goal the faithful representation, without addition or subtraction, of a given moral reality' (Durkheim 1974:75). As far as Durkheim is concerned, 'they teach us what passes in the public mind of one particular epoch and they must therefore be accounted for'; but on the other hand he recognises 'the existence of a moral reality beyond the minds of the philosophers who try to express it' (Durkheim 1974:76). He recognises that

> We all practise this morality without troubling, for the most part, about the reasons given by philosophers to justify it. The proof of this is the embarrassment we should feel if anyone were to demand of us a solid rational justification of the moral rules that we observe.
>
> (Durkheim 1974:77)

But in its way this is to restrict the terms of moral criticism. It reinforces a regime of obedience and subordination, if not to the way that society is now, then at least to what it is emerging to be. This undermines any Marxist sense that society might be organised in the interests of those who are rich and powerful, and that moral conceptions in large part legitimate this power. It also minimises the extent to which society can be recognised as working in the interests of men, enforcing the subordination of women. Its implicit rationalism tends to foster the idea that the rules of society are somehow organised in the higher interests of all.

It sustains the universalism of the Enlightenment that argues for a unified conception of 'society'. If there are sectional interests, they are 'functional' within this whole. So it is that if inequalities can somehow be shown to be in the interests of all, they can be legitimated. It stands in opposition to a vision that says a society might be judged through the ways that it accords dignity and respect to its least advantaged citizens, like those people who are old, sick or mentally ill. For this is to focus on the quality of life of individuals in a way that becomes oddly inadmissible. The focus in these rationalist forms of social theory lies elsewhere, in the rational organisation of the whole which is taken to be a concern of reason alone.

A weakness that emerges from Durkheim's holistic rationalism is the difficulty it creates for evaluating the quality of individual lives. It is as if we are left bereft of criteria with which to evaluate particular forms of social and personal relationships. What matters for Kant is the moral worth that individuals can accrue through acting according to the moral law. But this sense of the moral life is not available to Durkheim, though both rely upon a sharp distinction between reason and nature.

Both assume a structure of moral theory that is bounded by a distinction between egoism and altruism and both assume that if individuals followed their inclinations and desires they would irremediably be drawn towards selfishness. If the moral law is there to redeem individuals from a selfish nature, so society stands for Durkheim as a way for individuals to escape from the demands of their natures. In place for both is a Protestant denial of natural desire as inherently selfish and egoistic. We are to learn to look beyond ourselves as we grow up to *despise* our natures.

It is striking how social theory has remained faithful to these Protestant assumptions, so much so that much recent talk of desire in post-structuralist theory can feel empty and rhetorical. This is hardly surprising since, unless we are prepared to face these Protestant structures of denial, it is difficult to talk meaningfully of desire, let alone love. We often remain trapped within a structuralist opposition between an essentialist vision of human nature and an idea that experience, like individuality, has thereby to be seen as 'socially and historically constructed'.

This makes it difficult to explore the tacit workings of these Protestant assumptions within a supposed secular moral culture. This is a rationalistic dilemma, which paradoxically leaves us at considerable distance to the self. It leaves us outside and estranged from ourselves, unable to make the first step towards a fuller contact with ourselves. We are left with the hollow ring of discourses that are somehow supposed to be able to deliver our identities in all their live complexities.

These are different incarnations of the prevailing Enlightenment distinction between reason and nature. For as nature is given, so the form that it takes is provided by the categories of mind. Our emotions, feelings and desires, as part of an unredeemed nature, learn to keep their silence. They are denigrated as sources of knowledge or as ways of developing a fuller contact with ourselves.

For as rational selves we learn that we can only know ourselves through reason and that reason is the only way that we can guide our lives. We learn to *silence* our natures and so we also become deaf to the cries of others, learning to treat them as 'emotional' or 'subjective'. The link between rationalism and Protestant conceptions of human nature remains part of the deeper structures of social theories which, like Durkheim and Weber, find a particular inspiration in Kant.

The denigration of nature goes hand in hand with the denigration of women who are supposedly closer to nature. It also connects to the denigration of our inner emotional lives which are not properly treated as sources of knowledge. So much of this has been left implicit within the dualities, say between holism and individualism, structure and action, meaning and cause, that have dominated contemporary forms of social theory.

It has meant that the various challenges of feminist theory to traditions of positivism, marxism and phenomenology have largely gone unheeded, for we have failed to appreciate the level at which they are working. It is not simply that social theories have tended to illuminate the experience of men and not women, but that they have also served to legitimate a particular form of masculine experience.

In crucial aspects, different forms of feminist theory have challenged fundamental assumptions that have structured a modernity that has largely been cast in terms provided by the Enlightenment. In challenging the conventional distinction that we make between reason and emotion it has subverted the notion of the rational self that has been the guiding image of personal identity. It has worked to reinstate different forms of knowledge in a way that has brought into question both positivist and interpretative methods.

Not only has it served to indicate the partiality of the knowledge that sociologists have produced, but it has brought into question some of the assumptions upon which it was produced. It also helps us uncover different traditions of thought and feeling that have been lost under the dominance of an Enlightenment inheritance. It helps us rework the terms of modernity as we more fully appreciate its different sources and influences.

Chapter 2

Nature

MIND AND BODY

Conceptions of knowledge have been unwittingly tied up with notions of masculinity ever since the scientific revolutions of the seventeenth century conceived of themselves in terms of a new masculine philosophy. It is because we are used to the claims of science being made in terms of the universal and impartial language of reason that it has been hard to identify what is at issue.

The 'success' of scientific endeavours within the physical world has been enough to silence any opposition when it came to applying 'scientific methods' more universally to the cultural and human sciences. It has taken the emergence of an ecological movement to warn us of the dangers of a scientific tradition that sees progress as a matter of the domination and control of nature. In most cases this has led us to worry about the consequences of science in such areas as the greenhouse effect rather than its form and character.[1]

But we are slowly beginning to discern in different areas of life a subtle shift of emphasis as the mechanistic conceptions of self and nature which supplanted organic conceptions, largely because of the scientific revolutions, fail to carry the same unquestioned conviction.[2] This is not a matter of returning to a past that has long gone but of learning to appreciate values, meanings and intuitions with which we have lost touch in this paradigmatic shift.

In areas such as alternative medicine we are beginning to experience what can be gained from a more holistic sensitivity that brings us into a fuller relationship with the particularities of our health. We learn not to think of illness exclusively as a breakdown in a mechanical system whose symptoms can be treated impersonally and universally. Within a mechanistic vision, symptoms carry a signification that is supposedly universal, forming a language of signs, irrespective of the persons within which they are expressed. It is this conception, which might be appropriate in some areas, that is beginning to break apart at the seams.

To begin to grasp what is at issue in some of these differences, we need to context them in tensions we have inherited from the way that 'modern philosophy' was largely defined by Descartes. We will have to do this in quite other terms than those suggested by Derrida and those who have been concerned to define the present as a moment which is 'postmodern'.[3] We will address some of these considerations later. Their discussions are primarily focused upon the integrated vision of self that Descartes seemed to be suggesting, with his sense of a unified consciousness as the basis of our identities as rational selves. This needs to be placed in a broader context.

For Derrida, this vision of a unified self has gone along with considerations of 'presence', the ways in which we are assumed to be 'present' in our different experiences. It has been important for Derrida to render this problematic and to recognise ways in which we are fragmented and can experience aspects of ourselves as displaced, even lost. But by itself this recognition of fragmentation and dispersal is not enough, for it tends to move in the same universal terms as one vision of a unified identity is replaced by a recognition of fragmentation. For social theory this has meant a growing sensitivity to the ways that identities are not simply 'given' but are constantly being rearticulated and redefined through the different discourses we inhabit in different areas of our lives.

In recent years these concerns to do with fragmentation of identities have been used to marginalise some of the challenges of feminism. It has been thought that feminism was concerned with a unified vision of women in its talk of liberation, and so had been unwittingly caught up with a project of modernity.[4] This has encouraged some people to talk of 'post-feminism' while in truth we are only beginning to take seriously some of its challenges to forms of academic and institutionalised knowledges.

If this mood partly fits with the experience of a feminist movement which has itself fragmented so that it speaks with different voices of different concerns, this multiplicity has to be respected so we learn to hear these different voices. Otherwise the danger exists that the rationalistic terms of much of postmodern theory will go unnoticed, with its disdain for nature and emotional life, as it is able to marginalise potential feminist challenges. It could well mark an intellectual shift that presents its critique of western conceptions of reason in a way that silences others who have challenged its rationalism through a different appreciation of our emotional and sexual lives.

With Descartes we inherit a particular notion of the rational self that is set within an abiding categorical distinction between mind and body. It is not that the vision of consciousness and mental life that underpins this notion of the rational self is unified and whole, for it was fragmented from the very beginning. In its pure form it can be conceived of as a masculine self that has *separated* itself off from the supposed impurities of nature and emotional life. Descartes' vision of consciousness is essentially disembodied, as is the conception of the rational agent that flows from it. It is men who think. It is men who are conceived of in our western philosophical tradition as the rational sex, for they alone can take their reason for granted and so can escape from the demands of nature. It is in this setting that we learn to pay deference to the workings of a 'pure reason' that has been untainted by empirical investigations.

It is crucial to appreciate that for a Cartesian tradition, our bodies are part of a separate nature and so they are no part of ourselves. As rational selves our identities lie in our minds, for this is where we can be free to think our own thoughts and have our own memories. Within this tradition personal identity becomes an issue of memory and of being able to identify memories as 'mine'.[5] The relationship with different aspects of the self is taken to be possessive. There is an implicit relationship of authority where the mind is supposedly *in control* of the body and tells it what to do.

This sees control as essentially an issue of domination, for there is little to be learned from the body or from emotions and feelings which supposedly have their source within its province. The body is part of a nature that is deemed to be 'dead', for it only exists as matter and has no life of its own. The body does not have its own wisdom. If it does we are deaf to it, for we learn to live our lives as a matter of 'mind over matter'. We learn to pursue our ends and goals regardless of what our bodies might be saying to us.

For Descartes reason is sovereign. It is through reason alone that we supposedly discern the ends and purposes of our lives. For a crucial aspect of the dominance of this mechanistic world view that is so often rendered invisible through being taken for granted is that the natural world that we inherit is dead; for the Scientific Revolutions, in Carolyn Merchant's haunting phrase, went hand in hand with the death of nature.[6] In our vision of the cosmos, nature exists only as matter that is governed by laws that human reason is alone able to discern and control. This has left a profound legacy for our philosophy and social theory, for it means that we live in a world that is bereft of meaning and value.

Descartes learned to think of animals and nature in mechanical terms as machines.[7] Not only was the world disenchanted, as Max Weber has it, but it lost contact with its soul. It was in ridding ourselves of this archaic language of the supernatural that modernity was to take shape. As natural explanations came to replace theological explanations in terms of purpose, it seemed as if meaning was drained out of life. We were destined to live in a meaningless world that could not respond to our expressions, for it was supposedly dead. There was no echo to be heard within the world of nature. We were left alone, talking endlessly to ourselves. There was no one within nature to listen.

THE DEVALUATION OF NATURE

From within the terms of modernity it becomes difficult for instance to respect the North American Indians' reverence for the earth as their mother. This comes to seem quaint, fanciful and 'irrational'. So it is that we learn to use the language of 'irrationality' as a way of distancing ourselves. It is as rational beings that we inherit science as our own, even if we know precious little about it ourselves. Simone Weil tellingly talks of a white working-class man turning up in Polynesia being able to feel automatically superior to 'the natives' because he carries science as a guarantee of civilisation while they only have 'nature'.

It is this vision of rationality as a relationship of *superiority* that gets embedded within modernity and which helps organise our relationship with self within western culture. It creates its own tacit superiority as we learn to appropriate reason and science as our own. It worked to legitimate colonialism as it served to lower others in western eyes as being closer to nature and therefore as being in need of the 'civilisation' that only the West could bring.[8]

In reducing nature to matter, it also served to legitimate the inhumanities of the slave trade. For, instead of being able to recognise the different civilisations that existed in Africa, it was only able to see people as the embodiment of nature and so in the last resort as matter. It is important to reveal these connections, however briefly, since they work to provide the foundations for the Enlightenment.

As we learn to think of this as the 'bringing of light' into a Europe that was trapped in the darkness of traditional authorities of church and aristocracy, it is just as well to recognise the costs involved and the destruction that it wrought in individual and collective lives. What was being redefined was a magic circle of humanity with a very tight series of exclusions. It was to set the terms by which others were supposedly to enter. It was to define modernity as a western acquisition and so it was to set the terms for relationships of power and dominance between peoples.[9]

This vision of modernity was fundamentally set in masculine terms. That this is something that we still need to come to terms with is clear from the ways in which slavery tends to be marginalised in our histories of the West. This is equally true of the witch trials and witch burnings that left their wounds over much of Europe and North America.[10] If we learn about it at all it is as a moment of aberration and unreason, a regression from a period of science and reason.

But this is to blind us to the inner connections between these bloody and cruel movements and the scientific revolutions that were roughly happening at the same time. It has often been noted that such figures as Francis Bacon played a crucial part in both. It could be said that one served to legitimate the other, for it was Bacon who talked of torturing nature on the rack until she was prepared to give up her secrets. Nature was conceived of as a woman. Torture was supposedly a legitimate instrument to use in the search for scientific truth.

The scientific revolutions were formative in creating the terms of modernity. It involved a break with the past as people within Europe also lost a sense of the reverence they themselves used to feel towards nature. The land had also been conceived as a mother and mining the minerals of the earth had been severely restricted. It had been necessary to perform rituals before breaking into the soil for this had been tantamount to harming the mother.

With the Scientific Revolution the land no longer appears as sacred but it becomes a commodity like any other that can be bought and sold within a capitalist market economy. It is bereft of meaning, so becoming available to people to use at their will. It has no value or meaning apart from what people choose to give to it. But this also involves a loss of historical memory since people concerned to think of themselves in new terms as 'rational agents' can no longer identify with the practices and customs of their ancestors. They have come to live in a new world of modernity.

Women were to learn to identify with men as 'rational selves' or at least to seek reason in their lives through relating to them. They had to forsake their connection to those women who were burnt alive. This was to dismember their memory and themselves as they learned to treat these practices of healing and herbalism as 'irrational'.[11] This was to separate and estrange them from their own herstories, so teaching them to discount what they shared, at least officially, with other women.

But it was such a *separation* that characterises the culture of modernity. It gives a secular expression to the early separations and denials that have been part of a Protestant inheritance. So it is that we are supposedly *not* our natures, for these are evil and can lead us astray. Similarly we are not our bodies with which we sustain an externalised relationship, for they are supposedly equally part of nature. We learn to diminish and disdain these parts of ourselves both practically and theoretically and we do our best to construct and sustain our identities independently of them.

As nature is there to be used by people but carries no meaning or significance in itself, but only in relation to the purposes that people provide for it, so our bodies are there to carry us around. They are part of nature but not of ourselves. As rational selves we have to learn to *rise above* our bodies which exist independently of us governed by laws, as are other parts of nature. This is hardly experienced as a bifurcation of ourselves or our experience, for we learn to think of ourselves as conscious beings whose experience is conceived in mental terms alone.

It is as if we learn to live in the mental part of ourselves and as if this is allowed to exhaust our identities as rational agents. It is through reason alone that we learn to govern our lives and we tend to *minimise* anything that stands in the way of our being about to realise the goals that we set ourselves. We cease to be grounded in our somatic experience so we lose touch with its truths that could be communicated to us.

The ways that we are estranged from nature within the terms of modernity, learning to see progress in its domination and control rather than in learning to develop a *different relationship* with something that we are part of, are reflected in our relationship with our bodies. This relationship to our bodies is gendered and it brings out how dominant forms of masculinity are able to express the aspirations of modernity.

As men, we learn to treat our bodies as separate, as something that needs to be trained. Often we push ourselves because we can be testing ourselves against the limits of our bodies as some kind of affirmation of our manliness. Even if our bodies are carefully tuned instruments that are ready to obey our every command – the language itself reflects an education into authority and dominance – we can be left with little inner relationship to them. In part this reflects the limited relationship that we are encouraged to develop with our inner selves.

We are threatened by what our bodies might reveal to us, for they might reveal a weakness that can compromise our masculinity. It is as if we constantly have to prove our masculinity against a seemingly endless series of external tests. We can never rest confident in a sense that we are 'man enough'. We constantly have to be vigilant since at any moment we might be called upon to prove ourselves. Your masculinity is only as secure as your last competitive achievement. This fear of what nature might reveal is an endemic aspect of dominant forms of masculinity. It is built upon a denial of what cannot be denied, since it remains part of us.

As we do our best to construct ourselves according to a rationalist ideal we learn to discount and suppress emotions and desires that do not fit with the rational ideal that we have set for ourselves. We learn to suppress our fear, for instance, so that we cannot any longer identify the feeling for what it is. We have lived so long without acknowledging it that we do not recognise it when it makes its presence felt. We might feel uncomfortable, but that is a different story.

FEAR AND LEARNING

The traditional idea that human nature is malleable and its modern incarnation in the idea that individuality is 'socially and historically constructed' in their different ways legitimise this rationalism. They suggest that we are made or we can make ourselves according to the customs and aspirations of a particular culture or society. Within a functionalist tradition it is difficult to lay bare tensions between what institutions, such as schools, want from the children and what children might want and need for themselves if they are to learn.

We tend to accept with Durkheim that the rules of the institution have a wisdom of their own so that if children rebel, for instance, it has to be because they are 'deviant' or 'pathological'. We learn to blame the individuals, thereby removing the institutions beyond criticism. Often we are slow to explore the contradictions between say, a child's desire to learn, and the compulsory institution in which that child has to fulfil the desire.

It is difficult to draw upon a child's experience of school, for this is too easily discounted as 'personal' or 'subjective', simply recording how a child subjectively experiences the organisation of schooling itself. Rather we learn to discount this experience, as the child also learns to deny his or her bodily feelings as any possible sources of knowledge. If children are made to feel scared so that they cannot learn, we are assured that this is a personal response and we are blocked from acknowledging whether this is a shared experience of authority.

We are assured that these are subjective, emotional responses to an objective, institutional situation. If they tell us anything at all it is about the individuals themselves, not about the structured relationships of schooling. For there is a demarcation between the school that is supposedly organised according to the impersonal guidance of reason and the experience of individuals themselves. Experience falls on the side of nature and is to be discounted.[12]

Within a Protestant culture we learn to internalise this experience and turn it against ourselves. We also learn to identify this as a 'psychological' process that can tell us very little about the objective situations in which we find ourselves. So it is important that if a child cannot understand a teacher, that child will readily assume that it is his or her fault and that it must reflect some personal inadequacy.

The child will be tempted into this judgement *before* he or she has checked out how other classmates feel. We learn to keep our fears to ourselves, for otherwise they reflect badly upon us. We learn not to share with others in the competitive context of schooling if we think that it might give others some kind of advantage or some grounds to put us down. Often we are left with a sense of personal inadequacy enforced, as we are more often likely to assume that everyone else but ourselves can understand what is going on.

Within the sociology of education, it is rare to hear discussions of the fear that children feel in the context of school, even though for some this has been crucial to the way school works. It is also difficult to explore the connections between fear and learning. Where a functionalist paradigm has been challenged and there is an awareness of a gap between the knowledges that teachers have and the knowledges that pupils construct in a situation, this is often construed in cognitive terms. Somehow our knowledge remains disembodied and separated from our emotional realities.

It is as if we live in our heads and cut off, at least officially, from these different aspects of our experience. Often we are left with a relativism that is unable to judge fear as *undermining* genuine learning. The universalism of reason as embodied in the organisation of schooling assumes enormous authority when set against individualised experience. There is little surprise if parents and children end up feeling 'what is the point?', as everything seems to be stacked against them.

BODIES OF KNOWLEDGE

The body is conceived of as part of nature and so as separated from the realm of reason. Accordingly it has little to teach us. It has been silenced, as have other aspects of nature, governed by laws of its own. It is given and passive so without a voice in its own experience. It is uncivilised, if not dirty, and so it has to be *discounted*. It presents the threat of nature against culture and civilisation. Since we only inhabit civilisation as it has been defined by modernity to the extent that we live as rational beings, we learn to deny these aspects of our natures. We learn to live as if they do not exist at all.

With the identification of masculinity with reason, men become the protectors of and gatekeepers for this dominant vision of modernity. We set the terms on which others can be permitted to enter. Others have to pay the price of construing themselves as 'rational agents' in the particular ways this has been conceived.

As men, we learn to live a lie. We learn to live *as if* we are 'rational agents' in the sense that we live as if we live beyond nature. We learn to live as if our emotional lives do not exist, at least as far as the 'public world' is concerned, for this is where these identities are most securely lived out. It is as if modernity expects us to live, not as if our natures have been effectively controlled, but as if they did not exist at all. For to live out the ideal that modernity presents us with is to exist as rational beings alone. We learn to live in our minds as the source of our identities.

If we had our way as men it would be that our emotional lives did not exist at all, for they only serve to get in the way of our realising the goals and purposes that are set by reason alone. This provides the only meaning and dignity that our lives can have. Kant is clear that only if we act out of a sense of rational duty do our actions have any moral worth at all. To act out of our desires and inclinations, even if this be out of feelings of care and kindness, yields our actions no moral worth at all. For Kant we are simply doing what we want to do and this has to be selfish.[13]

But as Freud appreciated, this denial of nature cannot be achieved, for we cannot simply construct ourselves according to these rationalistic ideals. What is denied will return to haunt our dreams and fantasies. Freud recognised that modernity presents us with an *impossible* ideal for it suggests that we can exist as rational beings alone. It refuses to recognise the beings that we are and so it insists that we do injuries to ourselves to be able to live out these ideals. But these injuries go largely unrecognised, for they take place within an emotional life that has been silenced.[14]

In this regard, at least, Freud stands against structuralist forms of social theory that present this modernist dream in a new guise. Their antagonism to nature and 'human nature' is expressed as a rejection of 'biologism' and 'essentialism'. If structuralism has learned to speak of Freud and psychoanalysis, it is through a particular rationalistic reading provided by Lacan.

Freud refused to give up his emphasis on sexuality, for he recognised as one of his guiding insights the havoc that is caused in individual lives through the repression and denial of sexual feelings. In some way he recognised the integrity of our sexual expression and the 'naturalness' of our sexual feelings, leaving aside the different forms that this might take. To deny that we are sexual beings is to do an injury to ourselves and to repress our sexual feelings as shameful or disgusting is to move them into a different realm. By denying these feelings we do not abolish them.

At this level Freud sets himself against a modernity that has been established in secularised Protestant terms. With Calvin and Luther we are supposed to negate and eradicate these aspects of ourselves which reveal an evil nature.[15] We are to live as if these natural feelings do not exist at all, with the idea that if we do not give them any energy they will wither and die. Freud recognised that it was neither possible nor desirable to treat our sexuality in this way.

Freud is less clear about the embodiment of our sexual feelings and desires. He remains committed in effect to a Cartesian dualism that tends to treat sexuality as if it were a feature of our mental lives alone. He tends to work with a metaphor of mental life that works in spatial terms which banishes our unacknowledged desires and emotions to the unconscious. We can end up treating emotions and feelings as if they are mental states, as we so often do within the philosophy of mind.

Though Freud recognised the importance of *acknowledging* our sexual feelings as a way of opening up a space foreclosed within a Protestant tradition where the desire itself somehow confirmed the evilness of our natures, there is an important difference between acknowledging our sexual feelings and acting on them. What is crucial for Freud is that, in being more ready to acknowledge our feelings and emotions, even if these are feelings we would prefer not to have, we are helping to build some kind of bridge and relationship with our emotional selves. In this way at least, Freud stands critical of a Cartesian tradition which would assume that nothing was to be gained from building this kind of bridge with aspects of ourselves.

There is a great deal to be learned from our emotions and feelings about the situations that we face in our lives. Our feelings have an integrity of their own. It is quite wrong to judge them according to the logic of reason alone. It might be quite 'irrational', for instance, for me to feel jealous when my partner dances with someone else, but this can give me significant information about myself. It might be important to acknowledge these jealous feelings rather than to judge them before I have even allowed myself to become fully aware of them. In part this is to recognise that emotions and feelings have 'logics' of their own which need to be followed and learned from. It means that emotions cannot be reduced to thought or to aspects of mental life alone.

Within the Cartesian framework for modernity, our lives are split between mind and body. But since our bodies are part of nature we are destined to live out an externalised relationship to them. Our experience becomes a feature of mental life. There is no space for our emotional lives and if we continue within the framework set by Descartes and Kant, they are features of our bodily lives in the sense that they are aspects of unfreedom. They seek to interfere with and distract us from goals and purposes that have been set by reason and which are exclusively the source of our freedom and self-determination.

So it is that our emotions and feelings, if acknowledged at all, are torn between these two realities. It becomes impossible to acknowledge their autonomy and integrity. They cannot be aspects of our dignity and self-respect. In large part, different traditions of social theory have remained faithful to these modernist premises.

Freud made a significant break in his recognition of the integrity of our emotional and sexual lives. But it remains an issue whether the theoretical framework he developed allowed him to explore the full impact of his discovery. His scientific training meant that he also felt torn between these different poles. It is difficult to think of sexuality as a feature of mental life alone. His student Wilhelm Reich took an important step in the acknowledgement of the emotional life of the body. At moments Reich seemed to break with a dualistic tradition in his recognition that feelings and emotions can also be held in the somatic structure.[16] He acknowledges Freud's insight that reason cannot be separated from emotions and feelings without creating untenable and artificial distinctions that have no existence in reality. We can work to live out these separations in our lives, but only at the cost of building particular tensions in our experience. It is these tensions which Freud has helped us identify and give some name to.

When a teacher shouts angrily at a child in her class the fear that this can create can be held in the muscle structure of the child. If that child does not feel able to respond, or if he does not acknowledge this fear for what it is, say because it reflects badly upon his sense of self in front of others, it does not mean that this fear does not exist. It is not brought into existence simply because of our conscious awareness of it. Nor is it simply a feature of our mental lives.

This suggests the limits of intellectualist or cognitive theories that can only acknowledge this fear as a form of mental construction or classification. The dominant forms of masculinity that we grow into as boys can make it particularly difficult to acknowledge this fear. We might easily discount the whole experience or at least minimise its impact on us, out of a sense that it might compromise our male identity. As boys we learn to *separate* and *cut off* from emotions that might compromise us in some way. We learn that if we do not give them any reality, then they are not real themselves. This is not true, yet much of our social theory seems ready to go along with this.

Chapter 3

Reason

REASON AND EMOTION

Within an Enlightenment tradition we inherit a view of knowledge as 'objective' and it is through a faculty of reason, sharply demarcated from nature, that we strive for objectivity. Within this vision reason is sovereign and the source of knowledge. It is because reason is a universal faculty that it can yield us objective and impartial knowledge. It is the task of reason to discern the laws that govern the empirical world of nature.

It is partly because nature has been rendered as inert matter that gives it its particular reality. Nature is real but it is bereft of consciousness and of value. It exists as separate and independent of the consciousness that is attempting to grasp it, which establishes the realism of a positivist tradition. Fundamental to this Enlightenment vision is the abiding split between subjective consciousness and the objective world that it is seeking to understand. This is the prevailing distinction between subject and object.

So it is that we are estranged as subjects from the objective world that we seek to grasp. The social world understood in these positivist terms exists independently from human relationships and practices. With Descartes we exist as minds attempting to grasp a world from which we are estranged. It is as if, as natural selves, we are not grounded in the empirical world, even if our bodies are part of it. Our identities are established in our minds, or consciousness, that do not exist as part of the world they seek to comprehend. Our emotions and feelings exist as part of the empirical world as objects that need to be known, rather than as aspects of a knowing subject. It is only as rational selves that we exist as self-determining subjects.

It is reason that is the source of knowledge, while our emotions and feelings as part of our natural selves merely serve as distractions. They work to influence our behaviour externally for it is only with reason that we can have an *inner* relationship. So it is that the distinction between reason and emotions is reinforced as a distinction between 'internal' and 'external'. Emotions and feelings are personal and subjective, registering the impact of situations upon us but unable to yield any knowledge themselves.

In the medical context, for instance, the doctors have the authority of knowledge, since they have reason and the impersonal knowledge it yields of symptoms, while patients only have their personal experience that is easily discounted as 'subjective'. Within the classical model this experience yields interesting information at best.[1] It might or might not be taken into account. Doctors are secure in the impersonal character of their scientific knowledges. It was this science which, in the hands of men, initially replaced the power that women had in the sphere of healing. It involved a different conception of knowledge as well as a different order of human relationships.

It is significant that as children we are taught to be silent when the doctor is around, only to talk if we are specifically questioned. It is as if nothing that we know about ourselves could be of any relevance in this situation. Strangely, it is as if we have been estranged from the knowledge of our own bodies that no longer belong to us, but only exist as constituted through the categories of medical knowledge.

The only knowledge that we can have of our bodies can be discounted as 'subjective' and 'emotional'. It is personal and therefore inevitably partial. At most it yields opinion, but it can never deliver the supposed 'objectivity' of knowledge. It is hardly surprising that we are often left feeling that we have to apologise for ourselves when with a doctor. It is as if the authority of medical knowledge serves to make us feel 'stupid'. It comes as a shock to realise that somehow what is at issue in this situation is *our* health.[2]

We can be left feeling that we have been impertinent in even asking the doctor a question, as if this has to be somehow tantamount to bringing such authority into question. In what way is the authority of this medical knowledge connected to issues of masculinity? Is it an accident that men took control of medicine which as healing was largely the province of women? Is there a link between the impersonal character of these forms of scientific knowledge and the impersonalised character of particular forms of masculinity? Somehow it is the person in their full particularity that falls from view as the doctor learns to focus his or her gaze on the impersonal and universal nature of symptoms. It is as if reason can only work with the impersonal.

Similarly in Kantian moral theory, reasons for moral action have to be impersonal if they are to serve as genuine reasons for moral action. The condition of universalisability is tied into the rationalist characterisation of reason, for supposedly we are all equally susceptible to the obligations that flow from the moral law. What serves as a reason for me should be equally capable of serving for others faced with a similar situation.

The scientific revolutions helped to reconstitute particular forms of knowledge, according to the impersonal gaze of reason. Since these models of scientific knowledge seemed to work for discerning the laws of the natural world, where personal motives and intentions were to be eradicated, they were considered equally appropriate in the human and medical sciences. It was as if the terms of scientific methods could be equally applied to different realms of life. In themselves these methods were neutral, or so a positivist vision held. They were largely defined in terms of their universality and impersonality and so in terms of their *exclusion* from the realm of genuine scientific discourse of any personal or emotional features. They could only distract and interfere with the objective gaze of reason.

Under Foucault's influence the body has made a somewhat belated entry into social theory. We can now think more readily about the ways that it is disciplined and regulated.[3] It has been an important insight into the workings of power and subordination. The deference that, for example, we are supposed to feel for teachers is often reinforced and given form by our having to stand up whenever they come into the room. This is supposedly a show of respect, but it is much more as well. It instils an automatic response which we often act out blindly. This is the way that attitudes can be instilled which often last a lifetime. The attitudes that we *embody* in this way at an early age often have a powerful, if generally unacknowledged influence. It can mark the ways in which we relate to others in authority, as well as the ways in which we feel about ourselves.

In recognising the emotional life of the body we are challenging a Cartesian dualism and opening up space within our inherited traditions of social theory to recognise that we exist as emotional and spiritual beings as much as mental and physical beings.[4] If we are to recognise the interiority of these different aspects of our experience, we have to break with the reductionisms that we inherit. This is to acknowledge that 'rationality' should not simply apply to an independent faculty of reason. It is equally important to recognise the 'rationality' of our emotional lives. The pupil who challenges the teacher for the way that teacher shouted at him, scaring him stiff, is responding bravely to mistreatment. He might also be suggesting that school should not be a place of fear and humiliation and that this is not a context in which true learning can take place.

If the teacher insists that it is only by setting an example like this that he can motivate his class to learn, he needs to learn about the connections of learning to emotional life. Learning is not something that takes place completely independently, in a faculty of its own. Many primary schoolteachers have learned this from their own experience, but it is an insight that is continually being undermined and subverted within the dominant culture. If it were taken seriously it would involve profound changes in our educational theory and practice. It would be built around the life of the child in a more meaningful, and less rhetorical, way.

Within a voluntaristic theory we are made to believe that it is the easiest thing in the world to change our attitudes. Since we are free, so the liberal story goes, we can take up whatever attitudes we choose. This is part of a rationalist tradition that, having its source in Kant's idea of reason as an inner faculty of freedom, is given fullest expression in Max Weber's notion that we are free to give whatever meanings that we choose to our experience.

This idea has its source in the Enlightenment, particularly in its recognition that we live in a disenchanted world which is bereft of meaning. We are often presented within a structuralist tradition with an antimony between seeing values somehow waiting there in nature to be discovered and the idea that values and meanings have to be *created* by people themselves. This antimony has taken its place as part of a contemporary common sense in the human sciences. But it is a flawed choice that so easily misleads us about what is at issue.

It has tended paradoxically to perpetuate a particular humanistic vision that sees human beings as the source of all meaning and value. It denies value and integrity to animals and nature, as if they can only claim dignity and value through their relationships with human beings. This is partly the way that Kant thought. He thought that if we were insensitive and brutal in our relationships with animals we would be more likely to behave in these ways in our relationships with each other. It also tends to place humans in a relationship of *superiority* towards other animals, since we alone supposedly have a faculty of reason. To share emotions and feelings with animals was supposedly of little consequence. This is partly why it became so important to defend reason as if it were a unique and independent faculty. But with ecology it is harder to be convinced by these assumptions.

We can learn that it is not only our reason that works as the source of our values. Our feelings can provide the source of some of our most enduring beliefs. It can seem that it is those relationships that I have the most feeling for that I cherish most. This touches important questions in the philosophy of mind about the sources of our attitudes and beliefs.

Much of Wittgenstein's *Philosophical Investigations* was taken up with challenging the idea that our beliefs are inner mental states and his work remains the most significant challenge to a Cartesian tradition. He recognises that it was not enough to challenge Descartes' positions intellectually, as if they could be 'defeated' by reason alone. It was this kind of position that he was doing his best to expose. He recognised, in opposition to a rationalism that holds our attitudes to be freely chosen and therefore changeable, just how *hard* it was for us to change the ways we think and feel.[5]

Central to this is Wittgenstein's awareness that unless we can be *brought to acknowledge* and recognise how our experience is largely formed within an Enlightenment tradition, then we will be quite incapable of shifting it. This is not a matter of intellectual arguments alone but of recognising in all its complexity the ways in which we are tied up and live out these conceptions in our everyday lives. This is a slow and difficult process, for Wittgenstein has to build up our sense of the persuasiveness of these conceptions before he can begin to undo them.

Unless we begin to appreciate how deeply rooted are some of these conceptions, we will not be able to begin the process of shifting them. It is partly because Wittgenstein acknowledged the continuing grasp of Enlightenment modernity over contemporary culture and society that he thought that his work would be destined to be ignored or misunderstood. As far as philosophy and social theory are concerned they have not been ignored, but they have generally been assimilated into a rationalist conception of language that he was trying to dislodge.

Modernity has in large part been connected with a *spiritualisation* of reason, in the sense that it has sustained a vision of pure reason. This remains a secularisation of a particularly Christian vision, for the spiritual is set in firm opposition to the material and the bodily. So it is that reason is defined as an autonomous and independent faculty that should not be tainted by emotions, feelings or desire. It is the source of knowledge alone. It is this vision that feminist theory and practice help to question, as they suggest that reason *cannot* be categorically separated from feelings and emotions. At some level these distinctions have no basis in reality, though at another level they help construct the particular reality we live.

We learn to subordinate our emotional selves and tend to silence their impact upon the form and quality of our everyday lives. We learn to accept a certain hierarchy within ourselves which gives authority to reason and to the goals and purposes that it sets. Within a Protestant culture we can take pride in the sacrifices that we make in our emotional lives since this seems to imbue the ends we have chosen with a particular seriousness.

REASON AND AUTONOMY

We tend to accept that reason is the source of our individuality and so of our freedom and self-determination. Since we supposedly share emotions and feelings with animals they cannot help to individuate us as persons. It is as if they have to stand in the way of our process of individuation. Emotions can so easily be dismissed as 'childish' and so thought of as a feature of childhood dependence that we need to leave behind as we learn to move towards independence and autonomy. Our visions of autonomy are set in rationalist terms.

Cognitive models have become so well-entrenched in the psychological and human sciences that we are often blind to the philosophical assumptions about reason and emotions upon which they rest. We have become so used to the idea that a rational action is an action performed in the pure light of reason, untainted by any emotional considerations. Kant's idea that we are destined to have an externalised relationship to emotions and desire which consequently have a deter-mining effect on our behaviour conditions the categorical distinction between reason and emotion that has characterised so much of the philosophy and social theory of modernity.

Within social theory, this is reflected in Weber's theory of action which tacitly accepts that rational action is a higher form of human action. Since it is disinterested it stands superior to the partiality of emotional action. This vision of rational action is part of what establishes the universality of modernity and so its sense of superiority in relation to other cultural traditions that are caught within a moment of particularity.

It is because modernity can claim to embody a universal conception of human action and a conception of morality within which all can equally participate as rational agents, that it has assumed itself to be superior to other traditions of thought and feeling. Rather than recognise itself as a secularised form of Protestantism, it has accepted its self-conception to argue that as a secular tradition it can *make claim to a universality* that sets it equally apart from all religious traditions, including

Christianity. In this regard it claims to espouse a liberal conception of tolerance to all religious traditions, but the reality is otherwise.

Weber's studies within the sociology of religion are extremely interesting in helping us to think of the relationship of the West to other religious and cultural traditions. There are moments when the superiority of the West and its vision of instrumental rationality are assumed to be superior, so that the general questions concern the *failure* of other traditions to develop this particular form of rationality.

There are other moments when Weber recognises the crisis of values that is brought about by the process of rationalisation and means–ends relationships coming to dominate all aspects of social life. It is a fear that Weber struggles with because he tends to regard rationalisation as part of an inevitably historical process that will bring about the domination of western forms of capitalist rationality.[6] With the demise of centralised state planning within eastern Europe, it can seem that Weber was aware of the global implications of modernity.

At another level Weber tended to accept the superiority of rational action in relation to traditional or affective action. It is rational action alone that, in Kantian terms, is assumed to be an exercise of our freedom as individuals. When we act traditionally or affectively we are being determined emotionally. But this is to falsely assimilate different forms of action. It unwittingly legitimates the power of a particular form of masculinity that is assumed to act rationally, more or less automatically. So these different kinds of action presented as ideal types in neutral language serve to legitimate particular forms of action and denigrate or devalue other forms of action.[7]

It is men who can act freely while women are supposed to be tied to emotions and feelings. This enables men to use their power in relation to women when they devalue what women are saying by saying that 'they are rational while women are merely emotional'. In everyday relationships this is the way that men can silence the challenges of women by refusing to listen to their emotional 'outbursts' until they 'calm down' and learn to 'talk rationally'.

As modernity has worked to institutionalise the sovereignty of reason it has also *legitimated* the power of men, and men have learned to use their supposed rationality in enforcing the subordination of women. It is only if women learn to 'talk rationally' that they will be listened to, otherwise what they say will be denigrated – it will be treated as noise rather than as speech. It is as if language becomes 'rational' if it is deprived of its emotional intensity and power. It is not simply a matter of what we say but also of *how* we speak.

It was an insight of the early Women's Movement that women had been silenced and rendered invisible through the official forms of language. It was as if their language was being automatically judged by standards not of their own making.[8] They were being made to speak within contexts in which they could not find their own voices. Sometimes it was as if someone else was speaking.

REASON AND EXPRESSION

Within the context of consciousness-raising groups women learned to share their experience of subordination with each other in a way that helped connect language to experience. Out of a shared experience of denial and oppression it was possible to speak a truth that had long been lost to the women themselves. As reason could not be separated from emotion, so language could not be separated from experience as an instrument of reason alone.

As women were *moved* by listening to the stories of other women, they could not separate what was being said from the feeling with which it was expressed. It is as if truth is not simply a matter of what is said, but of the *contact* a person has with their experience. It meant that individuality has an emotional form that finds expression in language. Women learned to hear when a particular experience was being talked about in a loose and disconnected way – as if the pain that was tied up with the experience could not be released or shared if language stayed on a mental level alone. They learned to discern distinctions that were lost when language was conceived of as an expression of reason alone.

Sharing experience was a way in which the experience of each women was confirmed and *validated*. It created a sense of equality within the consciousness-raising group but also a sense of solidarity and sisterhood. These were all expressions of a new form of community that was new in many women's lives. It was created out of a sense that women could share their experience in terms of their own choosing, without feeling that others would interpret their experience for them from a superior vantage point. Many women had suffered at the hands of men who assumed that with a privileged relationship to reason they could say what was best for their partners, or what they 'really wanted'.

As men, we are so used to exercising control over reason and language that we barely recognise situations when we do this. We are so ready to offer solutions to that situation, assuming that this is what we are being called upon to do, that we rarely learn to listen. Often what our partners want is an experience of being *listened to*, but this can be hard for us to provide. We are so used to using language as a way of proving that we are right, or defending ourselves as men, that we automatically use it to 'solve problems'. We can feel hurt and rejected when our advice is not taken when it was not asked for in the first place.

Within consciousness-raising groups women created a space in which they could listen to each other and accept the feelings that emerged with the sharing of experience. They seemed to be less threatened with the sharing of emotions and feelings, since often not being part of the situation they did not have to respond defensively or in a way that would make these feelings go away. This is not to argue that women and men necessarily have different relationships to their emotional lives but that these relationships are formed within particular cultural and historical settings. This has changed over time and there were periods in which heterosexual men were more easily expressive emotionally with each other. I do not want to minimise these historical differences.[9] In fact it helps to place into context the development of consciousness-raising within a particular moment in the growth and development of personal and sexual politics.

As women learned to share with each other in consciousness-raising groups they recognised that what they had learned to hold as a private experience was in fact *shared* by other women. It did not reflect upon their individual inadequacy as people but upon their shared situations of subordination and oppression. It helped to break the spell of a liberal rationalism that had worked to *privatise* this experience and make it something shameful. Within a secularised Protestant moral culture it left people feeling unacceptable as they were. Their emotions and feelings were part of what made them feel *inadequate* and unacceptable within a moral culture of modernity which stipulated that only rational selves deserved to be visible and present within the public realm. Women learned to hide their emotional selves that only confirmed their inadequacy. Within a liberal modernity it was only acceptable for rational agents to guide their lives by reason alone.

Feminism helped to challenge this self-conception of modernity. Women learned to appreciate how much they could learn from sharing their experience with each other, by suspending the judgements that reason would otherwise bring to bear. They did their best to create a space in which the critical voice of reason was suspended, at least for a while. They tried to put aside the voice of men that they knew: fathers, teachers, lovers, husbands and partners. They found the space in which they could feel the confidence to find the words to respond in a way they could not in an original situation, when they had been brought up to accept these judgements as true beyond question. This did not mean that women did not challenge each other or the interpretations they went on to offer of what had happened to them or why that event had had such an impact on their subsequent lives. But the spirit in which this was done was new, for women recognised the courage that it takes to share themselves.

Within a liberal moral culture we are so used to treating emotions and feelings as if they are signs of weakness that it is hard to share with others without feeling that we are not letting ourselves down. Men probably feel this more intensely since they are used to identifying male identity with a vision of reason and self-control. We can feel threatened by the merest appearance of an emotion over which we have no secure control. Often we control this impulse within ourselves by putting others down and ridiculing them for behaving in ways that we lack the courage to do ourselves. We can tell ourselves that as men it is our task to be 'strong' – a rock that others can rely upon.

But if we never learn to share our feelings with those we are close to, thinking of this as a form of 'self-indulgence' that might be expected of women but is inexcusable for men, then we never really learn to *share* ourselves. And it is true that as men we are constantly holding ourselves back even from those with whom we are most intimate. I have talked about this as a fear of intimacy that has a tight grip upon many contemporary masculinities.[10] We pride ourselves on being able to do things for ourselves without the support of others, but this often means that

men are alone and friendless. At some level we often envy what women have
discovered for themselves through the Women's Movement.

Women learned that to share their vulnerability was a way of building understanding and connection with each other. They also learned that there was a
difference between accounting for their experience in rational terms and *sharing*
this experience with others. The latter situation helped to heal the cultural separation between reason and emotion. As they shared their experience they also shared
the feelings that were tied up with it. To have put the emotions aside would have
been to be false to their experience and to themselves. This in itself is an important
discovery which challenges the prevailing cultural distinction between reason and
emotion. It is part of what makes this experience difficult to share, for what happens
is often so rich, yet it seems to slip away as soon as it is described in conventional
terms.

In its own way this raises issues of meaning and interpretation that I will return
to later. For the moment, it is enough to draw attention to the ways in which it shifts
how we conceive the relationship between thought and action. As women recognise
that what they had taken to be a private and personal experience of suffering is a
shared experience that grows out of the subordination of women, they are not
simply interpreting their experience in different ways. There is an important shift
in their sense of confidence and self-worth as they learn, through the support of
other women, not to turn these feelings *against* themselves.

It is part of a process of *empowerment* as women locate or ground their emotions
in the material situations in which they find themselves in their relationships. If this
gives women greater confidence as they learn to identify and name feelings that
seemed to have no names, it is a process that affects their emotions and feelings as
much as what they think about themselves and the world around them. If this has
been talked about as a 'change of consciousness', this brings into question the
cognitive or intellectualist frameworks within which we have grown used to
thinking about 'consciousness' in both philosophy and social theory.

As women learn to draw support from each other, they learn how important is
this emotional and mental *support* in their being able both to question and to change
the situation in which they find themselves. This tends to bring thoughts and actions
into a different relationship with each other, as women recognise that as they take
action in their lives, for instance in validating their relationships with other women
and refusing to put these aside because of the demands that men make, so they feel
differently about themselves. As women learn to define what they want for
themselves they take a different kind of control of their lives.

Crucially this is not a matter of dominating their emotions and desires so that
they can do what they have decided through reason alone. Rather it involves a
challenge to this very rationalism, as women learn to appreciate their emotions and
feelings as helping them to define what they value and what matters in their lives.
What becomes important is the *relationship* that women are able to build with
themselves as they make more connection with their emotional selves. This is to

refuse to put these aspects of themselves aside – but to learn to appreciate them as sources of knowledge and value.

As women learn to appreciate what they can give to each other they learn possibly for the first time to value their relationships with other women. This can encourage them to question how little they really *receive* in their relationships with men. It can also help them appreciate the *feeling* with which actions are done. In understanding the nature of the support, what also matters is the feeling with which women acted towards each other. This sense of being cared for helped women to challenge existing patterns in their relationships. This was not simply a matter of the intentions that informed people's actions but of the *quality* of the actions that people were capable of in their relationships with each other. All this gave women a sense of self-confidence and helped them to develop an insight into the ways in which the self-confidence and self-worth of those who are powerless tends to be undermined.

RESPECT AND SELF-WORTH

Feminism has helped us to develop crucial insights into the ways that self-confidence can be nourished and sustained within a democratic community. This connects to an insight of Simone Weil's in *The Need for Roots* where she talks about how equal respect is not simply a matter of the attitudes that individuals take towards each other in relationships but it also has to be expressed in the way everyday institutions are organised.

An insight that separated Weil from Kant's rationalism grew out of a recognition that in the university she may have had rights and a sense of self-worth that could sustain the Kantian idea of dignity as an inner quality safe from social relations. But her experience in a factory proved to her the inadequacy of this Kantian conception, as it confirmed her in a sense that she counted for nothing and that everything could be taken away from her, including her sense of dignity and self-respect. This remained a crucial lesson for her about the power of social relations to undermine an individual's sense of self.[11]

Liberal theory which assumes that we exist as free and equal rational agents within the public sphere fails to learn from this insight. It assumes that we can always *abstract* from social relations of power and subordination to exist as equals in our personal relations with each other. It sustains a secularised Christian vision in its sense that the inequalities of earthly life have little consequence for the quality that we have as spiritual beings before God.[12] Because earthly life does not matter when it comes to salvation, the inequalities and dependencies that it creates cannot be significant since our individualities are supposedly sustained in individual relationships with God.

Similarly we are supposedly equal as citizens before the law which is supposedly impartial, existing in a realm of its own as the will to justice above the conflicts and contradictions of social life. As Simone Weil watched the workings of a court of law, she knew that the reality was otherwise. Individual lives were crushed within the machines of justice. As a poor person was unable to utter words, as the judge offered an elegant flow of witticisms, the relations of power were all too obvious.[13]

Contemporary feminism has also understood that if you undermine or invalidate a person's emotions and feelings, you undermine a person's sense of self. For a rationalist modernity our freedom and independence is expressed in our thoughts alone, for our emotions are supposedly shared not only by other people but also by animals. Feminism can help us grasp that our individuality is as well expressed in our feelings and emotions as in our thoughts and ideas.

As we have to *work* to establish our own ideas and thoughts, so that we are not simply repeating the thoughts of our parents and teachers, so we have to *work* to establish our own emotions and feelings. For many this might seem a hopeless idea, since however hard we try we are limited by the languages and codes of our culture and society. While this reminds us that we do not establish our individualities through isolating or separating ourselves from society, as we have already noted with Durkheim in Chapter 1, it is still important to recognise the movement that can be made in both our thoughts and feelings as we work *to define them* for ourselves.

Learning to express my own anger in appropriate situations can be as powerful an expression of my dignity and sense of worth as learning to identify what I think. A rationalist tradition which follows Descartes and Kant is misleading in suggesting that thoughts alone can be a source of dignity and self-respect. It is because of this that Kant is blind to the importance of the feelings with which we act towards others in our moral lives. For Kant, the motive has to be a rational one if our behaviour is not to be determined by emotions and feelings.

But this blinds us to the fact that intentions are sometimes not enough and that we have to work on the *quality* of our actions towards others. Sometimes people can have the best intentions but be quite false and empty in their response. Sometimes this is because of some unconscious resentment that has never been acknowledged, let alone expressed. This can subvert the action, with a person having barely a glimmering of what has happened. It is partly because we are taught to put these resentments aside if we are to think of ourselves in a good light. But as Freud recognised, this can be just to shift them to another level of our experience. Sometimes it is much more helpful to acknowledge the anger or resentment, as doing so might clear the way for a more honest response in our relationship with someone.

But this emotional work has been traditionally left to women in the culture and it is given little public recognition or value.[14] The ways in which we conceive human action tend to leave little space for these considerations. It is as if it does not matter how we are towards others as long as our motives and intentions are pure. But this is to sustain a Kantian tradition within which our motives and intentions are supposedly within our rational control. It is as if the will is a matter of reason alone, but this leaves room for all kinds of self-deception.

So for example, what matters for Kant is that I am visiting a friend in hospital not out of an ulterior motive that she will think well of me later, but because she is sick and we have a moral duty to visit the sick whenever we can. If it so happens that I do not feel like going because of some resentment I bear because of how she behaved when we last met, then it is incumbent upon me to put these feelings aside so that I can make the required visit. For Kant, the fact that I have to suppress my inclinations in order to make the visit reflects well upon the moral worth of the action. If I were going to visit her because I wanted to, rather than out of a sense of moral obligation, then this would bring into question the moral worth of the action, for it would be that I am acting out of selfish egoistic interests.

This sets the notion of moral action as altruistic too firmly against an undifferentiated category of 'selfish' or 'egoistic' action. The fact that I have feelings for this person and want to visit her should not, in my sense of things, detract from the moral worth of the actions involved. Kant's identification of morality with disinterestedness and universality needs to be reconsidered for it sustains a significant hold over modernity. This is not to discount the significance of these qualities, but to question the priority which they are automatically assigned.

The point here is that the fact that I have feelings for the person can add to the spirit in which I visit. It helps to particularise my response so that I can recognise the person herself. It is not simply a matter of making the visit, but of whether I am capable of being *with her*, in Buber's terms, when I am there. Can I listen to what she has to say, or do I constantly blot this out, giving her assurances that 'things will be better soon'? Am I doing this because at some level I cannot deal with these feelings myself?

Kant's ethical theory is flawed because he tends to suppress these considerations, leaving us to think that emotional considerations have very little to do with the substance of morality. If anything, they detract from the moral worth of our actions. This makes it impossible to give these considerations the weight they deserve within a moral theory that presents reason as our moral faculty and morality as a feature of reason alone. Kant reinforces the notion that we should put all these emotional considerations aside so that we can act out of a sense of rational duty.

As long as we are dealing with emotional issues we are supposedly taken with issues of particularity, for we are showing preference for one person over another. The Kantian appeal to an idea that if this ends up that I only visit people in hospital because I have particular feelings for them or share a particular relationship with them, this is surely less morally worthy than the person who insists in universal terms that it is simply our duty to visit the sick, whoever they are and whatever feelings we have for them. Kant wants to recognise the 'purity' of motive that is at work in someone who deems it their duty to visit the sick. As far as he is concerned, this sets an ideal against which other actions fall short. Its clear sense of obligation is what helps us bring into focus the nature of the 'moral' itself.

Chapter 4

Morality

REASON AND MORALITY

When we think in terms of an obligation to visit the sick, this is an obligation that is universally held, and it helps Kant question notions of moral relativism because it is important to recognise that this is an obligation that flows from reason. It is an objective matter which can be decided as a matter of reason, rather than left as a matter of individual opinion.

Initially Kant set himself against the cultural relativism of Hume, but his work continues to have powerful contemporary resonance as a refusal of the relativism that informs both the common sense of a liberal moral culture that holds that morality is a matter of individual opinion and its reflection in the human sciences in the notion that values are relative to a particular society and culture. This is an understandable reaction to an imperialist culture that appropriated the idea of civilisation to itself, and insisted on judging others according to its terms.

Kant insists on the importance of the notion of morality as a way of challenging historical and cultural relativism. He helps us to believe that if slavery is wrong, then it is wrong in all times and places because it is demeaning to the human being. But it is also important to context Kant's work in the Enlightenment rather than to abstract it as a set of timeless arguments, the significance of which can only be fully appreciated if they are separated from any particular background. This can be a weakness in the predominantly rationalist tradition of modern philosophy that assumes that issues can be solved through reason alone.

Wittgenstein's later writings can help us to question this Cartesian vision of reason as well as the notion of argument that tends to flow from it. The vantage point of reason is assumed to exist beyond the conflicts of social life in a noumenal realm of its own. Its impartiality in relation to the issues of empirical life is guaranteed through its universality. It treats everyone alike, whatever the particular conditions of their lives, and we stand equally before the demands of the moral law.

It is assumed in Kant's scheme that as we rise above our animal natures, identifying ourselves with our intelligible selves, we take up a position of selfless impartiality towards ourselves. It is a way of being objective in relation to ourselves. But for Kant, these visions of 'objectivity' and 'impartiality' are established in relation to our natural selves, our emotions and feelings. We are assumed to have reached a higher stage of moral development if we are capable of taking on this attitude towards ourselves. This is confirmed in the work of Piaget and the work he inspired in Kohlberg. It accepts a Kantian framework as setting the terms for our understanding of moral development as a series of discrete stages that mark our movement from childhood towards maturity, even if few of us reach the higher stages.[1]

We can learn from the differentiations that Kohlberg makes about significant features in our moral lives. He helps us to set distinctions that we might otherwise be blind to. His concern with the conditions for developing democratic forms of schooling that embody democratic principles in their everyday organisation opens up a crucial set of concerns.[2] For too long we have accepted that undemocratic and authoritarian schools can somehow prepare people to participate as citizens within a democratic society. But there are also weaknesses in a notion of citizenship that is organised around a notion of the rational self. It is as if our capacity to think in terms of abstract moral principles defines our existence as rational selves. This is to accept Kantian notions that see 'impartiality' and 'detachment' in opposition to our emotional selves. So it is that we are supposedly 'objective' to the extent that we have *separated* ourselves from emotional considerations and learned to consider impersonal reasons alone.

This is not to minimise the importance of notions of 'impartiality', 'detachment' and 'objectivity' but to question the ways that these have been drawn within a Kantian moral tradition. This is not simply an issue within moral theory, since these visions have guided traditional conceptions of 'objectivity' and 'science' within the human sciences. Carol Gilligan's work, *In a Different Voice*, has been important in showing how Piaget and Kohlberg's work was largely drawn from empirical work with boys. It is from boys' experience that these models of moral development have been drawn, for within our culture boys tend to think more easily in terms of abstract principles.

Boys learn to seek 'the right answer' and feel more comfortable if this can be 'proved' as a matter of reason and logic that does not bring their own experience into the equation. So, with the famous example of whether Hans should steal from the chemist in order to save the life of his partner who needs a drug that she cannot afford, boys might be more inclined to think that 'saving life' is a more important principle than 'the right to private property', so that in this kind of situation it might be justified to take the drug, even if it means suffering the consequences of breaking a law.[3]

So boys might think about this situation in impersonal and universal terms that have little to do with the personal relationships of the people involved. It is not a matter of the feelings that people might have for each other, for this would supposedly place moral decisions upon contingent grounds. It is a matter of setting out what 'the right thing to do' is as a matter of principle, regardless of the individuals concerned. I learned about this from the sharp end once when a colleague said that he was prepared to support the principle of having an extra person in the department, but he was not prepared to support me to have a job that I had already been doing for years. This was not an issue of the open competition for jobs, but of the way an impersonalised language of principles can be used as part of the language of power.

If an ability to think in terms of abstract moral principles defines our sense of morality, as it does for Kant, then it becomes an ideal towards which we all have to strive. But as Gilligan points out, this setting morality in universal terms works to render invisible and devalue the moral experience of women who often think in different ways. It encourages women themselves to discount their moral experience for it argues that only considerations that can be presented in impersonal and universal terms are relevant within a moral argument. This tends to simplify the complexities in our moral experience. It also silences women who are left feeling that what they might want to say in the situation is not relevant. It might be interesting but it is not relevant to a 'moral' evaluation of the situation.

This tends to create a hierarchy of moral experience. It also establishes particular relationships to power and authority. It tacitly legitimates the modernist identification of masculinity with reason that has rendered the masculine voice as authoritative because of its universality and impartiality. As men we have learned to speak for others, thinking that it is our task to say 'what is best' for everyone in the situation. In truth, we have often learned to use our voice to speak for others before we have really learned to speak for ourselves.

Somehow it is easier for us as men to be impersonal, saying, for instance, what would be best for the family to do this summer, than to say what we wanted for ourselves. Since we are being 'neutral', the control that we sustain in these situations is often concealed, for we have learned 'how to take the interests of others' into account. If others talk more personally about what they want, they are being 'personal', 'self-interested' or 'emotional' so that their voices can easily be discounted. It is the language of an impersonalised reason that assumes power and control in the situation.

If women more readily feel that they would want to appeal to the goodwill of the chemist before considering the situation in abstract terms of principles alone, they are appealing to the chemist's concern as a human being. They think they can appeal to his feelings for the urgency of the situation, so that the chemist might be prepared, say, to let them have the medicine, if they are willing to pay for it later. They are seeking some kind of arrangement. At some level there is a recognition that the issue cannot be settled at the level of principle alone, for it involves human relationships.

There is a sense that it would be much better if the chemist could be brought to accept that he should provide the medicine because of the gravity of the condition. If he responds that he is very sympathetic to their plight but that he has a business to run and that if he offered medicine to them then he would have to offer it to others in a similar plight, does this justify the chemist in refusing the appeal since he is universalising the situation, or does he stand accused of placing economic considerations above moral concern? Does this show the moral limits of market considerations which form a libertarian Right consciousness?

Do we think that if the chemist were a woman, she would be more susceptible to other considerations than those offered by the market? Is this a matter of scarce medical resources and their allocation? This resonates with the idea of the impartial moral observer who supposedly has information to make the right decision. But this presents it exclusively as a matter of distributive justice. What gets lost from view is the personal relationship between Heinz and his partner and the lengths to which he is prepared to go in order to save her life.

Is it being said that if he acts out of a sense of love for her, this makes it less morally worthy than if he is prepared to take similar action for anyone in such a situation? Within a Kantian framework it can be difficult to *give weight* to his feelings for his partner as a legitimate moral consideration. These feelings are too readily discounted as particular and personal and so as having no relevance to the moral decision involved. It will be readily acknowledged that it might be significant to the personal decisions that he feels ready to make, but does not enter the 'moral' decision involved.

MORALITY AND MASCULINITY

Gilligan draws attention to a morality of care and concern that helps to express women's moral experience. She suggests a particular relationship between masculinity and a morality of rights and principles. She draws this from her psychological data, but it is possible to make a similar point by drawing attention to a relationship between masculinity and a particular tradition of moral thought and feeling. As soon as you have an identification between masculinity and reason as we have within modernity, and a sense of morality as governed by an independent and autonomous faculty of reason, then it should not surprise us that there is a particular relationship between masculinity and morality. The universality of reason has suggested a universal conception of morality.

It is only when we begin to explore the workings of this universality and the ways that it is established *in opposition* to our natural selves, that we recognise its connection to particular forms of masculinity. When we get a little closer to Kant and take account of what he says about relationships between men and women, the family and sexuality – comments which have all too often not been translated within standard editions – we can recognise that it is men who have control of the gift of universality and reason.[4]

If we try and reinstate a morality of care and concern as a way of rendering visible women's moral experience, it is important to recognise that this cannot be promoted on equal terms without recognising the relationships of power and subordination that are at work. This morality of care and concern is continually being undermined in gender relationships as men have the power to *discount* what women have to say. Their power over reason can give them legitimacy in labelling what women have to say as 'irrational', 'personal', and so as 'beside the point'. It is a power to devalue the moral experience of women. It works to undermine women's sense of the *validity* of their moral experience to the extent often of making them feel uneasy and ashamed of sharing their perceptions.

The issue of abortion raises some of these issues in stark terms. Gilligan draws upon her study of the context in which decisions about abortion are made by men and women in relationships. Men sometimes regard abortion as a matter of principle, wanting to think in impersonal and universal terms as to whether it is 'right' or 'wrong'. Sometimes it does not get to this, as they might say, 'we are too young to have a child' or 'our relationship is not settled enough' or 'we simply cannot afford it'. These can all serve as impersonal reasons, suggesting that it would be quite wrong for others in a similar situation to go ahead with a pregnancy.

The point is that, presented in these terms, *personal* feelings do not come into the situation. Men will often talk as if they have taken all 'rational' considerations into account, so that it is now a matter of dealing with the emotional consequences of the situation. This is a 'subjective' matter which does not have anything to do with the moral decision that has been 'objectively' taken.

It marks a change for men to acknowledge that the situation has to do with them, even if they are ready to acknowledge that in the last resort it is for women to decide, because they have to carry the child. But it is important not to interpret a woman's right to choose as if it discounted the involvement of men in the situation. This would reproduce a traditional pattern in which men thought it had nothing to do with them.

Gilligan shows how women tend to think of the moral decision in terms of their relationships with others but also in terms of who will take what responsibility for the child. But these are not to be treated as pragmatic considerations that can somehow be contrasted as personal and particular with 'moral' considerations that are supposedly impersonal and disinterested. The point, in part, is that there is no such thing as a 'disinterested' decision, for whatever is decided will have an impact on the lives of all those concerned. It is not simply a 'rational' question that, once taken, can allow life to 'return to normal', for it inevitably has an impact upon the relationship.

A rationalist vision tends to argue that if you are clear that the 'right' decision has been taken, then it is 'irrational' to have feelings about it afterwards. This is simplistic because the impact that it can have on lives and relationships can be so different, depending upon the situation of the people themselves. For some people it might involve a period of mourning and sadness, while for others a sense of relief. The point is that it is particular to the lives involved, and cannot be abstracted from these lives as if it can be considered as a matter of reason alone.

Far from being irrelevant to the moral decision that is involved, it might be crucial for both women and men to work out their feelings about the situation they face. As men, we often tend to believe that things could be different by thinking of them in different terms, which is why subjectivist social theories that treat 'reality' as if it were a conceptual construction can be so appealing. In the past we have often enjoyed the power in particular relationships, to get others to accept 'reality' as we have chosen to conceive it. But with feminism times have changed for many.

Reality can be particularly painful to accept. As men, we can be so used to assuming that we can cast it in our own image that we can react like spoilt children when it resists and and we do not get our way. We are so used to this that it can take time to recognise what is happening. It can be particularly difficult for us to locate our *contradictory* feelings in a situation of a possibly unwanted pregnancy. It is as if we feel everything at once, so it can seem as if we feel nothing at all. It can take time and attention to bring some of these feelings into clearer focus and effort and courage to explore what these feelings mean to us in the context of our relationships and lives. If we are not used to this 'emotional work' it can come as a shock to be presented with a decision that affects not simply ourselves.

In such a period of potential emotional intensity many men are so used to withdrawing, wanting to settle the situation in other terms. Kantian ethics can help foster such a tendency, even if it is far from its intention. It can make us feel that where morality is concerned, there is no place for emotions and feelings. It is exclusively a matter of the cool workings of reason, and emotions can only get in the way and distract us from the moral task at hand. Sometimes we can even convince ourselves that it is best to sort out the issue in universal terms and then apply the solutions to our particular circumstances. To act otherwise seems to be to act in a self-interested, even pragmatic way.

Against this it can be argued that this cannot be settled in universal terms of reason alone, for the situation that people face is always different. The point is that it might be crucial for both women and men to explore and validate the contradictory emotions and feelings that they have because these are *relevant* to the moral decisions they take. It is not a matter of coming to terms with the emotional consequences, which are inherently subjective, of a moral decision which has itself been taken on rational/objective grounds.

It is important to stress this issue because it has an immediate bearing upon a whole range of issues which flow from the ways we conceive of the relationship between 'subjective' and 'objective' considerations. How people feel about a situation makes a material difference to that situation and the ways they might both cope with it. It is not just important for both women and men to feel they have had time and space to explore their feelings about the situation, but that these feelings can be part of the grounds upon which the decision is eventually taken.

If a woman feels that she is not really loved in the relationship and if this love has never been expressed to her directly, she might not feel the confidence to go ahead with the pregnancy. She might feel that the relationship could not sustain it. Being shown this love can help to transform the relationship, providing it with a quality it never really had. It might be in the process of working out their feelings about the abortion that people begin to appreciate what they have with each other.

This crisis might help them share parts of themselves that they had always left hidden from each other. So it might bring them closer to each other than they had been before. The expression of feelings can help to *build* trust and closeness that cannot be brought into existence through will and determination alone. I cannot choose to be close to someone, just as I cannot choose to love someone when I do not. Somehow we are able to acknowledge these as significant features of our emotional lives, without really allowing for a moral sensibility that would accord these facts the weight they have in our lives.

Similarly, learning to explore the emotions that have emerged through this unwanted pregnancy might help people recognise how little there really is between them. They might be prepared to face the fact that it is a fear of isolation that has kept them together, rather than anything they really felt for each other. It is through such emotional exploration that people learn and so generate knowledge about the relationship.

In some situations it is a question of dwelling upon these emotional considerations for them to reveal the truths they show about the relationship. This involves men learning to take greater responsibility for their emotional lives, rather than leaving it to their partners to interpret their emotions and feelings for them. This is often an emotional dependency that is hidden from men themselves, for it does not fit the conceptions they have of themselves as independent and self-sufficient.[5]

CARE AND RESPONSIBILITY

This allows heterosexual men to learn to care for themselves and others in possibly unfamiliar ways. If men are used to taking responsibility for others, this is often set in financial terms. It is as if it takes time for us as men to learn to particularise our vision so that we can care for others individually. In most families it seems to be women who more easily remember significant birthdays and who take trouble with presents. It is as if they have learned through their upbringing to express more individualised care and concern for others. Often this particularised vision is at the basis of compassion and love. It is a capacity to see people as individuals in their individuality, rather than as generalised.[6] This registers a different order of significance than most men seem to feel familiar with.

Since masculinity has been identified within modernity with reason and universality, it can be difficult for men to learn to care and love individually. It is because we learn to *discount* our particular emotions and feelings as we identify ourselves with our rational selves that we make ourselves insensitive to important aspects of our experience. At some level men have emotions and feelings of their own, but they are so used to discounting and devaluing them as sources of knowledge that they block their expression. It is partly because emotions are accepted as a sign of weakness that they threaten to compromise our sense of male identity that we learn to be wary of them.

This is not the same with all emotions, for with particular masculinities it can be quite appropriate to express particular feelings. Thus anger is often acceptable for men in ways that it has not been traditionally for women. But this can mean that a whole range of 'softer' emotions like sadness, tenderness, fear, are often displaced into anger because this can be seen as affirming rather than threatening our masculine identity. As we learn to *displace* our emotions in this way from a very early age, we never learn to discern and name the other emotions and feelings. It is as if they have died for us, for we have so little *felt experience* of them to go on with. We might continue talking about them but our language will often be disconnected and false.

This can help us recognise that it is not a matter, as Gilligan sometimes suggests, of there existing two distinct gender voices: the masculine which thinks in terms of rights and principles while the feminine works with notions of care and concern. Gilligan is saying more than this. But she leaves it up to others to work out the implications of the relationships of power and dominance involved. The expression of anger, especially within a relationship, can serve as an exercise of power. It might at some level block an expression of loss if it is occasioned by the disintegration of a relationship.

Men often feel that we can reassert control of a situation so that everything returns 'to normal'. We assume that there must be something that we can *do* to repair the damage and make things new again. It can seem 'rational' to us that if things have gone wrong, we should be given another chance to put them right. Within modernity we become attached to the idea that every problem has a solution that can be reached by reason alone. As long as we have the will and determination to do what is required, a solution is supposedly always at hand.

But it is not always so. Too much hurt might have been created in the relationship for there to be any room for going back. As men, we like to think that the clock can be turned back and we can start afresh. We learn within modernity that time is ours to use and we are used to struggling against it. Though we have a linear conception of time, it is a vision of time as something to be conquered and controlled. We think in terms of a battle against time and we often fight against the restrictions that it seeks to impose, thereby affirming our masculinity.

It is also because male identity can be so tied to physical prowess and strength that it can be hard to accept the waning of our strengths as men and the process of aging. It is partly because it threatens our sense of male identity that we can experience it as a gradual sentence of death. Since many older men will lose their jobs and with it the means to support their families, it can be bitter to realise that our strengths are beginning to wane.

If we sense that things are not right in our relationship, we will often resist this dawning awareness. Part of us will not want to know and if our partners try to voice some of their concerns, we will find ourselves using anger to silence them. Often men will withdraw into a sullen silence as, feeling that part of their world is being threatened, they will feel even less safe and secure to reach out for help. When things are not working in the relationship there will be a tendency to reinforce traditional masculine patterns, for it can feel crucial to hold our male identities intact when everything around us is beginning to feel shaky.

But this does not help to sort out issues in the relationship, for as we withdraw from any contact that might leave us feeling vulnerable we are likely to insist through anger that things are not so bad. We will not want to listen. We might feel a bitter injustice, aware that we worked so hard to succeed and provide in other areas of our lives. Since we are clear that we do all this 'for our partners and families', it is hard to realise how little they really get of ourselves in our absence.

As far as they are concerned, we are *not* there for them. As for our children, whatever the feelings we have for them, in reality we are 'absent' in their everyday lives, however much we attempt to make up for this at weekends. In our absence our relationships have thinned out, and consequently there is not so much holding us together. This is painful to acknowledge, especially if it means realising that it has caused too much hurt and pain for it to be a situation that can be healed.

What is important here is that because we have so little contact with our emotional needs and desires, constantly learning to put these aside within a male identity that is primarily defined within the public world of work, we become *insensitive* to ourselves. Since we learn to discount and silence these needs within ourselves, it is hard to acknowledge their presence in others. It is easy to experience our partners' expressions of need as yet another demand that is being made on us as men. We will do our best to meet it but it will have to wait in the queue along with everything else. Since this is the way that we learn to treat our own emotional needs and desires, if we acknowledge them at all, it is hardly surprising that we will respond in an externalised way to the expressions of others. It is often because we have no other models of relating that we cannot detect anything amiss with this.

If our partners feel that they are not being seen or heard in the relationship, it can be difficult for us as men to grasp what this means. We do not appreciate the ways our relationships have been *instrumentalised* along with the processes of rationalisation that have come increasingly to govern the advanced capitalist societies. We think that we are being quite fair and reasonable by saying that if our partners 'have a problem' then we will do our best to discover how to solve it.

As we have learned to be 'problem-solvers' at work so we automatically behave in similar ways in our personal relationships. It is hard for us to understand when it does not seem to be working and when our partners seem to be asking for something different. It is hard to make sense of what it is and too easy to dismiss it as 'emotional' and so as not really a rational demand that can be met. We choose to ignore it in the hope that, like other things 'irrational', it will go away.

Since we have learned as men to treat ourselves in impartial and impersonal ways, it is hardly surprising that we treat others in this way. Since we learn to discount our emotional needs and desires, learning to treat them as 'irrational' or as interruptions in a rationally directed life, it is hardly surprising that we are deaf to the expressions of others. But since the ways that we are have such social power, we think nothing, for instance, of sending an impersonal memo to our daughter, as this is the way we behave in the office. Since this is how we have learned to be efficient, this is the way we are in the different areas of our lives. It is hard to acknowledge anything wrong, let alone shocking in it. For many middle-class men it would seem as if life would be much simpler if it could be organised in the rational ways of the office.

As men, it is hard to acknowledge that the ways that we have learned to be successful in the world can also make us insensitive to ourselves in our emotional lives and relationships. It is because we have learned to *deny* our feelings and emotions as sources of knowledge that it is difficult to identify what is going on. This blindness is reflected in much of our philosophy and social theory which fails to find adequate ways of recognising the importance of emotions, feelings and desires. This is systematically connected to prevailing conceptions of masculine identity as they have been formed within modernity, and so reflected in our inherited traditions of thought and feeling.

Chapter 5

Freedom

FREEDOM AND MODERNITY

Modernity has largely been organised around a particular vision of the rational self who is able to guide his life through reason alone. We are intentionally talking about the lives of men, for with Descartes our inherited tradition of philosophy and social theory have treated reason as a masculine possession. Men do not have to prove their rationality for it is supposedly a gift of the gods that they can take for granted.

So it is that our visions of modernity have largely been cast to legitimate and confirm the visions of men. The universalism that goes along with modernity is an exclusive, rather than an inclusive, conception. It is a universalism that is grounded within the experience of men and it sets up this experience as an ideal that others have to fulfil if they are to be allowed, even temporarily, within the magic circle of humanity.

This is a Eurocentric vision. For it is Europe that has appropriated science and progress to itself that allowed it to define both 'civilisation' and 'modernity' in its own terms. It was able to define the rest of the world as *lacking* what it could take for granted as its own. It established a sense of the human being as a rational self defined in fundamental opposition to its inner nature. It was as rational selves that we were supposedly free and equal. It is reason that is the guarantee of our freedom.

This freedom is supposedly available to all as long as they are prepared to exist as rational beings, since it is the way in which a liberal moral culture defines freedom as a fruit of the Enlightenment. It is presented as available in universal terms. It becomes harder to recognise the *costs* of this freedom, as it is universally presented as involving gains in freedom and independence and only a loss of dependency and unfreedom.

We learn to accept a vision of our identities as rational selves. We lose a sense of the philosophical grounding upon which this is based, which might render plausible a different account of events. The Enlightenment proved historically victorious in advanced capitalist societies, so it was able to write history in its own terms. It was set as the victory of light over the darkness of the feudal period. Within this earlier period, as Tawney describes it in *Religion and the Rise of Capitalism*

(Tawney 1926), people's identities were provided for them by the position that they were born in in society.

This established a particular set of duties and obligations within the shadow of which people lived their lives. As they were born, so they would die, and their children would take on the duties that had accrued to them. Identities were given, they were not chosen. Within this account of feudal relationships, power and authority was divinely sanctioned and the social order was an expression of a great chain of being within which each creature and each social rank had its place. People learned to know their place and to accept it as a gift that should be gratefully accepted, whatever burdens it left them to carry.[1]

It was only with the breakup of feudal relations that individualism came into its own and people came to conceive of themselves as individuals who held their destinies in their own hands. There is a link between the development of capitalism and the fostering of particular forms of individuality. It was partly in response to the insecurities created by the growth of market relationships that influenced the growth of Protestantism, according to Tawney.

This was a thesis that Erich Fromm develops in *The Fear of Freedom* (Fromm 1991), where he tries to show that freedom is an ambiguous quality, for it brought with it its own insecurities. People no longer knew where they belonged within the social order. As Simone Weil claims, they were uprooted when traditional authorities of church and state were brought into question. This insecurity was one of the costs of freedom, as people found themselves competing with each other for whatever positions were available.

It was these competitive relationships that brought masculine identities into a new focus, since for a while at least women and children took on the status of their fathers. Patriarchal relations assumed a new significance as men had to strive for the wealth and power that they might achieve. Men had to *prove* themselves individually, now that their position in society was increasingly coming to depend, not on family and birth, but upon their individual talents and abilities.

Men had to prove themselves not only in their own eyes but in the eyes of others. It is as if men had to be continually ready to prove themselves because their position and success could never be taken for granted. It always had to be proved, so that if men could take their existence as rational selves for granted, in a way that was never available to women, they could never take their position of success for granted, for this was always at least partly dependent on the conditions of the market.[2]

Fromm draws a useful connection between the ways that people feel at once free but also powerless in the hands of the capitalist market, and the ways that they exist as individuals before God within a Protestant tradition, but whose natures are supposedly evil and irredeemable. People are radically to distrust their natures within Luther and Calvin, for the source of justice and morality lies externally beyond people's natures.

Within a Calvinist tradition we cannot trust our own inclinations towards morality and justice, for these feelings will inevitably lead us astray. We have to *eradicate* these aspects of our natures so that we can attend to a law that is inherently external. As natural selves we are irredeemable. It is only because we have a faith that we can place ourselves at the mercy of God and so find redemption. It is only by forsaking and sacrificing our natures, rather than reworking them through developing some kind of relationship with them, that we stand any chance of salvation.

Even though Luther helps to reinstate the Jewish Bible as a source of truth and revelation, it is still very much as the 'Old Testament' whose revelation has been superceded. He does little to accept the Jewishness of Jesus but insists on the historical denial of this. As our natures have to be denied, so do certain aspects of the historical past. Luther becomes fiercely anti-Semitic at the refusal of Jews to convert to Protestantism. He takes this as a stubborn refusal to accept this new revelation so that the Jews only have themselves to blame. They are to be victimised within Protestant theology and then blamed for their victimisation since they could supposedly have chosen a different path.[3] It is the sense of a unified truth that is available to all that sets the arrogance of modernity. Since a truth has been revealed, what others have has to be less than the truth. It is this intolerance that is also an aspect of a Protestant tradition that in some forms has recognised the virtues of tolerance. But there are different forms of tolerance, some of which only tolerate others until the truth will dawn on them. This is not the tolerance of a genuine pluralism that can recognise the validity of different traditions of thought and feeling.[4]

MODERNITY AND RELIGION

Protestantism has left a deep mark upon modernity for it has largely provided the terms that have been secularised. Its denigration of nature has been carried into modernity and it has played its part in establishing a vision of progress as involving the control and domination of nature. It has presented itself as a missionary tradition and so as the bearer of a truth that is supposedly universally applicable, whatever the traditions that are to be overcome.

Traditional societies in Africa, South America and Asia could not be respected, for they could not be fully 'human' without a Christian revelation. They were to be pitied because they were trapped in their 'natural' ways. They did not know what 'civilisation' was and this could only be presented to them through Christianity. It was the self-confidence that goes with appropriating truth as some kind of possession that fuelled forms of what so often can only be considered as cultural genocide. If these peoples were to be 'saved' their culture and traditions had to be eradicated, for they stood for nature and animality that had yet to be redeemed.

How was it that Christianity for so long legitimated the slave trade? This is a question that haunts the relationship between Christianity and modernity.[5] How did it conceive of these people as 'less than human'? Blacks, like Jews and women, were supposedly closer to nature, so they were deemed as closer to animality. In their different ways they came to occupy important positions within the unconscious lives of a modernity that had sacrificed and excluded its own nature.

As Susan Griffin has so beautifully illuminated in *Pornography and Silence* (Griffin 1980), the European mind learned to project its feelings of sexual desire and emotion that it could not accept in itself, on to others. It was a Protestant tradition that talked of the *eradication* of these aspects of our natural selves. So it was that our desires became signs of evil, of an animal nature that showed that we were still the evil 'good-for-nothings' that we had been accused of being as small children.[6] It proved that we had failed to make ourselves into rational selves and so other than the evil natures at some dim level that we still suspected ourselves to be.

I think it is crucial to connect to some of these religious themes, for they still echo within a secularised experience of modernity. Even if we were not brought up as Christians, these notions can still resonate with us. It is not a matter of conscious belief but of acknowledging those traditions that have helped form what Gramsci called the 'common sense' of modernity.

Gramsci recognised that it was quite misleading to present our consciousness as if it existed as a coherent intellectual construction. It is a weakness of a Weberian tradition that it tends to see meaning in unified terms, as an attempt to bring together in a coherent intellectual way the different aspects of our experience. It finds it hard to acknowledge the tension or contradiction between our consciousness and our experience, for it remains the heir to a Kantian tradition that treats experience as constituted through reason. Gramsci is able to recognise tensions between power and consciousness and so the contradictions that can exist between the ways we think and how we live. He knows that contradictions in our everyday social lives cannot be resolved in our consciousness alone.[7]

Gramsci recognised the fragmented character of our consciousness which does not exist simply as an intellectual or mental construction. It has different elements that are left over from different historical periods and traditions. These are traces that we might not be consciously aware of but which continue to influence the ways we think and feel. In this way Gramsci comes to terms with Hegel's insights into the historical character of consciousness but he refuses to see history as divided into discrete stages which mark the progressive realisation of reason. Rather, he helps to question this vision of history while refusing to consider as 'irrational' ideas which have a religious or spiritual source and so which might be superceded within a scientific culture, having their origins in an earlier time. He recognises them as significant aspects of a present reality which have to be grasped in terms of their continuing influence upon the ways people think and act.

Gramsci was also critical of an orthodox Marxist tradition that would also treat religion as a form of 'irrationality' that with time would be inevitably replaced by the 'rationality' of a scientific consciousness which only accepted explanations in terms of natural causes. This is to treat Catholicism, in the case of Italy, as an aspect of a backward ideology that cannot be explored in its own terms but only in terms of the workings of material interests. As far as people are concerned, their religious beliefs could be no part of their identity as rational selves. Such beliefs were evidence of a superstition that would gradually give way with the advance of reason and science. In this way, Marxism conceived as a science in orthodox terms had no way of engaging with religious notions in a serious way, even when they were a very significant part of history and culture.[8]

Orthodox Marxism, which conceived of Marxism as a form of economic determinism, has been cast within a positivist vision. It was too ready to treat those with religious beliefs as if they were 'backward' and 'irrational'. These ideas could not be taken seriously in their own terms but only as masking underlying material interests. In one aspect at least, it shared with a Protestant underpinning of modernity a sense that it was in possession of the *truth* about the workings of capitalist society and that other traditions of thought and feeling were living in darkness because they did not share the revelations of its science. Against this, Gramsci recognised that religion also served to fulfil real needs in people's lives that had in the first place to be acknowledged.

Catholicism could provide people with a way of sustaining some sense of order in life, amidst the difficulties and tragedies of individual lives. It could sometimes help people to a sense of the reverence of life within a culture that seemed to treat individual lives simply as a means to profit. So it was that Gramsci learned to take the beliefs and feelings of Catholicism *seriously*, wanting to grasp the different forms they took within the different orders of society.

Gramsci did not understand Catholicism as a unified set of beliefs that held everyone equally in its grip, even if it does this more than other religions, but as differentiated in ways that meant its significance had to be grasped in the context of individual and collective lives. Only as Gramsci came to appreciate its historical significance in Italian cultural life could he begin to appreciate how some of its strengths could be reserved within a different synthesis, which, for instance, helped people to a more active sense that they could collectively change the conditions of their material lives, rather than having to accept them fatalistically as somehow divinely ordained.

Gramsci helped to challenge the rationalism of an orthodox tradition of Marxism that saw Marxism as a form of economic determinism. To think of Marxism as setting out the laws of capitalist development which would inevitably lead to some kind of breakdown of the capitalist world and its revolutionary transformation, was to cast Marxism in fundamentally positivist terms. It is to construe Marxism as a science of history and politics, somehow radically separated from philosophy.

In challenging the tenets of orthodox Marxism, Gramsci was also providing us with a way of discerning the weaknesses of a structuralist Marxism developed by Louis Althusser, which was to come later. There is an echo in the ways that both scientistic traditions, one positivist and the other critical of both positivism and empiricism, conceive of relationships between modernity and identity.[9]

For both orthodox and structuralist traditions, Marxism is cast in fundamentally scientistic terms. They may dispute the character of its scientific practice, but both deem it to be realised in Marx's later writings. They are equally dismissive of Hegel and identify the strengths of Marx's analysis in the distance he is able to establish from Hegel. They break with Hegel's insight into the historical character of consciousness and so are blind to any sense of immanence within the development of individual and collective consciousness.

Rather, they are dismissive of any account of individuality, seeing it as a feature of classical accounts of social and political theory that supposedly rely upon essentialist accounts of human nature. Supposedly, a feature of theories of social contract is that people come together to form society to meet pre-existing needs and desires. This does not mean that people have to know the position that they would eventually hold in society, but that in Rawls' more recent vision a 'veil of ignorance' allows people to establish principles of social organisation that they can supposedly agree upon as free and equal rational selves.[10]

To what extent theories of social contract have to make assumptions about human nature is an issue that can be set aside. What Gramsci helps us identify are some of the traps set for our thinking when we accept some of the false dualities of modernity. He recognised the importance of working on the ways that Marx's later writings conceive of themselves as 'scientific'. But he thought it foolish to dismiss Marx's early writings as 'unscientific' because they supposedly rest upon considerations of human nature. This prevents us from thinking clearly enough about the *ways* they rely upon conceptions of human nature.

It does not have to be that human qualities are thereby assumed to be given, as if they are not shaped and distorted through the influence of capitalist social relations. We inherit a false duality between human nature as somehow 'given' – a feature supposedly of social theory before the dawning of modernity and its casting in terms of science – and the idea of people being 'socially and historically constructed'. In setting up notions of 'social construction' in this way, they remain flawed because of their inherent rationalism.

FREEDOM AND HISTORY

Gramsci helps us to question prevailing theories of 'social and historical construction', recognising how at some level they are built on a rationalist denial and denigration of nature. It is as if we can escape the conditions of our natures and with modernity shape external nature according to human aspirations. In his later writing Gramsci grows more wary of these visions of science and progress.

It is in part at least a masculine vision, for it is with modernity that masculinity is set in its identification with reason. As men, we learn to fear what our natures will reveal because they threaten to bring into question our masculine identities. We prefer not to know what our emotions and desires might reveal, for not only might they interfere with the plans and goals we have set for ourselves through reason, but they threaten to show us as more vulnerable than we present ourselves to be in the public realm.

Rationalism seems to offer a point of truth and objectivity from which social life can be neutrally considered. If we think of ourselves as individuals, within rationalist traditions of Marxism we supposedly show we are trapped within a 'bourgeois ideology' that fosters the idea that society exists as a collection of individuals, each able to determine the conditions of his or her own life and so each responsible for his or her happiness or misery. As we move from 'ideology' towards 'science', so we learn to take on an *externalised* vision as we recognise that individuality is 'socially and historically constructed'. We learn to replace individualised categories with the social categories of class, race and gender. Within a Marxist science of history and politics, these become the terms in which we can grasp our experience within a capitalist society.

We learn that, far from being free to share our lives as individuals, our lives are determined by these social categories. So it is that we learn to replace one vocabulary with another as we recognise ourselves within these social categories. For Althusser it is class that determines our experience most profoundly within a capitalist society, and while questions of gender and race might be significant at an ideological level that still controls the formation of identities, through language and culture, they are supposedly less significant at a material level.

Even if structuralist Marxism has had its day, its influence still guides in an implicit and unacknowledged way. So many of our analyses of gender and race still start with a critique of these as 'given' notions, watching for how they change as we appreciate that they are 'socially and historically constructed'. Something important is taught within this shift, but the analysis also traps itself, for it is far from clear what is meant by 'socially and historically constructed'.

Its vision is often too externalised and it can foster its own forms of arrogance as we are reassured that 'others' are trapped in these social definitions but 'we' have been able to free ourselves as we learn how these conceptions we once shared were socially conditioned. This is part of the excitement of social theory but it can often provide insights that come too easily. It seems to provide a meeting point between otherwise opposed interpretative and structuralist traditions, so it is readily defended. In part it is the 'externality' of masculinity that forms the implicit agreement.

There is undoubtedly a strength in being able to take up a position outside and beyond our own experience. But too often this vantage point of 'objectivity' is presented as readily available. This vision of 'objectivity' has a particular resonance with dominant forms of masculinity, for we learn as men to pride ourselves on our rationality, which often means being able to take account of the considerations of others. In truth it often means that we know how to *get our own way*, while presenting it as somehow being in the 'interests of all concerned'. Weber has brought some of these issues into focus with his notion of *Verstehen*, but this is a more difficult notion than is often presented. We think of this in universal terms as 'being able to take the point of view of another', to put ourselves in another's shoes and to see the world from their situation. It can be difficult to work out what is going on here, especially if we relate it, as we should, to issues of gender, class and race.

It may seem as if women more easily identify with the situation of others, which can mean that they place themselves in the situations of others. This is different from conceiving of things from the other person's situation. As Carol Gilligan has pointed out, it can be difficult for women to *include* themselves, to allow the individuality of their moral voice to enter. Thus in her study of abortion it can be easier to think how everyone else in the situation might be affected and to make a decision on this basis. It can come as a revelation to be aware of what they might want for themselves individually.[11] This marks a stage of moral development, to learn somehow to include oneself rather than to discount oneself more or less automatically. This is not a move towards egoism or selfishness, though these notions have often served to control much of women's moral experience.

As Alice Miller reminds us,

> Our contempt for 'egoists' begins very early in life. Children who fulfil their parents' conscious or unconscious wishes are 'good', but if they ever refuse to do so or express wishes of their own that go against those of their parents, they are called egoistic or inconsiderate.
>
> (Miller 1981:vii)

We carry these voices within us and they continue to echo differently depending on our early childhood experience. It can help explain some of the difficulties that women in particular seem to have in somehow including themselves in their moral considerations. If men learn to discount themselves, it seems to be in different ways.

It can be difficult for men to empathise with the situations of others, if they are constantly reassuring themselves that they would never get into the situation in the first place or if they are constantly focussed on giving solutions because they assume that this is what is expected of them. It can be hard to listen, even to our partners for instance, without feeling that we are somehow being accused or being held responsible for the miserable day they have had. It might be that they just want to be listened to so that they can feel that their experience is being validated. But as men it can be hard to recognise this, thinking that they *must want* to get rid of these feelings, so that they must really want some solution to their plight from us.

If we insist on dismissing notions of individuality through contrasting them with notions of collectivity, we too easily *reduce* the complexities of our experience. This danger seems present if we identify modernity with taking up an *externalised* view of ourselves. This promises a false vision of objectivity, for it fails to include ourselves in the situation. Gramsci breaks with these visions of 'science' and 'objectivity', having learned how orthodox Marxism had served to *pacify* working-class people since it had lost any sense of the connection between consciousness and action. It was too ready to dismiss people's everyday experience and culture as 'irrational' or 'ideological' because it allowed its vision of rationality to be defined by Marxism alone and this became the yardstick against which the experience of others was to be judged. Since Marxism was the possessor of truth, it was easy to judge the experience of others against it.

In this regard I have often been struck by the resonances between Gramsci's *Prison Notebooks* and some of the ideas Wittgenstein is working with in his

Philosophical Investigations. Both are working with their discontents with a rationalist vision of modernity that suggests that there is a single standard of rationality that helps place a particular notion of objectivity against which the 'subjective' experience of others can supposedly be judged. Both are re-evaluating in very different ways the relationship of experience to reason, *refusing* to see experience as constituted either by a faculty of reason or by language alone.

They question the sovereignty of reason that has been part of a tradition of modernity and which has conceived of it as a unified mental faculty. Both are working to revivify connections between thought and action or behaviour that had been rendered invisible within a rationalist tradition that saw actions as the outcome of reasons, if they were not to be considered irrational. Both refused to judge social practices by an externalised vision of reason, seeking to explore the particular rationality that was working implicitly within these practices themselves.

When Gramsci declares that 'we are all philosophers' he wants us to recognise that different philosophical traditions are at work within our everyday experience. This is part of a process of self-empowerment as we learn to take greater responsibility for the ways in which we think and feel. We do not have to accept a passive relationship to these traditions of thought and feeling as we become aware of how we actualise them in the ways we think and behave. This is part of a process of *critical self-awareness* as we become aware of the different levels of our experience and also of the different traditions and ideas that help form our sense of ourselves and our relationships with others.

As we take seriously the injunction to 'know thyself' in a way that connects the ways we think and feel with wider social and historical relations, we are already challenging traditional demarcations between 'subjective' and 'objective', for we do not simply know ourselves as a product or effect of these discourses and relationships. We gain a sense of the ways we can *change* ourselves as part of a process of transforming social relations within which we live.

In this sense our 'subjectivity' and 'individuality' is not 'socially and historically constructed', for we are active beings able to transform these relationships. We are not simply the products or effects of particular relationships or discourses. This is to take an externalised view of our identities in a way that *minimises* the responsibility that we also have for our lives. It is a strength of a dialectical grasp to keep alive the tension between who we might struggle to be ourselves, and what social relationships would have us be.

This refuses to grant a higher wisdom or authority to the social, seeing the individual in essentially egoistic terms. It refuses to set 'individual' against 'society' in these terms. It recognises the relationships within which individuals are forced to realise themselves without pretending, in Hegelian terms, that any kind of reconciliation might be possible. These contradictions remain aspects of our experience that cannot be wished away or reconciled through consciousness alone.

To present this less abstractly through an example: the difficulties that women might have in identifying and validating their values within a patriarchal society that constantly works to render their experience invisible are much worse when women are alone and isolated. The powers that are set against them can be overwhelming, and able to crush individual lives.

In Gramsci's terms, as patriarchy forms part of an unquestioned hegemony, people take for granted the superiority of men and the inferiority of women. This is institutionalised in the everyday organisation of social life as much as in the ways that men and women are brought up to think and feel about themselves. In a culture like Brazil, for instance, we can sense it in the way that some three-year-old boys hold themselves. It is as much an attitude of mind as it is part of bodily posture. Often the two are inseparable and equally difficult to shift.

Individual women in all periods and cultures have rejected the 'normality' that is presented as patriarchy. They have sometimes known that they carry a different truth within themselves, even if this is not given any public recognition. It is difficult to sustain a feeling for the integrity of their own experience when this is diminished and derided in so many areas of social life. Too often the idea that individuality is 'socially and historically constructed' tends to normalise particular individualities and particular values and experiences. It easily speaks the language of the powerful and unwittingly legitimates dominant definitions and identities.

It loses a sense of the tension and contradiction between who women are struggling to be and the dominant relationships of power. Often it is difficult to bring these contradictions into focus without a complex and textured grasp of experience. For sometimes a sense of who someone is struggling to be is inchoate and barely conscious. It might show in unspoken disappointment and resentment when for instance one is continually being passed over or not taken seriously as a person.

FEMINISM AND MODERNITY

Within the context of the Women's Movement women learned to draw support and strength from each other. These are not women's 'subjective' experiences but work to transform an objective situation as women grow in their own authority and strength. They no longer have to apologise for themselves or judge themselves by the singular standards of a modernity largely cast in masculine terms.

They can assert the *difference* of their values and beliefs, learning to respect the reality of their own experience and ways of knowing, rather than for instance dismissing or diminishing them as 'irrational' because they are based on feeling or intuition and so not based on reason alone. In recognising the validity of different forms of knowledge, feminism helps to challenge a modernity that privileges reason as the only source of knowledge.

We have been slow to recognise feminism as a challenge to modernity. Its refusal to accept prevailing distinctions between reason and emotion or between public and private life have not been appreciated enough as questioning a rational self able to guide life by reason alone. The public realm was supposedly the realm of 'reason' and 'objectivity' while the private was the sphere of 'emotion' and 'subjectivity'. This has provided a significant framework for modernity. Feminism has helped create a counter-hegemony in its recognition of different forms of knowledge and in its validation of different identities. It has sought ways of validating different forms of experience, rather than exclusively evaluating them according to reason.

In this regard feminism has been part of a refusal to privilege reason and science. It has been prepared to recognise the rationality, for instance, of discourses of morality and aesthetics, rather than deeming them as 'irrational' because they are not made up of factual statements alone. Within the realm of logical positivism, they were regarded in emotivist terms as so many forms of expression or persuasion, but they were not 'real' for they were not about the empirical world. Supposedly values were not part of the world. They only exist as matters of individual commitment and concern.[12]

Discussions around post-modernity have often been locked around issues of identity, wanting to see the modern as somehow defined by a universal Cartesian conception of reason and identity and the post-modern as a breakdown in this vision of the rational self. This brings a plurality of identities into being which refuses to give privilege to any, as they presumably come into prominence in different aspects of life.

But this vision of fragmentation and displacement is not as new as it is presented, and the vision of modernity against which it is set is often too rigid and static. Women have long lived this fragmentation, as they have sought to validate their experience within a patriarchal culture. So have blacks in the context of a white culture or Jews in the context of a secularised Christianity. Gay men and lesbians have also had to assert their own identities against a normalised heterosexuality. But if notions of post-modernity also want to remind us not to *fix* people into these identities, because, for instance, we are always more than our sexual or ethnic identity, they also have to consider the *weight* of these identities in our lives. This is especially so if they have been hidden for so long that people have learned to deny and feel ashamed of these aspects of their being.[13]

But those who discuss the post-modern often think that, in challenging the western notion of reason that characterises modernity, they have to dispense with the notion of truth. As identities not hitched to the conception of reason become fragmented, so does the notion of truth. We are presented with a plurality of truths and often with a relativism that does not seem to worry because it is not any longer set against an alternative vision. In the end we seem to be left with few ways of judging between the truths available.

Feminism in its different forms has been significant in sustaining a focus on the relationships between *truth* and *power*, knowing how relationships of power have worked to marginalise and diminish women's own experience and truth. This does not discount *differences* that exist between women or different elements of the Women's Movement. It has been crucial to learn how to appreciate the different oppressions that women suffer and not to subsume them unwittingly under a universal norm. But if black and ethnic minority women have had to discover their own voices more recently they can draw upon an awareness that feminism does not argue that those who are powerless and oppressed have a monopoly of truth and virtue, for it has long appreciated how relations of subordination can also work to brutalise and disfigure. But it has meant learning about the realities of racism and anti-semitism and the difficulties of talking about women in general. It has also raised crucial issues about the tenability of gendered identities, which we will need to consider.

If modernity sets in place the idea of reason as an independent faculty being the source of truth, it did not go unchallenged in its own terms. If we have learned to revere Descartes and Kant, we should not forget Herder and those who are seen as part of a 'counter-Enlightenment'.[14] The issues of identity have been crucial to these differences, for it was the Enlightenment that accepted the rational self as the moral self. But others like Herder were prepared to acknowledge different aspects of our experience, refusing to judge them according to the standards of reason alone.

As we are beginning to rethink the terms of modernity, rather than to accept it uncritically, it opens up new visions for our philosophy and social theory. It also sets old differences, like those between positivism and phenomenology, holism and individualism, Marxism and functionalism, in a new light. Hopefully it sets the terms for a renewal of social theory too long blocked in a debate between abstract oppositions.

Chapter 6

Identity

REASON AND IDENTITY

With modernity we have learned to think of ourselves as rational selves. This has helped to cast our experience in a particular light and has helped to shape prevailing traditions of philosophy and social theory. It has meant that our freedom supposedly lies in the goals and ends that we discern for ourselves through reason alone. As our reason is supposedly the source of our individuality, so it is also the source of our freedom.

This is shaped in masculine terms to the extent that it involves a denial of our needs. As men, we learn to take pride in *not* having any needs, especially emotional needs. It is 'others' who have needs that we have to be ready to support. Part of us continues to feel that others would do as well to curb their needs as we do, and so to exercise a 'self-control' that leaves them equally invulnerable to others. It is supposedly because women are more emotional that they find it difficult to do this.

In large part, our inherited traditions of philosophy and social theory privilege our existence as rational selves. It is when acting out of reason that we supposedly realise our higher nature as human beings. It is when we act out of a sense of duty that we are supposedly accruing the only moral worth that our actions can have. It is only as rational beings that our lives supposedly have dignity and we can respect ourselves.

Since we are supposedly free to see others as rational agents, it is possible to respect them as equal human beings. In *Kant, Respect and Injustice* (Seidler 1986), I argued that it is also possible to respect ourselves as emotional beings and to respect the integrity of our emotional, sexual and spiritual expression. As we can be false to the ways we think, so we can also be false to the ways that we feel or sense. These can all be different ways of *denying* what we experience. They can be different ways of forfeiting an inner truth.

I argued that a rationalist culture does not help us to respect our feelings, emotions or intuitions. Rather it teaches us that if we are able to 'take ourselves seriously' as 'rational beings' we will *discount* these aspects of our experience as 'subjective' or 'personal'. In never learning to take these aspects of our experience seriously, we fail to take ourselves seriously.

It leaves us with a fragmented conception of self as we learn to repress – even feel ashamed of – aspects of our experience that do not fit these idealised images of ourselves. We learn to suppress significant aspects of our experience and so to deny our reality as sexual and emotional beings. This makes us less sensitive to ourselves than we could be. It also makes us less sensitive to the injuries others endure.

Alice Miller in *The Drama of the Gifted Child* shows how these theoretical issues have a bearing upon the ways that we learn, as children, to respect others. She comments on how 'respect for others' is often said to be missing in self-centred people. She says how

> a child who has been allowed to be egoistic, greedy and asocial long enough will develop spontaneous pleasure in sharing and giving. But a child trained in accordance with his parents' needs may never experience this pleasure, even while he gives and shares in a dutiful and exemplary way, and suffers because others are not as 'good' as he is. Adults who were so brought up will try to teach their children this same altruism as early as possible.
>
> (Miller 1981:viii)

So a cycle is set in place that repeats itself from generation to generation. What is more, a Kantian ethical tradition finds it difficult to discern what is at issue in this difference. What the child might have been deemed to have lost cannot be treasured within its scheme of things.

For Kant it is important that we learn to do what is required of us, regardless of what we might feel about it. To make our moral actions dependent upon our feelings supposedly gives them an unreliable basis. But if consistency is important, as is the need to avoid favouritism or partiality, this cannot be secured by reason alone. Miller's experience proved to her that

> If a mother respects both herself and her child from his very first day onward, she will never need to teach him respect for others. He will, of course, take both himself and others seriously – he couldn't do otherwise. But a mother who, as a child, was herself not taken seriously by her mother as the person she really was will crave this respect from her child as a substitute; and she will try to get it by training him to give it to her.
>
> (Miller 1981: viii)

These are large claims and possibly different senses of respect are being invoked in the different instances, for the respect that is first suggested, as Miller knows, probably cannot be trained, for it relies upon a bringing together of thought and feeling.

The richness of psychotherapy is suggested in the issues it raises of what is involved in being taken seriously by our mothers, or for that matter our fathers. This involves not only our thoughts being listened to but also our feelings. If we are continually told that we cannot feel angry, for we have nothing to feel angry about, then our feelings are being systematically undermined. We are *not* being taken seriously. We learn to put our anger aside, for we do not want to be continually humiliated.

Within a rationalist tradition we are made to feel that we have to have 'reasons' for our feelings, for otherwise they become 'irrational'. This fosters its own displacement as we learn to search for the reason, before we allow ourselves to have our anger. But often the moment has passed and it is not expressed at all. We learn to welcome this in a culture in which anger itself, in whatever form it takes, can be treated as a sign of 'irrationality' and 'lack of control'.

Within a vision of modernity defined in rationalist terms, we learn to evaluate our emotions and feelings according to the externalised standards of reason. It is less a matter of whether, for instance, our anger is *appropriate* to the situation we find ourselves in, than whether we have sufficient reasons for it. This is to intellectualise our emotions and blocks us from learning from the information they potentially bring. Our emotions have a logic of their own which cannot be subsumed without working to displace them from the position they properly have in our lives.

It is quite misleading to think that we only need to resort to emotions when reason breaks down, somehow marking a fault in communication itself. Kant tends to reinforce this false understanding of our emotional lives in his suggestion that they are always externally determining our behaviour. That our anger, for instance, sometimes works in this way does not mean that it has to. It is more likely to do so if we have such little experience or relationship with it. The more that we allow it to have a place in shaping our experience, the more appropriate it is likely to be in its expression.

Within a Kantian tradition there is a particular view taken of self-knowledge that does not include experience of our emotions and feelings. It is as if we have to know ourselves as rational beings alone. This is what makes it hard for Kant to acknowledge the importance of love as anything other than a rational feeling. It is part of the spiritualisation that he inherits from his Protestantism that treats love as 'pure' to the extent that it is *separated* from the bodily and the sexual.

As we supposedly ascend from the animal, we leave these aspects of our experience behind us. Love is no more to be rooted in our emotions and bodily experience. As I have argued in *The Moral Limits of Modernity* (Seidler 1991), this serves to define a limit of modernity. Even if we continue to acknowledge the importance of love and falling in love in our lives, it is as if we have learned to discount it theoretically. It is as if a world with reason has become acceptable as a world without most forms of love.

Is it partly an issue that we are all supposedly equally capable of reason while it turns out that we are not equally capable of love? In what sense is our loving an expression of our individuality and a recognition of the individuality of another? Does love become more difficult as we learn to identify ourselves as rational selves, since this is conceived in ways that block the recognition and expression of our emotional selves?

This is akin to what Herder thought in his questioning of Kant. His vision of human beings as expressive suggested that our individuality is expressed in the ways that we feel and live as much as in what we think. This is not to deride the importance of reason and rationality in our lives, but to question the abstraction that allows it to exist as an independent and autonomous faculty. For Herder, this language of faculties has no existence in reality, for we cannot meaningfully abstract our experience as 'rational selves' from the totality of our experience. Not only is this abstraction false but it disfigures our experience.

What Herder is challenging is the ways that we exist for Kant as rational selves. It means we exist as complete and the only development that he imagines is in our growing identification with our moral selves as we learn to curb the influence of our inclinations. As we learn to act out of a sense of duty for its own sake, we undergo a process of transformation. This does not absolutely capture, for Herder, the expressive character of our lives. It is only as we discover a mode of activity which allows us 'to be who we are' that we can grow and develop as human beings.

In part this seems to mean discovering an activity through which we can most fully express ourselves, rather than settling for an activity that is chosen by reason alone. It matters for Herder that we have a feeling for what we are doing. This will make a difference to the *quality* of our expression. For Kant, it only matters that we are doing things that we have freely chosen as ends or goals. Supposedly, emotion and feelings could only get in the way, for Kant, of the clarity of the choices we make.

For Herder, our reasoning cannot be separated from our emotions and feelings. They grow and develop in relation to each other, since they are part of an 'expressive totality'. They have to find their place within our experience and this cannot be assigned in advance by a sovereign faculty of reason. In different areas of our lives our different abilities and capacities will be brought into play.

Somehow our philosophy and social theory has to break with a tradition of Kantian rationalism, so influential for both Weber and Durkheim, if it is going to be able to illuminate the richness and vulnerability of individual and collective life in society. It somehow has to find a place for the insights of Herder, as it has for an insight of Alice Miller that reminds us gently that

> A little reflection soon shows how inconceivable it is really to love others (not merely to need them), if one cannot love oneself as one really is. And how could a person do that if, from the very beginning, he has had no chance to experience his true feelings and to learn to know himself?
>
> (Miller 1981:ix)

As far as Alice Miller is concerned, most people live without any notion of his or her true self, somehow

> enamored of an idealised, conforming, false self. They will shun their hidden and lost true self, unless depression makes them aware of its loss or psychosis

confronts them harshly with that true self, whom they now have to face and to whom they are delivered up, helplessly, as to a threatening stranger.

(Miller 1981:ix)

She seems convinced that for most people 'the true self remains deeply and thoroughly hidden', which leads her to ask tellingly, 'How can you love something you do not know, something that has never been loved?'.

Within the context of prevailing traditions of social theory, such questions can seem awkward, even naïve. They seem to pose questions in a way that can strike us as sociologically and historically naïve. And yet they also have the power to haunt us, reminding us of something important that we no longer, in our false sophistication, seem able to talk about. It is a questioning that can still move us, suggesting perhaps that some of these insights, possibly commonplace in psychotherapy, might be important for our philosophy and social theory too.

IDENTITY AND SOCIETY

With modernity we have inherited a tight and exclusive view of reality. The Scientific Revolution of the seventeenth century has helped shape a vision of reality which has largely been sustained within our inherited traditions of philosophy and social theory.[1] The guiding traditions of empiricism and rationalism have set the framework within which much of our discussion takes place. It is as if they set the terms of the 'reasonable' beyond which other arguments and considerations are somehow beyond the pale.

We learn to accept that only what can be measured or quantified is real for, with Descartes, we are assured that reality is organised in mathematical terms. It is through reason that we can supposedly move beyond the realm of appearances to lay bare the structure of reality itself. So it is that within a rationalist tradition at least, it is the categories of reason that provide us with the categories of reality.

Within in empiricist tradition, championed in different ways by the writings of Locke, Berkeley and Hume, it is assumed that all knowledge has to have its basis in sense experience. There are no ideas which are innate and which help structure our consciousness as there are for Descartes, for everything that we learn has to be learned from our sense experience and from the impressions that we receive through our different senses. For Locke it is taken as obvious that we are blank slates upon which experience writes itself.

Within our social theories, especially within functionalism, this resonates with the notion that human nature is 'pliable' and can be 'moulded' according to the customs and practices of a particular society or culture. This was argued partly as a response to theories of natural differences which explicitly accepted the superiority of western culture in racist terms.

Functionalism, particularly in its structural-functionalist forms, has proved a powerful and formative movement within sociology. Having an important source in the writings of Durkheim, it sees society as *sui generis* and regards individual experience and social practices from the point of view of the function that they have for the larger society.[2] It tends to be less than tolerant about issues of individual identity, tending to view these issues as part of a 'psychologism' that it is doing its best to escape from. It is the society which is real and which in reality is reflected in the actions of individuals. This forecloses the possibilities of rebellion against oppressive relationships in any other terms than those anticipating future developments in society itself.

As Durkheim describes it in his discussion of 'Individual reason and moral reality',

> The individual can free himself partially from the rules of society if he feels the disparity between them and society as it is, and not as it appears to be – that is, if he desires a morality which corresponds to the actual state of the society and not to an outmoded condition. The principle of rebellion is the same as that of conformity. It is the *true* nature of society that is conformed to when the traditional morality is obeyed, and yet it is also the *true* nature of society which is being conformed to when the same morality is flouted.
>
> (Durkheim 1974:65)

As if we need to be reminded, Durkheim insists that 'In the sphere of morality, as in the other spheres of nature, *individual* reason has no particular prestige as such' (Durkheim 1974:65).

The repressive character of these assumptions has taken time to emerge. In Durkheim's case they have as much to do with a rationalist tradition and its belief in the universal character of reason and science. For Durkheim it is important that 'the intervention of science has as its end...the collective itself more clearly understood' (Durkheim 1974:65). In part, this breaks with an earlier Enlightenment rationalism that saw reason as a critical faculty before which institutions and practices had to legitimate themselves.

This assigned a particular critical authority to reason that it was to lose within a positivist tradition which identified reason with existing reality, either as it is or, with Durkheim, as it was becoming. This allows Durkheim to grasp conflict and struggle as features of a movement from mechanical to organic solidarity, which were the terms in which he conceived the move from 'traditional' to 'modern' society. These conflicts are short-lived and have their source in a period of transition.[3]

This appropriated reason from individuals themselves and placed it in the movement of society itself. For Durkheim, it is society that becomes sovereign and in its movement defines the limits of reason. In part, positivism is a response to Hegel's vision which recognised the antagonism between the 'real' and the 'rational' – that what exists cannot in positivist terms be identified with what is rational. The existing state of affairs, say, as it was characterised by slavery or class oppression, had to be *negated* so that the existing state of affairs could be made rational, namely a situation which supposedly allowed individuals to express their individual and collective freedom.[4]

Hegel's sense of the realisation of reason and freedom could, as Marx partly recognised, be repressive in a different way. It tended to give priority to the historical process as the medium through which reason and freedom will be realised. In their different ways Durkheim and Marx were still to prove crucial to an instrumental rationality that was eventually to dominate both capitalist and state socialist societies. In their response to the flaws of liberal individualism, they ended up in disempowering individuals, making them feel that as individuals little could be done as they stood before the mighty institutions of science and state.

Within a positivist tradition, individuals also lose a sense of the dignity that they might otherwise be able to claim for themselves within a rationalist tradition as rational selves. It is as if their reason has little weight or consequence. It is no longer a source of their freedom, that somehow comes to rest elsewhere, in the movements of society itself.

In this regard a positivist tradition has done much, despite its strengths in discerning patterns of social behaviour, to set the terms between individuals and state. It has existed in some tension with democratic theory for it has assumed the power of science to discern what is real, independently of the perceptions of individuals themselves. In its own way it has been repressive in its legitimation of an instrumental rationality. It has assumed that, crudely, 'society knows best' and that individuals would do best to conform to its movements.

As Durkheim expresses it,

I am not concerned with 'the literal meaning of reason'. On the contrary, this methodological application of the reason has, as its principal task, our release from the suggestion of 'reason'. This understood, in order to allow the things themselves to speak; the things in this case being the present condition of moral opinion in its relation to the social reality which it should express.

(Durkheim 1974:66)

This vision of what constitutes 'social reality' against which individual experience can seem to exist as a pale reflection, has had enormous influence. It sets the terms for understanding a particular relationship between 'individual' and 'society'. If it has strengths when set against a conception of society as a collectivity of individuals each able to determine their individual lives, giving credibility to the formative powers of social relations in organising individual lives, it also has weaknesses. It can work to disempower individuals and invalidate the truths that can emerge from their experience.

Durkheim's formulations echo in positions that have become familiar within structuralist traditions that define themselves in opposition to the sovereignty of the individual that is supposedly a feature of classical political and social theory. Against this it has become usual to talk about the ways language is able to constitute particular experiences, so that language is somehow speaking through us. Through articulating our experience it supposedly forms particular subjectivities.

In this way, structuralist traditions have been faithful to rationalist traditions and the ways they have served *to subvert* the reality of individual experience. As it was, the categories of reason and mind that had a reality able to constitute and organise experience in their own terms, so now we talk of language and discourse as constituting particular identities.

Here we might sense a certain kinship between Durkheim and certain notions of language that seem to be developed in Wittgenstein's *The Philosophical Investigations* (1958). But we have to be careful how to evaluate it. There is a shared challenge to the idea that language somehow emerges out of the agreements that individuals make with each other, and correspond to the meanings that people carry in their minds. Both are sensitive to the fact that we are born into a community of language users and that it is *within* such a community that we learn to know ourselves and the social world. We do not establish these meanings for ourselves individually, nor are they a product of reason alone.

But Durkheim would then be tempted to assign language, like society, a reality of its own which is both prior but also somehow sovereign in relation to individuals themselves. It is as if the terms of sovereignty have been reversed, and where the individual stood we now discover society. But this is to accept the same framework, only to reverse it.

LANGUAGE AND IDENTITIES

Wittgenstein, like Herder in some ways, also sees language in expressive terms. He wants to sustain the notion that individuals also learn to express and discover themselves through language. This helps to challenge a passive relationship towards language and blocks the idea that individuals are somehow the effects of language or discourse. For Wittgenstein however, there remains a more dialectical sense, in that, for instance, language in relation to pain tends to be an elaboration of natural expressions of pain. This helps to explain why this is such a crucial example in *The Philosophical Investigations*, for it helps to break with the rationalist distinction between reason and nature that would present language as an outcome of reason alone.

While Durkheim tends to sustain a rationalist view which presents language as an autonomous expression of reason, Wittgenstein crucially helps to question this view. That his work has been presented as part of a 'philosophy of language' has tended to hide this from view. It has been easier to misinterpret Wittgenstein's later writings to sustain a framework that sees language as providing a system of classification that serves to order social reality.

If we continue to think of language as constituting experience, then it becomes impossible to open up issues about the contradictions or tensions between our experience and the language in which we seek to express it. This is a difficult issue, since Wittgenstein has often been read as arguing that there is no experience with which our language can be compared in a one-to-one way to see whether it fits at all. He mentions for instance that there is no timetable in the sky, so to speak, with which the veracity of the timetable that we hold in our hands can be compared.

Similarly, we have no images in our minds with which we compare the cat standing before us to see if it is 'correct' or not.

In part, this can be read as a challenge to a theory of meaning in terms of ostensive definitions, as well as more abstractly and indirectly to a Platonic theory of forms. But it is important to put these examples in context, for they have been invoked to argue that Wittgenstein is saying that there is no experience that is somehow prior to language and with which language can be compared. There is supposedly, so the story goes, no experience that is not linguistic or discursive.

But this is misleading, especially when it is used to conclude that all experience has to be *linguistic*, so foreclosing any possible tension between language and experience. This tacitly works to assimilate Wittgenstein back into a rationalist tradition that he was doing his best to break with. We are back implicitly with Wittgenstein's early views of the *Tractatus* in which language is presented as a system of classification which helps order 'social reality'. These classifications are supposedly the work of reason so that in the end we find Wittgenstein being assimilated in to the Kantian inspired later Durkheim of *The Elementary Forms of Religious Life*. There might well be significant resonances here, and there remains something striking in the homologous relationship that Durkheim discovers between the principles of social organisation and the ways a particular cosmology is conceived. Even here, Durkheim sustains a sense of the independence of social life which is not seen in interpretive terms as the outcome of a particular mode of classification.

Where these issues are particularly important is where they serve to block any tension between language and experience. If we see identities as the outcomes of effects of language or discourse, then we can *discount* any experience that does not seem to fit. This resonates with a particular form of masculinity that insists on creating reality in its own image and in discounting as 'personal', 'subjective' or 'anecdotal' anything that does not seem to fit.

Within modernity the particular identification of masculinity with reason gives men a particular *authority* to make the world according to their image. Since it is reason that is supposedly the legislator of reality, it is easy to dismiss experiences that would bring some of men's ideas into question. Within the tradition of objectivist positivism this is all too clear, for it is the social laws that have been discerned by reason that are 'real' while experience can so easily be derided as 'subjective' or 'personal'. It is the 'impersonal' and 'objective' character of reason when set against the experience of individuals that gives it its authority.

But something similar is true with interpretive traditions in sociology that take their inspiration from Max Weber and Alfred Schutz.[5] Much of contemporary social theory has been set as a movement between Durkheim and Weber, between positivism and interpretive sociology. It sets issues of method within an endless debate between 'subjectivity' and 'objectivity' which years before Georg Lukács helped to identify as a debate within a shared framework of modernity – or, as he had it, within the 'antinomies of bourgeois thought'.[6] The ways in which Hegel and Marx were able to break with this framework through challenging the supposedly 'contemplative' relationship to social reality through an emphasis on social reality as an outcome of collective praxis will be discussed later. At the moment, at least in terms of methods, where Marx's notion of a revolutionary dialectic fits uneasily, centre stage is still largely taken by these issues of 'subjectivity' and 'objectivity'.

In relation to issues of identity and reality, this is significant because positivist theories supposedly view individuals as unfree and determined by external social forces. Individual freedom is seen as a significant myth, the boundaries of which are forever being challenged by the advances of science. Stuart Hampshire's *Thought and Action* takes this further into the realms of psychoanalysis and the unconscious, wanting to argue that they establish causal explanations of which individuals remain largely unaware.[7] Others argue on Kantian lines that as moral agents we remain free and self-determining, able to do good or otherwise, even if in much of our empirical lives we remain determined.

MEANING AND IDENTITY

Against the unfreedom of individuals that is supposedly an inescapable feature of positivism, a Weberian tradition has been able to argue that individuals are 'free' to the extent that social action has to be meaningful and individuals can assign meanings to their experience. Weber wanted somehow to reconcile this acknowledgement of the meaningful character of social action with the possibility of providing causal explanations. This partly depended upon, as Schutz argues, being able to provide independent criteria for the identification of social action.[8] He disputes whether these criteria can in fact be provided.

In so doing, Schutz provides an important bridge between Weber and a tradition of interpretive or phenomenological sociology that moves towards conceiving social reality as a subjective construction. Social reality comes to be very much what we take it to be, for there is no 'independence' or 'objective' reality with which our conceptions or classifications can supposedly be compared.[9]

This vision is strengthened in Weber's initial insight into the complexities of social reality which means that there can be no singular or 'truthful' way of representing it. There is no single narrative that can be legitimated as the objective view of reason and science. The way that we conceive of 'social reality' very much depends on the intentions and purposes that we bring with us to our task. This is part of what makes our vision of social reality 'subjective', for it depends partly upon the terms in which we are choosing to order, define or represent it.

It is partly because social reality is so complex that it becomes a subjective construction. It is also possible to question some of the positivist interpretations, say of crime or suicide, showing how these notions come to be constituted as one alternative, amongst others.[10] It can help bring to the surface certain moral assumptions that are left implicit and which serve to govern the judgements that we tacitly make about what constitutes a 'crime' or a 'suicide', or, for that matter, how it is that we might consider suicide as a crime.

It can be useful to set things out in such stark terms for it can serve to bring forward how much is in fact shared by what we usually take as competing or contrasting traditions. If it is a strength of interpretive traditions that they do not treat individuals as 'cultural dopes' responding blindly to the play of social forces, it has to be acknowledged that the limits to this freedom are set through being able to conceive of the social world and our actions in different terms.

It is a freedom and identity that is fixed in conceptual and rationalistic terms, for it is as 'rational agents' that we can presumably conceive of social reality in different terms. In this way our identities as creative and self-determining human beings remains circumscribed. It is then said, for instance, that phenomenological sociology sustains a vision of practice, since in coming to understand the world in different terms we are supposedly changing it. But as Marx grasped long ago, this is a very limited conception of individual and collective praxis.

In sociology, phenomenology has tended to remain within the Cartesian framework elaborated by Husserl.[11] It has proved much more difficult to integrate the radical critique which Heidegger made of Husserl's work and which he attempted in part to respond to in *The Crisis of the European Sciences*. Where this has been tried it has been difficult to make connections with the more empirical concerns of the discipline.[12] In part, phenomenological sociology has often limited itself to a unified vision of the individual consciousness as the source of meaning.

It is through consciousness that individuals supposedly assign meanings to their actions. It is as conscious selves able 'to bracket off' the terms in which the world presents itself, so able to discern a realm of essences, that our identities are conceived within phenomenology. Within sociology the intuitions of these essences is less significant than the capacity to discern the contingent terms in which social reality happens to be constituted.

As the emphasis shifts with Garfinkel and ethnomethodology from consciousness towards considering the rules of language themselves and the implicit moral connections they help to articulate, identity can be presented in more fluid terms.[13] We learn to think of identities as being constructed through language and the efforts that people make to present themselves in particular ways. Thus, in investigations of medical encounters, we can watch for the rules that are being created through language which allow, for instance, parents to construct themselves as 'responsible' when, as in David Silverman's work, they are discussing whether to allow their child to undergo an operation.

We can watch for certain rules that recur in the ways that parents present themselves and the ways that children are conceived of within these conversations.[14] This tends to focus upon the ways identities are contingent and are continuously being reworked and sustained. This is a useful perspective for it makes us sensitive to how identities are being continually questioned, threatened, sustained and reasserted. It makes us aware of the contingent character of identities.

But such work lacks a textured sense of experience, for it assumes that this is constituted through language itself. It remains within a rationalist framework even if it has found ways in conversational analysis of de-centring the subject. It can discern how particular moral rules are constituted through conversations but it assumes that language is the only reality that we have, for in traditional terms it repeatedly says that we cannot be sure of what is going on in people's heads. We cannot know their inner experience, only what is evidenced in the language they use.

We can watch, for instance, as doctors and parents constitute the experience of the child according to the tensions that exist between a medical discourse and a personal familial one. But through this process the child is *silenced*, and if she or he is allowed to speak, it cannot be in a way that might legitimate aspects of a particular discourse but only as generating yet another discourse that can be set against the others. We can simply watch as different identities are threatened and defended, say for instance when a parent nervously asks a doctor to explain the evidence that might suggest an operation.

Conversational analysis carries on within circumscribed limits, for it starts from the premiss that what is said is the only reality that we have. Those who might want to voice an unspoken tension or fear can easily be dismissed as 'humanists' who are attempting to appeal to experience that supposedly exists prior to language. Similarly, there is no way of drawing attention to how the child's experience, say, might be diminished or denied in the way that the doctor is discussing it, invalidating the fears they might have as 'emotional' or as 'subjective'. Language comes to assume an objectivity of its own, able to dismiss or deride other realities as 'emotional' or 'anecdotal'. Only what is said is supposedly 'real', 'reliable' and 'objective'. It is the only thing that can supposedly be relied upon as a source of knowledge. As emotional beings we only exist through the language we use.

I have wanted to explore just how pervasive is this vision of the rational self within competing traditions of social theory. In part, it reflects a masculinity that is confident that reality exists as we have wanted to conceive it, or as science has shown it to be. This sustains a particular notion of masculine authority that has to protect itself against the intervention of an experience that might bring its reality into question.

As men we often do not want to hear that women experience things differently from us, that for instance they feel dissatisfied and are not getting enough from a relationship with which we feel quite content. It reassures us as men if we can be sure that reason is on our side and that they are being emotional and will gradually come to see the relationship in the same objective light that we do.

In part, we have created social theories that are similarly self-enclosing and which legitimate our existing as rational selves alone. It is as if we do not also have an existence as bodily, emotional and spiritual selves. These aspects of our experience are silenced or denied as we enter the ground of public life, which is traditionally a masculine world of the rational self, in which our social and political theories have traditionally grounded themselves.

But it means that our traditions of social theory fail to illuminate important aspects of our personal and social lives and so fail to validate much experience that is potentially meaningful to us. It is to these issues of validation within modernity that we must now turn as part of enriching our visions of identity and personal life.

Chapter 7
Modernity

MODERNITY AND REASON

Social theory has largely been organised around the issue of whether objective knowlege of society is possible. Different traditions of thought and feeling conceive of this issue in different terms. Set within the framework of modernity it is presented as an issue of whether our knowledge of society can be compared in its objectivity with our knowledge of the natural world. A hermeneutic tradition has stressed the meaningful character of social life, which means that a method of cultural interpretation is appropriate to the historical and cultural sciences. I want to approach some of these issues in a different way since I think that once we grasp the failure of particular forms of social theory to validate particular aspects of experience, different questions will become prominent.

Laing's work *The Divided Self* has had a limited impact on social theory, but it raises some significant questions in an accessible way.[1] Laing was working with positivistic versions of psychiatry on the one side and traditional psychoanalytic theory on the other. He recognised weaknesses in both traditions when it came to validating the experience of people. In their different ways they were attempting to treat madness in terms of a language of reason. This led to the rejection and confinement of mentally ill people, particularly those suffering from schizophrenia. They had been objectified within the language of psychiatry that accepted the authority of reason to develop categorisations such as 'schizophrenic' or 'manic depressive', that were taken to be objective.

These became the categories of science determined by reason alone. They were able to set the standards against which people's 'subjective experience' was supposedly to be judged and evaluated. It became a matter of fitting people into these appropriate boxes so that within the terms of psychiatry they could be treated with the appropriate medicines for these supposedly organic conditions. Mental illness was conceived as a breakdown of the mind in very much the same mechanical terms as bodily illness was treated.[2]

Laing recognised the importance of Foucault's work, especially *Madness and Civilisation*, which seeks to grasp the significance of a brief period when mental hospitals emerged in different parts in Europe as places where the mad were to be confined along with vagrants, the mentally retarded and the disabled. Foucault recognised that in earlier times the mad were accepted as part of the community where their madness was also appreciated as carrying insights and wisdom that, even if set apart from ordinary mortals, could not be simply dismissed.[3] The knowledge that they shared was also familiar in dreams and visions which still held a place within early modern culture. There were also charlatans and tricksters but people sometimes learned to detect them. This did not underestimate the difficulties for the families having to cope with madness near at hand, but sometimes others could be called upon to support. People could also be cruel and baiting, but they did not feel that madness was necessarily contagious or threatening.

Madness and Civilisation tells the story of a shift towards modernity which, with the sovereignty of reason cast these different ways of knowing as exclusively forms of unreason that needed to be shunned. If they had sometimes been seen as the work of the devil this was not always so, and now this theme was set in secular terms. There was nothing to be learned from dreams and fantasies and the connections with madness, if acknowledged at all, were repressed. It was declared that reason was the only source of knowledge. It was a centralising notion that gave enormous power and authority to those men who could claim reason as their own.[4]

This involved a deep and lasting challenge to the church authorities who had traditionally assumed the position of legislators of knowledge. According to Isaac Newton, it was reason that could supposedly discern God's plans for the universe. It was only later that we were to understand the seventeenth-century scientific revolutions in secular terms as part of a conflict between reason and faith. Many of those involved did not see it in these ways since they saw developments within natural philosophy as revealing a divine order of things.

In some ways reason remained a democratic faculty, for it was a capacity that was shared by all, even if not to the same extent. Supposedly the advances of science could be confirmed by all, which was part of the significance of an invention such as the telescope. It shifted the terms of authority and it meant that knowledge was separated from the traditional authorities provided by Aristotle and the church fathers. This vision of a naturalised knowledge could help support the growth and development of centralised state authorities as existing independently from the church. They could claim the sovereignty of their own sources of knowledge as having an independent foundation in reason alone. This prepared the ground for the independent claims of a secular state authority. Within the new balance of power, state authorities could also unite with the religious authorities as they had in the development of slavery and trials of women accused of witchcraft. It was to be an authority set firmly in masculinist terms.

Foucault follows the processes through which these conceptions of reason and science became sovereign. They established knowledge as science, objective and independent, so existing as an authority that could be used coercively when set against people's experience that was increasingly discounted as a source of knowledge. So it was that 'the Age of Reason' provides a much more ambivalent inheritance than we are usually led to believe.[5] It involved bloody struggles for it to gain its unquestioned legitimacy, serving to transform quite radically people's relationships to nature, to themselves and to those who claimed authority. Modernity separated knowledge as existing in a sphere of its own, guarded and protected by reason alone. It set knowledge in fundamentally masculinist terms, for it insisted that white European men in particular had appropriated reason as their own distinctive faculty. So it served to set gender, race and ethnic relationships of power on a new footing. It gave dominant forms of masculinity enormous power and authority as the legislators of knowledge.

It was white men who could claim to have reason and knowledge on their side in their struggles against women and people of colour who were supposedly closer to nature. Masculinity was sovereign in relation to women and nature, for it helped to set the terms in which others were to make their claims to knowledge. The newly discovered scientific method that was proving so successful in explorations of the natural world was declared to be universally valid. It set the criteria according to which all forms of knowledge had to legitimate themselves; unless experiences could be replicated then they could not yield knowledge. At best they could yield insight and belief, but not knowledge. Somehow for knowledge to exist it had to exist independently and neutrally and it could not depend upon the personal qualities of the individuals themselves. This could only be superstition, for it rested upon personal premisses.[6]

Some of these features came into play in the struggle of the new science against healing which was stigmatised as witchcraft, thereby isolating women who had traditionally been predominant in these healing arts.[7] They had evolved a relationship with nature that recognised that there was a continuity between the energies that flow through nature and those that flow through ourselves as human beings. This involved a recognition of a relationship with nature that fostered the idea that people had to learn how to live properly with their own energies as part of living in proper relationship with nature. This involved a respect for the nature within ourselves as much as for the natural world of which we recognised ourselves to be part. It was partly in the disruption of this relationship to nature, as Rousseau sometimes grasped, that people would be made mad. Systematically to deprive people of their relationship to nature – both inner and outer – was to leave people uprooted from the soil that they needed to grow into themselves.

As men became the possessors of reason and knowledge, women were supposedly left with experience and emotions. The link between knowledge and experience was broken. It was remade within an empiricist tradition that treated knowledge as having its source in an externalised vision of sense–experience. Within this tradition knowledge was a matter of the association between these different elements of sense–experience.[8] Within our traditions of sociological method it yielded the idea of data as existing as discrete pieces of factual information that have to be brought inductively into relationship with each other to yield valid knowledge. This restricts the place to theory to an original hypothesis or to the manipulation of data.

With the development of rationalism it is only objective knowledge that can be validated. It has to be tested and confirmed and it has to be neutral and impersonal and so it cannot depend upon the personal qualities of people themselves. Insight and sensitivity only have their place in the generation of an initial hypothesis that has later to be tested. We lose a sense of wisdom within western culture as it is replaced by knowledge. We are wary of differentiating between the qualities of different individuals, thinking that it is inevitably elitist and that democracy involves holding tight to the notion that we exist as rational selves alone. But what then, for example, are we to make of the powers and qualities of healers which do not seem to be transferable? They become threatening to this new masculinist vision of reason and knowledge as essentially impersonal and objective. It has to be the work of the devil, and in any case it has to be fought as 'unreasonable' and so as an 'offence to reason'. As an offence it needs to be punished and gradually liquidated.

MEANING AND STRUCTURE

We learn to eradicate emotions and feelings that do not fit our conception of ourselves as 'rational selves'. These emotions are deemed threatening and we learn to live as if they *do not exist at all*. This is crucial for the ways that we have learned to treat ourselves within a vision of modernity that has largely been set in Protestant terms. In part, it recognises that as we learn in Kantian terms to suppress our inclinations so that we can increasingly act out of a sense of duty, our emotions and feelings become weaker in the hold that they have over our experience. Kant welcomes this development for he sees moral action as an expression of reason alone. This defines his vision of growth and development for us as moral agents.[9]

We learn to *eradicate* those aspects of our being that threaten this vision of ourselves and remind us of an 'animal nature' we had hoped to leave behind. This shapes our conception of inner growth and development, setting self-control principally as an issue of control *as* domination of our natural selves. This is to set it in masculinist terms which leave no room for any reconciliation with our emotional, somatic and spiritual selves, as somehow integral to a sense of inner growth and development. It is this path that is firmly established when inner strength is set in Protestant terms as a matter of mind over matter.

Foucault helps us to grasp how this vision of growth and development was associated with a particular vision of reason within modernity. The notion of reason as an independent and autonomous faculty somehow went together with a sense of the 'impartiality' and 'objectivity' of reason. Within traditions of social theory cast in these secular terms of modernity it comes to seem as if 'subjectivist' notions of reason provide the only coherent alternative. So it is that our discussions of method seem endlessly trapped within this polarity, each presenting its own vision of validation. Within interpretive traditions it can seem as if the insight that reality is 'socially constructed' soon makes it an issue of individual commitment, as if, in some sense, we choose the reality that we live. If there is a sense that this can help express something truthful, it soon gets lost as it is presented in generalised terms that fail to appreciate the significance of structures of power and subordination within which people live their lives.

This polarity is also reflected in traditional discussions within political theory which have helped define distinctions between 'left' and 'right'. We can be trapped by an idea that the structures of power and subordination exist 'objectively' so that individuals in their 'subjectivity' are quite unable to change the conditions of their lives. This seems to be a 'subjective' illusion that inevitably wastes people's energies, almost a matter of knocking their heads against the brick wall of necessities. This tends to disempower individuals as they are convinced that the sources of all their misery and unhappiness are exclusively externally produced. So it is only when these objective structures of power and subordination are challenged by collective action that their lives can change.

But often this is interpreted to mean that by ourselves we are powerless. Individual action, even in the context of our individual lives, is deemed useless. This serves on the Left to perpetuate a 'myth of individualism' that supposedly needs to be forsaken once and for all, if the conditions of collective action are to be prepared. Within the communist world Leninism took this direction. In the end it meant that the individual was despised in the face of the movement of historical forces. Recent events in Eastern Europe have forced a much-needed reconsideration of this whole Leninist direction of theory and practice.

Within a tradition of market liberalism the individual is made responsible for his or her own position in society. So it is that individual misery and unhappiness is largely set in terms of individual abilities and talents. If this talks in terms of individuals and their lives, it can serve to disempower them through a different route, through encouraging them to *internalise* their feelings so that they only have themselves to blame if they fail to find fulfilment and wealth. As this sense of failure is internalised, individuals turn against themselves since it seems as if they only have themselves to blame for the conditions of their lives. They have to carry the burden for their failures, for it seems to be impossible within a capitalist political culture to understand their lives in any other terms. If they have not 'succeeded' then they have failed.[10]

Within the liberal relativism that has come to dominate capitalist consumerist economies since the 1960s the harshness of these inner judgements of failure has been supposedly softened by the notion that 'success' is a subjective, individual notion. So it is often said that what counts as 'success' for me does not have to have any meaning to you. Success can supposedly be defined in individual terms. This supposedly makes it impossible to compare the experience of individuals since there is no longer a single scale against which they can be judged, as there is, for instance, in objectivist accounts of class that rely upon income as a measure.

We have to know the terms in which individuals themselves account for their experience and what meanings they assign to the different elements in their lives. But if there is some insight captured in this way of thinking, it is partly in the challenge that it opens up to a capitalist market economy that can only recognise wealth as an indication of individual success. It is as if other activities in life are automatically marginalised and the values that they might embody patronised.

In a capitalist economy such as has developed in certain urban areas of for instance, Sao Paulo in Brazil, you can watch such transformations in practice. In the early 1940s it was still possible for people to give some priority to their relationships with each other, but as the economic crisis deepens, relationships are increasingly fragmented and within the middle class there is less time and space for relationships outside the family. Even if familial relationships still remain strong they are also put under pressure. For years there has been considerable pressure, especially on middle-class men, to assume high-earning jobs and to consider themselves as having failed if they do not make it in these terms. Money comes to dominate everyday life, especially in a situation of inflation where exchange values seem to change almost daily. It is as if mental space is fully occupied by money.

It can seem rational for people to train in occupations such as engineering or computers which offer more income and to reserve their interests, say in music, as hobbies. The pressure to live one's life in this way can be intense within a middle-class world in which health care and education is privatised and there is constant fear of falling behind in comparison with others who have done well. But this needs to be identified as a particular form of capitalist rationality which works to subordinate a whole range of other values to monetary values. It produced a privatised medicine in which consultants expect to be paid in dollars rather than in the local currencies.

In the context of mass poverty that is produced in countries like Brazil, it seems impossible to highlight the smaller tragedies in individual lives where people are crushed because they fail to follow what they need to do for themselves. To give up an interest and love for music when this could be the guiding thread in an individual life, however, should not be minimised. It should not be discounted but has to be grasped as part of a larger situation in which human life is often so tragically wasted.

MODERNITY AND SELF-KNOWLEDGE

Social theories cast within the terms of a rationalist vision of modernity have in large part inherited thin and attenuated conceptions of experience. In their different ways they have derided experience, often in objectivist terms, by evaluating it through independent criteria and treating it as 'personal', 'subjective' or 'anecdotal'. It was a matter of reason yielding the categories of 'reality' and our experience being judged and found wanting according to their criteria. As Foucault illuminates it historically, our dreams, visions and intuitions are automatically treated as forms of unreason. They do not have truths of their own to teach us, for they are 'irrational'. They are not sources of knowledge, for it becomes axiomatic that for knowledge rather than belief to exist, it has to exist independently of us.

This sense of knowledge as 'independent' and so available to all was an important element in whatever democratic impulses existed within the Scientific

Revolution of the seventeenth century. It literally placed knowledge at arm's length and threatened to deny the possibility of a distinction between 'knowledge' and 'information'. Knowledge becomes something that we can accumulate as if it were akin to a commodity that can be stored. With modernity, as Cavell has pointed out, we have built our conceptions of knowledge around a knowledge of objects.[11] This has provided us with our critical paradigm against which different kinds of knowledge are to be assessed. In contrast to this, our knowledge of persons, especially as it grows out of visions of self-knowledge, has been traduced. It is as if we can only know persons to the extent that we conceive of persons *as if* they were objects. In large part, as Cavell recognised, this fragmented a western philosophical tradition and placed 'modern' philosophy in the image of Descartes and Kant upon different foundations.

An older tradition that goes back to the Greeks and possibly, if we go along with Martin Bernal's *Black Athena*, also to Egypt and India, bringing into question the belief that the autonomy and independence of a western tradition largely formulated within the nineteenth century has a different valuation of self-knowledge.[12] It refuses to fragment self-knowledge and knowledge of the world into separate and distinct spheres. It is this fragmentation that has defined a particular tradition of modernity as well as a dominant masculinity that has learned to shy away from self-knowledge, especially where it touches emotional life, as a form of self-indulgence. Supposedly it is only as objects that we can know ourselves, setting ourselves against standards that have been objectively defined.

In a gnostic tradition the injunction to 'know thyself' takes on a particular significance since it is through a deepened knowledge of self that one comes to know God. This recognises that self-knowledge is a process within which we gradually come to a deeper relationship with aspects of the self.[13] What remains vital for social theory is its grasp that cognitive or mental knowledge can remain at a superficial level of experience. Often it is when we have a *felt* experience and our feelings come together with our thoughts that we are in a process of change. In this sense, feelings cannot be separated from thoughts as if they exist in a subjective realm of their own. I might accept intellectually that a sexual and intimate relationship is over but it might take me a great deal longer to accept this emotionally. It might only be when this happens that space can be created in my life for a new relationship.

This helps to place a discussion of self-knowledge into a context that refuses to draw any categorical distinction between our thoughts and feelings. It helps us recognise the importance of the feelings with which we act in our relationships with each other. It challenges a utilitarian tradition that might say that it can only be hurtful if, for instance, we mention to someone in hospital that we did not really feel like coming that day. This would be to cause gratuitous pain, since as we had come anyway, is it not best to 'cheer the patient up' and so to 'put a good face on things'? Sometimes this might well be appropriate, when for instance a person would only feel rejected if you shared your feelings or possibly if they did not understand what you would be trying to say to them. But in other situations people might appreciate you communicating what you are feeling since they might well have sensed the awkwardness in your manner.

The point here is that it is not only what is said that is communicated, though linguistic theory in sociology often assumes that this is so. What is left unsaid is often as important in understanding the dynamics of a situation. Kant is misleading in suggesting that what matters is that we visit out of a sense of duty and that if we have to act against our feelings, this is more to our credit. But this is because he assumes, as does a whole ethical tradition shaped in his image, that our inclinations are 'given' and 'unchanging'. It is assumed that we cannot change what we feel but only what we think and how we act. This makes it hard to acknowledge that if we truthfully express what we feel, our feelings might well begin to change and our experience take on a different shape. Within a rationalist tradition it can be difficult even to talk about a truthful expression of our feelings since they supposedly influence our behaviour externally. We can supposedly only reach towards some truth by learning to hold our 'inclinations' in check so that we can listen to the voice of reason alone.

Subjectivist theories have largely been cast in a rationalist tradition. The fact that in large part they reject objectivist claims to knowledge does not make them any more sympathetic to emotional life. They tend to conceive of social reality in Kantian terms as a construction out of mental categories or representations. What matter are the systems of classification through which 'social reality' is constituted. This is the way that within modernity we assign meaning to an otherwise meaningless social world. Similarly, this is the way that our experience is also conceived as the outcome of particular mental forms of representation.

This makes it difficult within dominant rationalist traditions to appreciate any sense of *contradictions* within our experience, say, for example, for women between being workers and mothers, where there can feel as if their lives are being ripped apart as they can feel guilty while at work and inadequate while at home. It is as if these contradictions are not embedded in the way that we live and how society is organised, but supposedly in the mental ways that women choose to represent or give meaning to their experience. These contradictions, being supposedly 'personal' and 'subjective' in character, can be reconciled at the level of consciousness alone.

But it can be misleading to conceive of meaning in mental terms alone. We are left with accepting that there is a movement from mind or mental state to action and experience. This helps sustain an intellectualist form of hermeneutics that has lost touch with the initial impulse that was connected to felt knowledge. As the connection between knowing and feeling is broken within modernity, so the hermeneutic circle is presented in mental or intellectualist terms. Experience becomes an issue of interpretation and the possibilities of interpretation seem endless. There seems to be no way of breaking out of this circle, so long as it is presented in these terms.

If issues of validation emerge they are settled by the individuals themselves more or less pragmatically, depending on the purposes that inform the investigation. We are often left with a realisation that different groups choose to represent or interpret the situation in different terms. Within discourse theory we are left with the different accounts that people give of situations. Since 'truth' is often taken to be an effect of discourse we are left without ways of deciding between them. To think of doing so is taken as a sign of an aggressive positivism that needs to be resisted.

Wittgenstein, especially in his later writings, helps to shift the terms of this discussion, refusing to work at the level of a polarity between 'subjective' and 'objective' truths, patiently bringing into question the terms upon which such a distinction rests. This is part of the force of some of his arguments concerning private languages where he wants to show that, far from these being the tenable basis for any understanding of language, they are themselves derivative upon a shared community of meaning.[14]

But at the same time Wittgenstein helps us to challenge an interpretive tradition that would present meaning, and language itself, as if it were simply a mental or intellectual concern. It is not a matter of whether there is any 'correspondence' between what is going on in my mind as a mental state and what is happening, say, in the social world, as a state of affairs. Wittgenstein challenges such correspondence theories of truth. But along with them he undermines the traditional basis for this distinction between subjectivist and objectivist theories.

It is no longer a matter of whether, as realists have it, the social world can be said to exist independently of our representations of it or whether it is itself 'constituted' or 'constructed' through the categories or classifications by which we order it. We constantly get trapped by this polarity that is continually being expressed in different terms. As Lukács sensed in his critique of the antinomies of bourgeois thought, within modernity both these positions leave us in a fundamentally contemplative and passive relationship to social reality.

Lukács sensed an issue but he could find no adequate solution to it, wanting the subjective consciousness of the proletariat to provide us with an objective understanding of capitalist social reality.[15] Though there is something to be said for the understandings that are yielded to those who suffer from the oppressions of capitalist society, it was not something about which Marx, let alone Lukács, could give us a satisfactory account. Lukács was still trapped into the terms of classical theory, somehow wanting to reconcile the 'subjective' with the 'objective' and thus finding ways of rendering objective understanding of social reality.

If we were also to think about the ways the antinomy leaves us in a passive relationship to our experience, we would begin to develop some of the insights that have become familiar in recent feminist theory. Women learned that they would not solve the issues of low self-esteem and self-worth which they faced as features of their subordination through intellectual means alone. It was not simply an issue of using will and determination to think of themselves in different terms, but also of taking steps to *transform* their relationships.

CULTURE AND LANGUAGE

At some abstract level there remains a crucial resonance between some of these feminist insights that we will return to in more detail, and a direction in Wittgenstein's later writings. It has to do with a refusal to see issues as intellectual or mental issues alone. In its most general terms – which inevitably do an injustice – it has to do with learning how to *ground* the ways that we think in the ways that we live out our everyday lives. When Wittgenstein says that when we explore the meaning of a term we should look towards the complexity shown in the different ways that it is *used* in our everyday lives, he is returning language to its natural connection with everyday life.

He has learned that a rationalism that insists that the categories of reality can be defined through reason alone, with which our everyday usage can then be compared and found wanting, is opening up a false path. Wittgenstein knows this, because it was a path that he took himself in his earlier writings when he thought that philosophical problems could be solved in intellectual terms alone. Life taught him differently.[16] Problems of philosophy could not be separated out from problems of life. Marx had a similar insight that there cannot be one logic for philosophy and another for life, though he thought about it in quite different terms.

Wittgenstein is refusing to treat language as a feature of an autonomous faculty of reason alone. He grows wary of invoking reason as an autonomous faculty and so brings into question a guiding axiom of modernity. But to challenge reason in this way is to challenge a particular conception of reason and a particular vision of rationality that goes along with it. We have to *investigate* the workings of reason and rationality in the different areas of our lives. It does not exist in a pristine sphere of its own, setting universal standards against which different social practices, even whole cultures, can be judged and found wanting.

Positivism has helped reinforce an authoritarian vision of reason which has been used to legitimate forms of colonial oppression, since other cultures were in need of the 'civilisation' that only the West could bring, for 'progress' and 'modernity' were very much established within a western idiom.[17] This still largely holds true in large parts of the Third World, even if the mechanisms of cultural oppression have changed. The television has assumed a central position in even the poorest of homes.

Wittgenstein can be invoked against such positions, but it is quite misleading to regard him, or for that matter Peter Winch in *The Idea of a Social Science*, as exponents of a cultural relativism. It is important that values and meanings are returned to the cultural contexts in which they have emerged so that we can begin to understand the place that they have in people's lives. It is therefore a mistake to regard spiritual healing or witchcraft as lesser forms of what we already have in the West. We have to begin by suspending judgements as far as we can, in order to begin to grasp the meaning that these practices have in people's lives.

This is to refuse a functionalist path which might tend to assume that these practices are 'irrational' or 'lack scientific validation' so that we can only learn from the individual and social functions they play, for instance, as regards sustaining social solidarity or integration. But to understand these practices in the context of these communal lives need not mean either that this is the only context in which they could be appreciated or learned from. Rather, it is a warning against certain *externalised* forms of understanding in which we assume that *we* are in possession of truth while 'others' only have faith or belief or emotion.

When Wittgenstein investigates the meaning of particular concepts in *Philosophical Investigations* he is helping us to recognise the variety of contexts in which a concept might be involved, so warning us against accepting a single context as somehow paradigmatic for all other contexts. We are also continually reminded of childhood contexts in which we might have learned how to use a particular word or phrase. This is to recognise that these contexts are not exclusively linguistic but that language has a role, sometimes large, sometimes small, to play. This is crucial for it opens up a space of interplay and possible tension between language and experience and refuses to think of experience, as post-structuralist theories often do, as a linguistic phenomenon alone. It is part of *enriching* the conception of experience that has usually been allowed for within traditional forms of social theory.[18]

For instance, when Wittgenstein thinks about an activity such as remembering, which is often accepted as a paradigm for mental activity and as a basis for conceptions of personal identity thought about in intellectualist terms, he subverts this idea of remembering as exclusively a mental activity. He reminds us that when we are searching our drawers, unsure where we left a letter, this is all part of an activity of remembering.[19] It is as much a physical activity as a mental process, or rather we are quite mistaken in thinking that we can separate out these different elements and certainly wrong in assuming that priority has to be given to the 'mental' activity. Through this investigation Wittgenstein is challenging a Cartesian split between mind and body and so healing a fragmentation embedded in the ways that we both conceive but also live our experience. To remember is also to *ground* our experience for it brings us back to a sense of its richness and complexity.[20]

If I manage to find the letter that I have been looking for, does this mean that I have remembered correctly? Is this a way of validating my memory? But suppose that I come across the letter by going through a drawer: does it make a difference if I am searching this particular drawer with an intention of looking for the letter or if I just happen to come across it hours later when I have given up the search, so to speak? It is difficult to say, but it might be quite wrong to prioritise the intention as if this is what matters alone.

Wittgenstein helps to restore a sense of connections which are often lost to us when we think about remembering, say, in more abstract philosophical terms. It is in this sense that he perhaps thinks of his work as some kind of cure or therapy for ways of thinking that have become difficult to resist within modernity, for so much of our lives seem to be organised in its terms. The suggestion seems to be that if we get a little closer to investigating the contexts in which these concepts come most naturally alive, we will begin to appreciate connections usually lost to us.

Wittgenstein provides a challenge to a rationalism that suggests that there is a neutral position of objectivity outside of language from which its workings can be viewed. In this sense he stands against the kind of science of language that we find with Saussure and semiotics. It is this vision of language that has largely taken hold with structuralist and post-structuralist forms of social theory. It can be argued that if reflects a particular dominant form of masculinity which prefers to take an *externalised* view that it has learned to identify as rational.

As men we have learned to assess situations, for instance, to establish whether our emotions or feelings might be appropriately expressed within them. As I have already argued, we are anxious that our anger be considered 'rational' and so legitimate *before* we allow ourselves to have these feelings. This involves a subtle form of suppression and it can leave us estranged as we discover ourselves existing outside and beyond our own lived experience. It is as if we have become incapable of accepting, say, our anger for what it is, needing to legitimate it in terms of reason before it can be allowed to exist at all.

Aspects of post-structuralist theory resonate with this externalising in the ease with which they have it that we do not express ourselves through language, but that language somehow articulates our identities and experience *for* us. This sets the issue too crudely but at least it helps us to focus upon a passivity that such theoretical work presents as unalterable. It is misleading to present this simply in terms of being 'active' or 'passive' in relation to language, though these terms have been enormously significant since the time of Aristotle in defining gender relations. With modernity this was given a rationalist form as men alone were supposedly active in relation to reason so that women and children could only aspire to be 'rational' in relation to men.[21] This distinction has less significance for post-structuralism, which tends to see identities and experience as linguistically constituted. It is as if language speaks through us.

At this level of identity and experience, we can sense a resonance with a Hegelian tradition against which structuralism supposedly set itself so firmly. It rejected its characterisation of the historical nature of consciousness. But, paradoxically, both share a thin conception of experience, for with Hegel it is historical forces that are expressing themselves through our lives and we are simply the bearers of these forces. In some respects structuralism gave this a linguistic formulation, setting itself categorically against a humanist tradition that supposedly holds to an essentialist conception of human nature which finds expression through language. It tends to reject any sense of 'expression', sensing a humanist tendency that for structuralism needs to be displaced once and for all.[22] There is no sense in which 'I' can express myself through language, for there is no sense in which 'I' can be said to exist independently of the language that supposedly constitutes both my identity and my experience.

Wittgenstein works in different ways. He is more sympathetic to notions of expression, for instance, wanting to see language related to pain as an elaboration of a natural expression of pain. But it is crucial that expression does not have to take linguistic forms, for a cry of pain can do as well as a form of pain behaviour.[23] At the same time, Wittgenstein would probably have rejected the abstract contrast between 'individual' and 'collective' as much as the distinction between 'active' and 'passive'. He learned to be wary of distinctions that were so generally formulated and he would possibly have been critical of the mirroring that goes on within a structuralist tradition, tending to replace one set of contrasts with its opposites. Wittgenstein helps us to challenge the either/or duality that is such a pervasive feature of a rationalist tradition. He would often refuse the alternative when, for instance, he recognises that language can be both understood as emerging out of community as well as allowing for individuals to express themselves.

Wittgenstein shares the recognition that language is neither an individual construction, nor is it a creation of reason alone. It is not an issue of whether, in structuralist terms, individuals can be said to exist prior to and independently of language or whether they are constituted by it. This loads the issues in an unhelpful way, especially if it supposedly works to deny the existence of individual experience and qualities. It is crucial for Wittgenstein as it was for Hegel and Marx, though they took it in a different direction, that individuals grow up, and their identities are sustained, *within* the context of a community.

In this sense it is quite mistaken to set the 'individual' against 'society' in generalised terms, however useful this might otherwise be to limit the powers of the state in relation to the individual. Each in their own way rejects an externalised view that places 'society' independently as an object to be perceived or understood. In this regard at least they each bring into question a dominant vision of masculinity that feels more comfortable with holding both 'experience' and 'society' at arm's length.

In this way Wittgenstein, Hegel and Marx can be seen as challenging a classical tradition of social theory which sees society as existing independently as an object of study. This was to set social theory in fundamentally epistemological terms, be it in the objectivist traditions of positivism or the subjectivist traditions of interpretive sociology. Within modernism, both traditions were organised around epistemological concerns of whether objective knowledge of society was possible. Issues of consciousness became central since it was supposedly through the mind that we would come to know the world.

Within a Cartesian tradition we inherit a disembodied vision of consciousness that goes some way towards accounting for the poverty of experience that has characterised dominant traditions of social theory. Similarly, philosophy was presented as a mirror of nature and inherited disembodied conceptions of personal identity.[24] Both traditions worked to suppress our existence as emotional and sensual beings, relegating these to aspects of nature that had no connection to the claims of knowledge.

Chapter 8

Experience

HISTORY AND EXPERIENCE

Hegel helps to challenge a Cartesian tradition in his recognition that consciousness does not exist separately and independently of social life, but that we come to consciousness through the processes of social life. As I have already argued, social reality was not assumed to be rational so that we do not have to accept it as defining the terms of rationality. This is the mistake that a positivist tradition makes in identifying the 'real' with the 'rational'.

This is a limiting vision that narrows the focus of social theory to an exploration of society as it exists now and the laws which might help explain the shape it has taken as well as how it can be sustained. This is part of a conservative bias that has been identified as integral to a functionalist tradition.[1] In contrast, Hegel recognised that existing institutions, say of slavery or colonial oppression, have to be negated if they are to be made rational. But Hegel tended to see this as part of an historical process in which we could more or less anticipate the direction towards freedom and emancipation. History became the guardian of reason and freedom.

But Hegel assumes that society, or at least the state, presents the higher interests of individuals and that whatever conflicts exist between individuals in civil society will somehow be reconciled through the historical process. It is this belief in the historical process to which Marx gives a material form. But he recognises a weakness in Hegel's inability to focus on the significance of people's everyday material lives. What matters are not the everyday struggles of life but the salvation that is made possible through the historical process.

It is here that a secularised Protestantism can be sensed as working, for what matters is not our everyday earthly lives but the salvation that will eventually come. It is as if our individual lives do not have meaning or significance in themselves, but only as instantiations of a historical process. If there is a recognition of the contradictions in earthly life, particularly in relation to labour which was to be so crucial for Marx, these only have a temporary status since they will inevitably be reconciled as the dialectic comes to rest in the absolute of the Prussian state.[2]

If Marx refused this conclusion, his own sense of history and progress meant that he inherited some of the weaknesses of Hegel.[3] At some level he seemed to sustain some of its deeper assumptions, since it can seem as if our lives only have meaning as contributions towards a revolutionary progress. If Marx recognises that it is through labour that we realise ourselves as human beings, it was difficult for him to sustain this insight in the face of the analysis that he gives in *Capital* of the historical development of the capitalist mode of production. It is as if the dynamics of labour become central to the growth and development of the capitalist system which Marx increasingly wants to analyse in its own terms.

We lose a sense of labour as an aspect of the experience people have in their lives. It is as if it draws to itself the core meaning of people's lives since it is supposedly the realm in which people can be active. Aristotle's vision of masculinity is not far from the surface, as different areas of life can be discounted as areas of fulfilment and self-realisation. These are issues that are too large to be tackled here and we will have cause to return to them later.

Both Hegel and Marx help to shift the discussion around issues of validation which usually have their basis in epistemological conceptions. Hegel reminds us crucially of the *historical* character of consciousness so that we must be careful to ground particular ideas and conceptions within a particular historical context. He was also sensitive to the historical growth and development of ideas, recognising that they cannot be ripped out of context to be judged by reason alone as some kind of impartial and universal standard. Even if in the end he sees reason as identified with the historical process, in detail he is more sensitive to the different terms of rationality that exist within different contexts and periods. Here at least, significant resonances can be discerned between Hegel and Wittgenstein. This is not to deny the differences that are more obvious.[4]

According to Marx, there is a crucial insight that connects theory and practice to make the truth not something that has to be independently verified but also something that we have *to make true* in the ways that we live our lives. The truth has to be *actualised* in the ways that we live. This should remind us of the importance, as Havel puts it, of living in truth, but all too often this has been missing within an orthodox Marxist tradition that has tended to see the truth as a feature of class interests.[5] This had disastrous consequences when Lenin tended to define the truth as whatever brought the revolution closer. This served to legitimate many forms of devious and cruel behaviour as the revolution became the only legitimation for moral behaviour. This was not simply a matter of whether the means could justify the ends, for the issues raised cannot adequately be expressed in these Kantian terms.

Marx's initial insight has proved extremely difficult to sustain. Gramsci and possibly aspects in Walter Benjamin and the Frankfurt School come closest to sustaining it. It recognises that we have to validate the truth of particular notions through making them 'come alive' in the ways that we live. It shifts attention away from epistemological concerns that have shaped discussions of validation. In a different way this is also something that Wittgenstein seems to recognise. As a student in the early 1960s I came to Wittgenstein before immersing myself in Hegel and Marx. Part of me felt the resonance, though it was a considerable time before

I could say anything sensible about it. Wittgenstein remains crucial, for he helps us withstand the tendency within Marx and Marxism continually to foreclose itself, refusing to take seriously the different spheres of people's lives. Wittgenstein warns us against empty generalisations and the ease with which we can lose ourselves within theoretical discourse.

In reminding us of the complexities of our everyday experience, Wittgenstein is returning us to aspects of experience that we too often discount and devalue. It is as if in a Cartesian tradition we are continually losing our *ground* so that we have continually to find ways of grounding ourselves in our experience. Put differently, Wittgenstein returns us to a humanity that we have learned to forsake too often in the wake of modernity.

We have learned, especially as men, to identify with our minds and to separate and disdain our bodily experience. We have learned to value reason in a way that has estranged us from our emotional and spiritual lives. We have learned to identify progress with the domination of a nature that we can no longer feel at home in. As we no longer feel at home in our bodies, so we no longer feel at home with our 'natural' selves. Feminism has proved crucial in making these personal and political issues that have become central to movements for social change. It has helped people increasingly to trust an inner knowledge that they had learned to silence and disdain.

AUTONOMY AND EXPERIENCE

The Women's Movement provided a context within which women could share their experience with each other. Consciousness-raising was a process through which women could learn to validate an experience that in many ways they had learned to discount through learning to see themselves through the eyes of men.[6] At some level they had ceased, if they ever were, to exist as centres of their own experience.

Gender relations of power worked to leave women in a structured situation of subordination. The assertion of women's autonomy was a crucial challenge to the workings of these relations of power, for it meant a refusal to see their lives exclusively in relation to men and children. Women were to learn to become the subjects of their own lives, so learning to evaluate their experience according to terms that they had discerned to be true to their own variegated experience as women.

Feminism challenged the Kantian terms of autonomy that were set in rationalist terms alone. For Kant, we were autonomous if we could think for ourselves and act out of a sense of rational duty. This meant learning to suppress our inclinations that were an expression of our determination and unfreedom. To be autonomous we had to be rational, and to be rational meant learning to discount our emotional selves.

In large part this remains a masculine vision of autonomy that involves a *separation* from our emotional selves. But it was important that with the Women's Movement as it emerged in the early 1970s, consciousness-raising emerged as a practice that was *both* rational and emotional. As people shared their experiences, so they shared the feelings that were locked in with them. People trusted that they would be heard and that their experiences would be validated.

Men also learned from consciousness-raising although often it was harder for us to share our experiences rather than to simply talk about them in a way that removed ourselves.[7] It was difficult to share emotionally, for as men we were often far more estranged from these aspects of our experience. But for men it could be important to experience this sense of being locked into ourselves, being unable to reach out towards others. It could make consciousness-raising a frustrating experience for many, encouraging men to take more seriously expressive forms of therapy that they had themselves often derided as a form of self-indulgence.

Men learned to face a difficulty in expression that until then they had no name for, since it could easily be concealed under a veil of endless talk. It helped men appreciate that to talk was not necessarily to communicate, for language could so easily be a form of self-concealment. It could also help men become clearer about the inadequaces of forms of linguistic sociology or discourse theory that left themselves no way of recognising any tension between language and experience. A rationalistic tradition finds it hard to acknowledge that much could be spoken but very little shared or communicated.

More theoretically, an experience of consciousness-raising could throw into question some of the rationalist assumptions that informed Habermas' notion of an ideal-speech community.[8] These ideas were current at the time but they tended to assume that we existed as equal and autonomous participants within a speech community. Even if this was not true in reality, what mattered, or so it was said, was that we could abstract ourselves from the relations of power and subordination within which we lived our lives, to exist as free and equal rational agents within such a community.

The possibilities of abstraction were as important for Habermas' form of critical theory as they were for Rawls' in establishing the principles of justice in *A Theory of Justice*. In their different ways they held out the possibilities of constructing an ideal community which could be usefully compared with existing practices. Supposedly they could then help us legitimate claims to justice within the realities of power and subordination by which we were forced to live.[9]

If these rational constructions have their place, it is also crucial to learn from a feminist theory that is aware that autonomy cannot simply be achieved as an exercise of mind. Subordination does not simply work at the level of access to material goods, nor is justice to be thought about exclusively in distributive terms. If women did not have their own voice it was not simply a matter of giving them access to speak. Nor was it simply that some people had control of the means of communication.

Women had to discover *contexts* in which they could find their own voice, and for a time at least, consciousness-raising groups proved crucial to this process. Women had to create these practices that could help them to affirm and validate an experience that had long been derided. It took time and space for women to feel that they had every right to be emotional and that, along with insight and intuition, these could be important sources of knowledge. The fact that these were ritually derided within the dominant culture made these aspects of experience harder to validate.

Within a Kantian framework, autonomy is essentially a matter of will and determination. Feminist theory can help us appreciate the inadequacy of this rationalist formulation as it shows how people in their individuality can be undermined through the workings of power and subordination. It is as if women had to face the difficult reality that they no longer existed as people in their own right. Their identities had been fragmented and displaced, not as a result of any move towards post-modernity but as an aspect of oppression and subordination. It was a slow process for women to feel validated in the eyes of others in a consciousness-raising group as part of a process of revaluing themselves.

As women learned to validate their experience they learned to trust and believe in themselves. They learned to take risks which allowed them to explore their desires and needs, even when this challenged prevailing notions they carried about themselves. As women learned to draw strength and confidence from each other they learned to treasure what they were receiving from each other. As this exploration took place, *differences* also came into focus as women discovered that they also wanted different things out of life and to form different relationships.

But possibilities were often opened up as women experienced themselves as capable in a whole series of activities that had formally been closed to them. It also involved questioning some prevailing distinctions of a liberal moral culture that had for a long time been taken for granted. Women refused to accept that men's time was more important because it was waged and they learned to value their own time and space. This was no longer something that had to be justified.

PUBLIC AND PRIVATE

There was a tension within feminist theory and practice between arguing that women should have equal access within the public realm and a recognition of the value of the activities that women were traditionally involved in within the private sphere, such as childcare and homecrafts. Women wanted to bring into question the prevailing distinctions between public and private life which, within a liberal moral culture, tacitly accepted that what really mattered was what went on in the public realm. This was the realm of freedom, and traditionally it was thought that women would only achieve emancipation if they could have equal access in the public realm.

For liberalism this meant access to professions and jobs and a guarantee of equal legal and political rights. For Engels and orthodox Marxism, it meant access to the labour process so that women could struggle as equals with men to transform the conditions of capitalist production. It was generally assumed that injustice and oppression were centrally features of the public realm. It was here that suffering really *mattered* so that it was in the public realm that politics was defined.[10]

Since women were in large part excluded from the public realm to live out their duties and responsibilities in the private realm, they were excluded from the realm of politics. Politics traditionally became a masculine sphere, as it has largely remained. It was for men to mediate the political realm to women who were in large part not expected to take any direct interest in it because supposedly it did not concern them. Traditionally, it was the public realm that was to be organised according to the dictates of reason.

Since reason was conceived of as impartial, impersonal and universal, it seemed naturally suited to the public realm. The fact that reason had largely been conceived in masculine terms to reflect a dominant masculine experience was an issue that few men were concerned with. As the public realm was the realm of reason, so the private realm was conceived of as the realm of emotions and feelings. It was defined as a lesser realm since it was essentially bereft of reason and women learned to see it in this way. It was a realm that could safely be left to women.

In this context it was difficult for women to *validate* their experience in the private realm. There was a strong tendency, also present within the Women's Movement, which assumed that the path to emancipation was a path that left domesticity and childcare behind. It was thought that these activities were left to women because they could not be sources of fulfilment and self-realisation. It was these activities that women needed to be emancipated *from* as they gained access to the public realm of work.

But there were always other tendencies, represented by Dora Russell and others in the 1920s, which sought to validate explicitly women's experience as mothers and homemakers. They refused to deride these aspects of women's lives and they insisted that *within* these relationships were also embodied different ways of being and relating that provided a true challenge to the dominance of market values within the public sphere.[11]

Within this tendency of thought and feeling there was a recognition that women had to learn to validate their own experience and so allow values to emerge. Women needed to sustain their own communities that would help to embody these values and relationships in the face of a dominant patriarchal culture which would work to subvert them. This involved a recognition of the *difficulties* that women faced both individually and collectively in sustaining a sense of their values and relationships. It recognised the potential of love, care and concern that were available within the private realm as a potential challenge to the exchange values that dominated within the public realm. Women learned to appreciate an openness and honesty in their relationships with each other which was often missing within the public realm.

With the experience of the Women's Movement some of these lessons were taken to heart as women generally recognised that equality did not simply come with access to the public world, for this was to naturalise existing relationships. Women were insistent that they should be able to enter the public realm *on their own terms* as women rather than simply accede to the dominant terms of men. This was to force men to recognise the gendered character of institutions and relationships that they had been used to seeing in neutral and gender-blind ways.

It took time for men to realise that equality involves questioning the ways that they have traditionally organised things, say for instance in law, medicine and education. Liberalism had prepared the ground for saying that it did not matter whether it was a man or a woman who got a job, as long as 'the best qualified person gets it'. But this is to sidestep difficult issues about the structuring of opportunities and the demands that, for instance, children make on the opportunities women have for promotion. This is not to suggest that issues of positive discrimination are easy to settle, but the questions that have been raised cannot be avoided either.

Consciousness-raising helped women articulate the contradictory feelings they had, often feeling torn between the different aspects of their lives. It also began to open up an exploration of differences of class, race, ethnicity and sexual orientation. It created a space for exploration which held both emotional and structural considerations in an active tension. It helped women accept that, fixed within a contradictory situation, it is hardly surprising to have contradictory feelings.

As a woman is struggling to assert herself in her relationships, say with a man, basic patterns in the relationship will be upset. She might feel that there is still considerable feeling in the relationship but it also seems difficult for her to get the kind of time and space that she needs for herself. Within the context of a group, women were helped to recognise that these were not emotional issues alone for they connected with the larger structures of power in society. If a woman chose to end a relationship she was left with the difficulties of finding work and supporting her child. It was not an easy situation to face, and relations of class, race and ethnicity make a difference to what difficulties have to be confronted, though it might still be right for her.

FREEDOM AND CHOICE

The point is that within a rationalist culture a woman might feel that she should make a decision on the basis of reason alone. It might be said that it is a matter of weighing up what is important to her and in the last resort, giving weight to her different preferences. In part this is to turn qualitative issues into quantitative ones, thinking that this is the only way that they can be rationally handled. There are influential moves in both ethics and sociology to treat issues in this way. But feminism can help us grasp how a limited framework for rational choice theory is built upon an inadequate masculinist conception of choice and decision.

It is true that as a woman decides whether to stay in a relationship she has to weigh a whole series of different considerations. But it can also be important for her to explore the contradictory character of her feelings, possibly with the help of therapy, tracking them back to some early childhood experiences. It is partly *through* this emotional process that she sometimes *recognises* what is important to her. It is not through somehow putting these feelings aside, as rationalism has it, that she can come to a clear and unclouded rational decision.

It is partly for instance because of the difficulties of having her different feelings validated when she attempts to talk things out with her partner, that she has learned to appreciate the space that is provided by her consciousness-raising group. Her partner always seems to be telling her what she can and cannot feel. He says that she cannot feel angry because she does not have any reason to, since other people have things much harder than she does. All this confuses her because she can recognise that others have it much harder but this does not make any difference to what *she* is feeling. She wants to be *listened* to, not explained to.

In our example, her partner seems to understand the situation he is in so much better than she seems to herself that she often feels lost and even worse about herself. Their talks always seem to be pulled in the direction of who is right and who is wrong, as if in the way that her partner thinks this always turns out to be most significant. It seems important for men to prove that they are in the right, however long this may take.

This touches the issue of validation as it is often raised within sociological theory and method. It can often seem to be a matter of evaluating different accounts so that we can decide which are legitimate and which are not. Within sociology this is sometimes expressed as an issue of how to validate feminist knowledge so that it can thereby be related to more mainstream traditions. But it might be misleading to set things out in these terms, that can easily reflect tacit positivist assumptions that encourage us to be continually sorting out knowledge from different forms of belief or emotion. This pushes us to ask questions *before* they are really appropriate. Similarly, within a consciousness-raising group a woman feels that what matters is that she can be heard and her experience validated. It is just because women have been traditionally denied this time and space that it can be so significant for them. It is important in this process to suspend judgement so that women can feel safe to share how they feel about things. It is also important that a woman is free to set the issues in her own terms.

This does not mean that consciousness-raising is an uncritical practice or that the accounts that women give of their situation go unquestioned. A woman can feel that she has been heard and that she has been able to share how a situation feels to her. At some level she remains in authority but this does not prevent new light being brought to the situation as other women begin to share how they have experienced similar issues in their own relationships.

If this is a situation that they have been through themselves, they can share how the support that they received made a difference to the actions they took. This can be hard to bear, but it can also be strengthening to know that others have lived through a similar plight and seem to be coping, if not enjoying life in a new situation. It does not make the situation she is in feel easier to cope with, but it does put her situation into a broader perspective.

The point is that others in the group are ready and willing to *share* their own experience. This is the basis on which they *speak* expecting to talk at a similar level in themselves, so that they are prepared to make themselves equally vulnerable. It is not assumed that there is a neutral point from which the account that someone gives can somehow be evaluated, to establish whatever truth content it carries. It is misleading to think that each account somehow carries along with it its own rational core that can somehow be separated out as the basis of 'feminist knowledge'. Invoking a realist philosophical position can tempt us to work in this direction, for it suggests that some aspects of an account somehow correspond to an independent reality, while much of it will be made up of self-justification, if not exactly illusions.

FEMINISM AND VALIDATION

Similarly, a researcher sympathetic to feminism might feel called upon to share her own experience when she is interviewing. This might be part of sustaining a sense of equality in relationships between women. Within a traditional positivist method this would be frowned upon as bringing unwelcome bias and influence in what should supposedly be an impersonal and objective interviewing situation.

But there is a particular vision of 'data' that informs such a view. Sociologists supposedly take up a position of neutrality towards whoever they interview, suspending whatever personal feelings they have so that they can collect 'objective' data in a neutral and impartial fashion. Supposedly it is the methods followed, originally developed in the context of physical sciences, that guarantee the 'objectivity' of the data.

But we are learning that this positivist vision is flawed, partly because people change the way that they feel, say, about their relationships. This is not a static and unchanging situation, for the interview itself can serve to initiate a reconsideration or a deepened connection with some situation or event. A qualitative sociology should learn from such feminist insights and should shape its practice accordingly.

It should recognise that our understandings of situations change but this does not make them 'relative accounts', each attempting to articulate an independently existing 'state of affairs'. This gets the situation wrong for, say, with issues of abortion, a woman's feelings might change as she herself changes and develops a fuller or deeper connection with herself. She might have initially treated it as a straightforward rational decision, only reflecting perhaps years later, to be surprised when different feelings of loss began to emerge. These feelings might have begun as unexpected as they were unwelcome, but they were also part of her experience once she was prepared to acknowledge them.

It might be that an interviewer who recognises such feelings of loss from her own experience can help her validate these aspects of her experience. If others feel this way, it might be that she can be more accepting of her own emotions and feelings. To validate a woman's experience in this way does not mean 'biasing' what would otherwise be a quite neutral and impartial account.[12]

This is to reproduce a masculine assumption that emotions and feelings are inevitably, in Kantian terms, working to interfere with a situation that can be rationally assessed through reason alone. But the truth might be elsewhere, as the validation of feelings might help a woman to a fuller exploration of the decision she took. It allows her experience to fill out as aspects of her emotional life that had formerly been dismissed are acknowledged. Possibly, she had assumed that it reflected badly on herself, somehow demeaning her not only in the eyes of others but also in her own.

Taking a feminist standpoint cannot mean assuming that women are always right, for instance, and men are always wrong. But it can mean acknowledging the workings of relationships of power and subordination so that you do not unwittingly judge unfairly through simply abstracting from these material relationships. It means recognising that, for instance, men and women face different difficulties and situations in their lives, and that these are mediated by relations of class, race and ethnicity.

The fact that men enjoy considerable social power that they can use in their relationships with women does not mean that even middle-class men always have it their own way. It can be quite misleading to identify men with the dominant modes of masculinity, as if these cannot also be oppressive to men. The fact that men have relative power in society does not mean that there are not contexts in which they do not feel relatively powerless in their lives.

Some of these issues emerge acutely in the context of abortion. We have already argued that it can be crucial for men to *explore* their feelings about the situation as integral to being able to reach some kind of 'rational' decision with their partners. This does not have to bring into question women's fundamental right to choose, since it is they who carry the child, but it helps to put the issues into a broader perspective. Taking a feminist standpoint should not mean ignoring the experience of men or automatically taking the side of women in any disagreement. It involves a sensitivity to the *workings* of the larger relations of power which bring into question liberal conceptions of equality. This does not mean that there are not contexts in which men and women negotiate more or less as equals, but it is still important to place these communications within larger contexts.

It is easy to feel that those who are oppressed and so untainted by relations of power have a monopoly of truth and virtue on their side. This is a dangerous assumption, even if it carries some truth. As Simone Weil reminds us, people are also reduced by relations of power and so brutalised by these relationships. She was impressed by Marx's analysis of the capitalist mode of production and its power to crush and brutalise people's lives in a way that she thinks should have led him to question his trust in the proletariat.[13] She thought it quite misleading to think of truth as the monopoly of any single class or group of people. She was convinced that an emphasis on class morality could be corrupting if it took away responsibility from individuals themselves. It was crucial for individuals to learn to live in truth both with themselves and with others. Both fascism and Stalinism in the twentieth century remind us constantly of the costs of denying responsibility and the capacity for truth to individuals themselves.

Susie Orbach and Luise Eichenbaum write about the strains created by success in the relationships women have with each other.[14] However hard it is to hear, there can be a safety and security in taking on a victim position. The Women's Movement has changed the conditions of some women's lives in western societies and brought them to positions of power and influence. As Gramsci recognised in his thinking about what was involved in taking up a standpoint of the working class, this was not simply a matter of being prepared to view social reality from a particular point of view.

This was Mannheim's position in the sociology of knowledge but it encourages a false perspectivism. It regresses to a position where social reality is assumed to exist independently as an object of observation, and for Mannheim at least, this meant that different social classes, locked as they are within a particular position within the social structure, gain a partial view of social reality. It is only the intellectuals who, being free-floating, can move between these different structural positions, so constructing an 'objective' vision of social reality. It is intellectuals who have access to objective knowledge which they construct out of the partial perspectives of others.

Gramsci has a different vision of what he calls 'organic intellectuals' who have to live with the oppressed whose concerns they learn to accept as their own. It is crucial to start by encouraging people to voice their own experience as a condition for realising that this experience is not 'private' and 'personal' but a shared experience of subordination and oppression. So it is that Gramsci can help illuminate what might be involved in taking a feminist standpoint. This is less an issue of validating women's accounts as 'feminist knowledge' than of learning to *take seriously* the concerns and values of women in the particularities of their class, race and ethnicities, in their own terms.

As Simone Weil also recognises, the central issue is one of dignity, of *how* it is that we can help people to trust in their own experience and believe in themselves. This is part of a process of empowerment in which people in situations of poverty and oppression begin to recognise and value their own experience, rather than learning in different ways to diminish and discount it through evaluating it in terms not of their own making.

It is striking how difficult it can be for those who are powerless and oppressed to *take seriously* what they have to say. They are so used to being ignored that they learn to diminish their ideas before others have a chance to do so. Gramsci, like Simone Weil, sought to give voice to an experience that had been silenced, initially in terms that it chose for itself. People are so used to being *told* what they should think and feel that it can be difficult to be *listened* to for the first time by those outside your immediate community. This is something that a Leninist tradition continually failed to do because it felt that it already had the answers and it was the 'backwardness' of others that prevented them from seeing what the revolutionaries already knew. Both Gramsci and Weil in their different ways recognised the arrogance implicit in this politics.

The Women's Movement potentially provides an alternative more democratic vision. It found ways of validating not only the ideas of women, but also their experience. If her mind was recognised after generations of being despised, so were her heart, feelings and intuition. Women had long experience of being trapped and manipulated by their feelings and emotions, so they recognised the necessity for both mind and heart.

As women learned to validate their own experience, values and relationships, they were demonstrating that there were alternative ways of being and knowing than those legitimated by the masculinist visions of modernity. Different things were to be appreciated as it became recognised that exchange value was not the only source of value. These new feminist values needed to be embodied in different forms of relationships and ways of being that could sustain and nourish them. This is part of developing a broader vision of Gramsci's counter-hegemony that can be part of sustaining new visions of life.

We need now to explore some of the developments in feminism as they bear upon different forms of social theory. This can help us situate some of the challenges feminism makes to the ways our inherited forms of social theory have treated the experience of women. It also bears upon the ways we conceive relationships of power that exist between men and women. At the same time it helps us recognise the ways different forms of social theory have sustained particular dominant conceptions of masculinity. As long as masculinity is identified with reason and our inherited traditions see themselves sustaining a fundamentally rationalist tradition, this should hardly surprise us.

Chapter 9

Feminism

MEN AND FEMINISM

I want to explore how men's relationships to feminism over the last twenty years have helped shape some of men's explorations into inherited forms of masculinity. They have also helped to shape a sense of the inadequacies of prevailing forms of social theory which in part have helped sustain some crucial frameworks of Enlightenment rationalism. It is not simply that women's experience of powerlessness and subordination is rendered largely invisible within the traditions of positivism, Marxism and phenomenology, but they have allowed men to appropriate an impersonal and universal voice of reason.

The authority that men can assume in the larger society is reflected within the prevailing traditions of social theory which make it difficult for men to appreciate the gendered character of our experience as men. As I argue in *Rediscovering masculinity: reason, language and sexuality* (Seidler 1989), we learn to speak for others before we have learned to speak for ourselves as men. We have been slow to recognise it, but it has been feminism that has provided the challenge to modernity as we begin to explore connections between modernity and masculinity.

Since the early days of the women's liberation movement of the 1970s it has been clear that feminism is not only about women but also presents a fundamental challenge to men and masculinity. But from the beginning feminists were clear that their concerns could not be with the issues that were being raised about who men are and the nature and character of men's lives and power within the larger society.[1] Women had spent too long looking after the concerns of men, making the happiness and wellbeing of those men the focal point of their own lives. This was to be no more, and women were to learn to concern themselves with their own lives and relationships. Women were no longer prepared to give priority to their relationships with men nor to see themselves through men's eyes. Women were to learn to value their experience in their own terms, not in the terms provided by men.[2]

It has remained an important and consistent strand of feminist theory that women were to separate themselves from the dominant, essentially male values in terms of which they had been brought up to value and judge themselves. This involved a challenge to a liberal conception of equality of opportunity and the notion of rights which accompanied it, which asked for equal access to institutions that had formerly been closed to women.[3] This was to challenge a liberal conception of freedom and equality. Women were to demand more than access to jobs on male terms. Traditionally, this notion of women's rights only challenged men and masculinity to the extent that men limited access of women to occupations and professions.

It was possible to see the liberal market economy as gender-blind, so that, for instance, women should be able to be managers just as men should be able to be nurses. This presented the terms of work as if they were neutral, impartial and independent.[4] It took the women's liberation movement to raise questions about the *terms* upon which women were to enter these occupations. The rules and institutional practices of these organisations were to be fundamentally reformed so that women could participate on their own terms. This raised crucial issues of childcare which had formerly been neglected.

So it was that feminism involved a challenge to a liberal conception of rights. It was not simply that women demanded the right to compete equally for positions within the public realm. Since Engels, it has also been a powerful vision of the Left that women would gain equality through participating in the public realm of work, so escaping the confines of domesticity.[5] It was understood that it was women's restriction to the private realm of society that was the source of women's oppression and subordination. It was the wages that men earned as well as their access to the worlds of work and politics that seemed to give men power to dominate and control within the domestic realm.

When we conceive of equality in terms of a language of rights we see this fundamentally as an issue of access, and it renders invisible issues about the organisation of institutional power within work. Within this framework it is significant that it was relatively easy for men to support the claims of feminism and to think that feminism concerned the empowering of women without really challenging the rights of men. Even so, relatively few men supported feminism, as they felt threatened in terms of the power they assumed at work and in the home. Within the context of justice as fairness, it could be argued that women had not been given an equal chance at school, nor had they been given an equal chance to enter the workplace. In large part, this meant that women's rights was an issue that could be safely left to women and was not a particular concern for men.[6]

This framework has been challenged by the women's liberation movement which has insisted that the liberation of women would involve a challenge to men and to prevailing conceptions of men and masculinity.[7] Equality was not simply an issue to be settled within the public realm but affected the quality of everyday relationships between men and women. The personal is political in the sense that the personal sphere cannot be separated out as a realm which operates independently of questions of power and subordination. The character of the power relation between men and women is crucial to understanding what is at issue in the development of a distinct area of men's studies.

For it is this insight into the relationship of power between men and women that becomes disturbed if we begin to think of men's studies as having some kind of parity with women's studies, or as a set of studies that goes in parallel with women's studies. Even if it is not the explicit intention, it could still work to reinforce an intellectual framework that would render invisible questions of power and subordination that have been crucial to the emergence of modern feminism. Within a framework of role theory, for instance, it becomes possible to think that men are similarly restricted by prevailing expectations to the ways that women are restricted by their roles. But this yields a fundamental misconception about the challenges that feminism has made to men.

Feminism deeply challenged the ways that men are and the ways that men relate. It drew attention to the power men sustained in their relationships with women and showed that what liberalism conceived of as a relationship of equality with men and women operating in different spheres was in reality a relationship of power and subordination.[8] Recognising this involves more than a change of attitude on the part of men towards women, for it becomes clear that it is not enough to think of 'others' as equal with equal respect. It also has to do with the organisation of relationships of power that mediate between men and women in relationships. It is a material issue, though there have been considerable differences about how to conceptualise the nature and character of this materialism. Feminism challenges too narrow an economistic version of materialism but the extent to which feminist theories have allowed for a reformulation or break with Marxist conceptions of materialism is still an open issue.[9]

If men had to change they had to do this for themselves, for they could no longer rely on women 'to pick up the pieces'. Men were left to explore and investigate the nature and character of their inherited forms of masculinity. The crucial point is that feminism did not simply present a theoretical challenge to the ways men understood the world but a personal and practical challenge to *who* we are as men and *how* we relate as men both to ourselves and to others.

It was this personal challenge that men sought to meet in consciousness-raising groups, but often they were difficult situations because, as men, we were often so used to intellectualising and rationalising our experience rather than sharing it. Sometimes these groups died after a few weeks when it was not clear what men were supposed to talk about. It was difficult for middle-class men to *share* their experience with other men because we had been brought up to treat other men as competitors in a way that makes it easy to feel that showing our vulnerability would only be used against us.[10] It was not uncommon for many heterosexual men to say that they did not need consciousness-raising because they felt closer to women anyway, and did not find it difficult to talk to them.

This would often conceal a fear of sharing ourselves with men, a suspicion of men that had deep roots connected to homophobia and a fear of intimacy. This allowed men a certain identification with feminism while being able to disdain those men who involved themselves in consciousness-raising. This allowed men to sustain a feeling of superiority in relation to such men and also to avoid charges of feminists who would say, especially in the early days, that consciousness-raising was simply another form of male bonding that could so easily lead to a reassertion of male power. This fostered the misleading idea that all forms of male bonding were somehow equivalent to each other.

So it was that many men could identify with feminism through further marginalising men who engaged in consciousness-raising activity. It has to be said that the opposition of feminists made it more difficult for some of the work on men and masculinity to flourish until much later. It reinforced an image of 'soft men' or the idea that men who were doing this kind of work were somehow setting themselves up as 'superior' or 'more liberated' than other men, when, as women know, 'under the surface they are all the same'. Furthermore, it was often deemed 'preferable' to deal with traditional men and forms of masculinity because at least as a woman you supposedly knew where you stood with them, and in any case they were not trying to put one over on you.

There was also an issue, often left unspoken or at least publicly unacknowledged, about sexual attractiveness and how this was constructed. It was a matter of what male qualities were often found to be attractive to women which often did not correspond to their feminist aspirations. Relationships with men were only rarely explored within feminist literature, for it was often connected to feelings of guilt and uncertainty as if it were a matter of colluding with an oppressor. This was an issue that helped foster a feminist involvement with psychoanalysis and psychotherapy and helped develop a sense that the sources of desire were often located at a deeper, less conscious level, and that desire could not easily be transformed through a process of rational reconstruction. In part this was an important move, for it recognised the limits of a particular form of reason, of a particular Enlightenment notion that we could control our lives by reason alone. It helped to question the idea of feminism as essentially a rationalist project.

This is a difficult issue because it was important at the same time for women to be recognised as rational and intellectual beings in their own right, for it had been a feature of oppression that they had been treated simply as sexual objects. Rationality tended to be regarded in neutral and impartial terms and it is easy to see why this should appeal to feminism. It also explains the attraction of a structuralist framework to understand feminist experience, because this sustains a rationalistic framework. It can equally be said that part of the attraction of Lacan's psychoanalytic work is that it presents a reading of Freud that is fundamentally rationalistic in its conception of the unconscious as being structured according to language.[11]

This tempts us to think of desire as if it could be handled as an intellectual or theoretical construction, but it was also crucial for women developing a feminist therapy to recognise the contradictory character of desire and the ways in which it has a movement of its own.[12] This is threatening to a rationalist vision of control, for it means that in part we have to acknowledge or accept our desires, or at least we have to be ready to *name* them before we can begin to work with them. This is by no means the same as saying that we have to act upon our desires simply because we recognise them. This is not to be 'irrationalist' but simply to question the terms of rationality that we have inherited within an Enlightenment culture. Further, it is to question the relationship of masculinity to particular forms of reason and the ways this has been embodied within a lived experience of modernity.[13]

MEN AND MASCULINITY

A significant strain in the response of men to feminism has been a negation by men of their own masculinity. As masculinity was taken to be essentially oppressive to women and as being a structure of oppression, it had often to be rejected in the early writings of 'men against sexism'. This touches on something significant in sexual relationships, for it is a movement of denial that involves a self-rejection, often a loss of vitality and even sexuality. It is this response to feminism that was challenged in the writings of *Achilles' Heel*, which sought a reworking of masculinity as part of the project of men involved in consciousness-raising.

In fact, this self-rejection is often intensified because men have often failed to explore the contradictions of their masculinity. Rather, they have learned that masculinity is essentially a relationship of power, so that you could only give up your power in relation to women, and so no longer collude in women's oppression, if you were prepared 'to give up' your masculinity. This is a part of guilt and self-denial that was not an uncommon male response to feminism. In the end it is self-destructive but nevertheless it has to be understood.

It has often meant that men have given up on these issues and concerns completely, for they have often found no way through them. In some cases this has possibly fuelled a kind of anti-feminist politics, a threat or fear that women are somehow out to take away men's potency, and this has fuelled the politics of the Right. The move towards a men's rights position has grown to enormous strengths in the United States, often being larger than any men's movement grouping. This is in part why it is so important to rework and rethink men's relationships with feminism.

It was an important part of the *Achilles' Heel* project in England to look for more affirming and positive visions of masculinity, and so to challenge some of the sources of guilt and self-denial that had sometimes been part of men's responses to feminism. This involves a personal and theoretical quest. It could also be that the subject of 'men's studies', as it has developed in the United States, is also a move away from this difficult personal terrain and an attempt to deal theoretically, so that we will not need to deal more personally with the challenges of feminism.

This suspicion is partly fuelled by the strength of a positivist social science methodology within men's studies, which is probably related to the disciplinary strength of psychology and the ways that these issues can become 'topics' within a reworked social psychology. It is as if the claims of feminism, say around issues of pornography, could be 'tested' so that we could know what the 'effects' of pornography are on men, whether or not it makes them more violent and whether it influences the nature and character of their relationships with their partners.

Women would have grounds to be nervous about the testing of feminist claims set up within this kind of framework.

Of course, there has to be a relationship between empirical research and feminist theory, but we have to be very careful about it. It is too easy, given the struggle of social science methodologies, to imagine that the causal claims can be 'neutrally tested'.[14] For what about the fact that we grow up as men within a culture that is deeply imbued with pornographic images? How does this affect us? And is this not the larger context in which these 'experiments' are taking place? At the same time it might be argued that men have to be able to set their own agendas and, if this is the way they seek to investigate these issues, it has to be left to men to be responsible for the exploration of men and masculinity. But this raises questions and issues about the challenges that feminist theory makes to different forms of social science methodologies. These are often marginalised by claiming that they are only relevant in the exploration of women's experience.

On the other hand, what about the radical feminist assumption that 'all men are potentially rapists'? What does this mean about the conception of masculinity that underpins some feminist theoretical work? Is this something that men can challenge? If men are seen as an ontological category fixed in a particular position within a 'hierarchy of powers', what *space* is left for men to explore their masculinity? This is a question that feminists have to take seriously. It is also raised for men who would consider themselves as 'male feminists' or as 'pro-feminists', as is not uncommon in America. This raises the crucial question about *who* sets the agenda for research on men and masculinity.

These are difficult issues to resolve, for it is crucial to keep in mind that it has been the challenges of feminism that have made the dominant conceptions of masculinity problematic. In this sense men's studies has to have a close relationship with feminism, without thereby accepting that feminism can set the agenda for studies into men and masculinity. It is not unusual these days for men to pay lip-service to feminism and to women's struggles in their opening paragraphs, only to go on to ignore the implications of these studies for the work they are engaged in.

It needs to be taken seriously that many men have responded to feminism by internalising a particular conception of their masculinity as 'the enemy'. Since this masculinity was said to be 'essentially' a position of power in relationship to women, there was little for men to do but to *reject* their masculinity. So it seemed that to identity with feminism and to respond to the challenges of feminist theory involved an abandonment of masculinity itself. Often the analogy is made, which I think is misleading, with the position of whites in South Africa: the idea that the only way that whites could abandon their privilege was to identify completely with the black struggle. It seems as if there is no way that they could struggle as whites within the white community. It seems as if it makes no sense to work within this arena. So analogously it could seem that there is no point for men to work with other men, for this would be to work with the 'oppressor' and the only thing that could be justified would be to 'give up' our position of oppression.

Here again, there is a resonance with an orthodox Marxist frame of mind, even if this would not be acknowledged openly. Just as middle-class people could 'betray their class' and identify themselves with the struggles of working-class people against capitalist oppression, so it seems as if men can be asked to forsake their masculinity. In part, it is possible to change our class position and identify ourselves within a proletarian position, though there are difficulties with this vision of political struggle that was part of a 1960s inheritance. It often involved a denial of our 'education' and of our understanding of how capitalist institutions crush and distort working-class life and culture.[15] But why does an identification with feminism have to involve a *rejection* of our masculinity? If we adopt a conception of masculinity which simply defines it as a relationship of power, or as the top place within a hierarchy of powers, then we are tempted into thinking that it is possible to abandon our masculinity.

Similarly, if we conceive of 'heterosexuality' as simply a relationship of power that fixes straight men in a position of power and enforces the subordination of gay men and lesbians, then it can seem that 'heterosexuality' can equally simply be abandoned. This has often gone along with the idea of sexuality as being 'socially constructed', with the implication that it can equally be 'deconstructed' and different choices made. This fosters the view that sexual orientation is in the last analysis a matter of political choice. At another level, this reconstructs a rationalistic project that assumes that our lives can be lived by reason alone and that through will and determination, as Kant has it, we can struggle against our inclinations, to live according to the pattern that we have set for ourselves through reason.[16]

These are difficult and complex questions and they need to be handled with care and sensitivity. It might be that heterosexuality is a structured institution and that it enforces the conception of 'normality' that is taken for granted within the culture. This establishes important relationships of power that marginalise and, with Section 28 in English law, work to criminalise the sexuality of gay men and lesbians. It has been crucial to understand sexuality not as 'given' but as the outcome of a series of personal relationships, so bringing out the precarious character of all our sexualities.[17] This is part of the importance of recognising 'differences'. But it is one thing to understand the institutional power of heterosexuality and another to think that sexual orientation is a matter of 'political choice'.

In part it has been our sharp dichotomy, inherited as a defining feature of modernity and further inscribed within a structuralist tradition between 'nature' and 'culture', that has fostered this way of thinking, as if 'culture', in opposition to 'nature' as an outcome of reason is within our conscious control. This is one of the difficulties with the prevailing conceptions of social constructionism that, since the 1960s, are deeply embedded within the human sciences and which help foster a form of rationalism that gives us the idea that our lives are within our rational control and that through will and determination alone we can determine our lives. It forms our vision of freedom and morality which within a Kantian tradition are identified with reason.

This is part of an Enlightenment rationalism and develops a particular vision of self-determination, as if we *should* be able to control our lives by reason alone. So we begin to think that to say that our sexuality is 'natural' is to say that it has been given or that it is somehow beyond our conscious control. But this is to create too sharp an opposition. Freud helps us understand the organisation of our sexuality and how it has come to be what it is. He does not thereby think that it can be 'rationally reconstructed'. It is crucial for Freud that change comes through some form of *self-acceptance* of our sexual feelings and desires, even if these do not take the form that we would want or even that would be regarded as legitimate within the larger society.

Rather than judging these feelings and desires by external standards, we learn to acknowledge them for what they are and we learn to suspend judgement. This is part of a psychoanalytic process. It is crucial for Freud that within a rationalistic culture we learn to judge and often condemn our feelings and emotions because they do not fit in with the ideals we have set ourselves. Part of the originality of Freud, despite all the difficulties, is his break with the idealisation of culture and his recognition, however ambivalent, of the importance of validating our experience for what it is.

Similarly, we cannot simply *reject* our masculinity as if it is 'wrong' or 'bad' or 'essentially oppressive to women'. This is not to say that we cannot *change* the ways that we are. What is at issue is the model of change that we inherit within our culture, and in this respect Freud is critical of a Kantian-Protestant tradition that says that we can *cut out* or eradicate those parts of ourselves, of our feelings and desires that we judge as wanting, as if reason provides some kind of neutral arbiter or legislator for determining what is to be regarded as *unacceptable* to us.

This was also part of a 1960s inheritance which held that our anger or jealousy was 'unreasonable' and therefore unacceptable, and that it should therefore be eradicated. It was assumed that we could somehow cut out feelings of jealousy and behave as if they did not exist at all. Jealousy was 'socially and historically constructed' and so equally it could be reformulated according to our wills. If we insisted on our jealousy this just showed a failure of will and determination.[18]

This is part of a Protestant tradition that is still very much with us in the idea of 'mind over matter': that if you take your mind off what is troubling you, then the feelings of despair or sadness will somehow disappear. Because we live in a secular culture we are often unaware of the Protestant sources of many of our ideas and values. Freud and psychoanalytic theory move against this aspect of our inherited culture. It was part of the project of 'Achilles' Heel' to say that you could not *reject* your masculinity, but you could work to *redefine* it.[19] We would work to change what we are by first accepting the nature of our emotions and feelings rather than judging ourselves too harshly. This is to come to terms with the self-critical voice which too often stands in the way of our changing.

It is possibly because the culture puts such great force on the idea of 'self-rejection' that so few men have really taken up these issues. It is possibly because they have sensed that there is something self-defeating, even self-destructive in the path that they are being encouraged to take, by the early notions of 'Men Against

Sexism'. In part it is also up to a theoretical grasp of men and masculinity openly to challenge some of the conceptions of masculinity that are embodied within aspects of feminist theory; that is, to reject the idea that men cannot change and to show the ways that men can change might be an important way of questioning the notions that make masculinities seem irredeemable.

In working towards a transformed understanding of men and masculinity we have to recognise the injuries that were done by the idea that men should be guilty *as men*. At the same time we have to take responsibility for how underdeveloped the theoretical grasp of the diversity of different masculinities remains and how long it has taken for men to explore more openly and honestly their relationship to feminism.

MEN, POWER AND FEMINISM

If we think about the question of whether feminism is in men's interests we can say that clearly at one level it is not, in the sense that it is a challenge to the power that men have to make the larger society in their image. Liberal theory argues that men and women should have equal rights in society and, to the extent to which women are denied these rights, the society is unequal and unjust. So it is that men have been able to support the claims of liberal feminism without having to bring into question the inherited forms of masculinity. The Women's Movement has gone further in its challenge to the power men have to make society in their own image. It also challenges the dominance of masculine values and aspirations which are largely taken for granted in the institutional organisation of society.

Feminism in its new phase presents a challenge to men's power in society and also to the sources of men's power in sustaining personal relationships. It is a challenge to the ways that both public and private life are largely organised around the value of men's time and interests, and subsequently devalues and fails to recognise, or to give equal value to, women's time, values and aspirations. So the Women's Movement has encouraged women to recognise how much they have been forced to give up within themselves in order to see themselves through the eyes of men. It recognises the difficult tasks that women have of rediscovering their values and relationships in the context of a patriarchal society.

So it is important to keep in view the ways that feminism remains a threat to the ways that men are, without thereby insisting that it is up to feminism somehow to set the agenda for the reworking of dominant forms of masculinity. Within the framework of liberal feminism it could seem as if women could be empowered through being given rights in the larger society without thereby challenging the position of men.

With the Women's Movement it is not simply a matter of empowering women but it is also a matter of challenging the forms of male power and the kind of assumptions that men are ready to make about themselves.[20] This takes us much further than the liberal vision which would see feminism as the empowering of women to compete with men in the public sphere on equal terms. For there is a challenge to the idea of 'equal terms' once we realise that 'equal terms' are often 'men's terms', as if women are being forced to be 'honorary men' so that they can be accepted within a man's world.

Cynthia Cockburn's work shows how this creates more problems, or at least new problems for women, who in gaining positions of responsibility and power within institutions can often only be accepted if they abandon, or at least reshape, their femininity, so that it once again becomes 'acceptable' to the men in authority and power. It is possible for men to *co-opt* feminism in many different ways, to agree with it so as to displace its challenge. It can be said that once women have been granted promotions in firms they no longer have anything to complain about. They are expected then to defend the present organisation of hierarchy.[21]

It is quite common for men to be 'sympathetic' to feminism, finding some kind of security in the idea that feminism should be left to women, that women should be given space to set down their ideas and projects free from the interferences of men. This is not an uncommon response but it is also flawed, for it fails to take account of the challenge that feminism presents to prevailing forms of masculinities. Briefly, we learn to say 'the right thing' when we are around feminists; we feel that we are walking on thin ice and we learn to be careful. It is important to keep in view how feminism remains a challenge to the character and organisation of men's power in society, since this in turn challenges the parallelism that can so easily be drawn when we talk about 'men's studies' in relationship to 'women's studies'.

The idea that 'in the last analysis' or at some deeper level, feminism is in fact in the interests of men, has to be handled with great care, for this too can foster a kind of parallelism where it is also possible for men to assimilate certain feminist insights which they can then use against women. So it is that men can move into certain occupations, for example, nursing or midwifery, thinking that they have thereby absorbed a 'feminist critique' that allows them the sensitivity and feeling to do the job. But there might well be questions about the place of men in, for instance, midwifery, which go unrecognised. The relationship of women to birth might preclude the possibility of men working well in this area.

It becomes possible to give deference to feminism and to talk about the power which men have within the larger society without fully grasping the power of sociology to co-opt a feminist challenge. Even though a 'men's studies' paradigm has challenged the pervasive influence of role theory, the idea that gender exists as a pre-existing set of expectations of what men and woman are supposed to be and do in the larger society is very current.

It is easy, as the literature shows, to fall back into a much more refined form of role theory, which allows for greater flexibility in gender expectations but loses a grip on issues of power and subordination, because this is such a dominant paradigm within psychology and the human sciences generally. It is the methodology of the social sciences, largely unchallenged, which comes to provide the legitimacy for these areas of intellectual study. The critique that feminisms can make of an Enlightenment tradition and the forms of social theory and methodology that have emerged from it, tends to get lost. An empiricist sociology tends to take charge and begins to set the terms in which gender studies are to prove themselves as valid and legitimate.

In Britain there have long been suspicions that the intellectual and political challenges of feminism would be weakened as feminism entered the prevailing disciplines in the academy. There is a pervasive sense of the possibilities of feminist insights being truncated and its challenges softened once these have to be expressed within a social science methodology that is taken to be neutral, impartial and somehow beyond criticism itself.

This scepticism can be useful, for it becomes easy to think of the restrictions of the male role, so that a men's movement is conceived of as a removal of, or liberation from, these restrictions; so that it can be said that men can equally be loving, caring, compassionate people. Men do not have to be distant, detached and totally identified with individual ambition and success. At the same time it is crucial to keep in mind the power that men have in the larger society, even if this is not always shared or experienced by individual men.

We should not understate the importance of extending the possibilities that are available to men so that at long last men can live in closer contact with their feelings and emotions, but we also have to recognise that this can make men manipulative and exploitative unless they are also prepared to recognise the autonomy and independence of women. For it can free men from a certain kind of emotional dependency on women without getting men to acknowledge the power of sexist attitudes and values that their behaviour embodies.

We should also not underestimate the anger and resentment that many men feel towards women and the way that this can be easily channelled into an anger and resentment against feminism. This does not mean that feminism is beyond critique; nor does it mean that men are not entitled to feel angry at some of the images of masculinity that have been produced.

In the 1980s we certainly witnessed a 'softening' of the image of men and the appropriation by men of certain qualities traditionally associated with women. These are no longer conceived of as unmasculine. The boundaries between the sexes have been blurred but this can make it harder to identify the workings of power and subordination. This does not mean that men should always be conceived of as all-powerful in relation to women within the larger society. We should not be blind to the relationships of power that exist between men mediated by class, race and ethnicity, and the difficulties that men often face in identifying their own needs and desires and asserting themselves in relation to other men. It is because this is often done at the expense of women that it has been difficult to investigate relationships that men have with each other.

Within post-structuralist theory we have a vision of power as all-pervasive, that can undermine our sense of the nature of interpersonal power. This insight into the pervasiveness of power can be used to question whether it is right to say that men have power in relation to women, because it can be argued that both 'masculinity' and 'femininity' are interpolated within a particular relationship of power.[22]

We are offered the notion of identity as being articulated through particular relationships of discourses of power. This is the way that the notion of 'social construction' is often conceived within a post-structuralist framework. It rejects the idea of power as a 'thing-like commodity' that some people have over others, for it wants to insist that the pervasiveness of power means that all identities are articulated within particular discourses of power. In part, this accounts for the difficulties which Foucault has in illuminating gender relationships of power.[23] It also shows the way in which the influence of Foucault's work has tended to subvert some crucial insights into the relationship between power, identity and experience.

Part of what is appealing in this move is that it brings into the open the idea that men are not all-powerful in all spheres of their lives and that women are not always completely powerless or subordinate.[24] It helps to challenge the pervasive picture of a hierarchy of powers with white men sitting on the top of the pile. But this means listening to the experience of men and taking seriously the terms in which they present themselves. A structuralist framework *undermines* its own insight into the complexity of power by seeing experience as itself the outcome or product of particular discourses. The dialectic that exists between experience and identity and the continuous struggle that people are involved in, in trying to clarify their needs and desires, gets lost. The complexities and tensions of experience are often lost as they are presented as the effects of language.[25]

Nevertheless, the picture of the 'hierarchy of powers' so easily places woman in the position of victim, as being subordinated and oppressed, and so denies her her own activity and power to shape her own history. At one level a similar problem can be identified within post-structuralist theory because it assumes that subjects or identities are the effects of discourses. It tends to present people as passive. It is possible to question the ways in which a positivist tradition objectifies people, without thereby being able adequately to conceive of their active natures. Within a different tradition, Laing developed a powerful critique of positivism within psychology but in the end tended to see children as the victims of the families within which they found themselves.[26] Similarly, a phenomenological tradition has tended to conceive of meaning as something within an individual's control, but has been unable to conceive of freedom as practical, self-conscious activity.

This vision of people as victims has a powerful hold within different traditions of social theory. Sometimes the theory can be part of the problem, for it can place, say, women in a position of subordination and powerlessness that seems impossible to break. It can create its own forms of dependency and submissiveness and it can stand in the way of women being able to empower themselves. In this sense, structuralism has found a way of talking about identities, but it has been difficult to identify the ways in which it sustains a particular form of rationalistic theory. It sees identities as being provided externally and thereby subtly tends to reinforce a vision of women as being passive. We are back unwittingly to the idea that the powerless have to be rescued or that there has to be some kind of external intervention, say by the state, to save them. Even if this process of identity formation is seen as an ongoing active process within certain post-structuralist writings, it is difficult to make sense of this because experience itself is so often taken to be an effect of discourse.

It was an insight of the early Women's Movement also to stress the self-activity of women and to focus on the ways women can retain power in their lives. But this vision remains theoretically in tension with a vision that draws on the 'hierarchy of powers', as well as with a more general structuralist/post-structuralist tradition. It tempts us into thinking that we have to work for the whole structure to be turned upside down before there is going to be any movement. If this vision allows for righteous anger it can also become a tacit form of pacification. It can stand in the way of women changing themselves and it blinds us to the difficult issues of collusion in which women themselves can be involved. A certain therapeutic understanding potentially raises some of these difficult questions. It recognises a tension, different for women than for men, between who we want to be in our minds and the actual quality of our everyday experience. It does not take experience as either given or as socially constructed but recognises this as a false polarity.

It recognises autonomy and independence not as a linear process of development but as a process of working through an often painful and difficult history we might otherwise choose to avoid. A rationalistic tradition tends to assume that we can guide our lives through will and determination so that we can turn aside from difficult feelings that we would otherwise prefer not to acknowledge. Freud knew otherwise, for he recognised that feelings we would repress have a way of returning to haunt us. To banish the very notion of 'repression', as Foucault sometimes wanted to do, does not mean that the issues will go away.[27]

Again this involves difficult questions, for it questions images of moral purity that often go along with being a victim. It is as if those at the bottom of the pile, those who have been most oppressed, can do no wrong, or somehow have to be excused, 'for they know not what they do'. Their behaviour can somehow be excused because of the power they are up against. But this can sustain a passive vision of women as victims, even if it avoids difficult and painful questions of how people have sometimes colluded in their own oppression. This does not deny for a moment the reality of structures of power and subordination, but it does recognise the realities of projection and the ways in which anger and frustration will often be projected.

This reflects in another sphere an assumption of an orthodox Marxist position, that would see the oppressed as somehow morally pure. It is painful to recognise that the oppressed can not only oppress those who are in a worse situation than themselves but that in gaining power the injuries of long periods of oppression does not mean that people will act with greater understanding and humanity towards others. Simone Weil recognises this as a problem with Marxism. This can make it difficult within sexual politics to come to terms with the experience of both men and women, for it places men on the top of a hierarchy and so in some way to blame for whatever goes on supposedly beneath them.

This vision of a hierarchy of powers is often implicitly a moral hierarchy which somehow regards those at the bottom as the most unblemished and morally pure.

This can encourage men to take on responsibilities not only for the hurt and injuries they cause, but somehow to feel guilty for all the misery and difficulties in their relationships with women. It can create important blind spots where women can sometimes be tempted to hide their responsibilities for whatever is going on in the relationship. This has created particular difficulties in men's relation to feminism and is a source of the rejection of feminism that we find developing in many of the men's rights movements. It is also part of the silence we often hear in feminist discussions of heterosexual relationships, as if these relationships cannot really be openly discussed. As a point of collusion with 'the enemy' they cannot really be acknowledged for the importance they have in the lives of both men and women.

There has still been relatively little feminist discussion of relationships with men and of the ways women feel and experience their relationships with men. There is a recognition that the situation is more complex than was originally formulated exclusively in terms of a relationship of power and subordination. Originally the conception of power as some form of commodity made it difficult to really appreciate the workings of emotional relationships of power, and often feminism has been bereft of a moral language within which these contradictory relationships could be illuminated.

There are a number of issues that come up for men with this conception of the hierarchy of powers. If men are placed at the top of the hierarchy, what are we to say to men who experience themselves as powerless, or even to men who experience themselves as passive and unable to articulate their needs within a relationship? Is this to be dismissed automatically as a 'form of false consciousness'? If it partly reflects a lack of recognition of the power men hold in relationship to women in the larger society, how does it really help us illuminate the complexities of interpersonal relationships? This raises the issue of when we can accept men's accounts of their own experience. This has always been crucial for feminist methodology, which seeks to validate the experience of women but is uncertain about the experience of men. Is it to be said that men's own accounts are bound to be suspect, to say the least, because, following Jean Baker Miller's account in *Towards a New Psychology of Women* (Miller 1976), they talk from a position of power and so identify their own masculine reality as the only possible account of reality?

This could be part of an explanation of why men cannot understand what women are experiencing, what they are 'complaining about', as men might say. It was true, at least in the early days of the Women's Movement, that men often said that women 'should be happy' because middle-class women had for instance been provided with a home and a car, and thus everything in a man's eye that they could possibly want, and further, 'they didn't really have to work for it themselves'. This meant that there was no 'real reason' for the dissatisfaction or unhappiness that women were suffering, and that therefore it had to be their own creation. It was something that women were encouraged to deal with through seeking professional help, for instance through going to psychoanalysts.

Within such a utilitarian moral framework, where well-being is assumed to be about the consumption of goods, or the accumulation of 'satisfaction', it was hard to make visible the source of women's oppression. Within our moral theory it was difficult to illuminate that what women had forsaken was in some important sense themselves, a sense of their own worth and identity.[28] This could not be voiced because women growing up within a man's world had been denied, or they had never been able to develop a sense of what they wanted, needed or valued for themselves. Rather, they were brought up to see themselves through men's eyes and to value their own experience in terms provided for them by men. Within a rationalistic culture it was said that women had to be able 'to give reasons' for their feelings of unhappiness or sense of worthlessness. It was easy to be told that if you 'can't give reasons' then this unhappiness does not really exist and you should be able to recover from it yourself.

If men are in a position of power, are we then to *discount* their talk and feelings of 'powerlessness' as so much 'rationalisation' or do we have to be prepared to reconsider some of the conceptions of masculinity implicit in forms of feminist theory? This is not simply a remark about radical feminist theory, for it has been its strength to bring into focus issues of male violence and also the unspoken ways men can use their power in relationship to women: the sullen withdrawal, the tense resentment, the angry silence. What is more, in claiming the importance of women's culture and women's sense of value and morality as being grounded differently from men's, it also opens up the way to investigate men's relationships to their inherited conceptions of masculinity.

Further, radical feminism raises the issue of the extent to which all men are to be equally identified with the structures of male power and dominance, and dominant forms of masculinity, despite differences of class, race and ethnicity which divide the experiences of men. Although radical feminist analysis often tries to fix men in this kind of way, it in fact can help to open up the theoretical ground in which we can begin to recognise different masculinities and the very different relationships men can develop and very different histories that men carry in relation to the dominant forms of masculinity.

Chapter 10

Masculinity

MEN, EXPERIENCE AND FEMINISM

Why has it taken so long for men to explore their experience of masculinity? In part, the workings of masculinity within modernity have remained invisible as dominant men have learned to speak in the impartial voice of reason. This has been part of an Enlightenment tradition and is deeply embodied in western inherited forms of philosophy and social theory. So a man's voice assumes a pitch of objectivity and impartiality as it becomes an *impersonalised* voice, a voice that has 'authority' because it belongs to no one in particular while claiming at the same time to respect all.[1]

Thus it is hard to judge men's accounts of their own experience because often these personal accounts are not forthcoming. Traditionally, men have relied on women to *provide* them with an account and understanding of what they are experiencing in their emotional lives. It is as if men do not have to learn to take responsibility for their relationships, since this can traditionally be left to women within heterosexual relationships. Often men learn to put up with things since they have to learn to identify themselves with an absence of emotional needs, and so to centre their lives around the demands of work where male identity is supposedly constructed. But it is also that feminism has sought to account for men's experience in particular ways, most sharply in the radical feminist idea that all men are 'potentially rapists'. This is a challenging but also a damaging notion, for it works to *discount* differences between men as 'illusory', for as the story goes, all men are fundamentally the same. They 'have to be' because they all occupy the same position in the hierarchy of powers. They are not to be trusted.

This creates a difficult and tense silence, for it means that women often stay silent about their relationships with men. They can feel constantly critical, as if assuming blame is a way of assuaging an underlying sense that relationships with men can only be a sign of weakness. For men it creates a silence because it makes them feel that they do not know their own natures, that there is something to fear in them, and that their emotional lives and sexualities are full of danger.[2] This reinforces, rather than challenges, a traditional Kantian conception of masculinity as somehow dominated by an animal nature and as something that can only be curbed by the strong hand of reason. It also reinforces an idea that women somehow know what men are like better than they can know themselves. It does not encourage men to build a different, possibly more trusting relationship, to their own experience. It tends to encourage men to hide further, feeling that somehow they have to be guilty of all the issues and problems emerging in their relationships with women. It can make it easier for women to take the morally high ground and thereby refuse to recognise their own collusions and responsibilities for the way the relationship is going.

Guilt can help explain why it is not uncommon for men to take to heart and identify with this radical feminist vision of themselves.[3] But it is still in many ways a surprising fact that needs explanation. It tends to reinforce a negative vision of masculinity as a form of self-denial, even self-hatred, which is deeply embedded within a Protestant culture, as Nietzsche recognised. It also allows men to talk about masculinity as a relationship of power in relation to women and so it gives men a kind of security in being able to uphold this analysis. It gives men an overarching rationalistic analysis of the situation and somehow allows them to render their own experience invisible.

But this path hardly helps men to reflect upon their own masculinities, and it blocks any vision that men can really change their lives. It resonates with a feeling that men inherit, within a Protestant culture, that they really are not trustworthy themselves, that they do not know what they are feeling, and that what they come to feel cannot really be trusted. It can become a version of 'mother knows best'. But at the same time it allows men to feel that they are 'right' because they have thereby been able to *identify* with radical feminism. But it is a strange way to identify for it *discounts* men's own experience of themselves and their relationships, and it often says that men's accounts of their own experience are *never* to be trusted. Paradoxically it means that men do not learn to take *responsibility* for themselves.

Men can assure themselves that they have the 'right analysis' of 'patriarchy' but at some level this helps produce a form of self-rejection and self-hatred. There might be a tension between what men feel about themselves from their own experiences, namely that they are not 'potential rapists', and the pull of the cultural notion of masculinity which says that men 'should always have a go', that their masculinity is somehow being compromised if they do not make a move sexually. It reinforces a notion that men cannot help themselves and that sexuality is somehow some kind of irresistible animal urge.

If we are to deny this position and argue that sexuality is not 'given' but is socially and historically constructed, then we still have to think clearly about imposing a sharp modernist duality between 'nature' and 'culture' and about the nature and character of this 'construction'. We have to think about the ways men can come to know themselves and develop a different relationship to their emotions, feelings and sexual desires. We have to recognise the ground opened up by different forms of therapy which make it possible for men to work on their sexualities and so to change. All this is denied if we insist on automatically discounting men's own accounts of their experience and saying that 'in reality' men are always 'potentially rapists'.

This does not mean that men will always know best, for we have to acknowledge real differences between men and in the level of self-awareness and in the work men have been ready to do on themselves. But it does mean that we cannot automatically discount their accounts of their experience. We have to recognise this as part of a process, for men's perceptions of themselves, at least in personal and sexual relationships, are likely to be on the skew, defensive, superficial and many other things, because of the disconnections which often exist between inherited forms of masculinity and men's relationships with their emotions, feelings and desires. Men have for so long within modernity learned to discount the impulses of their emotional lives that it is difficult to forge this relationship simply as a matter of will and determination.

Often it is difficult for men to acknowledge that 'they don't know' what it is they are feeling because it is such an important part of masculinity for men to assume they 'have to have the right answer'. This is an exercise in humility, when men begin to recognise the injuries done to themselves in the cultural separations enforced between men and their emotional lives. Often as men we are bereft of an emotional language which allows us to identify and articulate our experience.

At some other level there is often an unspoken fear of women and of female sexuality and this has been touched by feminism. Men are often anxious not to say and do 'the wrong thing'. This can be part of a desire to be 'good boys' so that some men can fear a particular kind of emotional confrontation with women, sometimes because of the feelings they sense within themselves at another level. Again, therapy has helped create a safe space in which these feelings of resentment, hostility and disgust can somehow be acknowledged and worked on. Again, this is not something that needs to be worked on directly in relation to women, but it is something that men can work on with each other as they learn to take greater responsibility for themselves.

It is quite possible for these feelings to be worked on in a men's consciousness-raising or therapy situation. Sometimes an identification with feminism in the form of men assuming a radical feminist conception of masculinity can hide some of these deeper feelings of resentment that never really have to be faced or worked on. It is a paradox that men learn to assume a responsibility for others partly through providing financially before they learn to take emotional responsibility for their personal lives. Responsibility is often conceived impersonally since this is what men are often familiar with.

An identification with feminism in this way has to be considered carefully. It can so easily be a claim to 'difference', a feeling that I am 'anti-sexist' and so should be 'liked' or 'approved of' because of this. Often this goes along with the sense that some men have always liked women better, got on better and had closer friendships with women than with other men. Again, this can be part of a process of hiding or concealing more uncomfortable and negative feelings in relation to women. These are equally feelings for which men need to take responsibility. In this way an identification with feminism can serve as a kind of defence against these difficult feelings.

Sometimes men argue that feminism is 'in the interests of men' because it helps men to get in touch with their feelings and accept those parts of themselves that a traditional masculinity has led them to reject. There is something in this, but there is also something to be wary about, because it often leads to a denial of those feelings of anger and resentment that are taken to be *unacceptable* emotions because they are taken to be 'oppressive to women'. So men can curtail these responses and feelings and assume that it is always possible to have 'positive' feelings. But again this can be another way of denying responsibility in difficult areas of feeling in relation to women.

This partly explains my suspicion of the idea of 'feminist men', the idea that men can be doing 'feminist work'. This tendency has been stronger in the United States than in Britain, and it needs to be thought about critically. It connects to the issue of what men are trying to achieve when working on the relationship between men and masculinity. Are they doing men's sexual politics? If they are, how does this relate to what gay men have been doing for years and to the development of gay studies? Are there different ways of recognising that men are exploring the challenges of feminist work for traditional forms of masculinity?

If it is the feminist critique that has been so powerfully unsettling for who we are as men and the visions that we have inherited of our lives, do we want to say that feminists have somehow set the agenda for men's studies? For example, feminists have demanded that men consider the sources of male violence and in particular male violence against women. This is a crucial question, but the intellectual issues about the place of men's studies cannot be settled by saying it is for feminism to set the agenda while it is for men to work out their response.

This relationship to feminism cannot be right, for men have somehow to take responsibility for themselves and for the questions that emerge in their explorations of men and masculinity. Otherwise it can be too easy to be looking over our shoulders for approval, so to speak. But this begs the difficult question of the relationship of men's studies to women's studies and gay and lesbian studies, and the crucial importance of not undermining them even unwittingly through the development of an independent branch of work.

This is difficult because, since the early days of feminism, women have demanded that men take responsibility for themselves, but they did not really want men to take sides within feminist debates because this could be seen as dividing women. But it might be that various studies will bring into question assumptions that both socialist and radical feminist theory make about men. I think this is something which should be welcomed. It might well be important for men to consider the appropriate place of, for instance, anger, strength and resentment in their lives, rather than simply to discount these emotions and feelings because they can sometimes be acted out in relation to women. This is part of a re-evaluation of diverse masculinities and male values, and potentially even a recognition of differences between men and women. Too often we have thought of equality in terms of sameness so that it has been difficult to reconcile notions of gender equality with the recognition of differences that might not be socially produced.

This touches on complex issues that have emerged, particularly in the United States, with regard to the question of men's culture; whether for instance men will want to play with children in different ways from women and how, partly under the influence of feminism, men have sought to model their behaviour on the behaviour of women. So, for instance, is there something *distinct* in the nature of fathering, in the nature and character of the relationships men can have as fathers to their children, or is there simply something called 'mothering' or 'parenting' which is simply a question of dividing equally those care-taking tasks and responsibilities involved in caring for children?[4] Men who want to talk of themselves as male feminists might also be suspicious about defining particular qualities and responsibilities of fathering.

This connects to difficulties with a pervasive 'social constructionist' view within social theory, because it tends to assume that all our feelings and desires, as modes of classification or mental constructions, can somehow be 'remade' or 'remodelled' as an act of will and determination. This can discourage an exploration of diversities of men's own experience, say, of fathering, the particular tensions, frustrations and difficulties that men might experience in their relationships with children. While it is crucial for men to recognise what women have been obliged to put up with for years, this should not discount what men have to share about their experience.

It is also important to recognise the *differences* that exist between different men coming from different class, racial and ethnic cultures as well as the different needs that individual men might be fulfilling, given their own background and relationships with their fathers in taking on the responsibilities of fathering. We should be ready to recognise these differences but also to explore them critically, rather than to discount these differences in advance as if they have no basis in reality or in people's experience.

Another critical issue concerns heterosexuality and whether it is possible to conceive it both as a relationship of power in the larger society and also as a legitimate sexual orientation. So often the ways we conceive of relationships of power, particularly within a framework of a hierarchy of powers, has made it seem as if heterosexuality itself is somehow invalidated. Rather, what needs to be challenged is how this power is used against women, gay men and lesbians, and the ways it is 'normalised' so as to discount the validity of other forms of sexual orientation. A social constructionist view might tempt heterosexual men into thinking that, say, their feelings of sexual attraction are illegitimate and to be hidden and denied. But this is different from saying that these feelings should somehow be acknowledged and then worked on critically.

A social constructionist view tempts us into thinking that our sexualities can somehow be remade as acts of will, as if there were a question of political choice. This shows the depth of a rationalistic tradition within the Left and within sexual politics generally. This has produced enormous confusion as men have, for instance, been led to feel that an erection has to be an assertion of patriarchal power.

The only 'acceptable' form of sexuality is sexuality without an erection or at least without penetration. This produces and fosters a form of moralism that is not unknown in the culturally embedded idea that boys are *'bad'*. It is a notion that both working-class and middle-class men have been told since they were quite young.

As boys, we have often been told that boys are 'bad' and 'naughty' so we should feel guilty about our feelings. We have to learn to curb our natures, for otherwise we will 'lose control of ourselves' and 'do things' we will 'live to regret'. Since 'boys are bad' by nature we can easily assume that masculinity is something that can never be redeemed or changed or transformed, let alone enjoyed, celebrated or recognised as a source of pleasure and fulfilment. We have to take seriously men's accounts of their experience, recognising how they have learned to feel bad or guilty about themselves. We need to recognise some of the sources of these feelings within a Protestant culture in the ways they have grown up within the family.

There is a danger of feminism reinforcing a particular kind of moralism in relation to how men ought to be. This too easily encourages a simplistic antimony of being either for or against feminism and it can allow 'pro-feminist' men to take a stand of moral righteousness. This turns it into a matter of abstract principle, as if a clear and unequivocal 'stand' is being called for. As men, we often feel most comfortable when issues are turned into matters of principle, where they can be dealt with at an intellectual level as an issue of who has the best reasons on their side.[5]

But this itself shows how little we have understood about feminist method, for it is not an issue that can be decided by reason alone. For one thing we have to acknowledge the tensions and contradictions in the experience of men, even when a men's rights movement sees itself in opposition to the claims and still tenuous advances made by feminism over the last twenty years. It might also mean acknowledging dangers of a reaction against feminism that question the very existence of masculinity, rather than particular dominant forms of masculinity.

There is something misguided about a theoretical position which asserts that there is something 'wrong', 'defective' or 'inadequate' in masculinity itself, thereby leaving no space for men to change their experience as men. A rationalist construction of masculinity, whereby men see themselves as having to prove their masculinity constantly against some kind of ideal, is given a new form when men are attempting to squeeze themselves into a new mould, even one provided by feminism, of what 'a man is to be like'. This continues in a new form an old Protestant tradition that says that men are unacceptable as they are, that men's natures are somehow evil. This fosters a notion that men can only be acceptable if they forsake their masculinity.

This touches on the castration fears made visible within Freudian theory. It is the fear that the overbearing mother is about to overwhelm the son, taking away his potency. Even if this is no part of a feminist intention, it has often been an unwitting consequence of a feminist challenge which has left many men with a sense of 'not knowing who they are', or 'feeling inadequate in who they are as men' or feeling in the context of relationships that their partners 'know best'. This tends to make men defensive, rigid and stiff rather than providing a means for any kind of meaningful change. Men often feel threatened, withdrawing into a sullen silence, or acting out in violence. That this can be taken as further evidence of what men 'are really like all along' is simply another part of the problem that we are trying to identify.

It would be an unwelcome tendency in sexual politics if feminism simply supported a notion 'that women are always right', for they have the clear vision of being subordinate and oppressed, and 'that men are always wrong'. This is simply to reverse the traditional structure rather than to challenge it. Within relationships this can be played out, obscuring the power that feminism has given to some women over the last twenty years. Men can now be left feeling that they are not 'good enough', that they are not 'intimate enough', 'responsive and caring enough', so that if there are difficulties in the relationship it is for men to accept that they are responsible for them and that they are part of the problem, not the solution.

But this can be an unhelpful projection which turns men into 'bad objects' and says that everything that is 'wrong' in the relationship can somehow be placed at men's feet. All the sources of misery and unhappiness that a woman might feel are seen as having their source in the inadequacy of the men to whom they relate. The moral logic of this position can be reinforced by the idea that men are responsible for women's subordination, misery and oppression. This is complex because within a liberal moral culture that has now been deeply influenced by feminism it is easy for some men to buy this conception of themselves, having been brought up already to feel they are 'bad'.

So we have a tendency of men doing things to *please* or *placate* their partners, to feel somehow responsible for making them less miserable. This can connect to a masculine trait of feeling that men have to fix things, somehow make things better or make things right. But unless men are equally prepared somehow to acknowledge their own feelings and experience in the situation, this usually falls flat. As men, we often take a rationalistic position almost outside the relationship that can make our partners despair of being recognised or understood. Often this 'pleasing' behaviour is not genuine. Communication can further degenerate when men feel that their anger is not legitimate in the relationship since it is a form of coercion. While it is certainly true that men often pressure their partners in the very atmosphere they put out, it is important to acknowledge the poverty of our learning as men when it comes to contact and communication with others. We learn to accept an isolation and loneliness as if this is proof of our dignity and self-esteem as men.

This can help explain why many men have felt the need to put some distance between themselves and feminism in the 1980s, as if this distance is required for them to learn somehow to define their own experience. Sometimes this is expressed as an overt hostility to feminism, a sense of the injuries men have done to themselves in accepting the images of themselves as portrayed by feminism. Sometimes men feel the need to explore their own masculinity and discover what emerges for themselves. At least for a while this involves some kind of distance from feminism. This involves an exploration, both of traditional conceptions of masculinity, and also of the dominant conceptions of masculinity as men learn to deepen their trust in themselves in order to be able to share a vulnerability that can be owned as a strength, rather than as a sign of weakness and inadequacy.[6]

This can help us to question forms of social theory and the implicit conformism it fosters in the idea that 'socialisation' involves a conformity or adjustment to some preconceived model. The dominant forms of post-structuralist theory also tend, despite their sense of the ways that identities can be continually articulated and struggled over, to reproduce this 'externalised' vision, for they leave no space for an exploration of masculinity in the sense of individual men exploring their sense of self.

Part of what needs to be questioned is the pressure men feel of having to bring their behaviour into conformity with external rules and definitions. Some forms of psychotherapy can help open up the possibility for this kind of investigation through validating an exploration of emotional needs, values and desires. They recognise how a rationalist culture often stands in the way of the individuation and self-definition of men. It has fostered its own forms of suppression as men have felt the need to define themselves by external standards, if their very masculinity was not to be brought into question. It is part of the traditional inheritance that men can never take their masculinity for granted. It is always something that needs to be proved or defended.

MEN, POWER AND SOCIAL THEORY

Men often experience a tension between what they need for themselves and what the culture defines as their needs. It can be difficult to make this tension visible within modernist traditions of social theory. Part of this has been expressed as a 'going beyond' traditional role theory, that is, the idea of a fixed male social role that men have to conform to if they are not to be thought of as 'deviant' or 'abnormal'. This has traditionally built upon a sharp demarcation between 'masculine' and 'feminine' qualities that meant that men were supposed to be impersonal, career-orientated breadwinners providing support for their wives and families, a shoulder that others could depend on. This was a rigid formulation of the male role, and Joseph Pleck's *The Myth of Masculinity* set about establishing a more fluid pattern, a more multi-layered conception of masculinity. Masculinity was no longer expected to be one thing, it could be many things, for it could now allow for diversity. The dominant paradigm in academic work on men and masculinity has in fact been provided within a revised and flexible form of social psychology.[7]

A competing conception has been provided by sociology whereby social theory has begun to talk of the social construction of masculinity, to point out that masculinity is not simply given or provided for by biology but is something 'constructed' within particular social relationships. Both conceptions can operate within a particular social science methodology. They can both present themselves as being 'objective' and 'impartial'. Crucially they can often avoid issues of method that have been centrally raised within feminist theory. It might be useful to set out some of the issues which this 'gender perspective' framework, as it is often called, tends to avoid. This begins to set the scene for a different kind of exploration of men and masculinity, one which is more sensitive to the historical and philosophical sources.

First, these theories avoid the tension between the experience that men have of themselves and the way they are supposed to be within the dominant culture. If they illuminate the pain and confusion that is often felt, this is put down as transitional, as part of the movement from one social role to a newly defined and more flexible social role. Second, by talking about this tension in terms of 'social construction', we undermine people's trust in their own experience, in the ways that they might come to define what they want for themselves both individually and collectively. It encourages an externalised relationship to your male experience when you see it as the outgrowth of a particular construction. If it has helped shift the vision that gender is *biologically given*, it only does this at the cost of disorganising our understanding of the interrelationship, if it can be talked about like this at all, between 'the social' and 'the biological'.

Third, it displaces the issue of *responsibility*, for the role, like the construction, is provided for individuals 'by society'. It is not anything that I can help, nor is it anything that I can be held individually responsible for. This is important for men because it is important for them to learn to take responsibility for a masculinity that is so often rendered invisible. It is also important for men to think about the dominant position of masculinity within society and the ways boys are brought up into masculinity. Responsibility might well turn out to be a crucial issue for men, especially in relationships, for it can be seen that, even though men are 'responsible' in the public world of work where it can be a matter of following established rules and procedures, often in relationships men can be controlling, constantly *finding fault* with what their partners are doing, and feeling somehow estranged or outside of the relationship.

These patterns are not unique to men and have to be carefully specified in relation to class, race, ethnicism, age and sexual preference. But it is revealing to realise that men can often be seen as not taking the initiative within a personal and intimate relationship. The fact that middle-class men grow up to deny their needs, to see strength as a matter of 'having no needs', can build a falseness and inequality into a relationship, for men can often get into a position of providing for or pleasing their partners rather than negotiating from a sense of what they individually need or want for themselves. It is often difficult to identify our emotional needs as men because we are so used to suppressing them. This is generally so taken for granted that it is often difficult to identify the lack of responsibility that men have learned to assume for themselves and for their needs.

Often, men take little responsibility for their personal lives, partly because this has been taken for them by their mothers and later by their partners. We can be so used to having these needs met *for us* that we believe that it is a right, rather than an element in a gender relationship of power and subordination. It can seem to men as if love is shown by the fact that someone meets your needs without your first having to put them into words yourself. Often this is a rationalisation for the fact that men have never learned to communicate their personal and emotional needs and, fearing rejection, never learn how to take responsibility for themselves.

Fourth, these conceptions of masculinity make no sense of the contradictions that exist within men's experience. For instance, there is little sense that it is because men identify with their reason, because of the Enlightenment identification between masculinity and reason, that they are thereby estranged from their emotions and feelings. This is systematically organised and structured. It is a matter of the way a particular dominant form of masculinity and male identity is organised. So this sets up a particular tension between what men grow up to want for themselves, for example to do well at work and to be successful and achieve, and their feelings for what matters most to them in their lives.

As men learn to recognise their emotions and feelings they thereby learn what value to give to different aspects of their experience. They more readily recognise a problem within an Enlightenment modernity that assumes that values can be established by reason, or else that values are simply a matter of individual choice and will. For example, if a man has to cope with his child's accident, this might well bring him to recognise the importance of his relationship with his child and how little real *quality* time he spends, given how his life is organised. It might mean that, at least for a few years, he has to be less identified with work and less concerned with his career. This is a contradiction that women have learned to live with for generations but it is something which is quite new for men to discover.

Those men who are brought up within the terms of a protestant moral culture invariably assume that everything is possible if only they work hard enough for it. So often men are constantly pushing themselves against their boundaries and against their limits with a sense that if they only push a little harder then they *should* be able to meet all the demands that are being made on their time. This is a powerful myth and it is also damaging. The vision of masculinity as 'socially constructed' takes too removed and externalised a position and does not help illuminate the character of these contradictions and the ways individual men work this out for themselves. We tend to lose a sense of the crucial tension between an individual's growing realisation of what he or she wants for themselves and the definitions that are provided for them by social relationships. It is a tension which is central to the notion that 'the personal is political'. The attempts to reorder feminist theory on the basis of a social construction view have tended to lose touch with the power of this insight that can so easily seem marginal and rhetorical.

We have to be clearer about the tensions between the implicit theories of 'sexual politics', which are often left unacknowledged, and the explicit frameworks which are provided within the human sciences. It is possible that the attempt to present 'sexual politics' as a 'gender perspective' within sociology or, when dealing with men, as a sociology of masculinity, will mean a loss of crucial insights and understandings. This is particularly clear when we consider the nature of interpersonal power, or the ways sexual relationships are relationships of power, for it is so easy for power to be 'tacked on' as if it were some kind of afterthought. There is a tension between the social constructionist view that often tends to be externalised and totalistic, despite claims to the contrary, and a grasp of how power operates within the context of relationships. I have attempted to make some sense of this complexity in terms of heterosexual relationships between men and women, suggesting that there are difficult questions on both sides that have often remained concealed, for they tend to bring into question some of the larger theoretical commitments people have wanted to identify with.

It might be that we have to take more seriously the idea of sexual politics, particularly the idea that the 'personal is political', as the basis for a renewed conception of the dialectic between experience, identity and history. Feminists have long recognised that there is no way of squaring the contradictions whereby women have struggled for an autonomy and independence which is being constantly challenged and negated within the larger society. This is a contradiction that women have learned to live with, recognising the importance of the support they can receive from others. In this sense it is no different from men who are struggling to change patterns of behaviour that have been institutionalised. In both contexts we have to recognise the importance of a social movement for change as part of a redefinition of values and relationships, so that 'the micro' and 'the macro' aspects have to be brought into relationship. They cannot be separated off as independent levels of analysis as is often done within the human sciences.

So as men change it will have to be part of a movement for change which will transform the organisation of institutional powers *and* the forms of personal relationships. So it is that the 'micro' cannot be separated from the 'macro', nor can they be reduced to one another. This is an important feminist insight that men are in danger of losing if they take their theoretical starting point not from within sexual politics but from within the established social scientific frameworks. It is understandable that this temptation will be strong because movements for change have been relatively weak for men, understandably so because men have been so closely identified with prevailing relationships of power, dominance and authority.

But this also serves as a warning against thinking that the 'speculative claims' of feminist theory can somehow be tested against the causal claims that they seem to be making, say in the case of the effects of pornography on men's values and behaviour. This would be to take for men's studies the high ground of a refined positivist methodology, thinking that this is neutral and that it provides a secure base from which feminist claims can be evaluated.

If this temptation is to be resisted it will be because men have learned their own complicity with the dominant forms of social theory. They have learned to question the universality of these theories and methods, recognising the masculinist assumptions which they carry. Too often they are set within a rationalist framework that recognises reason as the only source of knowledge and invalidates feelings and desires as being legitimate sources of understanding, insight and knowledge. There are dangers for sexual politics in seeking legitimacy in terms of the prevailing paradigms of scientific investigation if this means losing the crucial power and value of feminist insight.

But this is not to say that a sexual politics of masculinity will not yield new questions that might challenge some of the notions of a developing feminist methodology. A study of men and masculinity will yield its own methodological concerns. These questions will not always lie within feminist theory, nor can we say in advance what they might be. They cannot be judged according to pre-existing feminist standards, but if they are firmly grounded they will also deepen our understanding of the sources of women's oppression and subordination. They will also illuminate the conditions and possibilities of changing conceptions of masculinity, if not also the conditions for the 'liberation' of men.

Chapter 11

Histories

MODERNITY AND MARXISM

Different traditions of social theory have largely been set within the rationalist terms of modernity, placed within a philosophical framework set by an ongoing argument between empiricism and rationalism. These have offered different ways of knowing the social world and establishing objective knowledge but they both accept the centrality of epistemological issues. We learn to think about *how* we come to know social reality in largely epistemological terms.

This helps to set up a guiding framework within sociology between positivism on the one hand as yielding objective knowledge which is guaranteed through following the impartial controls of a scientific method, and interpretive sociology that focuses upon the meaningful character of social action. This tradition supposedly sees individuals as free and self-determining, rather than externally constrained and determined as with positivism. So it is that the argument is often set, at least as regards issues of methods, between Durkheim and Weber.

It is also said that classical social theory remains an argument with the ghost of Marx. This is also true in the sense that a tradition of Hegel and Marx remains as a ghostly presence hovering in a disturbing and unintegrated way over many courses. In the context of methods there will often be lectures on the dialectic as a method but this fits awkwardly into the dominant framework, unless it is appreciated as a challenge, as Lukács grasped it, to the basic framework of Enlightenment modernity.[1] For it suggests that epistemological issues cannot be settled in their own terms but have to be related to practical concerns of changing lives and social relationships.

In the context of social theory Marx and the traditions that flow from him can command space and time, but often in ways that remain strangely detached. It often exists as a stream of work all on its own. It proves much harder to draw connections than we would often like to think. We learn to accept it as a 'perspective' within social theory that seems to provide a place to contain it. At least this is preferable to teaching it as a form of positivism or functionalism that used to be done before the 1970s. This has again been given credence with the development of analytical Marxism within a scientistic mould.[2]

As long as the dominant framework is set somehow between positivism and interpretive sociology, so crudely between objective and subjective accounts, the central methodological issues remain epistemological. If we think largely in terms of how sociological knowledge in its different forms can be validated or else in terms of whether 'objective' knowledge of society is possible, we are operating largely within an Enlightenment framework that sets consciousness against a social world it is attempting to grasp. The individual is set against society and their relationship is established in epistemological terms as an issue of mind or consciousness. We are left with a weak sense of experience which is construed in largely mental or cognitive terms, since within a rationalist tradition it is separated from any somatic or emotional life. It is only as rational selves that we are supposedly social actors or members of a larger society.

Hegel and Marx can help to challenge this epistemological framework. It is partly the influence of Herder that helps Hegel to challenge Kant's abstract rationalism.[3] He recognises that it is not only as rational selves that we exist as moral beings. But his analysis moves away too quickly from the contradictions of lived experience which tend to dissolve in the historical growth and development of reason. We have already gone some way to explaining the weaknesses this involves for his sense of experience, while at the same time acknowledging with Lukács that his discussion of labour prepared important ground for Marx.

This is an enormous debt to Hegel that Marx was ready to acknowledge, along with his debt to Hegel's grasp of the historical and dialectical development of consciousness. But along with this, Marx inherits an Enlightenment faith in progress and the progressive character of history that encourages him to think of capitalism as a progressive force because of the way that it overthrows feudal relationships of traditional authority and dependency. We inherit a vision of history as separated out into discrete stages each with its own logic and rationality, which within an orthodox Marxist tradition tends to get frozen into a preordained movement.[4]

But Marx also develops a sense of human beings as creative beings who need to discover a form of creative labour through which they can fulfil themselves as human beings. This contrasts with a Kantian tradition that assumes that our freedom comes from realising ends and goals that we have set for ourselves through reason alone. A Kantian tradition assumes that we have given wants and desires and that we can also set certain purposes or goals for ourselves. Its vision of the person is a vision of the rational self whose vision of growth and development is largely set in terms of the effective control of our inclinations. If we fulfil our desires we will find happiness, but the fulfilment of ourselves lies elsewhere in the moral worth that we accrue through acting out of a sense of duty. It is only as rational selves that we can transcend our natures.

Part of the importance of Hegel within western thought is his attempt to blend an Enlightenment rationalism with a rediscovery of the influence of the Greeks, particularly Aristotle. This reconciliation is only partly successful and in the end it is a reformed Enlightenment rationalism that wins out. Charles Taylor in *Hegel* talks of this as a reconciliation between Herder and Kant who were both important influences.[5] But the point here is that this opens up a space for the young Marx to explore our existence as creative beings who need to fulfil ourselves through appropriate forms of labour. At least with Marx, epistemological issues are placed in a less significant way, for it is as we change the conditions of our lives and the ways we relate to others that we come to think in different ways. The emphasis for Marx is on our existing as social beings, though this has proved difficult to illuminate. Too often discussions of consciousness and ideology take place, especially under Althusser's influence, that tempt us back into epistemological concerns.[6]

Marx's discussions of alienation and estrangement still manage to haunt much sociological discussion because they provide insights into *qualitative* conditions of being. It is crucial for Marx that alienation is not thought about as a 'psychological' condition, for it is inseparable from the material situations that workers find themselves in, separated from the means of production, within a capitalist mode of production. It is crucial for Marx that as wage labour we exist as commodities with a distinct price on our heads. We have to recognise that as far as capital is concerned, we exist as means which are dispensable as soon as the profitability of production is brought into question.

In learning to treat our labour as a commodity, we are left in a contradictory situation in relation to our existence as creative beings. This is because we cannot meaningfully separate our labour from ourselves as if it were a separate possession that we could use at will. It is Locke's vision of the possessive individual who can somehow be separated out as an *owner* of his or her qualities. It is this vision of the person as an owner of qualities that he or she is free to dispose of at will, that informs a capitalist ethic. It still sustains libertarian conceptions, such as that defended by Robert Nozick in *Anarchy, States and Utopia*.[7]

Marx contests this vision of the self and its relation to its qualities as part of his critique of capitalist notions of freedom. Marx's vision of people as creative beings suggests a discussion of needs, capacities and qualities that have to be fulfilled if people are to realise themselves. This is in constant tension with a rationalism that is attempting to construe such notions as 'fulfilment' and 'realisation' in externalised ways, as matters of achieving ends and goals that have been defined by reason alone. But Marx rejects these terms, since what matters is not simply our existence as rational beings but our growth and development as creative beings in all its different facets. This involves the fulfilment of our natures within this life, rather than the subordination of our natures for a salvation that is offered in the next. In this crucial respect it challenges the Protestant vision that tacitly informs modernity.

In Marx's early writing there is a recognition that our alienation from our activity – since we are working to produce goods that we do not control ourselves – is connected both to an alienation from others because of the relationships we have, and to an alienation from ourselves. Marx's discussions of estranged labour within the *Paris Manuscripts* is rich because of its refusal to separate these different facets out but to insist on holding them in tension with each other. They are all part of a material situation that is created through the centrality of wage labour to the capitalist mode of production. It is crucial that this is not a situation that we choose for ourselves, but as soon as we enter the capitalist labour market they define the conditions within which we have to work. Of course, the particular form that they take varies with our location within the class relations of power and subordination. Marx did not conceive of capitalism as a fixed system but spent much of his life investigating its historical transformation and the crucial part played in it by shifts in the labour process.[8]

But as Marx turns his attention to a study of the historical transformations of *Capital*, there seems to be a hope that these issues can be adequately expressed and worked through in the tension between use values and exchange values, as if a transformation of production away from exchange values will provide solutions. In part, Marx had welcomed the spread of exchange values as subverting traditional forms of loyalty and dependence while at the same time recognising how market values come to dominate all other values of life. He tended to identify the power of the bourgeoisie with the dominance of exchange values so that the overthrow of their power would not only create the conditions for more equal human relationships as private property would be socialised, but also open up a recognition of different forms of value and different, more equal forms of human relationships.

Possibly a foreclosing and narrowing of Marx's vision can also be detected in his earlier writing, though this requires careful investigation. There is in Marx a way in which our existence as creative beings gets channelled into our experience of labour and in time into a much narrower productivism than Marx ever intended. Marx's emphasis on labour, as Benjamin realised, is flawed because however important it is for people to discover an activity within which they can realise themselves, this should not minimise the importance of other areas of life. If Marx recognised in his vision of communist society that individuals will engage in different activities, it strikes an individualistic note.

There is little sense of the importance of human relationships, of learning how to sustain contact and love in relationships. This is because the personal and the emotional still tend to be relegated to the private sphere. They are not important in Marx's scheme of things. It is as if alienation from self and others takes place in the public realm alone. It is also that Marx inherits a rationalism that is antagonistic to what he can sometimes regard as our 'animal natures' and makes it difficult to develop his understanding of our existence as creative beings. There are moments in the *Paris Manuscripts* when it seems as if an independent faculty of reason remains the source of our humanity and the ends and purposes that are freely chosen an adequate expression of our freedom.

Marx is still important in helping us question the notion of the abstract individual with discrete wants and desires who enters, with others, a contract to form society in order to have these desires met. The liberal vision of society as a collection of individuals is subverted by Marx's refusal to think of society in abstract terms and his insistence on talking about particular societies at particular times. Similarly, we have to be careful to locate *who* we are talking about within what relationships of power and subordination, rather than to talk abstractly about individuals in relation to society. So it is that we learn that we are social beings who exist within a particular network of social relationships, that can often also be conceived of as relations of power and subordination. So it is that Marx provides us with a language of social relationships mainly focussed around the conditions of labour.

His sense of the relationship of theory to practice, of consciousness to social activity, can still help us question rationalist forms of social theory that would conceive of social reality and our experience within it as a conceptual construction. This is equally true of accounts of Marx's work which, following Althusser's structuralist work, would construe Marx's theory in largely rationalist terms. The emphasis is placed on a challenge to humanist versions of Marx that supposedly continue to rest on 'essentialist' or 'anthropological' accounts of human nature, failing to appreciate, according to Althusser, the epistemological break in Marx's move towards construing his work as a science of history and politics.[9]

It is this categorical rejection of essentialism, as we have discovered it already, that supposedly sets the terms for saying that 'individuality' or 'experience' is socially and historically constructed. This makes it difficult to illuminate the contradictions of our lived experience, for it forecloses a tension between who we might be struggling to be ourselves and the ways that our lives and experience are supposedly structured and organised through the dominant institutions of society.

HISTORIES AND IDENTITIES

It has proved difficult to substantiate Marx's notion that it is social being which determines our social consciousness. Either this has been grasped too reductively as if it were a contention of causal determination or else it has been allowed, as Korsch recognised in *Marxism and Philosophy*, to substantiate too crude and unhelpful a distinction between materialism on the one hand and idealism on the other.[10] Marx was not setting out to challenge the importance of ideas and values within social life but to question those who assumed they could be understood in their own terms without having to context them historically.

This was an aspect of a rationalist tradition that he was ready to question, as he was working for a recognition that it is in the context of *changing* the conditions of lives that we will learn to think differently. It is not as if our actions can flow directly from our intentions in a way that can always be clearly evaluated beforehand. This is an insight which feminism has regained for itself in its recognition that as women take steps to change the conditions of their lives – and as part of this overall process – they will begin to feel greater self-worth and inner strength. These are qualities that cannot be gained by will and determination alone, for they do not operate solely within the mental or conceptual reality.

If Marx can help us to situate our individual experience within class relationships of power and subordination, showing us that what we learn to think of as 'private' and 'personal' experience within a liberal moral culture grows out of a shared condition of subordination, the tradition he fostered tended to take an externalised view of individual experience. It unwittingly reinforced in its orthodox and scientific forms a sense of the powerlessness of individuals in face of the impersonal forces of history. It tended to think of *replacing* individual identities by class identities, which tended to shift responsibility away from individuals themselves towards their duties to the party or the revolution.

It was Gramsci who most clearly recognised the weaknesses of this tradition, not only for the passivity it tended to produce as it minimised the significance of working-class consciousness and self-activity, but also because it tended to disempower individuals in their own eyes.[11] It left working people waiting for a deliverance that would come from elsewhere. Authority tended to remain firmly in the hands of the party, rather than in the hands of the people themselves.

This is partly why Gramsci learned to insist that people had to exist as the centre of their own activity and consciousness. He learned to challenge a liberal individualism which claimed that beliefs and values were matters of individual opinion alone through asserting that we can all come to recognise the discontinuities and contradictions within our inherited forms of consciousness. At this level he did not seek to dissolve individuality into the social category of class, for he wanted to sustain a democratic impulse through recognising that we each have to understand the social and historical formation of our consciousness. This included a recognition of the tension that often exists between what we believe and the different 'logic' that often informs our actions.[12] If we are not to slavishly reproduce ideas and conceptions that we have passively inherited, then we have to become 'critically conscious' in Gramsci's terms. This is an important step in empowering ourselves, for it means learning to think and feel for ourselves.

The democratic impulse is sustained by the recognition that this consciousness cannot be delivered to us with the authority of science. It cannot be taught to us by party theorists in positivist terms. It was in this way that orthodox Marxism sustained a dominant masculinity that was confident in what *others* could rationally think and believe. It was the authority of reason that men had learned to accept as their own, and science in its positivist guises was formed within this image. This was no less true of Marxism, which after Marx's death felt it had to present itself in the scientific terms set out by positivism if it were to be taken seriously.

This meant separating the scientific analysis of capitalism as an independently existing object of investigation from the everyday experience of oppression, poverty and hardship endured by working-class people. This experience was 'personal' and 'subjective' so that it could have no place within an objectivist discourse of science. So it was that within orthodox Marxism the experience of working-class struggles that had formed the basic categories of Marx's work were actually excluded from the considerations of Marxist theory.

It is crucial for Gramsci that individuals have to go through the process of consciousness for themselves. Others might support the process and share their own experience of a growing 'political' consciousness but they cannot do it for us. We have to take the vital steps for ourselves, for it is a matter of reconsidering aspects of our personal and social lives. What shifts is our sense of ourselves but also our sense of our relationships with others. For Gramsci, this is a rich and continuing process, not something that is achieved once and for all.

It means that we grasp more of the social and historical sources of our individuality so that as we *empower* ourselves as individuals we become clearer in what we share with others, not only in the present but also in the past. It is here that there is considerable resonance with consciousness-raising as it has developed within the Women's Movement. As women learned to identify themselves with other women, they questioned ways that they had more or less automatically learned to discount their relationships with women when men were around. They learned that they could re-evaluate their relationships with women and so also with themselves.

The process of consciousness-raising was used by the Black Movement in the United States in the 1960s and it also developed independently in the Black Consciousness Movement in South Africa.[13] It was generally a space in which people could acknowledge the pain and suffering they had endured through learning to see themselves – and so devalue their experience and culture – through the eyes of the dominant society. To assert in the context of the civil rights movement that 'black is beautiful' was to challenge both the external structures of oppression but also the ways in which they had been internalised by black people themselves.

As black people began to see themselves through their own eyes, they had to accept how they had partly colluded in a process of self-rejection as they had learned to despise their own history, values and culture. This was not an experience that they were rooted in since it was associated with the shame of slavery. With consciousness-raising it was recognised that people could not simply turn their backs on this experience as 'past', since it continued to influence people in the present. The scars and inner injuries were still there even if people had learned to turn their backs to it.

Within a culture of modernity we very much learn to put history behind us so that we can live by the light of reason alone in the present. In this way we learn to *disconnect* from the past that was dismembered. It is as if we learn in the terms of a dominant masculinity that to dwell on the past is somehow a sign of weakness. We learn to harden ourselves against it as something we have 'overgrown' on the path towards freedom and independence. This is essentially Kant's conception. To be influenced by the past is supposedly to allow our behaviour to be externally determined. History is a source of our unfreedom, for it remains a sign of our determination.

This is true both in relation to class and race, since we learn within a liberal culture that to be 'free' and 'self-determining' means being able to think for ourselves without somehow allowing our 'backgrounds' to influence us unduly. We learn to separate and *cut off*, proud that we have 'improved ourselves', if at some level feeling guilty about what we have left behind. It is often a painful area of silence in our continuing relationships with our families.

Gramsci was aware that consciousness-raising, if we can use this term, was not an easy process. It involved facing a past that in many cases carried an inheritance of shame. Blacks recognised that slavery has to be faced for it cannot be turned away from without somehow continuing to undermine and block energies. It is a painful history but it has somehow to be accepted. The fact that it 'happened in the past' fails to appreciate how the past continues to live on in the present. We can only separate from the past, however painful, by cutting aspects of ourselves away. It makes our experience flatter and more superficial than it needs to be. To face the past with others who have shared its inheritance can be a powerful process that is at once emotional and rational. It is part of a process of coming to terms with yourself, for this is part of coming to terms with a shared history and experience.

Gramsci seems to have recognised the value of such processes. In this regard at least, he helps to challenge aspects of Marx's rationalism that might have been less tolerant. He also challenges a certain activism in Marx's writing that sees labour and creativity in active terms alone. It reproduces, as we have said, an older Aristotelian notion that identifies the 'active' with the 'masculine'. As men, we are often less accepting of our experience, especially in the past, learning to put it aside so that we can strive supposedly unhindered by attachments or involvements in the present. As part of a Protestant ethic which, in *Recreating Sexual Politics* (Seidler 1991a), I have argued informed how work was conceived within a Marxist tradition, there is a strong disdain for the 'psychological', which supposedly has no place within a political life. We learn, especially as men, not to waste time but to be constantly proving ourselves through our activities. Marxism has inherited this strain and for a long time the Left was suspicious of consciousness-raising that it never understood.

Rationalism on the Left has proved a powerful force and Marxism has largely been interpreted within rationalist terms. Even if Gramsci was very much living within this tradition, his experience of prison, as much as one can tell from his *Letters from Prison* (Gramsci 1975), makes him appreciate the details of individual lives. He recognised, for instance, the power and meaning of religion and was not prepared to dismiss it as 'mere backwardness'. I think he would also have been sympathetic, in his growing disillusionment with Leninism, with movements that were prepared to give people their own voice.

Consciousness-raising, particularly as it has been developed in the black, women's, gay and lesbian movements has recognised that individuals can grow in their authority if they have the courage to face themselves and their experience in this way. It can be part of a process of liberation in which people learn to accept and integrate aspects of themselves which they had learned to conceal in shame. Coming out in its different forms is a matter of sustaining dignity and self-respect as one learns to be proud of who one is and the relationships created with others.[14] It is crucial that individuality is transformed in creative ways rather than reduced or replaced by categories of class, race or gender. Some of the complexities of experience are accepted as people take pride in their history, experience and culture which was until recently despised and rejected.

REASON AND RULES

The subject of sexual politics has been important for social theory in the ways that it has linked issues of sexuality to questions of power. It has also sought to work with the contradictions of people's experience, allowing what is meaningful or significant somehow to emerge from this. In doing this it has refused the classifications supposedly created by reason alone that have been invoked to define and legislate notions of 'normality'. Durkheim's *Rules of Sociological Method* (1950) was an important statement, especially in its rejection of 'psychologism', of the ways that social life could both be understood and controlled. It effectively treated people *as if* they were objects since this is the way that their behaviour could be grasped as governed by laws. It was partly the conceptions of 'normality' and 'pathology' that this vision helped to sustain that made it so easy to begin to treat people as objects.[15]

It was the objective character of a scientific discourse when presented within positivistic terms which gave the categories invoked by science a particular power and authority in relation to people's lived experience. It is the categories which are 'real' and 'objective' since they are the expression of an impartial notion of reason. These categories come to exist in a space of their own while people's experience inevitably comes to seem thin and insubstantial since it is said to be 'merely personal' or 'subjective'.

Durkheim prepared important ground for this vision since his belief that society is *sui generis* is part of a sense of its higher moral authority. The fact that social rules have a legitimacy which is impersonal gives them a power to constrain individual lives. As with Kant, he tends to think of moral rules on an analogy with legal rules, so it is that Kant's vision of the moral law allows for the impersonality and universality of moral rules derived by reason alone. It is as if the moral law exists in a realm of its own which individuals can have access to through their faculty of reason.

One of the strengths of the Kantian view is that it does not leave individuals to work things out for themselves in each new situation. So it is that they can supposedly rely on social rules and institutional practices in a way that can make life simpler and more predictable.[16] So it is that individuals can learn to rely on rules that they have substantiated for themselves, rather than having to work things out from scratch each time. Since it is important for Kant that, in some sense at least, people legislate these rules for themselves, they can supposedly sustain their freedom and independence.

But then it is difficult to square such an account with a recognition of the potentially oppressive character of institutional arrangements, presented as universal and rational, but embodying patriarchal values and relationships. There is often a gap here that is difficult to close. For instance, the few women who might make it as doctors or teachers are told that their experience, in liberal terms, shows what is possible for any woman who is prepared to take the opportunities that are available. When you point out how few women reach the higher reaches of these professions you are often accused of being 'difficult', or of expecting changes to happen 'too quickly'.

Yet it remains important to situate the place of rules in relation to social behaviour. What we have said might question some of Kant's and Durkheim's formulations but the issues remain. Again, Wittgenstein might help, for within social theory we readily accept Durkheim's formulation that social rules are externally constraining and often backed by sanctions. For instance, at school we are told of the rules, which supposedly function in the interests of all, and we are punished if we infringe them. Of course there are good rules and bad rules and some seem to be made to give the teachers a quiet life, we might think, without any reference to the pupils at all. But supposedly these rules still have a rationality of their own which frees us from having to make decisions anew in each situation. But more than this, they can also help to provide a framework – a set of boundaries – so that pupils can feel confident that they know where they stand and that they will not be punished if they are careful to keep to the rules.

Something similar can happen in families. It can be preferable for a family to have some clearly defined rules, say about turning up at meal times and taking turns to help clear up, since otherwise children are left having to sense and respond to the particular moods of their parents or the available adults. It is as if children have to be continually tuned in because they cannot be sure in any situation how an adult might respond or be feeling that day. It can leave children anxious and constantly alert to signals that might come from adults.

Though parents or adults might be reacting to their own family histories in which there were too many rules that seemed pointless and children were never consulted about anything, it can be quite wrong to conclude that all rules are therefore authoritarian and deny freedom to others. It can be preferable for children to have clear boundaries established for them so that they can feel more secure about the environment they live in. They can know 'where they are' without having to feel anxious at any moment that things might change.

It can be important for parents to recognise a difference between having to exercise our authority as parents and being authoritarian with our children. To provide children with rules is not to treat them as objects. Somehow our conceptions of equality and sense of treating others as equals, whatever their age, has to be tempered by a sense of what children at different ages can be expected to cope with. We can often give children choices that they are not ready to cope with. A two-year-old is not given 'freedom' by being asked what he or she wants to eat for lunch where the choice is left supposedly open rather than, say, being offered a choice between two things. At the same time it is important to realise that rules might have to be different for children of different ages and that children will often have something useful to say about their formulation.

This tempers the notion that rules can be worked out by reason alone, since they can very much depend on the character of the children involved and their particular needs. But this makes it important to think clearly about the supposed 'impersonal' and 'impartial' character of rules. For instance, it might be important to treat children of different ages differently, somehow helping to underline that an older child is owed greater responsibility and freedom. It is not simply that to treat them alike might be to do them an injustice, but that somehow we have also to recognise the individuality of those children. This involves a different conception of rules that now have to be more related to the individuals concerned.

Wittgenstein has an extended discussion of what it means to follow a rule. His vision is less externalised than that which informs Kant and Durkheim, since he is critical of a notion of reason as somehow existing independently from the practices and relationships themselves.[17] He is critical of the vision of reason as an independent faculty that informs a Kantian vision of modernity. Reason cannot be invoked as if it can be used to legislate and provide rules that exist independently of experience.

At the same time Wittgenstein, in writing about children, talked of the absolute necessity of a parent who says *no* to a child, meaning it. It was important to be consistent and to mean what you say, rather than to give in to tantrums because it seems easier to give in, for example, and allow them sweets before lunch rather than to hold out. If there is a rule that you cannot have ice-creams before lunch it has to be held to. This does not mean that it is not also important for adults to admit when they have made mistakes. But it is important to be consistent.

It is not as if rules have to exist external to our behaviour, helping us to stay on track initially out of a fear of some sanction, though later becoming almost second nature. Wittgenstein seems to be working for a more constitutive sense of rules. So in learning to count we are learning how to follow a rule but reason does not dictate that there is only a single path that can be taken. It does not exist independently of the practice itself in a sphere of its own. This is clear when you watch the process through which children learn to read. There is help and practice but there is no set of rules that you can follow which will teach a child how to read. There might be different stages that you can discern but it is often difficult to predict when a child will be able to read.

Similarly, Wittgenstein is struck by the experience of learning to ride a bicycle, for this is learning that is not simply a matter of following certain mental rules, even if it might help to keep some tips in mind. This helps to challenge an intellectualist vision of learning and a sense of reason as a mental faculty alone. Often we cannot separate out different aspects of an activity and it is quite wrong and misleading to think that we should be able to make the attempt.

JUSTICE AND WORK

At some level both Durkheim and Wittgenstein seek to reinstate communal life and challenge a liberal vision that might see individuals working their lives out through reason alone. Despite crucial differences, there is a sense that it is in the context of a shared community of meanings, partly embodied in language, that we come to a sense of ourselves. But I think that Wittgenstein, like Simone Weil, would have contested a moral relativism that works to weaken our moral sense. Both had a sense of the ways you can be at odds with your times.

As far as Durkheim is concerned,

> Of all the moral rules those which concern the individual ideal most clearly demonstrate their social origin. The man that we try to be is the man of our times and of our milieu. No doubt each of us in his different way colours this communal ideal with his own individuality, in the same way that each of us practices charity, justice, patriotism etc. in his own way.
>
> (Durkheim 1974:68)

It might be true, as Durkheim says, that 'so far from the ideal being an individual construction, it is that in which the different members of the group communicate', but there might also be contrasting moral ideas available both in the present but also from the past and these might express quite antagonistic conceptions of social reality.

Durkheim both wants to say that just as 'the Roman had his ideal of perfection which was related to the constitution of the Roman city, just as ours is related to the structure of contemporary society', while also acknowledging that 'today traditional morality is shaken and no other has been brought forward to replace it. The old duties have lost their power without our being able to see clearly and with assurance where our new duties lie'(Durkheim 1974:68). But these are partly problems of transition and with time we will see the shape of things more clearly, though Durkheim is also ready to admit that 'we do not feel the pressure of moral rules as they were felt in the past' (p.64) for 'they cannot appear to us in their old majesty'. Durkheim seems to accept this with some regret, recognising that 'morality appears to us less as a list of duties, a defined discipline, than as an attracting idea, half glimpsed at' (p.69).

Part of the problem might be that if we see justice as an individual ideal that individuals live out in their own way, it takes our attention away from conceiving of justice in terms of the structure of wealth and power in society. Do we simply think of social justice as an ideal that is quite differently interpreted in different periods and societies or does it have a critical part to play in the legitimation and evolution of social institutions and practices? This is an important issue for social theory since they can often be conceived of as legitimating unequal social arrangements. It is a powerful insight of Marx that the dominant ideas in any society are the ideas of the ruling class, thus helping it to sustain and legitimate its position of wealth and power. In this sense Marx's discussion of ideology remains crucial for understanding the relationships of knowledge to power in different societies.

But it can be misleading to think of justice in exclusively distributive terms. Both liberal and Marxist theory have tended to treat justice as an issue of the public realm alone, as if this is the realm in which people can both find fulfilment but also suffer. But Marx did not treat expectations as if they were exclusively a matter of the distribution of surplus value, of workers getting less than they were owed for the work that they did. Exploitation was crucially related to the ways people were treated as wage labour by capital and the ways that they also learned to treat themselves within a capitalist mode of production. By learning to treat their labour as a commodity, people were learning to treat themselves as a means.

This was not a situation that was freely chosen for, as Marx shows in his analysis of the wage contract, this is not the free contract between equals that it is presented to be within liberal theory. People are forced to work to survive, and in many economies they can feel fortunate to find employment at all. It is still true that, deprived of control of the means of production, working people are left in a position of relative powerlessness and subordination. If this changes temporarily when labour is in short supply, it works to moderate the relationships of power and subordination.[18]

Marx was also centrally concerned throughout his life with the ways that people were treated within the labour process. Here, it was not an issue simply of private property so that the socialisation of private property in Russia after 1917 and later in eastern Europe did not mean the end of exploitation. This is something that Emma Goldmann and Alexander Berkman realised in their early disillusionment with the Russian Revolution.[19] It was also something that spurred Simone Weil into her own detailed investigation of the labour process in Paris in the early 1930s.[20] She realised that the defining feature was not ownership, since workers could be similarly treated within both state socialist and capitalist forms. She investigated the subordination to the rhythms of the machine that flowed from assembly-line production and, with Gramsci, was sensitive to the objectification of labour that was the explicit intention of Taylorism and scientific measurement. Gramsci also connects this explicitly to the reorganisation of the dominant forms of masculinity.[21]

It could be said that the ways that a Cartesian rationalism teaches us to estrange ourselves from our bodies, so treating them as existing independently of our identities as natural selves, prepared the philosophical ground for Taylorism and scientific management. Does this mean that as men we learn to treat our bodies as objects? If this is part of a process of estrangement, it concerns not only how we think about our bodies but also the ways we connect to them. This is not something that can be changed easily as a matter of conscious intention but it involves building more of a relationship with different aspects of our experience. As Reich grasped, being estranged from our bodies is part of a larger displacement of our emotional selves that we have also learned to treat as part of a separated nature.[22] It is partly because, as men, we are so used to treating our bodies externally, as if they are machines that need to be trained rather than a form through which we can learn to express ourselves.

In *Recreating Sexual Politics* I have explored some of the links between a Protestant ethic and dominant forms of masculinity (Seidler 1991a). I tried to explore some cultural and personal sources for the idea that men have got to be constantly proving themselves. It is because at some level we continue a Protestant inheritance that says our natures are evil, that we can be plagued by feelings of inadequacy, however much others might think we have achieved in our lives. It is this sense of proving ourselves that can so easily be used at work, as men take pride in constantly setting themselves against their own limits. This is to use one's body as part of the machine and so to fail to respect its limits. We learn to silence our bodies for we do not recognise them as sacred, as they are recognised in some religious traditions.[23] With modernity the body was treated as profane in western culture. It was available for use and as part of matter, for it had no voice or memory of its own.

We see nothing wrong any more in treating our bodies as objects, so it can be hard to feel that there is anything wrong when others want to so use them, so long as we have made a free choice about it. This prepared the ground for Taylor to conceive of the body in mechanical terms and to attempt to maximise its use in the service of capital. The only limits that are 'objective' are the physical limits of the body itself. This renders invisible the injuries that are done to people when they are shifted without notice from one position to another or from one job to another.

This is what Simone Weil tries to illuminate in her explorations of the experience of work. It is as if the fact that 'your time is not your own' renders you powerless to complain at the ways you are treated at work. For example, Weil recognises how people are forced to swallow abuse and torments they receive at the hands of a foreman, knowing that if they were to express the anger they feel, they would simply lose their jobs. The idea that you should be 'man enough to take it' produces a particular kind of resilience. Often this is at the cost of women and children who have to take the brunt of all this unexpressed frustration and resentment when men get home.

Weil is crucial in helping us extend our language with which we can illuminate the experience of work. The notion of alienation has proved helpful but it is also limited in the context of the rationalisation of work and the introduction of new technologies. This is where a phenomenology of work that is not merely descriptive but is in touch with the tensions that are built into men and women's everyday experience of work could be significant. It is as if the sociology of work has too often colluded in people's silence about work, wanting to leave it behind so that they can sustain themselves in their equality as consumers. It is not uncommon, for instance, for miners returning from the pit to refuse to talk to their daughters about the experience. It is not that they do not feel proud of what they do but they also know the hardships and humiliations that they would prefer to leave behind them until they are forced to return to the next shift. They might only say that they would wish 'something better' for their children.

Kevin Devaney's article, 'Mining – a world apart' in *The Achilles' Heel Reader* (Seidler 1991c:151–60) brings out some of the complexities and richness of a mining life. It helps us also to recognise the feelings of solidarity and companionship that are developed, and to appreciate the dangers of generalising from a particular class experience and the need to investigate different masculinities. It is within these mining communities, as the miners' strike in England in 1984 demonstrated, that different forms of support and association were developed. Women were able to take on much more active positions which were challenging to many men but it was clear that the strike was a struggle to sustain communities as much as jobs. These communities had long helped sustain more communal values, even if they have traditionally taken on a patriarchal form. The strike helped people recognise that different and competing values were being struggled over.

This is an important reminder since the Protestant ethic has tended to teach that salvation, like success, is an individual quest. Kant makes us suspicious of the help and support that we might receive from others since this might distract from the moral worth of our individual actions. If this ethic is particularly intense in the middle class, it does not exist there alone. We are often suspicious of our neighbours, which is why we have to be reminded so often to love them. It becomes easy within a capitalist market culture to see others as competitors somehow standing in the way of our individual success. We learn to use others for our own ends, thinking that it would be 'naïve' to do otherwise, or to make it clear that this is what we are doing.

As men, we can grow up being particularly wary of others. It is partly because, as I explore in *Recreating Sexual Politics*, within the middle class we tend to sustain a sense of masculine identity through comparing ourselves with others (Seidler 1991a). Somehow it seems difficult to develop much of an inner connection to self, when we learn to think we are doing well because we are doing *better* than others. We seem trapped in an endless cycle of comparisons. Even with our closest friends, it becomes difficult genuinely to wish others well, for their success seems to reflect badly on ourselves. We learn from an early age as boys not to make ourselves vulnerable to others, for this gives them opportunities to take advantage. With time, we cease to be connected to our own emotional vulnerability, since in public at least we are so used to putting a 'good face on things'. We do not let others know what we are feeling and we learn not to want to know ourselves, since emotions are treated as a sign of weakness and so are threatening to male identity. It would seem as if sharing our vulnerability will only make matters worse.

This aspect of male experience is significant because it can help us grasp why it is that our traditions of social theory tend to have such a thin grasp of relationships. It seems connected to the difficulties they have in working more qualitatively to illuminate the complexities of lived experience. This should hardly surprise us if these traditions in large part articulate the experience of men, and that they should share some of the difficulties that men have with these areas of our lives. As men we can find it hard to acknowledge, let alone name, these difficulties, so that it is hardly surprising if this is reflected in our traditions of social theory and philosophy. In the early 1970s it was still difficult to do serious work on the emotions. If this work was done at all it was usually done by women and treated as a 'soft option', for it had to be 'subjective' since it was less amenable to the 'rigours' of reason.[24]

As men, we learn not to dwell upon our experience and relationships. We treat this as a form of self-indulgence that is best avoided. It is only if things are 'going wrong' that we think our relationships need to be given any attention. If we have chosen well then we think that the relationship can be taken very much for granted, more or less as a background, since we have learned that what matters in terms of our identities are our achievements in the public realm alone. It is important to recognise this not as a personal matter of individual preference, as an interpretive tradition might have it, but as structured within a particular moral culture. Gramsci is helpful with this since he recognises that an issue with relegating experience to an ill-defined 'subjective' realm, and so as of little concern to science and politics that both want to see themselves as 'objective' and 'rational', is that we never recognise how certain tensions and contradictions are not of a personal nature but reflect much more pervasive structural features.

This can help us to recognise some of the difficulties that middle-class men in particular often have in changing. Even if we learn to give priority to partners and children it is easy for this to be lip-service because at another level, largely because of the ways male identities are constructed and sustained within the public realm, we can be plagued by a sense of inadequacy or failure. There seems to be a restless feeling, partly fed by the Protestant ethic, that we should or could do more. Whatever we do it never seems to be *enough*, so that it is hardly surprising if a sense of fulfilment constantly evades us. It is as if the day we end one project, rather than stop to enjoy the satisfaction, we find ourselves beginning to plan the next.

This makes it easy to interpret the demands that our partners make as complaints, failing to understand the pressures we are already under. We grow up to expect support to be non-conditional, so it is easy to feel betrayed when our partners seem to be adding to the demands that are being carried. And it is usually because we are already doing too much as a way of proving ourselves at work as well as meeting the objective demands of difficult economic times, so that it can be hard to hear what is being said by our partners. If our partners protest that we are taking them and the relationship for granted, it can take time to absorb. It is as if we are not prepared to believe in the seriousness of the situation, before it is almost too late to do anything about it.

Chapter 12

Relationships

EMOTIONS AND ISOLATION

If as men we learn to objectify ourselves, it can be difficult not to objectify others, even those we feel closest to. If as a white middle-class man I have learned that self-control means suppressing my feelings and emotions then it can be difficult to respond in an open and emotionally responsive way. If I have never learned how to respect my own emotions and feelings, experiencing them as signs of weakness, then it is going to be *difficult* to respect the emotions and feelings of others. It might be particularly difficult to respond to our partner's tears or expressions of feelings of inadequacy, assuming that as men we are somehow called upon to find solutions that might take these feelings away. Since this is the way that we learn to treat our own emoions, it is easy to assume this is what is expected of us by others.

We might feel puzzled when our partners say in heterosexual relationships that this is not what they want at all and that they feel unrecognised and unseen in the situation. It can be hard to acknowledge as men that they might be right, especially if we are feeling that we are 'doing our best'. But this is not the issue. It is, as we have mentioned earlier, that our partners may just want to feel that they are being listened to and that their experience is being validated. It might be that as men we either take such a legitimation for granted or else we are so used to living without it, that we do not recognise what is being asked of us. We might simply feel rejected since our own initiatives seem to be refused as out of order. It might be that we are so unused to *listening* to ourselves that it can be difficult for us to listen to others, even if at some level we want to.

Since male identities are to a large extent constituted and sustained within the public realm it can be hard to appreciate our emotional relationships with our partners or friends. It is so deeply embedded within a dominant masculine culture that somehow we have 'to make it on our own', that it can be hard to share ourselves with our partners. It might be easy for us to tell endless stories about work, but harder to *share* how inadequate this can make us feel. It is as if we learn to keep our negative feelings to ourselves, since we think that we are burdening others. Because we often experience the emotions of others as a burden, not knowing what to do with them, hoping unconsciously that they will go away if we provide a shoulder, we easily assume that others feel similarly about emotions and feelings. It is difficult to recognise that our partners might feel enormously relieved if we share more of ourselves emotionally especially if they had felt so little access to us recently.

Psychotherapy in its different forms can help people to greater access both to their own experience and to others. It can make people more aware of how they have learned to deny aspects of themselves and so weaken their sense of reality.[1] Men can learn how they might have studiously avoided any difficult feelings, always choosing to say that things were fine when they were not. Such tendencies can be fostered in particular cultures, but equally it can be underpinned by a fear of rejection. It is easy to feel that if we share our negative feelings then we will surely be rejected and left on our own. As boys we often learn to choose isolation out of a fear that we will be rejected if we reach out to others. We often learn to prefer to be on our own than to take the risk of making ourselves vulnerable to others.

It is easy for men to experience themselves as somehow locked within themselves, wanting to reach out to others but feeling unable. It is as if through the process of growing up we have learned to leave our emotional selves behind. Within modernity we have learned to identify ourselves as rational agents in a way that makes access to our emotions seem threatening, for it can challenge the image that we learn to sustain of ourselves, of being 'free' and 'independent'. Within the dominant male culture we learn to treat women as sexual objects and to put them down and diminish their experience as a way of asserting ourselves.

It is partly because of the suppression of our emotions and feelings that we are left with a thin relationship to our inner selves. We can feel strong and effective in the world of work where we know the rules and where we are constantly relating to others, but in our emotional lives we can find it much harder to express ourselves personally. We can be so used to the impersonal mode as a way of protecting our vulnerability in the public world that we do not know how to put this aside, even when we want to.[2] But these difficulties are often hidden because we learn to rely on women to do the emotional work for us.

We can be so used to constructing our experience according to how we think that things ought to be, that it can be difficult to acknowledge any emotions and feelings that go against these images. This reflects a cognitive constructivism that has become widespread within otherwise quite opposed traditions of social theory. It says that our experience is 'socially constructed', assuming that this is a strong position to take against the traditional idea that, for instance, gender roles are 'natural' and so cannot be changed, without at the same time recognising that this rationalism reflects another prevailing aspect of a dominant masculinity.

It means that we can shape our experience according to our will and determination, and that we are also free in liberal terms to relate to others as we choose. If our partners say that they feel we are taking them for granted, we assume that we can simply deny this because it was not our intention, since for rationalism it is often a matter of 'who is right' and 'who is wrong'. As long as we know that 'I am right' then this would seem to be the end of the matter. The fact that they continue to feel that way has to do with their 'personal feelings' or 'subjective experience', but it supposedly has no existence 'in reality'.

This can feel coercive to our partners who might well feel that they are not being listened to. They might feel that there is little real contact. As men we might hear this defensively, feeling accused that we must have done something wrong. It can be difficult for us to recognise that we are tacitly legislating what our partners can feel – for we are saying that 'they cannot feel taken for granted because we are not taking them for granted' or 'they cannot feel as if they are being treated as a sexual object for this is no part of our intention'. If they persist in feeling this way after they have been assured that their emotions or feelings have no basis in reality then they are being 'irrational'. As men we feel that there is little else to be done until our partners are prepared to 'see sense'. We might choose to put the issue aside, hoping that it will go away.

In *Recreating Sexual Politics* I have discussed some of the cultural conditions for men who often feel that they have to be independent and self-sufficient (Seidler 1991a). This is the way that, within a Protestant culture, we learn to affirm our male identity. Because of this it is easy to learn to live *as if* we do not have any needs, for we can easily experience needs as a sign of weakness. We learn to accept that others have needs, but that we ourselves are quite content as we are. This produces its own forms of cultural insensitivity for it blinds us to our own needs and so it maks us less sensitive to the needs of others. It can turn the screw of our rationalism that bit tighter as it becomes hard not to hear the expression of need as a sign of weakness. We can think back to Rex Harrison in *My Fair Lady*: 'why cannot women be more sensible...be like men'. Something still echoes from this, though few would want to acknowledge it publicly. If we are aware of a distance and a lack of understanding between men and women, we have learned to be more polite about it.[3]

As rational selves, we have purposes and goals that we want to achieve but it is much harder to acknowledge that we have bodies and souls that need to be nourished and fed. If we can think about these needs at all, they are relegated to the private realm of relationships. But as men, it can also be difficult to acknowledge our needs in our emotional and sexual relationships, for we can be so used to 'doing without' and drawing our sense of strength and pride from being able to do so. Since we learn to relate to ourselves as men and implicitly take this as some kind of model, it can be difficult to acknowledge that not only our partners individually, but also our relationships, have needs that have to be acknowledged and met.

It can be hard to learn to give time and space to our relationships, not just to meeting the individual needs of our partners. We can think that if a relationship is good it should not need much time and energy, but this is a mistake. It is partly because as men we learn to take *ourselves* for granted that it can be difficult to acknowledge that we often take our partners and relationships for granted. We can act defensively when our partners say they are just not getting enough from us, as if at some level we really do *not* want to hear what they have to say for it touches ways we have also neglected and forsaken ourselves.

THE PERSONAL AND THE SOCIAL

The way that we are accustomed to draw distinctions between personal and social relationships helps to render some of these issues invisible. We can feel that since they are 'personal' they can have no place within an academic discourse that is supposedly rational because it is 'impersonal' and potentially universal. We are used to thinking that personal relationships have to do with the relationships between individuals and these are the proper concern of psychology, while social relationships have to do with structured relationships of power and subordination and are the concern of sociology.

Durkheim helps to establish the *sui generic* character of these relationships and warns us against a 'psychologism' that would seek to reduce them to outcomes of individual relationships. It might also be thought that this distinction has proved itself more generally in helping us separate, for instance, the personal relationship between the owner of a firm and individual employees which might be friendly, even affectual, and the structured relationship of power within which they meet.

Some of these insights are important to sustain but we also have to be careful how we draw some of these distinctions if we are to learn that, with feminism, the personal cannot be separated from the political. This partly means that, just as knowledge cannot be separated from relations of power, nor can emotions and feelings. Foucault helps us to acknowledge one aspect of this but not the other. In classical sociology as well as in Marxism the language of social relationships has often been presented in rationalistic terms, as if emotions were no part of them. These have been pushed aside, where they have been acknowledged at all, as 'personal' and 'subjective'. Not only has it served to limit our understanding of social relationships, which have been set too crudely in opposition to the 'individual', 'personal' or 'psychological', but it has also served to protect and legitimate particular knowledges in their autonomy and independence.

If we think for a moment about a relationship between doctor and patient, we might be able to separate out the personal relationship between the two individuals and the clinical relationship involved. But it might also be that the clinical relationship works to *objectify* a woman in the way it relates to her body as an 'object' of medical knowledge. She might have feelings about this that she finds it hard to express, blaming herself for how hopeless she often seems to feel when she leaves the doctor's surgery. She feels that she cannot ask questions without seeming to threaten or bring into question his competence as a doctor – supposing him to be a man. He is prepared to talk in an open and friendly way but she feels increasingly frustrated that he will not really answer her questions, saying that she should not worry but trust his competence and training. He does not seem to listen to what she has to say about her symptoms, somehow treating what she says as 'subjective' or 'personal', and so as unreliable when it comes to the 'objectivity' of clinical judgement. Somehow she cannot help feeling small and inadequate in his presence.

With feminism she can gradually come to see the issues in different terms. She does not think it is a matter of his competence but of the way that medical knowledge more generally treats her body as its own.[4] It is as if her own experience and relationship to her own body does not count, for the symptoms that he is looking for are supposedly universal. They do not carry a particular significance or meaning in her case, so that emotional and personal issues would seem to cloud the clarity of his clinical judgement that supposedly draws upon the impersonal workings of reason alone.[5] She is doing her best to build more of a relationship with her body and to take more responsibility for her health, but she now feels that the otherwise good personal relationship she has with her doctor is getting in the way of her making changes in these areas of her life.[6]

She is beginning to challenge the autonomy of medical knowledge and clinical judgement, though she feels hesitant about doing this. She feels that what she is learning about her own symptoms cannot simply be treated as 'emotional' or 'subjective' but should make a difference to the clinical judgement that is eventually reached. She is beginning to recognise that the authority of her doctor partly rests upon the constitution of medical knowledge that he has inherited from medical school.[7]

She is also more aware that not all doctors agree. Some are more ready to make space for emotional issues but they still tend to treat them as 'subjective' consequences of 'objective' situations, so that if a woman is told that she has to have an operation they are ready to acknowledge that she needs to work through some of the emotional distress that this will cause. Doctors might even learn to expect these 'emotional reactions' and to be worried if they do not detect them. But this is still very different from acknowledging that emotional issues might be involved in bringing on the illness or in clinical judgements that need to be made in relation to it.

Priscilla Alderson has usefully shown how mothers' and fathers' knowledge of their children can prove important in helping doctors reach their clinical judgements when considering the advisability of doing open heart operations with young children.[8] She helps to re-evaluate parental knowledge that is so often devalued as being 'emotional' and 'personal'. This knowledge could also bring into question the autonomy of medical knowledge and the rationalised premises upon which this is based. If doctors were more aware, they might readily admit that what parents have said about how they are feeling has affected the clinical judgement they have made. This is not difficult to acknowledge in individual cases, though it might be harder to admit that such knowledge and the relationship out of which it grows is not only helpful but might well be indispensable to the clinical judgements involved. This brings parents into a different kind of partnership with doctors and it helps to redefine the terms in which medical knowledge is conceived.

Some of this is more easily acknowledged by holistic practitioners who are used to working with the idea that they 'treat the person not the symptoms'. In their practice they helped to question an Enlightenment modernity and the rationalist universality that has informed it.[9] It challenges the notion that symptoms assume a significance that is universal, recognising that if this is true of viruses, it can be misleading when applied as a general conception. The more that we can acknowledge that how a person feels about themselves can make a difference to whether they bring their own healing qualities to bear, the more crucial is a person's relationship with themselves. It means that illness cannot always adequately be thought about as an *event* that happens to a body, somehow regardless of our emotional relationship to ourselves.

So it is that we learn to challenge the dominant conception that illness is something that happens to our bodies in a way that is disconnected from the way that we live our lives. We learn to look to doctors to get rid of these symptoms. It is this notion of *eradication* that is sustained by Protestant notions of modernity. Like feelings that are unwelcome, we seek either to ignore or suppress them, since they threaten to bring into question the vision of ourselves that we strive to sustain. It is as though we learn that we can limit our misery or unhappiness by living as if these feelings do not exist for us. It is hardly surprising, then, if our lives assume an aura of unreality.

As children we learn to be quiet when the doctor is around and only to speak when we are spoken to. We learn that to question is tantamount to distrusting the doctor's authority. It is the doctor who has knowledge while we only have experience which is 'subjective'. It is as if, standing before the doctor, we are children, since we only have feelings and emotions while the doctor has reason. It is as if we have to put faith in his or her knowledge as we learn to put ourselves in the doctor's hands. We learn *not* to know, as if ignorance might show confidence and so help the process. Often we want the doctor to do his or her work and to take the symptoms away. Again it is a matter of *eradication* rather than conceiving of illness as a process and the symptoms as things that we can learn from. It is because our bodies exist somehow independently of our rational selves, that possibly we have not recognised this as a process of objectification. It is as if we cease to exist for ourselves in the doctor's presence but just as an embodiment of universal symptoms.

This accords with the visions of citizenship that were crafted within modernity. As Sartre brings out in *Anti-Semite and Jew*, within the liberal state it is as rational selves somehow abstracted from the conditions of our substantial existence that we exist as citizens.[10] We are supposedly the bearers of universal qualities of reason that sustains our existence as citizens. So within the workings of medical knowledge we are similarly uprooted, as Simone Weil has it, from the conditions of our lives. It is our symptoms that speak for themselves for they supposedly speak a universal language.

The fact that these symptoms have grown out of our lives and experience is taken to be a contingent matter within alipathic medicine. The symptoms do not need a grounding or context in our lives. For, as Foucault has it in *The Birth of the Clinic*, they exist on the surface of things (Foucault 1976). They yield themselves to a knowledge that is not ours but which rests with the doctors alone. In this sense we still live with the disempowerment that grew with the professional knowledges of modernity. The professions, which were predominantly male, knew best.[11]

Medicine as we have inherited it does not depend upon any inner connection that we might have to ourselves. Supposedly, it does not depend on our being able to tap our own inner healing resources for we are passive in its presence. It is the medicines which do the work. It is the doctors who are active but we as patients are supposedly passive. So it is that we learn to be grateful to them in our powerlessness. Supposedly, we have no inner knowledge which can be tapped to help the process along. It is this sense of interiority that has weakened with modernity.[12]

We lost connection with a Socratic tradition that wanted us to recognise *how much* we already know, even though we fail to acknowledge it. With modernity we exist as blank slates with a sense of how little we already know and therefore how much we must depend on the knowledge of others. It is the production of professional knowledges that have carefully built barriers to others that has characterised modernity. It is an aspect that undermined its otherwise democratic ethos. As regards knowledge, as Paulo Freire describes it, we are reduced to passivity. We are estranged from the sources of our own knowing.[13]

Within medicine this reinforces the authority of doctors who appropriate medical knowledge as their own. Doctors conceive themselves within a masculine language of battle and conflict as if they are standing alone to defeat the hold that illness has gained over our bodies. It is a matter of winning control. You only have to watch consultants do a round of a ward to witness how knowledge, authority and power are all centralised within a single person. Often it is difficult for 'patients' to get a word in, as if they are interfering in a process that really has nothing to do with them. Styles might have changed and efforts might be taken to 'keep the patient informed', but it has often been a slow and grudging process and exists at odds with the underlying masculinism of medical knowledge.

Until quite recently, especially in cancer wards, patients were not told of their condition. It was as if they were suddenly bereft of personhood as consultations took place with relatives who were suddenly given authority. It was thought that for patients to know could be unhelpful, for it might only depress them and so weaken their powers to resist. Aside from the issue of whether they have a *prima facie* right to know, there is little sense of how their knowing could be part of a process which brings their own healing powers to bear.[14]

To recognise the place of visualisations and consciousness within the healing process threatens to upset the objectification of the 'patients'. It brings them back as active subjects in a way that challenges the guiding Cartesian dualism that allows the body to be treated as an independent and separate site of illness. It promises to redefine the terms of a sociology of health and illness. The body can no longer be conceived in brute physical terms since it is interconnected with emotional and spiritual aspects.

This brings issues of attitude and consciousness into the centre of the healing process. It helps redefine the terms of modernity that have too often rendered people as passive through a process of 'objectification'. It becomes important to enlist the understanding and willingness of people as active subjects and participants in their own processes of recovery. We are not simply bodies to be worked on but active subjects whose health is part of our responsibility. It cannot be alienated and just handed over to others.

Is there a relationship to be explored between dominant forms of masculinity and processes of objectification? Simmel seems to suggest that there is.[15] As men, we conceive ourselves as rational selves in a way that makes us distinctly uncomfortable with the emotional aspects of life. This seems to be connected to the difficulties we have in treating others as people, rather than as objects. It is because we discount the importance of relationships that, for instance, it can be difficult to grant the importance of women being able to see the same doctor when they visit an antenatal clinic. This might be acknowledged as preferable emotionally, but it cannot have anything to do with the clinical situation. Supposedly, doctors offer a high quality professional service and within the terms of instrumental modernity this means that they are replaceable. So it should not matter, as regards the quality of the service you receive, or so the story goes, which doctor happens to be on duty.

This is connected to the assumption that doctors are more 'objective' when they are neutral and impartial in relation to their patients. This can easily legitimate an insensitive and uncaring manner since to explore a person's experience with them can supposedly bring emotional and subjective aspects to bear that can only interfere and cloud the objectivity of clinical judgement. In practice, these terms often have little reality but they also need to be reworked because they help to sustain an untenable model of medical practice. It is not a matter of 'patient management', as it is sometimes called. The issues go much deeper since they challenge an instrumental language and practice that would seek to treat the symptoms without reference to the people themselves. It is as if they recede into the background, barely relevant to the situation at hand.

But it might be that if women see the same doctor on each visit, not only do they feel greater trust and confidence but this enables them to share aspects of their experience which affect the clinical judgements that might be reached in their case. This is to show that it is not only a matter of being sensitive to the emotional needs of patients but that it is *necessary* to developing good clinical practice. But this involves transforming the ways in which experience is treated as 'subjective' and therefore of little relevance to a medical judgement that has to be 'objective'. It is the terms of this distinction that have to be redrawn as doctors learn to context their relationships with their patients in different ways.

It also involves becoming more conscious of the masculinist assumptions that doctors learn unwittingly to protect themselves with. It is striking that medical students often have their initiation to medical schools with a dead body that they have to learn to dissect. Anatomy still provides the core of their studies in a way that is quite blind to the emotional anatomy of the body.[16] Medicine is a matter of illness and the body is presented to them as dead. It cannot protest or talk back. As students learn to throw parts of the body around, joking in a defensive manner, there is little reverance for life that is transmitted.[17]

This prepares the ground for doctors to learn to conceive of their work in the masculinist language of success and failure. As men we learn to keep away from failure, for we learn that it can compromise the male identity we are doing our best to sustain. So research shows that doctors visit patients who they know are dying far less often, for such cases are regarded as 'failures'. Doctors even learn to avoid saying when someone is dying, preferring to say that 'where there is life there is hope'. But to be dying is not to be hopeless, without hope, as Kübler-Ross has helped us to recognise.[18]

In *On Death and Dying*, Elizabeth Kübler-Ross has helped us to recognise death as a process rather than just as an ending (Kübler-Ross 1970). Of course, even what she says about the different stages of dying can be misread mechanistically so that it can be taught in a way that is not sensitive to the individuality of the process. This is because there seems to be a tension between professionalism that defines itself in terms of the universality and impartiality of routines and the individuality of care. It is as if each occasion presents itself as an opportunity to bring a particular routine into play.

This is part of a dominant masculinity that finds it difficult to respond to the individuality of needs as they are expressed by people themselves. Kübler-Ross is constantly reminding us that respect involves a recognition that people need to die in their own way, often as they have lived. This involved a transformed vision of 'respect' and 'autonomy' and a break with the prevailing Kantian terms espoused within so much medical ethics. Though Kant talks of respect for persons, he prepares much ground for routinisation and objectification. This is partly because 'respect' and 'autonomy' are related exclusively to our existence as rational selves in a way that blinds us to our existence as emotional and spiritual beings.[19]

Dominant forms of masculinity can make it difficult for men to sustain relationships. It is as if we learn to break up experience into a series of discrete events or occasions. It is difficult to explain why this should be, but it seems to connect to the ways in which we often learn to *cut off* and *separate* from experiences that we find difficult. For instance, it often seems easier for men after an emotional argument or row with their partners to leave this behind when the front door is closed. Work provides an escape that men are often grateful for, especially if there are young children at home. Women often seem to find it much harder to leave things behind and they seem more likely to feel troubled and disturbed with the reverberations throughout the day.

This is not to express a judgement but to acknowledge that men often learn to *cut off*. Within relationships it is often men who want to 'leave the past behind', thinking that no good can come from uncovering old wounds and injuries. Often it is an evasion, not wanting to explore some of the sources of present difficulties in contact, in the hurts of the past. And when relationships end it can be men who 'want to turn over a new leaf', so cutting themselves off from past relationships. This might be why so many men from diverse backgrounds fail to sustain a relationship with their children after a divorce or separation. Sometimes this is not easy to do, but it seems also to connect with difficulties that we have as men in sustaining relationships.

TIME AND RELATIONSHIPS

Modernity has been largely cast in Protestant terms as far as time is concerned. Time becomes a scarce commodity that we have to be careful not to waste. We learn that to waste time is an unforgivable sin so that we are constantly setting ourselves against the clock. Traditionally it has been men's time that has mattered, for it has been waged time or else time spent within the public sphere. Men have traditionally had the power and authority to take women's time for granted. It is partly because of this that men have rarely acknowledged the time and energy that goes into the emotional work that sustains a relationship. As men, we assume that relationships, like cars, just keep going until they break down.

It is because as men we can be so aware of how hard we are working within the public sphere that it can be difficult to acknowledge what others need from us within our personal and sexual relationships. It is possibly because we tend to deny our own emotional needs as men that it can be hard to acknowledge the emotional needs of others. Because we learn to pride ourselves on 'not letting things get us down', so we expect others to act in the same way and we assume that it is a sign of 'weakness' or 'inadequacy' that they fail to do so. It confirms men traditionally in the notion that women are 'weaker' because they seem to have so many more emotional needs than men.

It can also seem as if women are constantly complaining or feeling dissatisfied when men seem to put their emotional lives aside to 'get on with the job at hand'. Of course, these are generalisations which need to be mediated by class, race and sexual orientation, but they can often help to highlight something significant. It says something about how in the conditions of modernity men learn to *displace* their experience. They learn to test themselves against the job at hand or against the goals that they have set themselves. As middle-class men, we seem much less prepared to describe our experience as we live it, treating this as another form of self-indulgence. At some level this can leave us dissatisfied as if we are not *living* our lives so much as conforming to a series of externalised demands. It can mean that, somewhat paradoxically, we make few actual decisions for ourselves but find ourselves in situations which seem to define *for us* what we should do.

Often we do what is expected of us or act in a way so as not to upset or hurt other people. In part this helps to sustain a particular image of ourselves as men, but it can also be to avoid conflict and have a 'quiet life' within the private sphere of a relationship. It is as if we leave this for our partners to organise, thinking that we are thereby being less controlling in the relationship. But often this is because we never learn to take responsibility for our emotional lives and relationships. We leave this up to others, partly because we have learned that what matters exists elsewhere.

Since we give very little time to ourselves as men, we can feel that it is wrong for others to complain that we do not give enough time to them. It is as if, within the terms of a Protestant ethic, we think that because we deny ourselves time and space, so should others. We learn that life is there to be got on with, not really to be reflected upon. For if we reflect too much we are in danger of wasting time. It is also that we learn to think of success and achievement in individual terms so that it is easy to feel that time and energy given to relationships is time taken away from our own projects. So it is that we can have difficulties identifying ourselves with our relationships and so with learning to care for others. It means that we constantly take others for granted in a way that reflects the ways we take ourselves for granted.

As boys we are usually cared for, especially by our mothers, so that we can look to our partners to continue the tradition. Not learning to identify and name our emotional needs, it can be difficult for us to take responsibility for them ourselves. It is as if being looked after is a right that we can assume as men. When women refuse to take care of us in these ways it is easy to sulk and feel rejected because it can be hard to articulate our emotions and feelings in a way that makes them a basis for negotiation. It is also that we can be so used to living out our own lives without the help and support of others that we never learn to recognise when it is that we have *lost contact* with our partners. This is not something that we have learned to value, so often it is not something that we know how to build. It is as if we have learned to live without this particular nourishment and support so that it is hard to understand what our partners mean when they say that it is absent in their lives.

As we grow up we never learn as boys *how* to sustain a relationship. We are assured that what matters for our male identities is what we can manage on our own. This gives us a guilty conscience about relationships, especially when it is a matter of accepting that we can receive from our partners. We can be so used to being self-sufficient and independent that we think that we have to be this way. This can make it difficult for men to have relationships.[20] It is as if we want them in some idealised form, but that we are quite unprepared for their everyday activity. We are so used to living without them, thinking that to be vulnerable is a sign of weakness, that it can be hard to live with them.

A kind of emotional re-education becomes necessary if we are to learn to care. It is only when we have learned to care for ourselves that we can properly care for others. Part of this is allowing space for our own emotions and feelings so that our experience of ourselves can begin to grow. As long as we insist on living as rational selves alone whose fulfilment comes from individual projects, it is difficult to respect and acknowledge our existence as emotional, sexual and spiritual beings. We are left with a thin and narrow grasp of our experience.

As men learn to define their emotional needs more clearly they sometimes begin to *revalue* their experience in relationships. This is important for social theory, for the poverty of men's emotional experience and relationships is reflected in the difficulties of creating a more qualitative methodology. It might be that a concern with the *quality* of relationships, a concern stimulated by both feminism and psychotherapy, could help shift the concerns of both philosophy and social theory.

For a time in the early 1970s moral philosophy was showing a greater sensitivity to personal relations and emotional life and this has slowly developed as a challenge to the dominant rationalist paradigms.[21] In social theory a similar concern with qualitative method has developed, partly shown in a renewed interest in life history and biographical methods.[22] But possibly it is with feminist concerns for the *quality* of a relationship as already explored that some of the most crucial work was initiated.

Time is important to the quality of a relationship though by itself it need not be sufficient. What matters is not only the time that we spend with our partners and children but the quality of that time. But we have to be careful about this because it also takes *time* and *energy* to build relationships and fathers who might spend very little time with their children can experience the difficulty. They might like to think of this as 'quality time', but if they have never really developed the relationship, they cannot merely as an issue of will take it up when they want. It is interesting that men think they should be able to do this, for this reflects a difficulty men inherit in handling relationships. There is a tendency to see a relationship as broken up into a series of discrete episodes. There is often little understanding of how relationships might grow and develop and the kind of efforts that they take to sustain.

Within Freudian theory the relationship to the father is seen in relation to a father's task in separating the infant from the mother. It is the mother's relationship to her infant that is crucial and supposedly the father's relationship has no independent existence.[23] The father is there in the background, ready at the appropriate time to separate the mother and child so that the child can make the proper transition from dependency towards independence. It is as if Freud connected development very much in masculine terms as a movement from dependence towards independence and autonomy. He prepared the crucial recognition of the early years and the emotional bonding, especially with the mother, but this tends to be seen as providing the crucial background for a movement towards independence and autonomy. But unfortunately these still tend to be defined negatively, as a matter of being able to thrive without the early dependency.[24]

Freud tends to see relationships as the projection of earlier desires, as if others exist as 'objects' of our desires. These desires themselves are seen as discrete, as if they exist in an unconscious sphere of their own. We unknowingly project these unmet and unacknowledged desires on to those around us who work as 'objects', allowing us a substitute gratification for desires which were initially unfulfilled in our early childhood relationships. The analytic session is often conceived in similar terms so that the analyst provides a kind of screen for these earlier projections. The analyst helps the patient recognise his or her frustration at not having been acknowledged or fulfilled in the primary situation, so helping to question an idealisation of childhood and parents that has often acted as some kind of defence against recognition of these unfulfilled desires. The analyst thereby helps the patient to make a transition that he or she was not able to make for themselves towards a freedom and independence that is not based upon a hidden dependency.

But still with Freud there is a limited sense of relationship. The analyst as a screen threatens to disappear in the situation, and of course a relationship exists, but it takes on a very particular form. Any kind of emotional involvement would seem to disturb the analytic projection and so supposedly prevent the analysis being successful. However important transference remains within psychoanalysis, it is easy to overdo the ways that it might be 'disturbed'. Often this helps to sustain the authority of the analyst whose own experience is hidden from view.[25] I tend to think this is a false notion of objectivity that in the end can make it more difficult for people to escape a dependency that can remain. Some of the people Freud himself analysed remained in a form of dependency towards analysis itself for the rest of their lives. These can either be treated as exceptional or help rethink some of the basic terms of the psychoanalytic practice.[26]

In a way that resonates with the analyst's existence in the background of therapy, fathers seem to exist in the background of their children's lives. Freud talked about how he regretted not having had more contact with his own children when they were still young. I do not know whether he meant this in terms of what it might have taught him about analysis, or more personally. Traditionally fathers have been absent – even if powerful absentees – in the lives of their children. They have often threatened their children harshly, seeing it as their role to provide authority and discipline. Reading Kant's *On Education* gives you some sense of the lengths that people had to go to to discipline the supposedly 'animal' nature of children. Here it is a matter of staying distant and uninvolved so that one's authority as a father is not compromised. There is a sense of the obligations of parenthood but not of the joys that a close relationship can bring. There is little sense of fathering as fulfilling needs within men themselves and providing a possible enrichment to their lives.[27]

As long as relationships are tacitly identified with dependency, then growth and development can be seen as a linear path away from dependency. This vision informs Freud as it does the very different moral psychology of Piaget and Kohlberg. It becomes difficult to explore relationships as a source of meaning and value within our lives. This is reflected within social theory that can often define social relationships in contrast to personal and individual ones. At different times Marx seems to open a space for acknowledging that people are important to each other, not just the accumulation of individual power and wealth. A sense of the value of human relationships supposedly affords us a vision of socialism in contrast to capitalism that fails to give such a recognition.[28] But still it has been difficult to realise this vision, and orthodox Marxism was too ready to argue that it would come into existence automatically with the abolition of private property and the socialisation of the means of production. But history has taught us otherwise.

In their different ways it has taken feminism and psychotherapy to remind us both of the *value* of relationships in our lives and also of the time and energy that it takes to nourish and sustain them. If we took some of these insights to heart our lives would have to change, for we would, for instance, begin to create cities and neighbourhoods that would be fit for children. As we learn to listen and respond to our own 'inner child' so we would want other children to grow and thrive. It would also transform our patterns of work as men come to recognise that if they are to have a meaningful relationship with their children it has to be every day, not just at weekends.

As men we would endeavour to be more in touch with our emotional selves, recognising that we need to take time for ourselves. How otherwise can we hope to build quality into our relationships with others? We would begin to appreciate that our children do not want to be bought off with things, however technologically sound, but want us to be there for them, rather than constantly thinking that 'we have something important to do'. Our children too often learn to give up on their fathers and to look elsewhere for sustenance. Often they become angry and withdrawn, if not both, feeling that they are somehow being cheated out of what should be theirs.

Our understanding of socialisation within social theory has often been too narrow and adaptive. We have expected children to conform to society as it is and learned to silence them when they demand a world which is fit for children and which recognises and validates the individuality of their emotional and spiritual lives. In seeking to adapt and prepare children for society as it exists, reassuring ourselves that, according to cultural relativism, different societies will organise a different conception of childhood, is to turn our eyes from the injuries that we do to our children in the ways that we bring them up and seek to educate them.

In many cases we are too busy to listen and we have ways of diminishing what they have to say as 'child's talk'. We learn to fob them off with excuses, for there are always more important tasks that need to be done. As children have low status in an adult world, so a sociology that reflects the assumptions and concerns of that world has been slow to respond to them. In thinking about relationships, children should be a core concern for any viable social theory. Perhaps we should start by thinking about our relationships with our children or with the 'inner child' that we all carry and that we have learned to silently protect from the hidden injuries of our own childhoods.

Chapter 13

Language

MEANING AND LANGUAGE

When Wittgenstein in his later writings discusses the meaning of concepts, he asks us to think back to childhood when we first learned how to use a particular concept. But childhood often does not provide the kind of transparent content that Wittgenstein might have hoped for, since not only were we often lied to but we were often told what we should feel and think.

Wittgenstein was contesting a linguistic rationalism seeking to ground the natural expression of some of our emotions. He was wanting to grasp how language develops as an elaboration or substitution for more basic behaviours. Thus, for instance, a cry of pain is a natural expression that we might later learn to express linguistically.[1] But it is also crucial, as has been remarked many times before, that boys are still often told that 'boys don't cry'. We learn to *inhibit* what might be taken as a 'natural' expression and in some sense to go rigid in organising ourselves against our tears. Sometimes these unwept tears are turned inside so that others cannot see them.

How are we to understand this? Is it that boys do not allow themselves to get upset or feel scared because this will compromise them in the face of others? Are we to say that, in Weberian terms, they can choose to give their experience a different meaning, for as far as they are concerned 'it was nothing'? The fact that another boy pushed them over and took away the ball that they were playing with supposedly did not upset them *because* they did not cry. Supposedly this is proof itself and it is reinforced by the praise that he was given by adults who admired him for 'taking it like a man'. In his own eyes he had proved to himself that he was not a 'sissy' or 'wet'. He could hold his head high with the other boys.

This is a familiar story and we might say that it goes some way to showing how 'experience' and 'individuality' are socially and historically constituted. This is a point at which a structuralist and an interpretive account might find some agreement, though it will be more significant for a Weberian to stress the freedom that exists for the boy in the situation to assign his own meaning. He supposedly makes some *choice* as to whether to see it as a situation which is 'upsetting' or not. The fact that it is not upsetting for him is what matters and is a sign of his freedom in the situation. It shows that his behaviour is not determined, as positivism might have it, by external forces, since its existence as a social action is marked by the meaning that is assigned to it.[2]

There is a point here where we can witness Weber's account resonating with a traditional conception of masculinity that stresses the importance of men showing 'self-control'. This often means that we have to be careful to sustain a particular meaning for our actions, so that we do not compromise ourselves in the eyes of others. Weber, following Kant, assumes that as rational selves we can curb and dominate our feelings, desires and emotions which by themselves are not sources of meaning. It is through the workings of reason alone that we can give meaning to our actions and experience. If we want to discount the tears that are welling up inside us then we are quite 'free' to do so, for within a Kantian framework they threaten to challenge our freedom and autonomy as rational selves. If these feelings can be said to be 'natural' in the situation this is of no consequence at all, since it has no bearing upon the meanings that we can assign to our actions as rational selves.

Again, I am less concerned to establish what Weber might actually have argued in such a situation than to follow through a certain tendency of thought and feeling that finds a general expression within an interpretive tradition. Wittgenstein can help us to challenge some of the Kantian premises that underpin such an account and which flow from a prevailing distinction between reason and nature. As I have already argued, Wittgenstein in his later writing is working to subvert such a distinction and the notion that meaning and language are an expression of reason alone. This sustains the idea of assigning meaning as an inner cognitive process. Kant saw reason as an 'inner' faculty which alone is the source of our freedom and autonomy for we have an 'external' relationship to our emotions, feelings and desires. They are not aspects of our autonomy but are seeking to determine our behaviour externally. This partly affirms reason as the source of meaning, for it is through the interior faculty that we assign meaning to our actions.

Wittgenstein works to undermine our grasp of this Protestant distinction between the 'inner' realm of reason and the 'outer' existence of our emotions, desires and actions. He questions this cognitive rendering of meaning as an inner process and helps us to recognise how the 'inner' and 'outer' cannot be isolated in this way. It is not as if we can assign meaning to our actions through some inner process of mind. Wittgenstein is challenging this Cartesian vision in the philosophy of mind. It is part of the significance of his considerations of private language arguments. He shows that we cannot assign meaning through comparing an object in the world with an inner representation that we carry in our minds. It is partly because a Cartesian tradition has left us as rational selves that we are estranged from the natural world, including our bodies. We exist as minds who are reflecting upon a natural world that is independent of us and whose existence we can bring into doubt. Supposedly the only condition for certainty is our existence as thinking selves.[3]

Wittgenstein's later writing, particularly *On Certainty*, is concerned with questioning the idea of foundations for our knowledge that are grounded in conditions of certainty (Wittgenstein 1975). He was carefully exploring the different issues that it made sense to question, recognising the particular conditions that might render, for instance, questioning what my name is or whether the earth existed before my birth, meaningful. It was as if there were no one set of foundations that exist for knowledge, but in the different areas of our lives different criteria are brought into play.

The point was that Wittgenstein was working to shift the centrality of epistemology within modern philosophy. He was suspicious of generalised questioning about, for example, the existence of the external world, and was learning from G. E. Moore's struggles with these issues.[4] It was a matter of recognising that it is only from the position of actively living our lives with others that questions of what we know and how we know become intelligible. To place the world at some distance from ourselves and then to question how we know of its existence is of limited value. But this temptation was deeply set within modern philosophy and it was no easy task to shift it.

If we are to challenge the distinction between 'inner' and 'outer' and the notion that it is the categories of the mind that order, classify or represent the 'outer', natural and social world to us, we are questioning a Kantian framework that has powerfully influenced classical social theory through the writings of Durkheim and Weber. Put crudely, we can say that as regards a sense of ourselves as practical beings who come to a consciousness of our lives as part of the process of living, Wittgenstein can be said to stand with Marx against the dominant Kantian tradition.

They both in very different ways help to question a notion that often lives on in structuralist and post-structuralist work, that there is a framework which is largely conceptual in character through which we order or classify social reality. This is to place 'social reality' at a distance and so to estrange ourselves from the different activities and practices that we live out in everyday life. For Wittgenstein, it was important to remember the idea first mentioned in the *Exodus* chapter of the Jewish Bible that in the beginning there was the deed. It is our actions that come first and through our actions we reach understanding and awareness.[5]

Much of this is expressed too abstractly to be useful and what is at issue might only become clear with a careful reading of Wittgenstein's later writings. Within social theory we are often too ready to resort to labels as a substitute for thought. Hopefully I have said enough to question the idea that since Wittgenstein rejected the idea of foundations for knowledge he settled for the other alternative, which is to say that our concepts are conventionally defined within a particular society or culture.[6] Wittgenstein was keen on imagining different societies and showing how what were familiar concepts to us might operate quite differently in such contexts. Such examples worked to show us the particularities of context that make a particular concept or practice intelligible. Usually these conditions are taken for granted and so are lost from view. Wittgenstein helps us appreciate the particularity of the contexts in which our concepts come to life in their appropriate contexts.

Wittgenstein is aware of the specificity of contexts so that when we are born into a community it is not simply a linguistic community which shares its meanings.

This is the mistake in thinking about his work as a form of linguistic convention-alism, for he is out to question the autonomy of language as an expression of reason alone. This is also what is misleading in assimilating his work to a 'philosophy of language'. He shows that speech is an *aspect* of a larger practice but that it does not define the practice itself. But he does want to challenge the individual con-sciousness as the source of all meaning. This Cartesian view, developed in a rationalist form by Kant, is challenged, because meaning exists as a feature of a particular practice and has to be grasped within that context. This context is not provided, as it is by Saussure and a tradition of semiology, by discourse alone.[7]

When the small boy stops himself from crying when his ball has been taken away, he is interrupting what might otherwise be a natural response. It is inadequate to claim that we cannot say this with forms of cultural relativism, since within western societies at least, boys learn not to cry in situations like this. Weber colluded in this form of masculinity in reassuring people that they have the freedom to create their own meanings, so that if he says that he was not upset then we have no cause to question it. This resonates with a dominant form of masculinity that insists that it can create reality in its own image and which appropriated to itself the power to dismiss any experience that might count to the contrary.

As far as phenomenological sociology is concerned, reality is held to be a subjective construction, for it cannot be said to exist independently of the meanings that we assign to it.[8] This seems to treat individuals as the sovereign source of meaning, especially if it is a phenomenology that is cast within the Cartesian terms of consciousness, as it was for the early Husserl.[9] Wittgenstein helps us to question this view through making us aware that we grow up within a particular society taking for granted particular ways of doing things and ways of making sense of our experience.

But Wittgenstein can also help us question a rationalist tradition so that we can appreciate that in curbing his tears, the boy is interrupting a 'natural' expression. This does not mean that there are not different ways of expressing his hurt, but if the hurt is denied completely it does not mean that it can be eradicated through reason alone. We cannot treat our emotions and feelings in this way, as a rationalist theory such as Weber's might suggest. This is something that Freud also recognises and it might be part of Wittgenstein's appreciation of Freud's work. Freud knew that if we suppress our feelings they return in different forms. It can also be that in talking out this incident the boy begins to recognise this as part of a whole pattern of events with this other older boy. Somehow he had turned this blame on to himself, thinking that he must have done something to bring it on. The circle of this internalisation, familiar enough within a Protestant culture, can be broken as the boy recognises it as an instance of bullying.

Identifying the incident as bullying can help to shift the incident in the boy's eyes and help him feel that he has been wronged and that it is quite legitimate for him to feel angry, if not still upset. This can help to give a reason for the feelings, as if in rationalist terms we can *allow* ourselves to have these feelings once we have been convinced that we have 'reasons' for them. This step is consonant with masculinity. It is yet another step, one possibly threatening to the dominant masculinity as it is experienced, to acknowledge that you feel hurt and upset by what happened. If a boy allows himself his tears, he still has to deal with the rejections of those around who might not be so understanding.

If he takes it further and is ready to assert to others that there is nothing wrong with boys crying and that if they have been hurt it is quite natural to do so, he can be asserting himself in a clear and forthright way. The point Wittgenstein makes, however, is that we do not have to go through such a mental process, drawing as a conclusion a permission to cry. This is an intellectualism that Wittgenstein is out to question. It is quite 'natural' to cry when we are hurt and we should not have to explain it.

Freud works to explain the workings of repression, showing for instance how this unacknowledged hurt might show itself in revengeful behaviour in our dream life. He tended to make repression an issue of unconscious life. Foucault is less tolerant of a language of repression, believing that it commits him to a hydraulic conception of emotional life with feelings that are denied and pushed down waiting to be expressed.[10] But neither Freud nor Reich has this conception. More significantly, it helps Foucault to assert an opposed position, one which carries some important insight. He is wary of declaring that there is a position within which people are not repressed as if the structures of repression can be released once and for all. This version of Reich was around for a short period in the early 1970s, encouraging people to think that if they could only break through the 'armour' that they had created as a protection for themselves against feeling, then they could live a life of free emotional expression. But Reich appreciated how important were the defences that people had learned to construct for themselves and how careful you had to be in working with them. This was not the place where you should begin to work since people could quite properly react against such intervention.[11]

Foucault has been important in challenging a particular vision of revolutionary politics which held that, for instance, repression or ideology are features of capitalist society alone, having their source in private property so that with the socialisation of the means of production we will live in a society without ideology and without repression. It is as if power and necessity are features of a capitalist society alone which will wither away with socialism, to be replaced by a regime of freedom and equality. Foucault had learned to suspect these characteristic modes of thought and recognised how easily one regime of power with its structures of regulatory powers could be replaced by another.[12] He had learned from Althusser that ideology would exist within socialism, even if it takes on a different form.

But there is an issue of ideology in its relationship to truth and language that needs to be explored. An orthodox Marxism had held that truth was in large part ideological within bourgeois society, working to sustain particular material interests. So it was that the language of truth and freedom had constantly to be scrutinised for the material interests it was working to legitimate. Language is itself powerless to communicate meanings and truth, destined as it is to express the dominant ideologies. If truth existed, it was supposedly a 'possession' of the working class and of Marxist theory itself. Truth did not exist in capitalist society, which was itself torn apart by contradictions of class. Within a Leninist tradition, truth became the possession of the party and so was centralised in a single source. It was the duty of the party to bring this truth to the working class who could not reach it through their own experience within the factories, which at best could only yield a 'trade union' consciousness.[13]

Foucault helps us to challenge this centralised vision, showing us how truth exists as an effect of discourses encoded in the different institutions of society. His studies of medicine in *The Birth of the Clinic* (Foucault 1976) and of regimes of punishment in *Discipline and Punishment* (Foucault 1975) show how different knowledges help to create and sustain their own truths. This was an insight that Foucault already knew in his *Madness and Civilisation* which argues against a liberal notion that says that gradually with time, as we learn more, our treatment of mental illness is becoming more rational and humane (Foucault 1971).

Foucault rejects this premiss, showing how different regimes of treatment have replaced each other, each with its own conception of 'mental illness'. He challenges the identification of reason with progress, showing that history is in no helpful sense progressive. Not only does this help displace a Hegelian tradition which sought to treat history as the realisation of reason, but it also helps us to question a liberalism that assumes that history brings progress in its wake. For Foucault, it is very much a matter of one system of regulation with its own conception of 'truth' being replaced by another. There is no neutral point which allows these different systems of regulation to be compared, for truth is seen as an effect of a particular regime of power and regulation.[14]

TRUTH AND EXPERIENCE

If language can express truth, it is only as an *effect* of a particular regime of power. As knowledge is always related to power for Foucault, so also is truth. His vision, which is helpful in so many ways, shares with orthodox Marxism a certain disdain for claims to truth. It does not look towards material interests, which for Foucault are conceived too reductively, but to regimes of power. But, unlike orthodox Marxism, truth is not held by any particular political party or group but is dispersed through all the discourses that are invoked in society.

If Foucault learned to question his early conceptions of truth as an effect of discursive practices, wanting to relate knowledge to discipline and power, he could not escape a relativism that at some level subverts any language that claims to be truthful. Foucault did not seem to worry about this, aware as he was of the harm caused through history by those who claimed to be in possession of a truth that had been denied to others. He was familiar with the history of the crusades, to go no further. But he was less aware of the difficulties of living without a conception of truth at all. At the same time he was able to acknowledge in his later writings significant resonances with work done by the Frankfurt School as critical theory.

The Frankfurt School has been important in exploring how an instrumental conception of reason has come to dominate modernity.[15] We learn to think of reason in terms of a means–ends relationship in a way that restricts our vision of truth to efficiency. Horkheimer recognises how notions of reason and rationality which were known to the Greeks and which related rationality to the ordering of the whole society, were narrowed within modernity to be defined as an inner relationship between a Cartesian consciousness and the goals or ends it chooses for itself.[16]

Horkheimer was concerned to show that there were alternatives to this vision of instrumental rationality that had become so dominant that it was taken for granted as defining rationality itself. If this vision of rationality is an effect of particular regimes of power, it is important to be able to discern alternatives that are still potential. This is something that Foucault has difficulty with, since he is prepared to dispense with the notion of truth which is always constituted within a particular discourse or the effect of power.

Weber tended to treat rationalisation as an inevitable process in the West, even if he regretted it because of the ways that it undermined a serious consideration of values. It was only the emergence of a charismatic leader that might temporarily be able to hinder the growth of rationalisation. Lukács, a student and friend of Weber, thought this conception too fatalistic and came to see reification to be a particular feature of capitalist society, rather than a feature of industrialisation as such.[17] For Lukács we live in a society where the relationship between people has taken on the form of a relationship between things. It was only with the proletariat that the truth of these processes could be revealed. It was not within the system itself that any alternative vision could be created. Supposedly for Lukács, the dominance of exchange values was complete.

The Frankfurt School was struggling to escape some of the conclusions of Lukács' *History and Class Consciousness* (Lukács 1971) while at the same time being influenced by its analysis of reification within capitalist society. They saw this as a way of characterising social relationships more generally, as did Lukács, rather than in the more orthodox Marxist terms as characterising productive relationships exclusively. It opened up ways for thinking about how experience had been reified and how relationships had taken on a particular form.

But unfortunately Lukács has only a few examples, for instance when he talks of the ways in which the truth of a particular event are traduced by journalists who have to get a 'good story' out of any situation. He recognises how this distorts the story and corrupts the journalist as truth gets lost from view. He also talks about how making a 'good' marriage can be separated from the loving relationships of the persons involved, having to do with wealth and family connections. But these remain scattered examples within an otherwise dense text which is largely rationalist in form. It sees truth, not in terms of experience, but exclusively in terms of reaching an 'objective' understanding of an independent capitalist social reality. In the end Lukács takes refuge, as we have already noted, in the idea that the subjective consciousness of the proletariat will somehow yield an 'objective' grasp of social reality.[18]

Horkheimer's formulation of critical theory in his essay 'Traditional and critical theory', relies upon bringing to bear a wider conception of reason that is connected to social justice and therefore provides terms within which to evaluate both the 'negative' and 'positive' aspects of, say, the Enlightenment tradition.[19] Unlike positivism which he thinks of as a traditional theory, Horkheimer holds a vision of truth and justice, thinking they can be sustained through a vision of reason that can evaluate not only means but also ends. He is looking for a more substantial vision of rationality that is able to make the 'ends' of human action subject to critical evaluation. For Weber, the dominance of instrumental rationality had put a discussion of ends beyond the pale of reason. They were largely a matter of individual opinion and commitment. It was generally accepted that the ends, say of a particular organisation, are given, and that rationality comes into play in working out what would be the most efficient means to reach these ends.[20]

Weber, significantly, connects the rationalisation of society with the growth of bureaucratic organisation. In his earlier work *The Protestant Ethic and the Spirit of Capitalism*, it would also seem possible to connect it to particular dominant forms of masculinity (Weber 1930). For it was the Protestant ethic that helped to educate a masculinity into accepting that achievement comes from realising goals set by reason alone. It teaches men to be suspicious of their natures as inevitably leading them astray from the goals they set for themselves. Men learn to take pride in their achievements and in the denial of their natures, which only affirm their masculine identities.

If there is a truth to our experience it is to be revealed in our individual success and achievements that have to be striven for. Where Protestantism talked of salvation as providing the meaning of life, a capitalist ethic learned to insist on similar denials of intrinsic need and satisfaction for realising the goals of wealth and power. It was wealth and power that were to be the measure of individual success and so to provide meaning for life.

This can help explain why men in particular seem trapped in an endless circle of activities, and can seem as if their very existence is threatened if they stop working. Activities give meaning to masculine identity even if at the same time not offering much of a sense of fulfilment. It can be difficult to feel fulfilled and take enjoyment in what we have achieved if there is always the next task on the horizon waiting to be done. It seems to beckon before the last job was even finished.

Marcuse recognised this in some of his earlier studies, particularly 'On Hedonism', and is also aware of how important it is to sustain a moment of happiness.[21] It is as if the category of happiness as part of a lived experience had been forsaken within modernity only to be represented in the externalised terms of a utilitarian calculus. Possibly it was Marcuse's relationship with Heidegger that helped him breach a prevailing rationalism that worked to subvert the possibilities of intrinsic pleasure and satisfaction.[22] This was also something that Adorno could write about in a telling way in *Minima Moralia*, though he was more readily aware of happiness as an illusory possibility, making people feel guilty and responsible if they could not achieve it.[23]

But the more theoretical formulations in critical theory tended to take solace from a reconstituted conception of reason. In part, it remained confined by their own rationalism, though this was tempered by an interest in Freud and psychoanalytic theory. They tended to affirm the primacy of theory in a period in which the prevailing social conditions had forsaken the possibilities of emancipation.[24] It was the task of theory to keep open possibilities of transformation that seemed to have been foreclosed in practice. It was important to sustain a discourse of truth and justice but supposedly both these conceptions were to be guaranteed by a more substantial conception of reason. It was reason that was to bring light into the world and they were constantly vigilant against what they took to be signs of 'irrationalism'. But this distinction was possibly drawn too sharply. It was perhaps one of the reasons why they failed to develop a full enough conception of experience and the contradictory forms through which this is lived.

Somewhat paradoxically there is a similar difficulty with Foucault, who helps sustain the notion that experience is socially and historically constituted. He maintains, in this regard at least, the structuralist opposition which says that it is either 'given' or else it is 'socially and historically constructed'. Since it is language that is said to constitute experience, this *forecloses* the possibilities of tension between language and experience. Partly because of this, contemporary social theory has in large part been left bereft of a conception of morality and conscience.

This foreclosing also helps to situate sources of difficulty in the relationship between feminism and social theory, since in large part feminism was premissed upon an exploration of the shared experience of women's subordination. This was not to assume that experience was provided for by language. It is with feminism – when it refuses to be reworked within a structuralist tradition – that social theory has recently been able to engage with issues of experience and oppression. It should be possible to draw insights from this work into identities and power without surrendering to its particular masculinist form of rationalism. For without a conception of experience, social theory was left unable to illuminate the workings of oppression and empowerment.

If Marxism has thought in terms of oppression, this is usually in the externalised terms of the expropriation of surplus value. This is how exploitation tends to be conceived on the assumption that it is only if it can be quantified that it can be validated. This has influenced the discussions of class and stratification within contemporary sociology which have found it difficult to bring together objective studies of wealth and power with the subjective perceptions of class. It is rare to find studies such as Richard Sennett and Jonathan Cobb's *The Hidden Injuries of Class* (1970) or Lillian Rubin's *Worlds of Pain* (1976) that are also able to illuminate the lived experience of class. It is partly because the dominant traditions have shied away from moral categories, thinking that this brings a 'subjective bias' into an otherwise objective account. We have already explained how this is exacerbated by the ways that experience tends to be treated as a 'subjective' category.

Foucault's *Madness and Civilisation* can help us trace the process through which our grasp of experience has been narrowed and foreclosed (Foucault 1971). He shows how a western conception of reason and rationality was set in opposition to our natures. So it was that within modernity our dreams and fantasies were deemed to be no part of our experience, which came to be conceived in terms of reason alone. As aspects of our experience were sensed and invalidated as 'irrational', they no longer had an existence 'in reality'. But in learning automatically to denigrate aspects of our experience in this way we are denying certain truths about ourselves. But Foucault cannot help us to adequately appreciate ways that our experience grew more thin and attenuated as we learned to think of ourselves as rational selves and to accept a conception of reason set in sharp opposition to nature. At some level he remains trapped by his own rationalism.

A greater sympathy for Freud and psychoanalytic work than Foucault had, could help us to reach such a conclusion. It would at least draw to our attention the idea lost to Foucault, that sexuality can only be repressed through a particular cost to ourselves. A rationalist tradition tends to deny our existence as sexual and emotional beings, thinking that these aspects of our being could safely be denied or at least we could live our lives according to reason alone. Freud tends to accept our existence as sexual and emotional beings, recognising these as natural forms of expression that we only deny through *displacing* them into our unconscious lives. Freud was anxious to sustain his focus on sexuality and the costs of its denial within western culture. He learned that what we repress returns to haunt our unconscious lives.

Foucault is less sympathetic to notions of the unconscious and to a Freudianism that tended to carry with it a strong sense of normality. It was rightly important for Foucault that people should define the terms of their own sexuality and not have this imposed from the outside. He was suspicious of a sexual politics which argued that the 'truth' of ourselves lies with our sexualities and so that could have supported the argument for the priority of a gay or lesbian identity, for instance, over others.[25] At the same time this made it difficult for him to fully appreciate how important and in some sense irreversible was the process of 'coming out'. It is hard for Foucault, with the theoretical framework he provides for himself, to say why this should have been such a significant experience that helped shape a person's sense of identity and relationship with others.

This touches on another aspect of Freud's work. For it can be said that Freud, like Wittgenstein in a different way, opens up a space for investigating the relationship between language and experience. They both challenge the idea that language can constitute experience and that there is therefore no way of appealing in any meaningful sense to experience that is not discursive. It is important to question this idea along with the notion that experience is 'socially constructed'.

Freud might have developed psychoanalysis as a 'talking cure' but he was well aware of the way in which speech can be used as a form of avoidance. He would have known that Foucault's idea, that the existence of discourses about sexuality somehow showed that repression did not exist, could equally be used to show the reverse. As I have argued elsewhere, speech can become obsessive in the absence of feeling or relationship. Freud is in fact helping to question an instrumental use of language that characterises particular masculinities.[26] As men we often learn to use language as a weapon with which to assert ourselves and defeat others. We learn to use language to get our own way and to prove to others, including our partners, that reason is on our side.

But Freud recognises the way that language and feeling can come apart so that language becomes more or less automatic and works to conceal how we have been affected by particular experiences. Wittgenstein talks in different terms but he is also aware of how language loses meaning as it works without making any difference – it is like a part of a machine that keeps on working once it has been separated off. In their different ways both recognise this as a difficulty that needs to be healed. Wittgenstein talks of philosophy as a form of therapy and – though it is hard to be clear what he meant by this – it partly meant returning words that had lost connection with their natural contexts back to those contexts, so that we could recognise the full complexity of their connections. As we learn to *ground* our language, so we help to ground ourselves. We should be less susceptible to illusions and false consolations but also hopefully more in touch with the springs of our own existence. Simone Weil shared a similar aspiration, for she equally recognised that the problems of living could not be settled by intellectual or philosophical means alone. She also recognised the inescapability of moral concerns.[27]

Though Freud sought to reconcile us to our emotional and sexual natures, he was much more suspicious of morality and spirituality in general. He tended to think that they had a source in the primal history of sexual repression and this increasingly became a concern of his towards the end of his life. It was part of a move away from clinical work. But if Jung and others refused this reductionism of spiritual concerns they had all learned from Freud's insights into the ways experiences can be buried and emotional affect blocked depending on how language is used. It is as language is drained of its meaning that it offers merely a form of empty distraction. Freud was well aware of how language is often used to *displace* reality so that people learn to avoid painful or difficult feelings. But in avoiding these feelings we are avoiding greater contact with reality. We make our experience more superficial than it needs to be. We lose touch with reality as we lose contact with ourselves.

MEANING AND EMOTION

Freud learned to use language to bring people back to themselves. He recognised the power of connecting to emotions and feelings that had been locked away with painful childhood experiences. Through a process of regression some of these memories come back into view and some of the effect that was tied up with them could be released. Not only did this help to connect people to experiences they thought they had lost, but it gradually helped to develop a person's sense of connectedness with themselves.

As people learn to speak, say of their relationships with their fathers, they can learn to *feel* a hurt that they had learned to diminish. They might have thought that this relationship did not matter to them, only to become aware of how these ideas worked as some kind of defence for the feelings of pain and neglect they felt. They had possibly long reconciled themselves to receiving very little from their fathers, but this was also part of a process of rationalisation. When they return to some of their childhood scenes a different story comes into focus.

People learn to avoid the truth about themselves and their relationships. This was a crucial insight of Freud's, for it questioned an Enlightenment vision that sought to represent people as constantly in search of truth. Freud knew otherwise. He learned that the avoidance and displacement had to be handled carefully, for people had found ways of defending themselves against feelings and knowledge that they did not want to know. He also knew that if change were to be possible, language had to renew its connection to feelings.

In part, he was working with a pathology sustained by a modernity that insisted that reason and emotion be pulled apart as reason alone exists as a source of knowledge. Freud knew as a crucial insight that people could know something intellectually while refusing to acknowledge it emotionally. A woman might know, for example, that her father has died but would have learned that it was pointless to mourn, for she could not bring him back. Mourning rituals could barely be sustained within a culture of modernity which declared emotions and feelings to be a sign of weakness and which denied them an existence in reality. As people learned to take an instrumental view of emotional life, it became increasingly difficult to acknowledge its importance. Mourning had been displaced within a regime of reason.

Freud was dealing directly with some of the hidden injuries sustained by an Enlightenment rationalism. Since this was a tradition he still largely identified with as providing the fruits of civilisation, he wanted to ameliorate its worst consequences.[28] He sought to acknowledge our existence as sexual and emotional beings, since he recognised the injuries that were inflicted when these aspects of our existence were repressed and denied. He recognised the pain and misery this caused in people's lives and refused to discount this misery as 'subjective', for he knew that it was no less real and damaging. He also refused to discount suffering because it was a feature of private life and personal relationships. In asserting the significance of emotional hurt and suffering, he was quite prepared to challenge traditions of liberal and Marxist theory that could only validate suffering within the public realm. Freud wanted to reinstate our emotional and sexual lives as being of no less reality.

Knowledge has different springs, and felt knowledge has yet to be acknowledged in our philosophy and social theory. Weber sustains a rationalist tradition within interpretive sociology with his vision of meaning as a process of reason or consciousness alone. He helps sustain a dominant form of masculinity that insists that 'reality' exists as its own subjective construction. An interpretive tradition can sustain dominant masculinities in the sense that constructions they choose to make of 'reality' are their own concern alone. This can confirm men in an inherited sense that reason is a masculine appropriation. Since men are supposedly rational, they assume that they are 'right' unless some aspect of the logic of their argument can be shown to be faulty. This is in line with the way that men often learn to relate to language as a means of self-assertion and as a way of proving themselves in the eyes of others.

Freud has an appreciation of *felt* knowledge, of the way that we can come to know something through our emotions and feelings. This helps to challenge a rationalism that says we can 'know' through reason alone. It helps to shift the conception of truth we construe in the objective terms of correspondence. Of course it can be important to know whether an event that we remember did really happen, but it can be quite misleading to think that our feelings about the situation can be treated as 'merely' subjective and so of little consequence when it comes to issues of truth. Freud recognises that our emotions and feelings can equally be truthful and he learns that truth can involve a *process* of awareness so that it is not simply a matter of making a mental decision to be truthful. For Freud, in contrast to Weber, does not think that we have sovereign control over the 'meanings' that our experience has. This authority that we supposedly have cannot be cast adequately in rationalist terms.

This is also an issue that Wittgenstein touches on, for he is concerned with establishing the authority that we sometimes have over our own knowledge. Can I be mistaken about whether I have a toothache or not? Is this something that others can correct, or is it something that I have apodictic knowledge of? In questioning this way, Wittgenstein is helping to question a Cartesian inheritance which thinks that doubting is intelligible, where Wittgenstein thinks that it is not.[29] He makes us aware that there are moments when it makes little sense to doubt and that we are continually working with assumptions that we readily take for granted in the different areas of our lives. Like Schutz, Wittgenstein is aware of the tacit assumptions that we are continually taking for granted, though he does not tend to present them in cognitive terms as 'knowledge' that is tacitly assumed.

As men, we tend to assume that our particular relationship to reason gives us a particular authority in relation to our knowledge. Not only do we assume that we know about our own lives but we can readily feel that reason gives us authority to comment on anything going on in the lives of others. It is hard to accept our boundaries and to acknowledge that others do not need our comments and opinions but, as feminism makes clear, can get on quite well without us. As men, we can feel that our ideas and opinions are indispensable, so we can be shocked to be told by others to mind our own business since it is none of our concern. Reason can make us assume that everything is our concern. It also gives false confidence, thinking that as long as we apply ourselves there has to be a solution to any well-formulated problem. This was part of the promise of the Enlightenment and is a challenge that men have often accepted as their own.

Freud recognises that in our emotional lives there are often few solutions. A rationalist tradition can help us think that solutions lie in eradicating feelings we do not want or find unacceptable. We learn not to show our feelings, especially with others. Partly because of this, men can often be impatient with therapy, wondering what it is all for and what the point of it can be if it does not promise 'solutions' or 'cures'. If you cannot solve a problem, we learn as men that the best thing to do is to forget about it. We can even think that if there is no solution then it cannot be a 'real' problem, simply one of our emotional or subjective making. But as we deny these aspects of our experience, even if this is generally culturally encouraged, we weaken a sense of our own reality and connection to ourselves. It works to curtail the sources of our own felt knowledge.

It is through a process of therapy that we come to *accept* aspects of our experience and relationships that we had learned to reject because they did not match the ideals and images we have for ourselves. This is part of a process in which we learn to transfer some of our childhood feelings before we gradually learn to accept them as our own. Therapy becomes a matter of learning to accept greater truth in our lives as some of our rationalisations fall away. For example, a woman might feel that her father is busy working for the family so that she feels no justifiction for feeling angry at his absence. Therapy can help her recognise these feelings of anger, without worrying so much about whether it is 'rational' to feel this way. In accepting that she *does* feel this way, whether it is rational or not, she is accepting more of her own experience. This is part of a process of learning to be true to her own experience.

When her father dies it might take time to accept this emotionally. As she allows herself to grieve and mourn she can gradually accept his death. This is a process that takes time, and different religious traditions have rituals which can help mark different stages in the process. In the Jewish religion you traditionally return for a stonesetting eleven months after the death as a way of marking the end of a period of mourning. There is a wisdom in this process, for it acknowledges a dimension of time largely denied within a rationalist modernity that asumes that knowledge can be instantaneous. Sometimes it can take years to appreciate the significance of a death in our lives and this process has its own movement and integrity. This is not, in interpretive terms, simply a matter of replacing one interpretation by another, but of reaching a deeper connection with oneself. This is the path that psychotherapy seeks to tread, but not without its own difficulties.

Chapter 14

Sexuality

LANGUAGE AND SEXUALITY

Freud learns to interrupt the flow of language to allow more reality to enter. Sometimes it is through the entrance of unrecognised feelings that reality is felt. He understands how emotions and feelings can operate at an unconscious level and so beyond our conscious awareness. This was an important discovery that helped question the hold of a rationalism that insists that reasons we are aware of provide the 'causes' for our behaviour.[1] This connects to a particular vision of masculinity that identifies masculinity with reason, and forms the *control* men often assume themselves to have in relation to their experience. Since as men we learn to account for our behaviour in terms of reason, we learn to defend ourselves in similar terms. Since we can explain why we have acted in a particular way, we can make ourselves invulnerable to attempts to explain our behaviour in different terms.

If Freud helps to question this vision of rationalism, recognising that we are often moved by emotions and feelings that operate beyond the level of our conscious awareness, he does this in a way that keeps these dominant notions of masculinity intact. He wants to broaden the scope of men's emotional lives *without* losing the control men learn to take for granted. It sets different terms for this control, for it acknowledges the existence of unconscious emotions and desires that would otherwise be repressed out of existence.

Freud recognises that the Kantian terms set for modernity involved too sharp a domination of our emotional lives. It set individuals against themselves in refusing to acknowledge our existence as sexual and emotional beings. It insisted that self-control could only be gained through the domination of our emotional and sexual lives.[2] Freud sought a different accommodation with our natures. It was to recognise that repression remains a condition of civilisation, but that civilisation can be sustained by shifting the terms of this repression.

We can learn to acknowledge our emotions and desires without thereby acting upon them. This is a space that is foreclosed within a Protestant tradition, as I have discussed in *Recreating Sexual Politics* (Seidler 1991a). We learn for instance that to feel sexually attracted towards a woman when we are already in a relationship proves our evil natures. It is as if the feeling itself serves as proof of what we 'are really like'. It proves that we are the 'animals' that our parents accused us of being. To avoid this knowledge of ourselves we learn to put these emotions aside, so eradicating them from our conscious lives. We do not let these desires enter our conscious lives and so we learn to live as if they do not exist at all. This allows us to sustain the image that we have of ourselves. It is a way that men learn to create reality in their own image and to deal with any uncomfortable emotions or experiences that might interrupt these definitions of 'reality' that we do our best to sustain.

Freud can help us acknowledge these emotions as he opens up a *space* through getting us to recognise that there is an important difference that needs to be sustained between 'having' these feelings and 'acting' upon them. He recognised that the act of verbalising such desires can give us a different way of creating control in relation to them. It can be a relief as we acknowledge these feelings to ourselves and also possibly to others. It is as if the effect that is tied up with these desires can somehow be released.

So it is that Freud helps open up a critical space between emotions and actions that is so often foreclosed within a Protestant culture. He is also thereby challenging an important aspect of a Kantian tradition that holds that our emotions and desires externally determine our behaviour. He softens the distinction that Kant draws between 'reason' and 'inclinations' through his recognition that by acknowledging desires, rather than repressing them, we can gain a form of control in relation to them.

The famous case of Dora shows how Freud sustains important masculinist assumptions. This is a significant case, for it marks a crucial shift in Freud's work and it remains a crucial text for psychoanalytic training. It reveals the different ways that Freud tended to think of male and female sexuality when Dora was approached by Herr K who was a friend of her father and whose wife, Frau K, was having a relationship with her father. At the same time Freud could say, 'This was surely just the situation to call up a distinct feeling of sexual excitement in a girl of fourteen who had never before been approached' (Freud 1974, 7:28).

Dora, only 14 years old, is deviously approached, as Masson brings out in his important chapter on Dora and Freud in *Against Therapy*[3]

> by a man old enough to be her father (and with two children of his own), married to a woman who is having an affair with her father, and she is expected by Freud immediately to yield, ecstatically and without hesitation, to his sudden, un-wanted sexual advance. Dora's behaviour, then, is for Freud *proof* that she is suffering from hysteria, that she is denying (or repressing) feelings she should have had.
>
> (Masson 1989:92)

> In this sense...the behaviour of this child of fourteen was already entirely and completely hysterical. I should without question consider a person hysterical in whom an occasion for sexual excitement elicited feelings that were prepon-derantly or exclusively unpleasurable.
>
> (Freud 1974, 7:28)

What gives Freud the power to label Dora's behaviour as 'entirely and completely hysterical'? What gives him the right to use language in this way, especially when he also realised that Dora had been forced into treatment by her father in the hope, as Freud says, 'that I should "talk" Dora out of her belief that there was something more than a friendship between him and Frau K' (Freud 1974, 7:109)? Freud saw his task differently and agreed with Dora that she had not imagined, as her father claimed, the scenes she shared with Freud about Herr K's attempts to kiss her.

At the same time, Freud did agree with the father that Dora was ill and in need of treatment. At the same time he acknowledged Dora's characterisation of her father as deceitful (*unaufrichtig*) and dishonest (*falsen*). As Freud remarked,

> I could not in general dispute Dora's characterisation of her father; and there was one particular respect in which it was easy to see that her reproaches were justified. When she was feeling embittered she used to be overcome with the idea that she had been handed over to Herr K as the price of his tolerating the relations between her father and his wife; and her rage at her father's making such a use of her was visible behind her affection for him.
>
> (Freud 1974, 7:34)

In an illuminating footnote, Masson recognises that it is peculiar that Freud cannot allow his recognition of Dora's correct perceptions to stand without a challenge. It might be because Freud at some level had recognised that she had been handed over to Herr K so that in some way he had colluded in an exchange. This might explain why Freud felt obliged to add somewhat awkwardly that

> At other times she was quite well aware that she had been guilty of exaggeration in talking like this. The two men had of course never made a formal agreement in which she was treated as an object for barter. Her father in particular would have been horrified at any such suggestion.
>
> (Freud 1974, 7:34)

This is a masculine voice of authority that is coolly able to detach itself and recognise the 'exaggerations' of others. It suggests a formalism of principles with which men often learn to defend the institutional power that they hold. But as Masson insightfully says,

> What Dora said was no exaggeration of the reality at all; on the contrary, she was merely highlighting for Freud the deeper emotional reality of her father's behaviour. She was being 'insightful' and 'analytic', whereas Freud was insisting on being 'literal'. Dora, clearly, did not believe that there was a written agreement between her father and Herr K, but this hardly diminished the impact of the emotional trauma on her of being selfishly and callously used by her father, and Freud knew that she was perfectly correct.
>
> (Masson 1989:89)

But then, of course, this also raises the issue of why Freud took the case in the first place.

What seems to have embittered Dora most was the readiness of her father to disbelieve what she told him about the sexual advances that Herr K made to her on a walk after a trip on the lake. This undermined her very sense of what is real, for as Freud noted,

> None of her father's actions seemed to have embittered her so much as his readiness to consider the scene by the lake as a product of her imagination. She was almost beside herself at the idea of its being supposed that she had merely fancied [*eigebildet*, imagined] something on that occasion.
>
> (Freud 1974, 7:46)

At some level, Freud also colluded in this situation in the way that he conceived of his analytic task. For he understood that for all these years Dora had really been in love with Herr K so that her refusal had somehow to be explained. As Freud asks, 'If Dora loves Herr K, what was the reason for her refusing him in the scene by the lake?' (Freud 1974, 7:46). Since he was, according to Freud, 'still young and of prepossessing appearance (*einnehmendem Äusserin*)' (Freud 1974, 7:29), her behaviour still needed to be explained since it was assumed to be 'irrational'.

It seemed that Freud needed to return to explain why Dora was so angry at having her memory of the scene by the lake treated as a fantasy. In his words to Dora that seemed to clinch the analysis for him in an interpretation that confirmed his view that women are always in love and want to marry, he told her:

> You will agree that nothing makes you so angry as having it thought that you merely fancied the scene by the lake. I know now – and this is what you do not want to be reminded of – that you *did* fancy that Herr K's proposals were serious, and that he would not leave off until you had married him.
>
> (Freud 1974, 7:29)

In another useful footnote, Masson draws our attention to the fact that Freud deliberately uses the word *einbilden* in two different senses here:

> the first time to refer to Dora's 'imagining' the scene by the lake, and the second time (*sich einbilden*) to refer to her pride that he would ask her to marry him. By means of this pun, Freud entirely took away from Dora the full meaning of her concern with a validation of her perceptions. Freud in effect told Dora that she merely imagined the whole scene, not in the real sense of the word 'imagine', but in what he regarded as the deeper sense, namely that she had the proud notion that she would be married to Herr K. Freud substituted for Dora's legitimate concern with the truth his own limited view of what women really want.
>
> (Masson 1989:95fn)

I think Masson is also quite right to say that

Freud had just trivialised her deepest concern, and had demonstrated a total inability to understand her search for historical truth. It is not that he denied that the 'seduction' took place, but he stripped it of any significance, by giving it a totally different meaning, by 'interpreting' it. He treated her like a patient, not like a human being. Freud had never believed that Dora could be concerned with external truth.

(Masson 1989:95fn)

This is a striking insight that says something important about psychoanalytic psychotherapy. Why could Freud not recognise how painful it can be not to be believed about an incident of sexual assault so that it must be neurotic, serving some kind of defensive function? Her intense feelings about this has to be an internal pretence. As Masson has it, 'Freud's interpretations of Dora's behaviour (most of them made, let us remember, directly to her) were in the service of disavowing the apparent reality in favour of his deeper reality' (Masson 1989:96).

Freud assumed that the fact that Dora found the idea that she had imagined the situation so hurtful meant that these thoughts were charged with energy from other, deeply repressed and unconscious, trains of thought. Freud thought that Dora was identifying both with her mother and with Frau K because she was in love with her father. As the story goes, for Freud she wanted her father for herself, for she wanted him to love her to the exclusion of all others. This insight somehow took precedence over the fact that Dora needed *protection* from her father which he was incapable of providing, for he was also directly responsible for the danger that she was in from Herr K. The fact that her father refused to accept what she was saying was all the more hurtful because he was her father. If she could not look towards him for protection, who could she be expected to trust?

In the face of Freud's idea that Dora fell ill because she was in love with too many people and loved them too much, it was difficult for him to hear that she did not want, but was repulsed by, Herr K's sexual moves towards her. The fact that Dora had a 'violent feeling of disgust, tore herself from the man' (Freud 1974, 7:28) became on Freud's assumptions something that needed to be explained. Even though she avoided being alone with Herr K, Freud never seems to have believed Dora's conscious 'no', believing also that 'there is no such thing at all as an unconscious "no"' (Freud 1974, 7:57). It was one thing to reconcile himself to her father's refusal to hear what she says, but she also had to accept that Freud was no longer prepared to accept that her distress could have been brought on by the attempted seduction and then the recognition of her father's collusion. For Freud it remained a distress of her own making, for what becomes significant is not the seduction that falls into the background even when it is acknowledged, but her individual way of responding to it.

EMOTIONS AND REALITY

If Freud shows us the existence and effects of emotions that exist outside the sphere of conscious awareness, say in the feelings of love, jealousy and hatred which

Dora's dreams reveal that she was otherwise not consciously aware of, there is still a critical issue of the extent to which her unconscious feelings are anchored in reality. As Masson says, 'If her dreams revealed that she was disappointed she had every right to be disappointed' (Masson 1989:100).

If Masson tends to think that therapy is essentially flawed and coercive, for it ends up by substituting a person's conception of their own reality with that of the therapist, he does identify important questions about the validation of people's realities. Dora knew that her father, the person who should have stood by her, had failed her, so that it was hardly surprising, as Freud reports, that 'She was constantly comparing me with him consciously, and kept anxiously trying to make sure whether I was being quite straightforward with her, for her father "always preferred secrecy and roundabout ways"' (Freud 1974, 7:118). Freud was concerned not with corroborating her vision of the world but with proving the correctness of his own psychological theories. But it can be misleading to say, as Masson does, that 'he simply ignored one kind of reality in his search for another, for one that *he* regarded as deeper' (Masson 1989:101).

It could have been possible to confirm Dora's reality and the feelings she felt at the betrayal of her father, with an exploration of Dora's feelings about the people involved. This did not have to be a matter of substituting one reality for another, but it is crucial to recognise that whatever her feelings, she could say *no* to the sexual advances. Freud failed to support Dora when she needed it and in the end offered 'interpretations' that pushed her to accept the solution that society wanted of her which was to close her eyes to what was happening around her. Masson is surely right that

> If Freud could not take up the struggle on her behalf (and on behalf of other women patients similarly abused) he could at least have walked away from their tormentors in disgust and washed his hands of the emotional and intellectual corruption that surrounded him.
>
> (Masson 1989: 102)

Discounting a person's reality and substituting a psychological task for it so easily becomes a flaw of psychoanalytic method. It cuts the inner processes from an ongoing relationship with external reality and so separates the 'inner' from the 'outer'. It can thus seem feasible to say that the workings of psychoanalysis have to do with the workings of these inner mental processes and the 'realities' that they help to sustain. It is not that external realities are denied but that they are simply not the guiding concern of psychoanalytic practice. So it can be said that it is not Freud's concern to deny the reality of Dora's seduction, for whether it happened or not is beside the point for psychoanalysis. It is supposedly not part of its legitimate interest since in any case it would still have to deal with the inner mental processes that cannot be grasped, as some would think Masson does, as reflections of external processes.

This is a powerful argument that was often heard against Masson's early book on Freud, *The Assault on Truth* (Masson 1984). I am sure that Jeffrey Masson's more generalised assault in *Against Therapy* will make it easier for many to ignore the substance of the crucial issues he raises. Whether we think that it is the abandonment of the seduction theory and the recognition of the power of suppressed fantasies and infantile desires that makes what we know as psychoanalysis possible, the form that psychoanalytic psychotherapy has taken has largely been set in this break. I think that Masson has hit on something important, if terribly uncomfortable.[4] We have had to take seriously the deafening silence of psychoanalysis upon questions of sexual abuse and its difficulties until very recently in recognising the reality of these traumatic experiences and the damage to lives. There is a continuing tendency to recognise these as events within the 'inner lives' of women, rather than with the difficulties of transforming relationships in a way that makes abuse less likely.[5]

Psychoanalysis, in its attempt to present itself as dispassionate and objective, thinks that it can work without having to take sides. The case of Dora shows that this is not possible and that in such situations moral judgements simply cannot be suspended or put aside. It has to be said that the sexual abuse of children should not happen and that the child is *never* to blame. Freud tragically made it possible to blame the victim. Psychoanalysis has refused to take sides and in taking this stance it has unwittingly taken sides with the powerful.

Freud never seemed to appreciate, as psychoanalysis has failed to since, that it is crucial for Dora and others who might be similarly abused to hear the truth spoken and to know that they have nothing to blame themselves for. A psychoanalytic tradition that can only deal with 'psychological truth' and can only deal with this in personal and subjective terms, fails in this crucial regard. This is not simply an error of individual judgement but it points to the structure of the theory itself.

At some level this has to do with psychoanalysis' relationship with morality. It has a difficulty, in some ways shared with Marxism, in distinguishing between morality and moralism. Freud had good reasons to be suspicious of a moralism that had dealt so harshly with questions of sexuality. But if moralism can be connected to issues of sexual repression, the same thing should not be said about morality. Freud tended to identify morality with the super-ego and with the workings of authority. He knew that authorities use morality to defend their own powers in society. Freud wanted to use science against morality very much in positivist terms.[6]

This made it difficult for Freud to say to Dora that what had happened to her was terrible and should not have occurred and that her father should have supported her in the situation. But this would be deemed to reflect a lack of objectivity and professionalism. At best, it might be conceived of as a personal opinion that should not be allowed to intrude into the objective processes of therapy.

This connects to the methodological issue that allowed Freud, whenever Dora complained about anybody, to turn it back against her:

A string of reproaches against other people leads one to suspect the existence of a string of self-reproaches with the same content. All that needs to be done is to turn back each particular reproach onto the speaker himself.

(Freud 1974, 7:35)

This is a technique that goes well beyond psychoanalysis and is often invoked in traditional forms of psychotherapy. If it often yields important lines of emotional investigation it can also distract people from the source of their anger, resentment or frustration. In support of this it is often said that 'we cannot change the world' so it is not a matter of working out whether it is right or wrong, but simply our responses to it. Often this is useful advice, say for example, in bringing us to realise that it is often hopeless to wait for our parents to change, but that possibly *we* can learn to relate to them in different ways. This might help us to accept them as they are, rather than as what we might have wanted them to be.

It might also be true, for example, that if we allow ourselves to express the anger and resentment we feel for someone in a management position at work, we will simply lose our jobs. It might be better to recognise this as we learn different ways of dealing with the situation. But at the same time it can be important to develop forms of psychotherapy – if this remains the right term – that do not at the same time *invalidate* our own anger, resentment and frustration by turning it against ourselves or by tacitly accepting that we feel angry with our boss *because* we have never resolved an issue of authority in our relationships with our fathers. This can unwittingly mean that we shift our focus away from the everyday relationships at work to their 'true cause' in our unresolved relationships with our fathers. This is often easy to do since most of us never seem completely to resolve these parental relationships, however hard we seem to work on them.

In some situations it might be important for therapists not to take sides so they can work, for instance, with a couple that is having difficulties in relating. It is not a matter of apportioning blame and responsibility and sometimes this cautions a response which seeks to attribute blame on the assumption that this goes to the heart of the matter. A therapist might refuse, preferring to explore how both partners are involved in maintaining the relationship as it is. If it is a mater of the couple deciding upon whether their relationship will continue, then this is a choice that they will have to make for themselves.

It can be important in such contexts for therapists to refuse to play judge and so it might seem important to put their moral judgements aside. But then again a therapist's views about feminism, for instance, no less than Freud's, can have a significant impact upon what he or she might say in the situation. What is more, if these views are never allowed to the surface as having no relevance to what is going on in the sessions, then it becomes impossible for people to make clear judgements about the kind of therapy they want for themselves.

If Freud was to conclude that Dora had a hidden agenda, wanting to take vengeance on men and, more generally, on the hypocrisy of adults, this was no less true of Freud who, in patriarchal fashion, often assumed that he knew what was best for people. Freud had decided that a good outcome for all concerned would be for Herr K to divorce his wife and marry Dora once she reached the age of 16. This was the masculine voice of reason that allows men to legislate what is best for others. In this regard at least, psychoanalysis serves to reformulate a masculine and rationalist project. It sets different terms by including what is going on below conscious awareness to provide a revitalised model of rationality. In this regard Freud learned to displace the 'surface' of Dora's experience, for he was convinced that she was moved by forces which operated beyond the level of her emotional awareness.

This seems to excuse Freud from taking seriously the 'reality' as Dora experiences it, or presents it, for he can argue that his concern goes deeper to Dora's 'true interests', not as she happens to experience them herself. Like many fathers, he would claim to know what was best for her. But Dora had got to this conclusion before Freud, for she had recognised, as Masson put it, that 'Freud *was* like her father. He cared about his own interests far more than he cared about hers' (Masson 1989:102).

Dora had good reasons to distrust men and adults in general. She had put her confidence in people, only to have it betrayed. Freud saw it as taking revenge but it seems more a matter of courageously confronting the adults with the reality of what they had done to her. Once she had established the truth she was through with them. She told Freud that she had confronted her parents with the historical truth, but it was hard for him to recognise this as courage rather than 'acting out' or 'revenge', since all along it had been important for Freud to use Dora's case to convince Fliess and his other colleagues that the cause of Dora's suffering came from internal fantasies, not external injuries. For Freud, the true source of Dora's hysteria lay in the fact that she had masturbated as a child. At the end of the case, almost as an appeal to Fliess, as Masson notes, Freud concluded that 'it is the therapeutic technique alone that is purely psychological; the theory does not by any means fail to point out that neuroses have an organic basis' (Freud 1974, 7:113).

According to Freud, Dora is sick because she cannot feel love for Herr K and she cannot do this because she cannot acknowledge her love for her father. She has not passed through a normal development stage of a slow disillusion with her father, a slow detachment from exclusive sexual love for him. In Freud's 1896 paper on hysteria this premature libidinal fixation was usually accounted for by seduction, but this proved very unpopular, and with masturbation it was much easier to reject the external genesis of neuroses and to blame it on the patient herself.

Masturbation, especially in women, was a familiar theme in medical literature in Freud's time. Dora allowed Freud to prove this revision of his theory and as Philip Rieff has pointed out in his introduction to the Dora case,

> Freud is not interested in all truths, and certainly not in Dora's, except in so far as they block the operation of his own. Because Dora's insights are part of her illness, Freud had to hammer away at them as functions of her resistance to his insight.
>
> (Rieff 1963:11)

Dora's truth had to do with the anger that she felt towards Herr K and towards her father for betraying her and using her for his own sexual ends. But this is not an anger that she is allowed to have, for it signifies something other than the meaning that it has for her. Freud seems convinced that her anger has to be 'interpreted', for as far as he is concerned it is not appropriate to the situation. It is not a rational response to a sexual advance, especially as Freud surmised Dora was in love with Herr K. For Freud her behaviour had to be motivated by emotions that Dora was not consciously aware of for, as Freud holds, 'how could a girl who is in love feel insulted by a proposal which was made in a manner neither tactless nor offensive?' (Freud 1974, 7:95).

Freud was somehow convinced that Dora's anger and revulsion were not legitimate reactions to an external situation but to an inner movement of feeling of which she was unaware. Her anger needs to be explained – and so explained away – for it is assumed not to be rational. It is in this regard that Freud's interpretations serve to invalidate Dora's experience and so work to diminish her in her own eyes. Freud can respond that his primary response cannot be with the validation of her experience, for he is concerned to cure her illness. Freud has to look beneath the level of her experience and conscious awareness to reveal the unconscious processes that are at work to determine the shape that her experience takes. To restrict psychoanalysis to a validation of people'e experience in the terms that they conceive of it themselves is supposedly to block its investigations before they have really got going.

There is something to be said for this and for the idea that Masson is in danger of short-circuiting a process by too readily assuming that therapy involves the substitution of the therapist's sense of reality for the client's who has come in search of help. This move is made too quickly, and sadly it probably means that many people will be deaf to the very real and important challenges that Masson makes in *The Assault on Truth* and *Against Therapy*. But there is something else here too, for Masson is quite right to insist that Freud fails to validate Dora's experience in a way that she could legitimately expect. She has a right to hear that she need not tolerate sexual advances that are not welcome to her and that if she says no it is important that her 'no' is understood and respected. Freud can so easily be read as unwittingly perpetuating the notion that 'when women say "no" they mean "yes"'. It is as if he undermines Dora's trust in her own judgement by saying that 'if she really thinks about it she will discover that she is in love with Herr K and so really at some "unconscious" level welcomes his advances'.[7]

This is a pernicious line of thought that is so easily used to undermine people's sense of trust and confidence in themselves. It abuses the language of the unconscious in a way that is used against the people themselves. This is a dangerous power that lies in the hands of the analyst who speaks from a position of power and authority that within modernity is shaped by the particular identification of masculinity with reason. The analyst so easily presents him or herself as the person who knows our unconscious feelings and desires. This authority can be particularly difficult to resist within a Protestant culture in which women are constantly being told that 'they do not know their own minds'. As we learn to distrust our natures as 'evil' or 'animal', so we learn that 'others know best'. This is an authority that our parents and teachers are used to claiming as their own. Since they supposedly have our 'best interests at heart' we learn to listen to them before we really learn to listen to ourselves. Psychoanalysis unwittingly exploits these masculinist relationships of power and authority. This power is reinforced in the silence of the therapist, who can wait patiently for the 'patient' to reveal, while they remain silent themselves.

SEXUALITY AND DEVALUATION

In Masson's chapter on 'Dora and Freud' he points out that

> It is not, really, that Freud disagreed with Dora. He simply ignored her needs in service of his own, which was to find more evidence for the correctness of his psychological theories. His task, he felt, was not to corroborate her vision of the world (even when he shared it), but to probe beneath and behind it, in short, to interpret: 'He that has eyes to see and ears to hear may convince himself that no mortal can keep a secret. If his lips are silent, he chatters with his finger tips; betrayal oozes out of him at every pore.'
>
> (Freud 1974, 7:18; Masson 1989:101)

At some level the issue remains as to whether Freud's conception of his task of 'interpretation' allowed him to hear what Dora was saying. I do not think that Masson can so easily surmise that no doubt Freud 'would have agreed that the world, certainly Dora's world, was precisely the way she saw it', only to say 'but that kind of vision did not interest him very much' (Masson 1989:101). I do not agree with Masson that, as he puts it in another context, 'It is in the nature of therapy to distort another person's reality' (Masson 1989:247). But I do think real issues are raised in the way Freud conceived of 'interpretation'. Here it is not simply an issue of whether 'patients' are 'ready' to accept the interpretations that analysts offer, but the ways these interpretations connect and engage with a person's own experience.

When Freud says of Dora that she is really in love with Herr K, it is easy to hear her denial as a form of 'resistance' to a truth he has independently discounted since he has an access to her unconscious life not available to her. Since these forces operate at a level supposedly 'deeper' than the level of her conscious experiences, Freud does not really have to dwell upon the ways that she might experience things herself. Freud was often more sensitive than this and the complexity of his case studies testifies to the fact that he did not cover up the complexities he saw. But the objectivity that Freud built into his concept of 'interpretation' meant that a distance could be sustained as the analyst learned to conceive of his or her task in neutral and impersonal terms.

This can make psychoanalysts less likely to validate a person's experience out of a fear that this would be to 'take sides' or to become 'personally involved'. The analysts in traditional Freudian analysis learned to be detached. They can be so keen not to interfere with the process of transference that they do not want to intrude personally to affirm an experience. Their task is to act as an impartial mirror, the silent, if benevolent, father who is ready to hear whatever the child has to say. If this process serves to infantilise the 'patient' who remains powerless in the situation, it is said that this is proof of the potency of transference.

Freud used the Dora case to set out some of his initial notions of transference within the psychoanalytic process. This provided for ways of shifting attention away from the suffering of Dora herself and served to deflect any dissatisfaction she could be feeling through a failure to be recognised in the analysis itself. Freud assumed, as Masson has it,

> that *any* negative qualities Dora could find in him that were reminiscent of Herr K would be due exclusively to the transference; that is, they would be fantasies. But the evidence seems to suggest that Dora did, in fact, perceive similarities between Herr K and Freud that were *not* the product of her imagination. They were real. Freud was not interested in Dora's truth any more than Herr K was.
> (Masson 1989:114)

Freud acknowledged that he had failed in his goal to get Dora to see her own complicity in the tragic situation she was in. It is often said that only by accepting her own responsibility would Dora have been able to free herself from her situation. But it might be that it is only if Dora had felt *recognised* in her anger and pain about the assault that the door might have been open for this kind of awareness of her own involvement. This is an insight of feminism and consciousness-raising. It might well have been that Dora needed to be supported in her sense that what happened should *not* have happened, whatever her involvement might have been.

For Dora, complicity can in no way excuse the behaviour of Herr K and her father towards her. It is only if the truth of the abuse is fully recognised and her feelings of anger and pain validated that she might go on to investigate other aspects. But Freud would not acknowledge the truth of her feelings for he wanted to discount the effects of the attempted seduction. He did not want to account for the intensity of her feelings as an outcome of such an external trauma. It was important for him to establish psychoanalysis upon different foundations.

Freud attributed his failure to the fact that he had not fully acknowledged the negative transference, that is, the fact that Dora ascribed to Freud qualities that really belonged to Herr K, and as Masson says, so 'was bound to treat Freud as she wished to treat Herr K: vengefully' (Masson 1989:113). This failure allowed Dora to 'act out' these memories rather than talk about them, by deserting Freud 'as she believed herself to have been deceived and deserted by him'. But this serves to protect the analyst and serves to infantilise the person who is supposedly not acting freely and independently. It so easily becomes a way of holding on to the client, who cannot leave without such an accusation being levelled. It leaves the analyst innocent in the situation, able to tell him or herself that they are just trying to help.

It is a way that systematically absolves the analyst from having to take any responsibility for the ways they behave during the course of the analysis. It is as if it is never legitimate to be angry at them, for this *has* to be an 'acting out' to do with the workings of transference. It allows the analyst as the person in power to feel unchallenged. It is another form of the powerful being able to blame the victim and being absolved from having to take critical responsibility for the power they exercise in the situation.

The powerful have language at their disposal to treat the powerless with contempt. The fact that analysts supposedly work as screens to allow a transference to take place can easily blind them to the power that they hold. If there is frustration and anger expressed at them it can always be deflected, for its real cause always lies elsewhere. Once Freud had stopped believing in a 'real' seduction as the origin of hysteria, he placed the source of neurosis in the child's fantasies. Later analysts were to speak of Dora with contempt. As Ernest Jones, Freud's English biographer, said of her many years later, setting the seal of history:

> Dora was a disagreeable creature who consistently put revenge before love; it was the same motive that led her to break off the treatment prematurely, and to retain various hysterical symptoms, both bodily and mental.
>
> (Jones 1958:287)

Significant light is thrown on some of these issues by the secret diary of Sandor Ferenczi, for many years one of Freud's closest associates and acknowledged by Freud as having more compassion for his patients. Ferenczi was beginning to wonder about what Masson calls 'the covert sadism in psychotherapy' (Masson 1989:117). In what amounts to a startling and unparalleled confession, Ferenczi wrote in his diary on July 27:

> We greet the patient in a friendly manner, make sure the transference will take, and while the patient lies there in misery, we sit comfortably in our armchair, quietly smoking a cigar. We make conventional and formulaic interpretations in a bored tone and occasionally we fall asleep. In the best of cases the analyst makes a colossal effort to overcome his yawning boredom and behave in a friendly and compassionate manner. Were we to encourage our patients to real freedom (of expression), and to overcome their anxiety and embarrassment towards us, we would soon learn that patients at some level are acutely aware of all our real feelings and thoughts.
>
> (Ferenczi 1932/1985:246)

Ferenczi is aware of how the relations of power work to make people feel anxious and embarrassed towards the analysts in a way that blocks their own awareness and understanding.

As Masson reports it, Ferenczi felt that

> Something of the hypocritical, harmful atmosphere of analysis was caused by a wrong theoretical expectation, namely that patients could not distinguish between what really happened to them and what they imagined happened to them.

This, in Ferenczi's opinion, was Freud's greatest initial error, which had started psychoanalysis in a wrong direction, and from which it had never really recovered.

(Masson 1989:123)

Masson thinks that Ferenczi brings the very nature of therapy into question. I am less sure, though it is clear that he challenges the power relations implicit with traditional psychoanalytic practice, and questions the character of the transference they sustain. He recognises the importance of validating a person's experience and comes to realise that it is wrong for therapists to present themselves as the source of all knowledge. It is this masculinist vision that is embodied in the idea that the analyst is the source of reason and that he or she can alone discern what is 'real' and 'unreal' in the situation. It is a power that is also invoked by doctors and teachers and all those who see themselves within the terms of modernity as exclusively the source of knowledge.

We learn to be silent in the presence of those in authority and to speak only when we are spoken to. Analysis provides something different, as Ferenczi makes clear, but it often fails to deliver what it seems to promise. The analyst learns to stay aloof, since the clarity of a rational vision can so easily be threatened by the emotional confusions that the client or patient offers. If the rigours of reason are to be sustained, the analyst must be careful not to get emotionally involved with a subjective experience that can so easily threaten the objectivity of his vision. As Ferenczi wrote in his diary on 13 August,

Index of the Sins of Psychoanalysis (reproaches made by a woman patient): Psychoanalysis entices patients into 'transference'.
Naturally the patient interprets the (imagined) deep understanding of the analyst, his great interest in the fine details of the story of her life and her emotions, as a sign of deep personal interest, even tenderness. Since most patients have been emotionally shipwrecked, and will cling to any straw, they become blind and deaf to signs that would show them how little *personal* interest analysts have in their patients. Meanwhile the unconscious of the patient perceives all of the analyst's negative feelings (boredom, irritation, and hate when the patient says anything unpleasant or provokes the analyst's complexes).

(Ferenczi 1932/1985:232)

It becomes difficult for a patient to challenge an analyst without having this challenge turned back so the analyst is left strangely invulnerable. Because of this relationship of power, as Ferenczi describes it,

Analysis is an easy opportunity to carry out unconscious, purely selfish, unscrupulous, immoral, even criminal acts and a chance to act out such behaviour guiltlessly (without feeling guilt), for example, a feeling of power over the number of helplessly worshipful patients, who admire the analyst unreservedly; a feeling of sadistic pleasure in their suffering and their helplessness.

(Ferenczi 1932/1985:232)

Ferenczi goes on to conclude that

> As a result of infantile experiences similar to this it becomes impossible for patients to detach themselves from the analysis even after long and successful work... just as it is impossible for a child to run away from home, because, left on its own, it would feel helpless.
>
> (Ferenczi 1932/1985:232)

This is a powerful recognition of the way that analysis can submerge people in an infantile relationship of dependency from which they cannot escape. To say that this is just the point since it is the transference that allows for these infantile emotions and feelings to be faced and dealt with, does not resolve the issues of power and dependency presented here.

Ferenczi recognised that a therapist cannot be an indifferent spectator to the suffering being relived in his or her presence. But if one is to take it completely seriously, then one must really, as Masson reports it, 'enter the past with the patient, that is really believe in the reality of the event. "Freud would not permit me to do this," Ferenczi complained. He wrote that to remain on an intellectual plane, without allowing one's feelings to enter, is subtly to encourage the patient to feel that the event could not have taken place' (Ferenczi 1932/1985:126). Analysis seems simply to continue a denial that so often surrounds the child already. As Ferenczi reports,

> In most cases of infantile trauma, the parents have no interest in engraving the incidents in the memory of the child, and, quite the contrary, almost always employ a kind of repression therapy: 'It is nothing'. 'Nothing happened.' 'Don't think about it any more.'....The events are silenced to death, the hesitant hints given by the child are not taken in, or are resolved as impossible. And this is done so systematically and is in such conformity to what everybody else believes that the child's own judgement cedes.
>
> (Ferenczi 1932/1985:72)

It says something about Dora's courage and tenacity that she did not let go of what she knew to be true. This was not a matter of 'psychological truth' but her sense of what abuse she suffered in reality. She knew that it was not her fault or something that she somehow imagined or brought on herself. It also says something important about Freud and psychoanalysis that he did not appreciate how *important* it was for Dora to be believed. Once the truth of her assault had been acknowledged it might have been possible for her to acknowledge other feelings in the situation. Freud tended to think that if he had focused on the counter-transference,

> her attention would have been turned to some detail in our relations, or in my person or circumstances, behind which there lay concealed something analogous but immeasurably more important concerning Herr K. And when this

transference had been cleared up, the analysis would have obtained access to new memories, dealing probably with actual events.

(Freud 1974, 7:118)

But it was partly because Freud could not or would not validate Dora's experience of 'actual events' that the analysis did not succeed.

EMOTIONS AND MEMORIES

This remains paradoxical, for in many ways Freud is concerned to help people accept the truth of their experience rather than to deny it. He works for instance to help people accept the reality of their feelings of loss and grief which are so often invalidated within a utilitarian culture that teaches that mourning is 'useless' because it cannot bring people back. Rather than distracting people from their misery and pain in a set of activities, Freud recognises the need for time and space within which people can experience their loss. So it is that he helps people to respect rituals that acknowledge the importance of mourning in people's lives. He helps people to validate an experience and give voice to their feelings of loss and bereavement. It is important, as I have already argued, to have rituals that can help with expression and support people through. Freud knows that a utilitarian language that disdains these experiences and encourages a notion of strength as denial will often make matters worse for people in the long run.

If language can serve to invalidate particular emotions and feelings, it can also be used to bring people into *contact* with these aspects of their experience. But this involves healing the separation between language and feelings and refusing to see language as a rational tool somehow able to form reality in its own image. But again it is important to recognise that we cannot say in advance how a person will feel for it will very much depend upon the relationship they have had with the person who died. It might be that there is guilt and remorse about how they treated them when they were alive so that it is difficult for this mourning process to take place. It is as if people can be locked into a permanent state of mourning. At some level this is their 'reality'. It might be said in interpretive terms that we have to accept the meanings that people have chosen to give to their experience.

But the issue of meaning is not so straightforward, and Freud can help us rethink the rationalist terms of a Weberian interpretive tradition. There are times when Freud helps us acknowledge that if the mourning seems endless and goes hand in hand with an idealisation of the person, then we can suspect that the person is not being fulfilled or satisfied through their mourning and that something else is stirring beyond the reaches of their conscious awareness. Linguistic theorists often say that we cannot speculate what is in people's minds but we can only draw the meanings they give to their existence from the language they use.

Freud helps us recognise this as a limited vision of language in its relationship to experience. He wants to say that we do not have to invalidate a person's experience, nor do we have to replace one sense of reality with another, as Masson has it. When we draw their attention to the frustration they feel and the ways they never feel satisfied or completed in their mourning, this can help put them in touch with this experience themselves. They might also reflect if there are other areas of feeling that they are not touching or allowing to surface.

It is possible for people literally to eat themselves up with remorse, unable to face the guilt that they feel at the ways they treated someone when they were alive. Sometimes this is a process that is not susceptible to therapy for people prefer to live with their idealisations, possibly unable to face the anger that was expressed towards them in the dying weeks of a person's life. They might insist in the face of these facts that they always treated the person well and that they were always loved and respected themselves. This might be the 'truth' that someone prefers to live with, even if at the same time they are being incapacitated with remorse.

But if this is something that they are not prepared to acknowledge themselves, refusing all forms of help offered, then there is little that can be done. But this is not simply a 'reality' which they have constructed for themselves that is somehow to be placed on a par with other definitions of reality. For at some level it is also a choice to live out a lie, to insist that the relationship with the dead person was other than it was. It is the consequences of these different 'visions of reality' that an interpretive tradition has failed to track and illuminate, both for the individuals themselves and for the relationships they sustain.

Thinking about a different situation, it might be that a woman has idealised her father who has recently died, because of the difficulties that she has facing up to the way she was physically and emotionally abused as a child. She has learned to minimise what happened to her partly as a way of coping with it, but also, as Ferenczi illuminates, because of the way these experiences had been 'silenced to death' within the family. As her 'own judgement cedes' her experience is invalidated and she comes to exist in relation to others. She learns to please others but is left with a weak sense of her own identity. She finds it hard to share herself in relationships, for if she were to open up these memories would come to consciousness. She learns to live as if they did not happen at all. She says that she is not interested in exploring her past but has learned to put this aside so that she can live in the present. Even if this approach is culturally encouraged within modernity, Freud can help us discern some of its costs.

But at some level Freud seems less tuned into issues of relationships as he tends to focus his attention on the individual's emotional life, seeing relationships as projections. It is as if others exist as 'objects' for our libidinal desires. When Freud thinks of sexuality he thinks in terms of desire, not in terms of the quality of our relationships with others. This somehow falls into the background as we are encouraged to focus on tracing the movement or otherwise of our desire.

It can foster the idea that fulfilment is bound to elude us, for our relationships are in the service of a return to primary ties, either as an attempt to rework them or else to taste something that we still miss. It is partly because development is seen in masculinist terms as a move from dependency towards autonomy as rational independence in a modified form, that female sexuality and relationships come to seem enigmatic for Freud.[8] It seems hard for him not to see women in terms of the experience of men, for supposedly, as we are all individuals, there has to be a single line of development.

Ferenczi reports that the child who had been abused often attempts to protect herself by saying 'it cannot be true, that all of this happened to me; for surely if it had, somebody would have come to my assistance'. This seems to explain why it is so important for a therapist to believe in the reality of the event. But is this possible to do if the analyst stays, as Freud suggests, on an intellectual plane, and is Ferenczi right that without allowing our feelings to enter is, as Masson reports it, 'subtly to encourage the patient to feel that the event could not have taken place' (Masson 1989:126)? Of course, there are different ways of allowing one's feelings to enter and there is always a danger of over-identification with the person's pain. But having said this, it can still be crucial to affirm and validate a person's pain and the reality of the situation they describe. The therapist cannot take the pain away but he or she can be there with the person as they relive aspects of this pain.

Since it is so important for a person to feel heard, for as Ferenczi notes, when a person has been the victim of trauma she or he needs an enormous amount of genuine love, it is important for therapists to admit when they cannot take something in. But this is what makes therapy so difficult, for people cannot simply be trained to listen in this way. If this is an intellectualised listening that cannot take the emotional content to heart it can simply continue the denial. It would be better, and more honest, to break with the impersonalising of the analyst, to say, as Ferenczi suggests, 'I have so many personal difficulties of my own that it is only with great difficulty that I can hear about yours' (Ferenczi 1932/1985:72).

The analyst learns to smile in a friendly and encouraging manner but often this is false, especially if the analyst is not continually working on himself. Ferenczi questions the idea of a training in analysis as a once and for all experience. As he confesses,

> I have yet to see a single case of a training analysis, my own included, that was so complete that such corrections, both in life and in analysis, would be unnecessary.
>
> (Ferenczi 1932/1985:73)

It is because children are so often lied to that it is crucial for therapists to be truthful. But this is far more difficult to achieve than an attitude of mind and it involves therapists learning how to be true to themselves. In large part, dominant traditions of social theory, as we have explored them, have lost a sense of the importance of truth in people's lives and will often treat these issues pragmatically or in post-structuralist terms as the effects of power. In large part, psychoanalysis has sustained a masculinist rationalist tradition that sees the analyst as the source of truth while the patients only have subjecive experience and emotions. It is partly because of these epistemological assumptions that traditionally the analyst does not see him or herself as *working with* people to sort out the truth of their experience.

Rather, it is traditionally a matter of delivering 'interpretations' that will hopefully yield insights into the patient.

Chapter 15

Dependency

LANGUAGE AND EMPOWERMENT

Sandor Ferenczi helps us to understand how psychoanalysis constructs a situation that so often perpetuates a dependency at the same time as it takes itself to be preparing the conditions for freedom and autonomy. He believes that this has to do with the relationships of power and authority which it embodies. It encourages those in authority to present themselves as in the possession of truth, thinking that this allows a transference to take place.

It makes it difficult for therapists to share their own experience and doubts out of a fear that this might 'interfere' with the transference. But when Ferenczi admitted to a patient his doubts and fears 'that the whole thing will be a failure and that you will end up insane or will commit suicide' he got the response that

> Had I, early on, been able to bring my father to make such a confession about the truth, and to recognise the danger that I was in, it would have saved my mental health. For this confession would have shown me that I was right when I spoke about things that seemed to be impossible.
>
> (Ferenczi 1932/1985:86)

This led Ferenczi to wonder whether 'the whole plan of "mutuality" was not...an unconsciously sought antidote against the hypnotic lies of childhood'. Without underestimating the experience a therapist has which probably has as much to do with the ways they have worked on themselves as it has with a theoretical grasp, Ferenczi formulates his ideas of mutual analysis in a way that brings them closer to the practice of consciousness-raising. It had to do with challenging the prevailing analytical relationships of power. As he describes it in his diary on 13 March,

> Certain phases of mutual analysis represent the total giving up of all force and all authority, on both sides. They give the impression of two children of the same age, who had been terrified, and who tell each other about their experiences. Because they have the same fate, they understand each other completely and instinctively seek to comfort one another. The knowledge that each has experi-

enced a similar fate permits the partner to appear totally harmless, a person to whom one can safely entrust oneself.

(Ferenczi 1932/1985:106–7)

It is difficult to build up trust if there is fear of the analyst and the traditional relationships of authority tend to foster anxiety, as can the silence of the analyst. If this supposedly gives 'material' for the analysis, it also takes it off in a particular direction. Ferenczi thought that 'to undo infantile amnesia, one must enjoy total freedom from fear of the analyst'. If you are left with a feeling that you might not be believed it is difficult to trust and share yourself. You learn to do what is expected by the therapist so as not to disappoint them or to leave yourself feeling that you have failed again. If the therapist is more prepared to share his or her own experience, it can help to give reality to the situation. It leaves you feeling less isolated and alone and it can also help you to feel understood. It can help to empower you as you realise that people 'in authority' also have difficulties in their relationships.

It was part of the value of consciousness-raising that women learned that others shared similar feelings and experiences. It helped to break the fragmentation and isolation that is so much part of urban life. This is also the strength of group therapy in which you can empathise with the struggles of others and also be moved by their different experiences. It is partly the authority relationships that can make it hard for therapists to hear what is said, as they are often tacitly looking for interpretations that often resonate unknowingly with their own experience. It is partly because they are trained to hold back to take an objective stance that they can be locked into their own perceptions. Because they share so little of themselves they often get little from the encounters, since it is so much a one-way process. Like others in relationships of power they are often isolated, and learn to resent and disdain those who are dependent on them.

Ferenczi recognised that analysts, like others in positions of power, can so easily use people to satisfy their own neurotic needs. He felt, according to Masson, that he had been so treated by Freud and that this sensitised him to the harm that can be done. 'He felt that Freud had treated him as he had treated all his patients, with a certain callous indifference to their *real suffering*' (Masson 1989:129). He remembers certain statements Freud makes that bear not just on Freud himself but on the difficulties of the traditional analytic relationship. They also have to do with the disdain that is so often the other side of masculine power and authority. Again, it is not just that the analytic relationship can be abused, but that it is constructed on false assumptions which often serve to disempower the very people they are supposed to help. This does not discount the experience of the many people who have been genuinely helped through these relationships.

In a remarkable passage in Ferenczi's diary (1 May 1932) he writes of Freud that

He said that patients are only riffraff. The only thing patients were good for is to help the analyst make a living and to provide material for theory. It is clear that we cannot help them. This is therapeutic nihilism. Nevertheless, we entice patients by concealing these doubts and by arousing their hopes of being cured. I think that in the beginning Freud really believed in analysis; he followed Breuer enthusiastically, involved himself passionately and selflessly in the therapy of neurotics (lying on the floor for hours, if necessary, next to a patient in the throes of a hysterical crisis). However, certain experiences must have first alarmed him and then left him disillusioned....The discovery of the mendacity of hysterical women, since the time of this discovery, Freud no longer likes sick people. He rediscovered his love for his orderly, cultivated superego....He is still attached to analysis intellectually, but not emotionally.

(Ferenczi 1932/1985:148–9)

It can be difficult to share in the pain of others, especially if you have few opportunities to share your own. This is why it is so crucial for therapists to keep working on themselves. It can also mean changing the way that the therapeutic relationship is conceived as bringing in the 'mutuality' that Ferenczi mentions. Therapists can learn to share relevant aspects of their own experience in a way that can help to validate what the person has shared.

Unlike Masson, I think such changes are possible at least within psychotherapy, if not within traditional psychoanalysis. Of course this relates to the conceptions we have of how people change and the relationship of change to empowerment. It is these questions which feminism has raised in suggesting that it is possible to have authority while treating others as equals. But this is a natural authority that grows out of experience and out of a readiness to share one's own vulnerability. It is not an authority that Freud seems to have believed in.

To what extent can social theory be empowering? Feminism has shown how important it is for women to have learned that what they had taken as a private and individual experience is in fact a shared social experience. As women learned to remake themselves, they learned to remake the relationships that sustain them. Women learned to speak for themselves and so grew in their own authority. It helped them question authorities that they had always learned to take for granted. Women learned that the ways that they feel about themselves individually cannot be separated from their position of subordination within the larger society.

Since Freud has insisted on viewing women's sexuality in masculine terms as lacking, it has been important to challenge the terms of psychoanalytic theory. Juliet Mitchell and others have looked towards Lacan, arguing that he helps to give symbolic form to the powerlessness of women so that, for instance, penis envy symbolises an absence of social power.[1] But whether this is tenable has to be doubted in the face of the way Lacan conceived of the issues facing Dora:[2]

As is true for all women, and for a reason, that are at the very basis of the most elementary forms of social experience (the very reasons that Dora gives as the ground for her revolt), the problem of her condition is fundamentally that of accepting herself as an object of desire for the man.

(Bernheimer and Kahane 1985:99)

Feminism has been insistent in its argument that women can change their lives and redefine their values and aspirations. Different strands of feminism have shared a sense that inner change and transformation cannot be separated from changing the conditions of women's everyday lives. The inseparability of the 'inner' from the 'outer' which argues that the autonomy of inner emotional and psychic life cannot be separated from our fulfilment within our everyday relationships is a theme explored by Jean Baker Miller in *Towards a New Psychology of Women* (Miller 1976). It remains sceptical of traditional psychoanalytic assumptions and presumably of attempts to reclaim Freud.[3]

This opens up important issues for social theory, for it raises difficult questions about the relationship of personal change to larger political and structural changes. It sets different terms from those that have traditionally separated the dominant frameworks of positivist and functionalist theories that tend to see individuals in relation to structures, rules and norms, from interpretive traditions that tend to insist that people are free to give meaning to their experience. The inadequacy of inherited traditions of social theory to illuminate predicaments we face is part of the appeal of post-modern theories which forsake the search for underlying theoretical grounding.[4]

Freud became increasingly sceptical about the possibilities of change. He was rightly wary of giving people false hopes, which he recognised as a danger of orthodox Marxism. In part, he recognised how difficult it was for people to come to terms with themselves, knowing how readily people escape from themselves. Freud can help us reconsider how difficult it is to gain satisfaction and fulfilment in our everyday relationships. In crucial respects he is right to wonder how we can think of changing the world if we have not yet learned how to find happiness ourselves. Even if these warnings are heeded it is still important to take seriously Ferenczi's notions of Freud's development:

> His method of treatment as well as his theories result from an even greater interest in order, character and the substitution of a better superego for a weaker one. In a word, he is becoming a pedagogue....He looks like a god above his poor patient, who has been degraded to the status of a child. We claim that the transference comes from the patient, unaware of the fact that the greater part of what one calls the transference is artificially provoked by this very behaviour.
>
> (Ferenczi 1932/1985:148–9)

Ferenczi argues that after a wave of enthusiasm for the psychological, Freud 'returned to biology; he considers the psychological to be nothing more than the superstructure over the biological and for him the latter is far more real' (Ferenczi 1932/1985:148–9). This helps explain how Freud lost a sense that people could change, which is why it is difficult to invoke him in defence of a feminism he never supported himself. He tended to think that all reforming activity, legislation and education in relation to women would founder on the fact that 'nature will have appointed women by her beauty, charm and goodness, to do something else' (E. L. Freud 1961:90).

Once Freud no longer believed in these early traumatic experiences of seduction he posited a biological explanation for their having been fantasised. They are, as Freud argued, universal fantasies. As Masson then explains it,

> They cannot, therefore, evoke in the therapist any degree of real compassion for real human suffering. The therapist's only task is that of the educator, to explain to his patient that these apparent memories are nothing but biologically determined fantasies; they are mistakes in perception. Therapy, Freud maintained, does not require any deep emotional commitment, but merely a certain intellectual grasp of theory. In effect, said Ferenczi, Freud's heart was no longer in therapy, because he could no longer believe in the uniqueness and the reality of each separate human being's experience of suffering. He had universalised suffering, thereby robbing it of its power to move us individually.
>
> (Masson 1989:131)

For all the difficulties I have with Masson's general thesis that it is therapy itself that has to be questioned, this strikes me as an important insight. It connects to a dominant masculinity that in its modernist rationalism is constantly universalising. It is as if, as men, the way that we learn to see others makes it difficult for us to care for them individually. But this is not a facet of biology but of culture, and as men we *can* learn to relate in more caring ways.[5]

Ferenczi had learned, as he says in his diary on 18 May, that 'no analysis can succeed in which we do not succeed in really loving the patient' (Ferenczi 1932/1985). An aspect of this was being ready to hear what they say about their abuse. But Freud could not do this any more and Ferenczi knew, as Masson says, 'that Freud had lost something uniquely valuable; the greater tragedy is that, with its loss in Freud, it seemed to have been lost to therapy in general' (Masson 1989:131). I do not think it helps to generalise in this way, though it may capture something important about how traditional psychoanalysis is flawed. If Ferenczi is right about the need for therapists really to love their patients, this is connected for him with a need to be truthful at the same time. If they learn to simulate these feelings, this is bound to be recognised at some level by their clients. Unless they can learn to be truthful with their own emotions and feelings, it is difficult for them to be truthful with others. According to Ferenczi, Freud could no longer tolerate the suffering of childhood and so denied its reality.

When Ferenczi, admittedly after 37 years of analysing patients, attempted to convince Freud that his patients had been telling him the truth all along, he was dropped by Freud. As Masson puts it, 'Ferenczi had become, at last, and like his patients, somebody whose knowledge made him unwanted' (Masson 1989:132). He had wanted to deliver his paper entitled 'Confusion of tongues between adults and children', in which he argues that women who had told him they had been sexually abused as children were telling the truth. He insisted on meeting Freud who was against his delivering the paper before the Wiesbaden Congress of Psychoanalysis in 1932. Freud insisted that he had given up the seduction theory and told Ferenczi that he was being deceived by his patients and that what had been reported to him were fantasies, not memories. Ferenczi insisted on giving his paper, but he died soon after and with him many of the issues he sought to raise.

In an unpublished letter to Eitingon on 28 August 1933, Freud helps to confirm the idea that Ferenczi must have been paranoid because he believed what his patients told him about their childhood. 'But what one really gets', as Freud has it, 'are the fantasies of patients about their childhood, and not the (real) story. My first great etiological error also arose in this very way' (Masson 1984:182). Ferenczi was acknowledging that real traumas can give rise to fantasies, but that these fantasies derive from a real event; they do not replace it. This is the truth that Ferenczi refused to forsake. His refusal was met with isolation and character assaults as he was accused of being 'paranoid' to believe his patients when they said that parents could be cruel and sexually violent to their children. A similar fate has been dealt out to Masson for raising some of these issues again.

In the last few years we have been much more aware of the incidence of childhood sexual abuse. This has helped therapists such as Alice Miller[6] and Dorothy Rowe[7] to acknowledge the importance of the questions Masson raises, if not with the general conclusions about therapy. They have also recognised that to fail to listen and accept the truth of what children report of their experience can be another form of abuse. The medical profession and psychoanalysis have not come out well in all this, for they have colluded in silence for so long that it can be difficult to take seriously their recent changes of heart.

More questions still need to be asked about their fundamental epistemologies and approaches and the ways they have been shaped by masculinist notions of modernity. It has been feminism that has helped to raise these issues about the authority of professional knowledges in its insistence that women can share and validate the truths of their experience. Women learned to tell the difference – as Ferenczi has it in his last paper:

> Patients do not react to theatrical phrases expressing compassion but only to genuine sympathy. I do not know whether they can tell the difference by the sound of our voices, by the choice of our words, or in some other way.
>
> (Masson 1984:288)

The point is that feminism helped women to recognise how the truth can empower in important respects. Initially it was a movement against hypocrisy, for it was built on a recognition that women had been lied to for so long, not only in their personal relationships with men but in the scientific practices that had for so long legitimated their subordination as 'natural'.[8] They learned to doubt when men said that they were working for them and the family, recognising how much time and validation men had for themselves but of which women were deprived.

Feminism questioned the epistemological ground of a positivism that presented its knowledge as 'neutral' and 'impartial' when it served to legitimate their subordination and oppression. Psychoanalysis was initially conceived as part of this apparatus of power, though later many women softened their views of it, thinking that it could be treated as reflecting their powerlessness within a patriarchal society.[9] It is still an open question whether particular traditions of psychoanalysis can be redeemed to illuminate the experience and struggles of women, gays and lesbians.

KNOWLEDGE, MORALITY AND POWER

In different areas of social life women have learned that they have to question the theoretical formulations that have been established as 'neutral' and 'universal', as part of a struggle to find their own voice and reclaim their power and identity. In this sense at least, feminism has learned that power cannot be separated from knowledge. This helps illuminate how our inherited conceptions of reason and knowledge have largely been set to reflect an experience of men. It is because the dominant culture has accepted the neutral and universal claims of reason that it has encouraged people to deny differences in learning to judge meaning implicitly according to standards that are not of their own making. Women learned to evaluate themselves accordingly, and so to feel inadequate and disempowered. Because women tend to fail according to these apparently neutral criteria they supposedly only have themselves to blame for their inadequacies.

Carol Gilligan' *In A Different Voice* has provided important evidence to challenge a prevailing idea that women are somehow less moral or principled than men.[10] According to the work of Piaget and Kohlberg, as we have already mentioned, women tended to come lower on the scale of moral achievement for they were less likely to think in terms of universal and abstract moral principles.[11] With the Kantian assumptions informing Piaget's research, it seemed as if an impartial scale was being created, little recognition being given to the fact that this was largely research carried out with boys. It seemed as if the ability to abstract oneself from the contingencies of the situation you faced, to think about it in terms of abstract principles, designated a higher stage of moral development. If girls were less able to reach this stage it simply reflected upon themselves, since the stages had been developed through a supposedly impartial investigation.

But if it can be shown that women, for whatever reason, tend to conceive of moral dilemmas in different terms so that they think more concretely in terms of the people concerned, then there is a danger that a Kantian tradition which identifies morality with reason will fail to illuminate the particularities of their moral experience. This would be to judge women according to standards that are not appropriate to their moral experience. As Gilligan has it, women are more likely to invoke an ethic of care and concern whereby their decisions are influenced by the people affected. Men are more likely to think in terms of abstract moral principles, wanting to sort out the issues in principle before they return to the details of the particular case.

This seems to be confirmed in early psychological research that shows that boys will stick very firmly to rules, while girls seem more ready to give up a game if it seems to be threatening the personal relationships involved.[12] Of course, there are issues about how such research is evaluated. I am also suspicious of the idea that there are two ethics at work, one to do with care and concern while the other, more identified with men, has to do with rights, justice and principles, as if it is simply a matter of reinstating an ethical tradition that has been subordinated and silenced. But again, crucial issues are raised that will not go away until they are seriously addressed.

What seems significant here is that as feminism gives women the courage to voice their own experience they also seek the appropriate terms within which to validate it. Feminism has taught women to be suspicious of the prevailing forms of universality, knowing that these have traditionally worked to silence women and to invalidate their experience. Of course as women find their own voice, differences between women with different experiences and histories will come into focus.[13] But this is something that feminism has often been aware of so that the attempts of post-modernity theorists to argue that feminism itself depends upon a unified conception of women as a category is misplaced.[14] This attempt to place feminism as another discourse of modernity fails, as I have argued, to recognise the ways it also challenges the rationalist terms of modernity.

Possibly what matters here is the balance that feminism can help retain between reason and emotions, between mental life and inner emotional life. Theorists of post-modernity often set themselves against a totalistic and unified conception of reason without being able to explore the *particular* form of rationality within modernity that sets itself against nature and emotions. It is unable to identify *what* makes this a masculinist notion of reason so that we do not have to speak against reason itself but against the ways it is traduced through setting itself so firmly against the body and emotional life.

Theorists of post-modernity have only been able to present a fragmented and relativistic conception of different rationalities in the face of the unified visions of modernity. They are often crucially silent on issues of gender. If they had learned more from the history of feminism, they would also have given more weight to the disempowerment that goes along with being excluded from reason. This was why it was so crucial for feminists such as Mary Wollstonecraft to insist that reason was equally theirs, however 'unreasonably' it was being defined within the rationalist terms of modernity, rather than a category which men possessed alone.

It has been a continuing theme of feminism, in its different forms, to assert that women could think for themselves. They did not need their fathers, teachers or even analysts to think *for* them. They could think out what they wanted or needed for themselves. They insisted on questioning a rationalist universalism that worked to subsume their experience as a 'faulty' or 'inadequate' form of masculinity that tacitly provided the measure of all things. They did not want to give up on reason but simply to redefine it. It might be because men have learned to treat reason as a masculine possession that they can talk so easily, within theories of post-modernity, about forsaking or deconstructing it. Women have suffered through being considered 'irrational', and consequently through not having had their experience validated – for if women are continually told that they are 'irrational' what is there to validate? This makes women rightly suspicious of post-modernist theories that in their questioning of western forms of reason seem so ready to dispense with notions of 'reason' and 'rationality' completely.

Women, being less identified with reason, also have more experience of what it is to be overwhelmed by emotions and feelings so that it is difficult to reassert control in relation to one's life. If they know that feelings and emotions have to be validated as sources of knowledge and empowerment, they can also recognise the need for some balance between ideas and emotions. It is not a matter of choosing between them but of somehow learning to give them a proper and balanced place in everyday life. This involves challenging a rationalism that has refused to validate our inner emotional lives as sources of meaning and fulfilment. What matters is not simply the realisation of goals and purposes set by reason alone, but the quality and meaningfulness of our everyday experience and relationships. This involves a challenge to prevailing forms of social theory that in large part refuse to acknowledge the importance of a dialectic between what authorities expect of us and what we discover about our own needs and desires.

INADEQUACY AND EMPOWERMENT

Issues of empowerment are hard to formulate within a Protestant culture that can leave us constantly struggling against feelings of inadequacy or against a sense that whatever we do is somehow not good enough. Not only do we seem destined to compare ourselves with unrealistic standards that we set ourselves but we can feel torn through constantly comparing ourselves with others, silently feeling envious of their success. This touches on issues of self-esteem and self-worth, as if nothing that we do really provides us with any sustenance or nourishment.

It is partly because, as men, we often have such little relationship to our self-esteem which can feel like a neglected inner child that somehow never feels acknowledged, that we can experience ourselves as constantly striving to prove ourselves. As Weber seems to recognise, this placed issues of masculinity at the heart of a capitalist moral culture. It is as if we are destined constantly to be striving without ever really experiencing the joy of fulfilment.

If we have no real feeling for what we do, but are constantly acting out of a sense of obligation, we will never feel satisfied or fulfilled. If we have learned within a Protestant culture to prove ourselves through our deeds so that we can somehow feel good about ourselves, often we will never do enough to assuage the sense of inadequacy we carry. In the end we will resent giving so much and, with Freud, resent those we are supposedly helping. As professional teachers, doctors or therapists we are often trapped into thinking we can help people, if only they put their trust in us. We take it to be part of the service we provide as professionals. Because the knowledge is ours, all they have to do is to receive it. But this is a trap of authority. The isolation it leaves you in often gets you so little for yourself that it easily breeds resentments. This is also connected to a dominant conception of masculinity that fosters the idea that, as men, we do not have any emotional needs of our own, especially at work. It is part of a myth of invulnerability. But the truth lies elsewhere for, whatever our class, race or ethnicity as men, we are neither invulnerable nor invincible. We are human and have emotional needs like any other human being.

Feminist theory and practice, particularly around questions of health and women's relationships with their bodies, have recognised just how disempowering these traditional forms of masculine authority can be. Male doctors have long assumed that their patients want them to act as authorities, so much so that, as we have already discussed, they feel threatened if they are asked too many questions. Women have learned to reformulate their relationships with their doctors, often preferring them to admit their doubts and worries about the situation. This is an honesty that doctors have been trained out of as they assume their unquestioned authority is part of the burden they have to carry. They learn that it would only upset patients to be told the truth about their condition and only recently has it been considered as a right that patients can claim. The point is that people might want different things from their doctors and it can be very misleading to generalise about 'patients'. Feminism has had its influence in the fostering of more equal relationships which have allowed women forms of dependency to reclaim their bodies as part of themselves.

As women have learned to take greater responsibility for their own health, they have learned to exercise a different vision of freedom and choice in relation to their doctors. They have learned to separate out issues of knowledge and experience from the traditional relationships of authority and dependence this has gone with. They have questioned forms of medical knowledge that systematically discount their own feelings and experience. Women have learned to voice more of what they are feeling and to trust the knowledge they have of themselves, rather than constantly to defer to an autonomous masculinist conception of medical knowledge. It takes considerable courage to speak out in contexts in which you can so easily be made to feel small and stupid. In consciousness-raising groups women learned to share and validate knowledge that they were developing of themselves. They learned to trust their experience as a source of knowledge and so to empower themselves.

The ways that professionalism connects to dominant forms of masculinity still need to be investigated. It connects to the autonomy of professional knowledge that serves to devalue what others experience. So, for example, in the context of education, parents can be told that their child is well able to cope with going into juniors, even though they have just moved, since the educationalists assume they possess the relevant knowledge. They see how the child is coping in class and because they think that he or she is bright and relating well to his or her peers, that is all there is to it.

What parents have is 'mere experience', which should not be able to interfere with a supposedly autonomous educational judgement. Similarly, doctors will listen to parents while discounting what they say, for they will insist that whatever experience they have cannot, as we have already discussed, be relevant to their clinical judgement. But parents have to live with their children outside of school and often have to cope with different strains and tensions that they are going through. They know in a way that teachers or doctors cannot what anxieties children carry home with them which *should* influence the educational decisions being made. Parents should be partners in these decisions, learning also to take account of what children have to say.

If you are made to feel that what you know or feel is of little relevance or concern, you can so easily feel small, dependent and disempowered. It is often hard for middle-class men to appreciate what women and people from ethnic minorities are up against, since the difficulties they face are so often rendered invisible. Since middle-class men often take for granted the right to speak, they are unaware how easily others are silenced and what courage it takes to speak. Liberal democratic theory has yet to learn from the insights of feminism into issues of power, autonomy and dependency for its form of representation.

It is not enough for opportunities to be provided, only to blame people for not taking advantage of them. You have to create institutions, often small-scale, in which people can learn to feel confident to share themselves. This is what feminism attempted to do with consciousness-raising groups. It provided a context, as we have explored it, in which women could speak, knowing that they would be heard and their experience validated. This was a rare situation within a society in which those who are socially powerless are used to being put down.

It takes courage to express what you feel or know if you can expect to be ridiculed or ignored. Within a patriarchal culture this is an experience familiar to women whose language has for so long been devalued. Women learned to keep their thoughts and feelings to themselves and consciousness-raising groups provided a rare space and time where they could speak in the belief that they would be heard. It helped to validate the spoken word and so gained them an appreciation that through a sharing of one's experience, connections could be made between an inner sense of self and the relationships in our lives. To have one's experience validated as we have explored it does not mean that others would have to agree with what you said, but it is a matter of people listening to the way that someone has experienced an event. It is because of the *trust* that this helped establish that people could then go on to explore different levels of feelings, so becoming gradually willing to share more of themselves.

In this way, feminism learned from movements of black power in the United States to challenge central aspects of a Protestant vision that encouraged people to conceal aspects of themselves and their experience that they cannot feel proud of. As people learn to do what is expected of them by those around them, they *discount* what it is they are experiencing themselves. We often learn to be sensitive to what others might think of us and to fear rejection if we do not act according to the norms and rules of a particular social group. In this context it can be a liberation to share more of what we feel ourselves and so begin to strengthen an inner connection to self.

Of course, a Protestant tradition has been significant in sustaining a sense of interiority, but this inner self has often been detached and isolated from the ways we are with others. It helps produce a schizophrenic culture in which we outwardly conform often out of a fear of rejection while we are left feeling alone and isolated and believing that no one really understands who we are in ourselves. It is this split that can be healed as we find courage, both as women and, in a different way, as men, to share more of our experience and emotional lives with others.

In large part, our prevailing traditions of social theory have failed to sustain a connected sense of interiority or a sense of the tensions and contradictions between who we might be for others in our relationships and the ways we experience ourselves. Within a Durkheimian tradition it is the social rules that provide us with a higher vision of ourselves, so that we can feel constantly guilty for not living up to standards that we have made our own. We inherit a vision of 'socialisation' that incorporates the notion of the external rules and norms somehow becoming internalised and made our own. Lacan's structuralist notion of psychoanalysis tends somewhat paradoxically to operate in similar terms as external relationships are interiorised. But if this helps to acknowledge the power and weight of social relationships in people's experience, it does this in a way that normalises this process so that we never have a way of illuminating the injuries suffered. We are left bereft of a moral language with which to explore the workings of power and dependency.

It is in the context of a feminist discussion of women's oppression that new terms are formulated and our prevailing traditions of social theory challenged, as women, gays and lesbians have learned to identify their oppression. The ways people have learned to discount their experience and reject aspects of themselves have been crucial to their oppression. As people have learned to take pride in aspects of their experience and sexualities they had before learned to deride, people found their own voices and means of expression.

It was not simply that people were prepared to share aspects of themselves that they had learned to conceal and feel ashamed of, but they formed a different relation to their language and to themselves. They learned more of what it meant to be true to themselves, rather than to think of language in structuralist terms as sustaining a particular version of their truth and experience. But this involved grasping the nature of oppression not only as an external process of constraint, but also as an inner process of shame and self-rejection. To come to terms with this we need to explore how modern western traditions of philosophy and social theory have in large part been silent about the notion of oppression.

Chapter 16

Conclusion

Masculinity, power and modernity

FREEDOM AND OPPRESSION

Those supporting the traditions of social theory have generally found it easier to think about the power that some groups or classes have in society than about how some people are systematically oppressed in the way that society is organised. It might be because we inherit visions of sovereignty that encourage us to believe that authority has a single unified source, for example, the Queen in Parliament or the American Constitution, from which flow all other forms of legitimate power and authority. Weber has helped consolidate such a vision of legitimate authority within classical sociology and encouraged us to think about the different forms that this authority can take.[1]

Modernity, for Weber, is very much characterised by the dominance of legal–rational authority. Since within the liberal democratic state we supposedly all, as the people, sustain this authority and, within Kantian terms, legislate these rules and laws for ourselves, there is little space for considerations of oppression. It might well be that some people come out of this much better than others, so that according to Weber there are prevailing inequalities of class, status and power, but this does not amount to oppression.[2]

For Durkheim, the rules and norms of society represent a higher source of duties so that people have to learn to conform to what is expected of them. To do otherwise is supposedly to act in a selfish and egoistic way. Society is the guardian of our moral selves and a protection against our otherwise selfish natures.[3] As people learn to do what is expected of them they are supposedly fulfilling their higher natures. At some level this externalises people's relationship with themselves and leaves them a thin connection to their inner selves.

If people feel dissatisfied with what they are expected to do, then they only have themselves to blame. Durkheim helps to reinforce a sense of 'normality' as somehow sanctioned by some higher authority. If people fail to conform to these legitimate notions of normality it can only be because there is something wrong with them or that they are inadequate. So it was that a powerful tradition within social theory learned to treat those who failed to conform as pathological. Their suffering was to have no legitimacy in itself.

As children grow up they learn to see themselves through the eyes of the dominant culture and institutions. A vision of sociology as a science seems to go hand in hand with a strong and unquestioned sense of the 'normal'. Within a Protestant culture in which we learned that our natures were evil or bad, it was easy to grow up with a *fear* of difference. To be different was to be 'abnormal' and there was enormous pressure, on boys and girls in different ways, not to stand out as different. People learned to minimise those aspects of their experience that drew attention to themselves in an effort to present themselves to be 'like everyone else'.

This was a paradox within a liberal capitalist society that J. S. Mill acknowledged, realising that while people supposedly treasure individuality they seem at the same time to be haunted by a fear of difference.[4] This seems to hark back to humanist assumptions and the ways they were cast within a Protestant tradition. As human beings we are supposedly 'all alike' so that any difference, whatever its source, turns out to be threatening because it seems to bring our very humanity into question. Again, this connects to the fact that it is as rational selves that we exist as human beings for Kant and an Enlightenment tradition of modernity.[5]

With emancipation, for instance, Jews were permitted to enter professions and institutions of higher learning that were formerly closed to them. They were allowed to live outside the confines of a ghetto. They used to be oppressed *as* Jews since they suffered legal and political restrictions. With emancipation, they were allowed to exist as free and equal citizens who were guaranteed the same legal and political rights as other citizens. Supposedly their oppression ceased as they were allowed to compete on equal terms for positions within society in general.

But as Sartre points out in *Anti-Semite and Jew*, the cost of this emancipation was to be the recognition that our Jewishness is an incidental and contingent matter of individual belief (Sartre 1960). So it was that, in Germany for instance, Jews became Germans of the Mosak belief. Jewishness became a matter of religious belief alone and as Germans first it was important that they participated as free and equal citizens. There has long been tension and uneasiness with these terms of emancipation, for in part they meant that Jews learned to see themselves through Christian eyes. For when we talk about equality as 'rational' selves this vision of rationality was firmly set within secularised Protestant terms.[6]

There was an abiding *tension* between modernity and difference. We learned to treat differences in a particular way. We learned within a liberal moral culture to treat them as incidental to who we are as human beings. At most they are issues of individual opinion and belief. As rational selves we can claim to exist as free and equal citizens, and for a long time, as I have argued in Chapter 9 on feminism, it was possible to think of women's subordination, for instance, as the denial of specific legal and political rights that were enjoyed by men. As women were to struggle for equal rights with men, so they were gradually to assume an equality with men. This proves that the 'differences' that can be said to exist between men and women are arguably artificial and have no existence in reality. It reinforces a liberal position that says it is pointless and misleading to think of ourselves in gender terms, for we are all people. It is as rational selves that we are citizens and have rights, even if it has taken many years of struggle to reach this point.

Marx helped to contest this liberal position while arguing for an abstract universalism of his own. I think this comes out in Marx's relationship to his own Jewishness and this turns out to be a significant test case, for the terms of emancipation were initially set out in relationship to Jews. Marx sustains a vision of humanism that assumes that Jews would want to be emancipated not only from their oppression as Jews, but also from their Jewishness.[7] In this sense Marxism embodies a universalist dream that sets people as human beings, somehow separating them from their history and culture. Marx shared the universalist dreams of the Enlightenment while questioning its vision of human beings as rational selves. He wanted to reinstate our species as being practical rather than simply contemplative.[8] But if this was a recognition of labour as a source of human creativity and involved a break with an Enlightenment rationalism that saw people as complete as rational selves, it fostered a similar universalism.

To this extent Marx echoes a Kantian tradition, at least in his vision of freedom as involving an emancipation from the particularities of history and culture. All forms of particularism were treated as 'backward-looking' and essentially as compromising to our freedom as human beings. So it was that for Jews to learn to *separate* themselves from Judaism was seen as a move towards freedom and emancipation. To identify ourselves with a limited and particular history and culture when we could take up the standpoint of an international working class, for example, was tantamount to a stubborn refusal. This in truth is a secular form of a Christian response to Judaism which offers the universalism of the Christian church to a Jewish particularism. For Jews to refuse this new revelation is treated as backward-looking, for it is to identify with a revelation that has supposedly been surpassed. In this sense, Judaism only exists as a historical anachronism rather than as an autonomous tradition with its own vitality and contradictions.[9]

It is such universalism that is supposedly embodied in the universal task of the proletariat. It is a unifying vision that is intolerant of differences, for it is supposedly as 'human beings' that we can be emancipated. This can help account for the particular significance which Marx gives to class oppression and it has allowed an orthodox Marxist tradition to reduce forms of race, ethnic and gender oppression to forms of class oppression. Not only do these forms of oppression and exploitation have a 'material basis' in the ownership of wealth and power but they supposedly provide a 'common basis' upon which working-class people, whatever their gender or ethnicity, can unify. An orthodox Marxist tradition has been intolerant of the *different* interests that these different groups might have, thinking that this was divisive of the movement. It wants people to identify primarily as workers, and whether they were Jewish, black or Asian was somehow irrelevant in the struggles they faced. Rather, they assumed that these distinctions have no basis in material reality and so they must be artificially produced and sustained by ideologies that are in the interests of those who rule capitalist society.

Marx was more helpful in his critique of rights and in his examination of the workings of class relationships of power. He argued that capitalists and workers do not meet on equal terms so that the wage contract is not the contract between equal parties that it is presented as within classical political economy. Marx recognises a class relationship of power that flows from the unequal ownership of the means of production. It means that capitalists have power over the lives of working people.

It is a relationship of power and dependency because the ruling classes can organise the larger society according to their own image. This is Marx's crucial insight about the ruling ideas of any society being the ideas of the ruling class. It refuses to see class as a market relationship in which some people are more wealthy and so have more opportunities than others. Marx challenges a liberal moral culture that assumes that individuals stand isolated, autonomous and alone, able to make their position in the larger society.

For Marx, it is crucial that we are born into particular relationships of power and dependency. These are not relationships of our own choosing or of our own making. This is what works to frustrate the notion of equal opportunities, as people learn to identify how things have been stacked against them. But working-class children sent to grammar schools can also be struck by an abiding sense of difference. It is as if they do not fit in, however hard they try. They can be left feeling inadequate and isolated, unable to explain to themselves why their families live in such poor housing and impoverished conditions. Gramsci believes that a sense of class consciousness can emerge out of this experience of difference.[10] Within a Market ethos poverty is tied to a sense of failure so children can learn to feel ashamed of their parents, seeking a success that seems to have been denied them.

This feeling of shame and inadequacy seems to exist as a shadow of oppression. Gramsci, like Simone Weil, recognised how important it was for people to respect themselves in their own eyes. If people were to learn 'who' they were they had to learn where they came from. In this way a sense of working-class history and culture can be so very important for it teaches people not only where they come from but also that they have a history and a culture. This is as true of women's history as it is of black or Jewish history. Gramsci recognised how an orthodox Marxist tradition had lost a sense of the importance of culture, education and consciousness. It had assumed that people could learn about capitalism as an external set of institutions and practices without first discovering their place within it.

Gramsci recognised this as a moral and political task, as much as it was a task of science. So it was that Gramsci recognised the growth and development of political consciousness and awareness as an issue of morality. He saw morality and politics as inseparable, which is not the same as reducing morality to a form of politics. As people come to an awareness of themselves in relation to others, so they begin to grasp the weakness of a liberalism that thinks of society as a collection of independent individuals.

Gramsci helps us to think about the relationships of individuality to power, for he recognises the ways we come to a sense of ourselves within particular relationships of power. As we develop what Gramsci calls a 'critical consciousness' we question ourselves as a product of these relationships, as a functionalist theory has it, and we begin to discern tension and contradictions between who we want to be and how we aspire to live our lives and the ways of thinking and relating that we have passively adopted from our background and culture.

So it is that Gramsci can help us question Foucault's post-structuralist assumptions that treat truth as an effect of power. For Gramsci this can only be part of the story, for it is possible for people to contest truths that they have inherited along with the social relationships that sustain them. As we come to consciousness of these relationships of class, gender, race and ethnicity, so we become aware of the difficulties that we face in transforming them.

Coming from Sardinia himself, Gramsci was also acutely aware of issues of ethnicity and marginalisation. He sought to reassert the values of different cultures and so to question the empty universalism of abstract talk about culture in general.[11] He recognised that these differences had to be *valued* and the traditions they embodied sustained, rather than treating them in orthodox Marxist terms as artificial divisions of a fragmented working class. As he learned to take pride in his own cultural inheritance he learned how easy it was to feel shame in the face of metropolitan cultures that presented themselves as the embodiments of universal truths.

Even though people in Turin might have looked down on Sardinia as backward and provincial, Gramsci knew to value what he had inherited.[12] He could feel proud of this cultural inheritance, even if it was going to take time for others to appreciate it. It helped him to question the rational universalism of orthodox Marxism. He knew that it was mistaken to think that people had to forsake their traditional forms of ethnic and cultural expression to replace them with a scientific discourse of Marxism. This involved a betrayal of Marxism as he grasped it.

Marx's ambiguous relationship to his own Jewishness made an Enlightenment universalism seem an attractive option. He was less tolerant of different ethnic and cultural traditions and the importance, as Gramsci had it, of developing a critical relationship towards them. It is partly because of this that Marx was also less sensitive to issues of racial, gender and ethnic oppression. He was very concerned with questions of colonial oppression, but he tended to cast these discussions in largely economic terms.

Since emancipation was largely conceived in the universal and masculine language of the 'brotherhood of man', it was assumed that distinctions of race and ethnicity were part of the problem, not the solution. If Jews, for example, were not emancipated *from* Judaism, then their emancipation could not be complete. It was difficult to question, say, the patriarchal and racist assumptions that can inform a particular historical tradition while at the same time acknowledging it as a viable and autonomous tradition of thought, feeling and action. It was impossible to recognise the oppression, for instance, of Jews who felt that their Jewish consciousness was inadmissible, since as equal citizens it could only be a contingent aspect of their identities.

Colonialism was not only an external structure of power and oppression, for it also involved an inner organisation of people's experience. This was to come into clearer focus with the writings of Albert Memmi and Franz Fanon which themselves evoke themes that had been raised by such writers and activists as Aime Cézaire and Paul Nizan. It was partly in the struggle against colonial oppression that a language of oppression and liberation was initially formed. Power could not only be conceived in externalised terms.[13]

Somehow the workings of social power had to be connected to the inner processes of consciousness. These could no longer be separated out and our inherited forms of philosophy and social theory which insisted on analysing these separately could not come to terms with issues of oppression. This is partly because of the crossing of boundaries with the recognition that oppression is at once a moral as well as a political category while at the same time being both a psychological and a social conception. A social theory that sought to present itself in scientific terms by setting itself against morality and a discourse of values and which defined itself in opposition to psychologism found too many boundary issues being raised at once.

Again, Marxist theory often found it easier to think in terms of exploitation because this seemed to provide an objective measure that could be relied upon. Marx's vision of exploitation was more complex and less tied to positivist visions of science. He refused to separate the scientific from the moral and recognised not only the dependency that was created through class relations of power but also the ways people were degraded through factory production. When we say that workers within the capitalist mode of production are not only exploited but also oppressed, we are saying more than that they are deprived of control of the processes of production.[14]

This points not only to questions of surplus value but to the capacities, emotions and imagination of people themselves. It is that people's capacities are crippled and distorted and somehow they are demeaned in their own eyes. It is as if people come to see themselves, at least partly, through the eyes of those who have power and influence in society. They learn to blame themselves for the conditions of their lives, thinking that if only they had worked harder or been more able, they would be in a different situation.

Traditions of social theory that are largely cast in the images of men have difficulty reinstating any sense of interiority and emotional life. It was this that men, at least publicly, learned to do without in place of the privileges and powers they gained within modernity. As men from different class backgrounds, we can share a sense that we need to be *in control* of our lives. It is often important to persuade ourselves that we are in control, even if we are not, since otherwise our very sense of male identity is threatened. As men we learn to 'take it' and often this means that we learn to *minimise* the hurts and indignities that, say, we have suffered as children. If our treatment at the hands of teachers was bad, we tell ourselves that it could have been a lot worse and we can recoup a sense of male identity by showing that we are not wingeing or complaining. As the saying goes, 'we are man enough to take it'.

IDENTITY, DIGNITY AND POWER

Part of this belief is reflected in traditions of social theory that are less than tolerant of the 'subjective' or the 'personal'. They see their task in discerning a rational order out of this emotional disorder. This is integral to the rationalist quest. It is for men to be the guardians of 'reason' and 'objectivity' and so to refuse to be drawn into the unbounded and the chaotic that, like the feminine, can so easily overwhelm. Social theory and philosophy has to stay within the limits of reason, learning to stay within the province of what can be clearly said.

Often this means, as Jean Baker Miller has suggested, that it unwittingly speaks the language of the powerful, for often they can only recognise their own reality and look towards theories that can reflect this back at them.[15] But the experience of those who are marginalised or powerless, such as women, lesbians and gays, Jews or blacks, is always more *ambivalent*, for they have to live in different realities. Things are not so clear if you live one reality at home and another at school, as do many children from immigrant families. There is not a single reality that can be described in clear and unproblematic terms. Reality is contradictory and you have to discover ways of living with these contradictions.

This has ramifications in different areas of social life. There is no solution that can be provided by reason alone that will settle the contradictions that many women feel, for instance, between their relationships to their children and their careers. It is all very well for men to say that there is no point in feeling guilty about leaving your children since these feelings make no difference, but this only goes to show that they do not understand the situation. It is easy for a rationalist to assume that contradictions only exist in the ways we think about things because they are essentially features of our consciousness, for they fail to grasp how these contradictions are also *lived out* in everyday life and relationships. It might well be that there is no perfect solution, but this does not stop many women feeling ripped apart. To say that it is a matter of making choices and establishing preferences that can then be quantified, is again to miss the issues involved.

Similarly, a working-class person can be confronted with the issue of taking on a foreman's job and so be seen as 'getting on' at work whilst also feeling that they are betraying their workmates by taking up a management option. Many people refuse promotions because they experience them as a betrayal of where they come from and because they want conditions of working-class life to change, rather than to escape them individually. This is a contradiction that is systematically created within a class-divided society.

It is not a problem that reason can solve alone, nor can it be said that a person with 'ambition' or 'initiative' would know what to do, so that people only have themselves to blame for not taking an opportunity available to them. As Gramsci recognised, this is a moral and political issue, not one simply to do with individual preferences and values. It is a difficult decision which reason alone cannot resolve. It is also a decision that middle-class people who have never had to face it find it hard to grasp. They prefer to ignore the discontinuities of social life created by class, race and gender relations of power. Within liberal moral theory it is supposedly only as individuals that we can face such issues.

If we are to understand the contradictory situation that, for example, black people find themselves in within a white society, it is important to understand racism not as an issue of individual prejudice but of the institutionalised relationships of power.[16] This also reflects the ways that black people feel about themselves and the inner relationships that they develop with themselves and their culture. This is all the more acute when black people are regularly blamed for the situation in which they find themselves.

Michael Harrington in *The Other America* says that white people think 'the racial ghetto reflects the "natural" character of the negro: lazy, shiftless, irresponsible, and so on'. This allows whites in traditional liberal terms to think that blacks somehow 'prefer to live that way' since all inequalities are somehow chosen, as Kant was forced to maintain. But as Tom Wicker states in his introduction to the Report of the US Commission on Civil Disorder:

> What white Americans have never fully understood – but what the negro can never forget – is that white society is deeply implicated in the ghetto. White institutions created it, white institutions maintain it, and white society condones it.

If people are further blamed as victims of their own oppression, this can fuel anger and hatred. For many years blacks have been taught to see themselves through the eyes of white society, so becoming defensive and ashamed of who they are. I know from my own experience of my Jewish identity the ease with which you unwittingly slip into self-hatred, for in learning to devalue, for instance, Yiddish culture and history, we are in fact learning to devalue and diminish ourselves. As Ernest Stephens wrote of his experience as a black student in American universities,

> Instead of encouraging racial pride through analysis and discussion of black people's rich cultural heritage, the black student is told that he is 'culturally deprived', while western culture is shoved down his throat. In history the horrors of slavery are watered down and sketchily covered so as not to enrage the complacent black student, while the period following reconstruction is covered as if the negro had strangely disappeared from the face of the earth.
>
> (Stephens 1967:133)

Gramsci realises how important it was for people to struggle to see themselves differently, so learning to take pride in aspects of their own experience and culture that had been systematically denigrated within the dominant culture. He recognises this as an aspect of class relationships of power and subordination but also in the area of culture and ethnicity. This is part of a process of recreating a sense of individual and collective dignity and self-worth. It is an inner struggle that cannot be separated from transforming the material conditions and relationships of everyday life. It is a task that links psychology to history and politics, for it involves a rethinking and reworking of inherited conceptions of history and culture.

People can learn to *ground* themselves in their own history and culture, refusing to see themselves through the derogatory perceptions of the dominant culture. This can be a slow and painful process, for it acknowledges that even if slavery remains a problem of white institutionalised racism, it is also something difficult that people of colour had to learn to relate to. It is an experience of universal significance, while it carries particular meaning and pain for black people. It cannot be separated off as an aspect of history that is long past, for it continues as a shaping presence in the present. It is only in acknowledging and working through this period, however fraught and painful, that it can become part of history. If it is ignored, as Freud grasped, it weakens our identities and gives us less of a relationship with ourselves.

I can speak more directly of the need for Jews to face the experience of the Holocaust or possibly more accurately, the Shoah. This is an issue not only for Jews but for Christianity in general which helped to produce an atmosphere that made such crimes possible. But these feelings are difficult to deal with for Jews and Christians alike, and it is a significant reflection on our post-war traditions of philosophy and social theory that they have failed to deal with these events. They have continued with established traditions as if these events did not take place at all. This says something important about western culture which we have yet to face.[17]

The re-emergence of anti-Semitism in both western and eastern Europe in 1990 suggests that people deal with these historical crimes by somehow continuing to blame the victims. This was part of the thesis of Claude Landzmann's film *Shoah*, which showed how the continuation of anti-Semitism in Poland was in part a way that people had learned to deal with the horrors of Auschwitz and Treblinka that had taken place in their midst.

When blacks come to terms with the history of slavery, as when Jews have to face how they were largely abandoned by others who should have acted differently, there is bound to be anger. There is also shame and resentment. These feelings cannot be displaced from a historical consciousness that has the potential of transforming the self. As Gramsci and Simone Weil knew in their different ways, this is also a *moral* task, for history, like politics, is inseparable from morality. This is not a matter of morality as a discourse of values, but the focussing of what Gramsci calls 'moral individuality'. This is a difficult path, as it is the path of learning that touches the self.

But in large part this is a process that our inherited traditions of social theory have failed to illuminate. They have either insisted on a Weberian tradition where we have control of the meanings that we give to our experience so that there is nothing there to surprise us, or else that they are products or effects of existing relationships. As men, we grow up wary of change, accepting the notion that 'you haven't changed at all' as some kind of compliment. History is waiting there as an accumulation of facts and interpretations. It is rare for it to touch us, let alone for us to grasp the ways it informs and sustains our identities.

It is partly because the dominant traditions of classical social theory have been set largely within the framework of an Enlightenment modernity that they have tended to split science from morality, the 'objective' from the 'subjective', theory from experience. I have argued how this is tied up with a vision of dominant masculinity and the rational self. In part we need to break with these traditions and with an orthodox Marxism that is equally set within this mould if we are better to appreciate some of these new social movements. In their different ways they *refuse* to accept these antimonies, seeing the process of gender, ethnic or racial consciousness as connected to integrity and self-worth. They have insisted on validating these processes of change rather than seeing them as 'personal' or 'subjective', for they know the difference that these changes make to the ways people live and relate.

In large part these movements and the writings that have emerged from them have been marginalised within social theory. They remain pertinent to specific areas, say to do with race or ethnicity or with sex and gender, but in large part they remain peripheral to social theory. It is partly because they are treated as particularistic within a tradition that has largely agreed to differ around an implicit identification between reason, objectivity and universality. This has established the framework within which *differences* can be argued out. It is also, as Lukács recognised, because they work to question the methodological ground laid out between 'subjective' and 'objective' theories and, like Marx, want to connect understanding the world with changing it. In this regard feminism has learned from black movements about the importance of changing yourself as part of larger processes of change. It helped towards a recognition that unless we can change ourselves to relate more truthfully to ourselves and others, how can we hope for more equal relationships in the social world?

Feminists also touched on the levels of anger, in their case towards men who had sustained patriarchal institutions and relationships at the cost of women's own lives and dignity. There was anger because women had been told that these arrangements were somehow in their interests as well. It was part of the dream of universalism. So if women felt bad about themselves, they only had themselves to blame. They were often told to see a therapist, for the problems supposedly lay within themselves, rather than in the way that their relationships were structured and organised.

Women learned to question liberal notions of equality as somehow serving the interests of men. It was not enough for women to be respected as equals unless they could also live as equals, which meant that the tasks and responsibilities of domestic life had to be shared. Feminism taught how the personal could not be separated from the political. Love could not be separated from power. They learned to recognise that the process of feminist consciousness involves both moral and political changes as women were left with a different vision of their own lives and their relationships with others. They saw their lives in society in quite different terms, though this did not mean the everyday difficulties that they faced would disappear. In fact fresh difficulties seemed to emerge with this new consciousness.

It was difficult not to blame men for the oppression they suffered and somehow to hold individual men responsible. This anger was to be expected, for it was the power which men held within a patriarchal society that oppressed women and had largely set the terms in which they understood themselves. This was a power that individual men could make use of even if they might question the subordination of women theoretically. In this context, the analogy is often drawn with the fate of white liberals in South Africa.

But I think this is misleading. It has been important for whites to speak out against the injustices of apartheid and to take sides with black struggles against institutions of white supremacy. The point that a radical feminist analysis seems to stress is that a white person cannot know what it is to suffer the oppression of blacks in South Africa any more than men can really identify with the sufferings and oppression of women. It is important to recognise that people cannot escape the contradictions of their own situation but it is also misleading not to recognise that people can learn and change.

But as Charles Silverman recognises in *Crisis in Black and White* (1964), anger is part of a process of coming to terms with a history of oppression. It is often the oppressed who are expected to be reasonable when they have been treated unreasonably for so long:

> People can gain their freedom and self-respect only in the process of fighting for it. Thus, the very militancy and stridency that whites find so upsetting is indispensible if negroes are to shake off their traditional dependency and become truly free and equal, if they are to respect themselves and to be respected by whites. When whites express a yearning for 'responsible' negro leadership, therefore, the question must be asked, Responsible to whom?
>
> (Silverman 1964:149)

The long history of the struggles against colonial oppressions should have taught such a lesson. As Steve Biko recognised in the case of the black consciousness movement in South Africa, it is crucial for blacks to appraise their own history and culture as well as the injuries suffered because of oppression. This is a painful process, for it means coming to terms with a history of suffering and oppression. It is inescapably a moral process as people learn to see themselves through their own eyes, so feeling dignity in their survival and values.

Social theories have in large part sought to separate morality from science so that, for instance, they feel easier with objective measures of exploitation that can be developed within orthodox Marxism, than with the moral language of oppression. It is when the integrity of individuals has been subverted and undermined that we can no longer conceive of society in contractual and market terms. Simone Weil recognised the ways that relationships of power *reduce* people to matter, so that their dignity as human beings is attacked. She does not see power as a commodity that some people have over others for she recognises, as Foucault does, how power helps to constitute both parties in a relationship. It is partly because of this that you cannot simply talk about the redistribution of power or about reasserting human rights that have been abandoned. It is as if we are at the limits of liberal moral theory when we recognise how relationships of power and oppression damage individual and collective lives.

Weil's vision of power is in many respects more helpful than Foucault's, for she recognises the suffering that is a consequence of power.[18] She insists on connecting power to morality, while Foucault seems to have forsaken this connection until the last years of his life with his vision of power being ubiquitous and being a source of truth.[19] It is his earlier relativism that was prepared to see truth as an effect of power which remains a flaw within post-structuralist theories.

At the same time, what Foucault helps dispel is the idea that the powerless are virtuous and so can claim a moral purity. He fosters the notion that, for instance, both 'femininity' and 'masculinity' are constituted through relationships of power so that it is not that women are oppressed because men have power that should be theirs. But saying this tends to *dissolve* gender relationships of power and subordination, the specific character of which gets lost. We are left with a strangely disembodied notion of power. Not only is power inescapable but we are left feeling strangely incapable of analysing its gendered character.

Nancy Hartsock in 'Foucault on power: A theory for women?' raises the question of whether relations of power between the sexes are comparable to other kinds of power relations, or whether we need a new theory of power to account for them. She argues that we must

> distinguish between theories of power about women – theories which may include the subjugation of women as yet another variable to be considered, and theories of power for women – theories which begin from the experience and point of view of the dominated. Such theories would give attention not only to the ways women are dominated, but also to their capacities, abilities and strengths. In particular, such theories would use these capacities as guides for a potential transformation of power relationships – that is, for the empowerment of women.
>
> (Nicholson 1990:158)

Foucault finds it difficult to talk about capacities, abilities and strengths but, to be fair, so do our inherited traditions of social theory. It is partly because to enter this discussion is to challenge the vision of the rational self and the distinction between reason and nature that have structured our visions of modernity. This is crucially because modernity has been shaped to reflect a dominant masculinity.

Theorists of postmodernity such as Derrida, Rorty and Lyotard fail to take these moral and political issues to heart in their arguments against the totalising and universalistic theories we inherit from the Enlightenment. This is because they want to argue against a faith in universal reason that has informed 'modern' philosophy and social theory without challenging the dominant forms of masculinity which have sustained these conceptions. It is partly because modernity has been identified with reason and set against nature in the Kantian tradition that such writers have felt that to abandon reason because of its universality, we must also forsake morality.[20]

They get trapped in the idea that morality, like truth, is an effect of particular relations of power. It is because of this that they can talk of different rationalities that are constituted within different discourses, but not of the way that the universalism of reason was connected to its appropriation by the dominant masculinity. It is also because our capacities, abilities and strengths are supposedly constituted within particular discourses that it becomes impossible to develop any critical relationship to them or any sense of how they are 'distorted' or 'damaged' through the workings of relationships of power and oppression. This is something that Simone Weil can give us important insights into. She is aware that questions of power cannot be separated from issues of morality.

This is part of the weakness of the conceptions of difference that we find within discussions of post-modernity. We learn to think about difference as a way of *not* having to think about oppression and subordination. For it is partly in the context of oppression that we can begin to grasp how people's sense of themselves is undermined and their sense of worth and dignity destroyed. This is why it is so important, as Weil learned, to restore a person's sense of pride and dignity since this helps prepare the ground upon which people can act for themselves.

It is a strength of Hartsock's discussion that she recognises the political nature of differences as they have emerged among women, recognising that 'Issues of difference remind us as well that many of the factors which divide women also unite some women with men – factors such as racial or cultural differences' (Nicholson 1990:158)

Because of this,

> We need to develop our understanding of difference by creating a situation in which hitherto marginalised groups can name themselves, speak for themselves, and participate in defining the terms of interaction, a situation in which we can construct an understanding of the world that is sensitive to difference.
>
> (Nicholson 1990:158)

Though Simone Weil thought less in terms of difference, this resonates with how she conceived her task in her later writings.

NATURE, CULTURE AND POWER

An aspect of the workings of power is that the relatively powerless can always be *blamed* and held responsible for the failings of the powerful. Simone Weil knew from her experience of factory work how easily a foreman could always pass on his frustration and irritation. They had the power to let others have it, while the workers at the end of the line, so to speak, had to swallow their own resentment at this mistreatment, knowing that if they protested they would lose their jobs.[21]

Often such insights are lost in our investigations of hierarchical or authoritarian organisations, though the literature on sexual harassment at work helps to bring such issues into focus. It is as if those in power expect others to be available to them and if they complain they are accused of being 'hysterical' or of 'not having a sense of humour'. If others fail to believe what happened, not wishing to confront those in power, it can make you feel worse as your reality is denied.

In heterosexual relationships men often learn to blame women for what they are feeling themselves, as if it is the woman's task somehow to take the resentment or frustration away. It is also because men learn to be constrained and to take pride in being able to put up with things that women are often left carrying the emotions for the relationship. This can confirm a sense of the man's superiority as he learns to see his partner as 'emotional'.

It might well be that if we, as men, learned to take more responsibility for our own anger and resentment, even if this reflects on the image we like to sustain of ourselves, then our partners would not need to carry so much of the anger themselves. That the emotional economy works out this way partly grows out of the power that men have in relationships to withdraw and seem unaffected. In itself this is an exercise of power, though it is rarely appreciated as such. As men, we learn to pride ourselves on 'staying cool' and not getting 'too involved', thereby reaffirming our supposed superiority.

Psychoanalytic theory makes much of these processes of projection, but it is often less aware of the cultural processes that help to sustain them. It is part of a relationship of power to allow those with authority somehow to sustain the images they have of themselves by projecting emotions and feelings on to others. It means, as Jean Baker Miller points out, that men have traditionally been able to expect women to do their emotional work *for* them and that women have grown up to accept this as their task, so much so that they can feel guilt and responsibility if their partner is not feeling happy. It means that they must be failing in their duties and that if they only worked harder at it, they could make him happy. It means that as men we rarely have to take responsibility for our emotional lives. More than this, often we have only the slightest notion of what we are feeling, since we learn to discount these aspects of our experience. It is often regarded as wasting time and as a distraction, which is allowable to women but not to men, from getting on with the task at hand.

It is important to recognise ourselves in some of these processes, for projection has been a crucial aspect of modernity. We can only grasp this theoretically if we also have some sense of *how* it works in our experience. It is possible for men to present themselves as rational because women are treated as emotional. As men, we learn to discount our emotional lives. This was why Rousseau insisted in *Emile* that boys and girls should have a very different education. It is crucial to appreciate how liberal visions of freedom and equality have been conceived in terms of men, as have our unified visions of humanity.[22] For Rousseau, women's sexuality existed as a threat and so as 'other' to the independence and autonomy of men. Women existed as closer to nature and as nature was conceived as a threat to the rule of reason, so women's sexuality had to be curbed as a threat to men. So it was that women were to be seen in relation to men and their capacities, abilities and qualities. In the end their place was in serving the needs of men.

As Susan Griffin has explored the issue in *Pornography and Silence*, men have learned to deny their natural selves that were defined as a threat to their existence as rational selves (Griffin 1980). But since these aspects of our being could not be wished away in reality, as they are in theory within a post-structuralist theory that would construct them out of existence, they are constantly finding ways of reasserting themselves. Freud knew this as part of the mechanism of repression, so that our dreams and fantasies are constantly reminding us – or bringing us back – to aspects of our being that we have learned to ignore, denigrate or dispense with.

Griffin recognises that it is partly through exercising control over women that men learn to *curb* these feelings in themselves. It is as if exerting control over others becomes a way of maintaining a form of self-control, as domination of inner nature is such a crucial feature of dominant forms of male identity. I have traced some of the sources of this pervasive distinction within modernity between reason and nature, but Griffin helps to show how women, blacks and Jews have all been identified in different ways with a threatening nature. She helps establish the centrality for modernity between anti-Semitism, racism and misogyny.

Nancy Hartsock makes a similar point when she argues that

The philosophical and historical creation of a devalued 'other' was the necessary precondition for the creation of the transcendental rational subject outside of time and space, the subject who is the speaker in Enlightenment philosophy.

(Nicholson 1990:160)

I have shown how this distinction between reason and nature that helps to form the conception of the rational self is also tied to the devaluation of inner nature. With the dominant forms of masculinity there is a *loss* of interiority and connection with an inner self. Emotions and feelings are defined as 'other' and they are systematically denigrated as sources of knowledge.

As men, we learn to separate from these aspects of ourselves and the dominant forms of philosophy and social theory reflect this movement. These aspects of life are feared as 'soft' and 'unsystematic' and it remains the task of reason to salvage whatever is of worth, just as it is the task of science, in Bacon's terms, to wrest and torture whatever truths nature will reveal. Nature, like women, supposedly conceals what it knows and it is only through force that she will yield her secrets. So it is that violence and rape were to haunt the masculine unconscious as some of the dominant metaphors of modernity.

The relationship that Albert Memmi explored in *The Colonizer and the Colonized* helps to focus the ways that women are created as Other (Memmi 1967). As Nancy Hartsock has learned from Memmi, 'The Other is always seen as "not", as a lack, a void, as lacking in the valued qualities of the society, whatever those qualities may be'(Memmi 1967:83).

So it is that the humanity of the Other becomes 'opaque'. Memmi recalls that colonisers can frequently be heard making statements such as 'You never know what they think. Do they think? Or do they instead operate according to intuition?'. Like women who were thought of as having no souls or being capable of reason, the 'others' are constructed as marginal in relation to the rational self at the centre. The 'colonised' are not seen as individual members of the human community, but part of an anonymous collectivity since they carry 'the mark of the plural'.

Memmi describes this process of dehumanisation as the colonised ceases to be a subject of history and becomes only what the coloniser is not:

> the colonialist stresses those things that keep him separate rather than empha-sising that which might contribute to the foundation of a joint community. In those differences, the colonised is always degraded and the colonialist finds justification for rejecting his subjectivity. But perhaps the most important thing is that once the behavioural feature or historical or geographical factor which characterises the colonialist and contrasts him with the colonised has been isolated, this gap must be kept from being filled. The colonialist removes the factor from history, time and therefore possible evolution. What is a sociological point becomes labelled as being biological. Or, preferably, metaphysical. It is attached to the colonized's basic nature.
>
> (Memmi 1967:85)

This can help illuminate the ways that women are defined as emotional in a way that supposedly exhausts their being. Similarly, men claim reason as their own. It becomes difficult for men to hear what women are saying, poised as we often are to have our say. As men, we take it as our task to 'know better' what others should do. Women restricted to emotions supposedly cannot know at all.

As a Tunisian Jew, Memmi knew the coloniser as well as the colonised, and so 'understood only too well [the difficulty of the coloniser who refused] their inevitable ambiguity and the resulting isolation; more serious still, their inability to act' (Memmi 1967:xiv-xv). Nancy Hartsock tries to argue that this is a position that characterises Foucault's writings and partly accounts for his blindness to systematically unequal relations of power which tend to vanish from his account of power. As she has it, this is 'in part because power relations are less visible to those who are in a position to dominate others' (Nicholson 1990:165). This is particularly pertinent in men's relationships to feminism and the difficulties men often have in recognising their individual experience as an experience of mascu-linity.

This is an insight of consciousness-raising that connects theory to experience. It recognises the tensions and contradictions created between who we struggle to be as individuals and the social relationships which sustain our identities. But this is an insight lost to Foucault, who tends to treat experience as an effect of discourse, and this tends to leave his claim that wherever there is power there is resistance with little to support it.

Feminists have rightly drawn attention to a vision of men's studies which, according to Christine Griffin, would use 'an uncritical dualism which separates the intellectual/theoretical from the personal' (Griffin 1989:104). But within a structuralist tradition it is difficult to sustain a critical feminist insight about the relationship of theory and personal experience. This is one of the difficulties of Foucault's conception of power which would stress its systematic nature and its presence in multiple social relations. It has worked to marginalise and to some extent subvert some crucial aspects of feminist theory which otherwise had appreciated the inseparability of morality from power.

At the same time, it can be important to learn from Foucault's challenge to the notion of power as a commodity that one group or class uses to dominate another. As far as he is concerned, individuals 'are always in the position of simultaneously undergoing and exercising this power' (Foucault 1980:48). But if this helps us illuminate how men might be relatively powerless at work while at the same time exercising their power in the home, his account fails to come to terms with gendered, racial or class relations of domination.

This leaves him with a somewhat abstract vision of individuals who are constituted by power relations, but not specifically being brought up as boys, say, within a mining community. As Foucault has it, individuals are not to be seen as atoms that power strikes, but the fact that people are constituted as individuals is an effect of power. This threatens to lose the emotional complexity which is revealed in an experience of consciousness-raising to replace it with a complexity of its own. It can be persuasive in what it helps to argue against, but it leaves people strangely powerless to illuminate and transform the conditions of their oppression and subordination.

Nancy Hartsock recognises that Foucault 'takes yet another step toward making power disappear when he proposes the image of a net as a way to understand power' (Nicholson 1990:169). For, as she has it,

> The image of the net ironically allows (even facilitates) his ignoring of power relations whilst claiming to elucidate them. Thus he argues that power is exercised generally through a 'net-like organisation' and that individuals 'circulate between its threads'. (Foucault 48). Domination is not part of this image; rather, the image of a network in which we all participate carries implications of equality and agency rather than the systematic domination of the many by the few.
>
> (Nicholson 1990:169)

Again, Foucault seems to be clearer in establishing the weakness of unified conceptions of power which have started with a centralised vision of sovereignty and with the question of why we should obey. But his vision of disciplinary power, even if it wants to focus on issues of domination and subjugation, fails to illuminate them. It allows him to illuminate how power is ever expanding and he suggests an ascending analysis of power, starting from the 'infinitesimal mechanisms', each with their own history. But this helps us to identify the workings of power in families, mental hospitals and prisons in ways that the binary opposition between rulers and rules failed to illuminate.

But if Foucault senses the inadequacy of the binary oppositions, say, between capital and labour which worked within orthodox Marxism to marginalise other forms of misery and oppression, he leaves us with manifold relations of force which then become the basis for 'wide ranging effects of cleavage that run through the social body as a whole' (Foucault 1979:98). This is not enough, because it fails to appreciate how the 'personal' and the 'political' are related to each other so that our individual relationships are *shot through* with the realities of class, race and gender. If feminism helps us to rethink the relationships between 'micro' and 'macro' levels of analysis, it does this crucially at the level of experience. Hartsock tends to miss this in her vision of epistemology and her concern to show that objective social knowledge is possible. But to show this adequately involves a fuller exploration of the tensions between Marx's work and feminism.

In some of Foucault's later writings he seems to have focussed most specifically upon issues of individuality and subjecivity, so it is misleading to write as Hartsock does that

> Rather than getting rid of subjectivity or notions of the subject, as Foucault does, and substituting his notion of the individual as an effect of power relations, we need to engage in the historical, political and theoretical process of constituting ourselves as subjects as well as objects of history.
>
> (Nicholson 1990:170)

If she is to avoid the construction of another falsely universal discourse, she has to explore the complexities of feminist conceptions of subjectivity. If this is to avoid a stifling moralism it has to connect with the illumination that psychotherapy can bring into the ways that, for instance, women carry their injuries and humiliations from the past. Consciousness-raising also opens up the possibilities of recognising that personal suffering emerged out of shared conditions of subordination, as well as a recognition that healing these wounds would take time and space, if not also attention and love.

MODERNITY, EMOTIONS AND OPPRESSION

Feminism and psychotherapy connect in their recognition of the personal nature of oppression. It can be difficult to sustain this personal voice without being made to feel 'subjective' and 'untheoretical'. But this is a mistake, for it is an *impersonalisation* of personal and emotional life that has marked philosophy and social theories formed within the images of modernity. But reason does not have to be impersonal if it is transformed through a relationship with emotional life. Habermas tries to defend the emancipatory potential of Enlightenment reason which to him is the *sine qua non* of political democracy. As Andreas Huyssen has written about it in 'Mapping the postmodern', 'Habermas defends a substantive notion of communicative rationality, especially those who will collapse reason with domination, believing that by abandoning reason they will free themselves from domination' (Nicholson 1990:253).

Habermas is trying to salvage Enlightenment modernity against those such as

Lyotard who seem determined to liquidate any trace of the Enlightenment modernity inherited from the eighteenth century. In this, Habermas differs from Adorno and Horkheimer who, as an earlier generation of the Frankfurt School in *Dialectic of Enlightenment* (1973), challenged the dominance of instrumental rationality. Even if they were more pessimistic than Habermas, they still held on to a substantive notion of reason and subjectivity which much postmodern theory has abandoned.

I have tried to show how arguments about modernity are set in different terms if you acknowledge the particular relationship of reason to a dominant form of masculinity. This takes the issues that feminists have raised about the relation of reason to emotion, the 'personal' to the 'political', to the heart of current discussions about the crisis of modernity. It is also an awareness of the workings of power in relationship to language that raises difficulties for Habermas' conception of communicative rationality. He tends to assume, in Kantian terms, that we can abstract from relationships of power and subordination in order to relate to each other equally as language users. But as I have argued in *Kant, Respect and Injustice*, this Kantian vision which also informs the writings of Rawls and Dworkin cannot be sustained and that Kant himself had great difficulties when thinking about relationships between rich and poor in upholding this vision of equality as rational selves (Seidler 1986).

Feminism has helped us to acknowledge the ways that power and subordination can reduce people to silence. This is something that Simone Weil also appreciates in her discussions of power. She acknowledges the difficulties people have in believing that they count for something if they are constantly treated as if they count for nothing. Different feminisms tend to share an appreciation of the ways women are undermined and made to feel worthless by the workings of relationships of power and subordination. They record the processes through which people cease to exist for themselves and only exist in relation to others.

Consciousness-raising has helped many women disentangle some of these threads, but they often have less grasp of the psychological processes of change, often falling back on the idea that with the support of other women and with will and determination, changes will come. The move towards different forms of therapy was partly motivated by the insight that changing the conditions of one's life and relationships did not always mean you changed the ways you felt about yourself.

There are also the difficult issues of how to take greater responsibility for your emotional and material life. Since women had learned to blame themselves for how they felt, let alone for how their partners felt, it was possible in turn to blame their partners, for it was men who seemed to hold all the power in the relationship. But it was also possible for both women and men to find themselves locked into such a position of blame, unable to leave the relationship behind and explore new directions. This is an issue affecting women and men in different ways. The fact that men seem to locate their identities in the public world of work can blind them to the dependency they feel in an intimate relationship. At some levels men often expect to get their way in relationships and can blame their partners if they do not. This power is often exercised through an emotional withdrawal or a menacing silence. It is important to name this power for what it is, and I know myself how resistant and defensive I can be when this is pointed out to me. The fact that these forces of power operate in subtle ways can make them even harder to recognise. It is partly because male identity is so tied up with conceptions of control that men often resist identifying the controlling behaviour when it is pointed out to them.

It seems important to hold on to a recognition of the sources of power that men maintain in heterosexual relationships whilst also being able to recognise the ways men and women collude with each other in sustaining relationships as they are. A radical feminist analysis would reject this train of thought, thinking that it is the power that men hold that is the source of women's oppression and subordination. They argue that it is only in separating from relationships with men that women can discover the sources of their own autonomy and independence. Since they often argue that sexuality is a political choice, it is only will and determination that stands in the way of women being able to make these choices for themselves. It is partly because women have been left feeling as if relating with men is consorting with an enemy that there has been so little writing relatively on the issues of heterosexual relationships.

The ways that women are oppressed in personal and sexual relationships cannot be separated from the ways they are invalidated and their experience devalued within the institutionalised oppression in the larger society. So it is that the personal cannot be separated from the political and treated independently in a realm of its own. It is this insight that can also help transform traditions of psychotherapy which treat individual suffering and emotional life as a feature of personal relationships alone. Often they over-emphasise the extent to which people *can* be held responsible for the reality they create. This is partly an over-reaction to the idea that people are the products of situations and are powerless to change them. Therapy can broaden the options available and help people take more responsibility for themselves through recognising that even if they cannot change the way their boss is, for instance, they can at least change the ways they relate to their boss. But again all the issues of sexual harassment make this a very difficult issue for women.

Simone Weil helps to recognise oppression as both a moral and political category. It has to do with denying to people a sense of dignity to which they are entitled. So it is that women are denied a sense of the dignity of their emotional lives and within a rationalist culture are made to feel that it is only as rational selves – where this is defined in masculinist terms as the subordination of emotions and feelings – that they are deserving of respect. The Women's Movement has been important for women in supporting the idea that women can do whatever they want to do rather than be confined by the expectations of a patriarchal culture.

This has helped women explore capacities, talents and qualities that were devalued within the dominant culture and to value their emotions and intuitions as sources of knowledge. It has recognised how important it is for women to *believe* that they are capable, for it is a mark of oppression to feel that you will always fail.

If this is the message that a young girl was constantly given in her family, it will be difficult for her to believe that she can achieve anything in the world.

How is it that we learn to feel confidence in ourselves? In *The Moral Limits of Modernity* I have argued that this takes on a particular form within a Protestant moral culture in which as children we are constantly told that we are 'good for nothing' (Seidler 1991b). If we are told this by those we are close to, it is difficult not to absorb this. Ronald Laing's work is very important in showing how a sense of self-esteem and self-worth can so easily be shattered within a family. He recognises how our very sense of reality is at stake in the ways in which our experience is affirmed or invalidated within our relationships.

It is this focus on a 'sense of reality' and the ways it can be undermined or sustained in each encounter we have that gave Laing's work a resonance and originality in relation to orthodox traditions of psychoanalysis.[23] He also took the focus away from the individual in isolation with his or her emotional history and placed individuals within the context of familial relationships. If the Frankfurt School had recognised the importance of the family as a mediator of the dominant ideology, it never discovered an adequate way of investigating how often people were left feeling disempowered and self-blaming.

The pressure on another person to adopt one's own fantasy of the situation is what Laing calls 'induction', and once we have a family with a shared fantasy, transpersonal defences really come into their own. Laing illustrates this in his essay 'Persons and experience':

> If Jack succeeds in forgetting something, this is of little use if Jill continues to remind him of it. He must induce her not to do so. The safest way would be not just to make her keep quiet about it, but to induce her to forget it also.
>
> Jack may act on Jill in many ways. He may induce her to feel guilty for keeping on 'bringing it up'. He may *invalidate* her experience. This can be done more or less radically. He can indicate merely that it is unimportant or trivial, whereas it is important and significant to her. Going further, he can shift the *modality* of her experience from memory to imagination: 'It's all in your imagination.'. Further still, he can invalidate the *content*: 'It never happened that way.'. Finally, he can invalidate not only the significance, modality and content, but her very capacity to remember at all, and make her feel guilty for doing so into the bargain.
>
> (Collier 1977:31)

Are these different forms of invalidation connected to the nature of the power men have in relationship to women and the ways that they can claim reason to be their own within modernity? It would be interesting to investigate whether women within relationships of power are vulnerable in particular ways. Laing was concerned with the workings of unequal relationships, particularly in the context of the family where he often focussed on the mother–daughter relationship, as for instance in the chapter on 'the churches' in *Sanity, Madness and the Family*.[24]

Though the mother asserts that she has always got on well with her daughter, the daughter's account is that this is because the mother is a domineering character and she prefers to submit rather than to argue. Her mother replies, defending her own fantasy structure, that 'When you *are* an organiser in business you sort of carry it a bit into the home as well....But we seem to have got on very well throughout the years', and that 'you [the daughter] never like a lot of fuss, do you?'.

As Andrew Collier points out in his study of Laing, without actually denying the facts as seen by the daughter (indeed, her reply confirms them), 'she is redefining them such that the problem disappears' (Collier 1977). We no longer have a domineering mother and a daughter who submits but rather an efficient organiser and someone who does not like a lot of fuss. At the same time the mother reasserts her own view that 'we get on very well' and leaves it up to the daughter to disagree if she can. Laing comments,

> We wish to emphasize here not so much the mother's evident *intra*-personal defences but that she has to defend herself from the evocation in her of her own feeling by acting on Claire to muddle *her* up, to render *her* speechless, to obliterate *her* memory – in short, by introducing a disorganisation *in her daughter's* personality. That Mrs. Church's actions serve this function does not of course mean that they necessarily have this intention.
>
> (Laing and Esterson 1970: 94–5)

A child is particularly vulnerable if her parents insist, for example, that what she thinks she perceives and remembers, she actually only imagines. If traditional psychoanalysis persists in this mode of operating, presumably it can have destructive consequences. Children in particular have few ways of checking their own experience other than their parents' confirmation of it.

But feminism can help to broaden the context in which we can explore some of Laing's findings, for men also have power to muddle and confuse since they claim that their relationship to reason gives them a particular access to what is best for others. This is what so often makes men 'unreasonable' in their reason. It is the very impersonality of this conception of reason that allows it so easily to speak for others. It has become the dominant voice in our conceptions of philosophy and social theory within modernity. It has a self-confidence that is partly derived from the authority that reason has within the larger society to discern in a disinterested and neutral way what the best outcome for everyone would supposedly be.

But it has not gone unchallenged, nor has its vision of life and relationships. With feminism, psychotherapy and ecology we have social movements which have challenged the terms of modernity, showing how unreasonable a reason separated from nature could be. As we challenge the visions of power, progress and history that we inherit within modernity, we open up to different possibilities in ourselves and social relationships. As we move beyond the rational self, finding ways to honour our emotional and spiritual lives, so new forms of social theory which can illuminate human suffering and oppression as well as sources of joy and fulfilment begin to be sensed. Different visions of freedom and equality grow to sustain moral and political life.

Notes

1 INTRODUCTION

1 For some helpful discussions that illuminate the connections between the Enlightenment and the emergence of different traditions of social and political theory, see Hawthorne 1976; Giddens 1971; Zeitlin 1968; Gouldner 1970; Nisbet 1967; Marcuse 1986; and Hulme and Jordanova 1990.

2 Useful reflections on this relationship between culture and nature which are sensitive to its bearing upon gender relations are provided by MacCormack and Strathern 1980; and Griffin 1980. See also Sherry B. Ortner, 'Is Female to Male as Nature is to Culture?' in M. Z. Rosaldo and L. Lamphere 1974 and P. Brown and L. J. Jordanova, 'Oppressive Dichotomies: the Nature/Culture Debate' (Cambridge Women's Studies Group).

3 Discussion of Weber's relationship to our visions of modernity are provided by Mac-Intyre 1981. See also discussions of Weber's work provided by D. MacRrae (1977); Parkin 1982; Stammer 1971; Lash and Whimster 1987; and Brubacker 1984; and Mommsen 1974.

4 To place Durkheim in historical and cultural context, see, for instance, Gouldner 1970; Giddens 1978; Lukes 1983; Thompson 1982; Nisbet 1967; and Pearce 1989.

5 For an introduction to Kant's ethics which draws out some of these implications for social theory, see Seidler 1986. See also Taylor, 'Kant's theory of freedom' (1985: 318–37), and Hans Fink's brief discussion in *Social Philosophy* (1981).

6 Feminist discussions of liberal conceptions of freedom, equality and rights are usefully explored in Moller Okin 1980; Kennedy and Mendus 1987; Jaggar 1983; Grimshaw 1986; Elshtain 1981.

7 Useful introductory discussions to the issues surrounding distinctions between modernity and postmodernity are provided by Foster 1985; Huyssen 1986; Bauman 1991a and 1991b; Lash 1990; and Berman 1982.

8 A sensitivity to issues of race, ethnicity and gender as they emerge in the context of the Enlightenment and the ways that this subverts historically received notions of the Enlightenment as exclusively the source of reason, freedom and progress is to be found in *The Enlightenment and its Shadows* (Hulme and Jordanova 1990). See also Griffin 1980, where some important connections are made between issues of gender and race because of their both falling on the side of a despised and denigrated nature; Davis 1989 and 1990; Jordan 1980; and Poliakov 1974.

9 Simone Weil's discussion of oppression and dignity is a theme in Blum and Seidler 1984, Chs.4 and 5. See in particular some of Weil's early formulations on these issues in Weil 1978, and her later essay entitled 'Human Personality' in Weil 1962.

10 Some of these themes are helpfully explored within a tradition of critical theory by

Herbert Marcuse (1986). For a somewhat different interpretation of Hegel, see Taylor 1978 and his shortened *Hegel and Modern Society* (1979).

11 Simone Weil discussed the relationship between sciences and the humanities in the wake of modernity in *The Need for Roots* (Weil 1988). It is an important theme for her as she seeks the validation of different forms of knowledge. It is partly the integration of conservative themes into her particular radical vision that makes her writings difficult to place. At the same time it is partly her rejection of the ways that left and right have traditionally been conceived since the French Revolution that makes her so pertinent to our times. She certainly helps to question the easy ways that modernity and postmodernity are often conceived.

12 Simone Weil's appreciation of Descartes upon whom she worked for her dissertation is to be found in McFarland and Van Ness 1988. It helpfully challenges the simplistic terms in which Descartes and Cartesianism are so often identified. For other useful introductions to Descartes' writings, see Rée 1974; Kenny 1968, and Williams 1978.

13 Useful introductions to structuralism as it emerged within post-war France are provided by Mark Poster 1975; Descombes 1980; Jameson 1972; Hawkes 1977; Sturrock 1979; Benton 1984; Eagleton 1990.

14 For some interesting discussions about Durkheim's relationship to Kant at different times in his life see, for instance, Lukes 1983; Woolfe (ed) 1964; Bellah 1984.

2 NATURE

1 The scientific revolutions of the seventeenth century are usefully introduced by Burtt 1932; and Whitehead 1958. See also Farrington 1969; Easlea 1981, Ch.3; and Ehrenreich and English 1979, Chs. 1,2 and 3.

2 The shift from the organic to a mechanistic conception of nature is introduced in Capra 1975. See also Bateson 1979; Sheldrake 1981; 1988; and Merchant 1980.

3 A useful introduction to the writings of Derrida is provided by *Writing and Difference* (Derrida 1981). See also a variety of assessments offered in *Derrida and Deconstruction* (Silverman 1989), while the notion of the postmodern is discussed in a helpful way by Bauman 1991b and Smart 1983.

4 Discussion of different feminists' relationships with modernity are provided by Craig Owens, 'The discourse of others; Feminists and postmodernism' in Foster 1985. See also Nicholson 1990, in particular pieces by Nancy Fraser and Linda Nicholson, 'Social criticism without philosophy; an encounter between feminism and postmodernism' and Susan Bardo, 'Feminism, postmodernism and gender-scepticism'.

5 Discussions of personal identity that help illuminate some of these issues are provided by Williams 1973. See also the paper 'Persons, character and morality' in his later collection *Moral Luck* (1981: 1–14). See the useful introduction by Noonan 1991.

6 Merchant 1980 gives an important historical grounding to the complexities of relationships with nature and how they interact with inherited visions of the self. See also Thomas 1971, which also provides many historical insights into these profound cultural transformations.

7 Descartes' conception of animals is helpfully discussed by Midgley 1983. See also useful discussions in Regan 1988; and Clark 1977 and 1982.

8 The complex relationship of modernity with colonialism is illuminated in different ways by Fanon 1967a, 1967b; Memmi 1967; Sartre 1960 and Nizan 1960.

9 The relationship of the Enlightenment to the legitimations of the slave trade has been partly explored by David B. Davis. On the problems of slavery in the Age of Revolution, see also Williams 1964. See also more recently broader discussions in Young 1990 and Said 1990.

10 The relationships between the growth of science in the seventeenth century and the witch

trials that spanned western Europe and north America have been explored by Ehrenreich and English 1979. See also Brian Easlea 1981.

11 Mary Daly has explored some of the implications of the witch burnings within western culture in *Gyn/Ecology: the Meta-ethics of Radical Feminism* (Daly 1978). See also *Beyond God the Father (1973)* and *Pure Lust* (1984).

12 Attempts to take more seriously children's own experiences of schooling are to be found in Holt 1969 and 1970; Dennison 1971; Graubard 1972 School of Barbiana 1969. This is an important literature that is too easily categorised as 'permissive'. As certain forms of structuralist Marxist theories gained ascendancy in the 1970s it became more difficult to recognise the significance of this writing which was often dismissed as 'humanist'. With the return to more traditional teaching methods in the 1980s it proved difficult to draw upon this literature creatively.

13 Kant's treatment of altruistic emotions is usefully treated by Lawrence Blum in *Friendship, Altruism and Morality* (Blum 1980). See also Bernard Williams' insightful paper, 'Morality and the emotions' in Williams 1973: 207–29.

14 Freud talks about the repression of sexuality and emotional life in more broadly cultural terms in *Civilization and its Discontents* (Freud 1961). For helpful discussion of these themes in his writings see Rieff 1965; Mannoni 1991 and Gay 1988.

15 Erich Fromm provides an interesting discussion of Luther and Calvin in his *Fear of Freedom* (1946). While drawing on the writings of Tawney and Weber he helps extend a sense of the protestant underpinnings within a secularised vision of modernity. It reaches beyond preparing the ground for capitalist motivation, as Weber tends to have it.

16 Reich developed ways of working with the emotional life of the body, thinking that in large part he was remaining faithful to Freud's earlier energetic conceptions of the libido in his notions of sexuality. Interesting introductions to Reich's work are provided by David Boadella 1988 and Sharaf 1985. For a grasp of Reich's complex relationship to Freud, see Reich 1974 and 1967.

3 REASON

1 Foucault's *Birth of the Clinic* is helpful in laying out some of the implications for this changed conception of medicine. He does not give attention to the gender implications and the reordering of gender relations that served to legitimate the horrors of the witch burnings. Exploring connections between dominant forms of masculinity and forms of knowledge seem indispensable if we are to illuminate these cultural and historical transitions.

2 Interesting discussions of the nature of medical knowledge in its relationship to people's control of their own health are provided by Armstrong 1983; Foucault 1976; Ehrenreich and English 1979; Roberts 1991; Kidel 1988; and Rose 1991.

3 Discussion of Foucault's conception of the regulation of the body can be found in Foucault 1975. It is also a theme discussed in some of the interviews with Foucault collected by Gordon (Foucault 1980). See also discussions in Turner 1984 and 1987.

4 For some interesting discussions of the emotional life of the body, see, for instance, Lowen 1963 and 1972; and Boadella 1976; Kellerman 1974 and 1975; Dychwald 1978.

5 Introductions to Wittgenstein's work are provided by Norman Malcolm, *Ludwig Wittgenstein: A Memoir* (Malcolm 1958) and his more recent study of the continuities in Wittgenstein's philosophical writings, *Nothing is Hidden* (1986); Hacker 1972; and Kenny 1973. See also the useful essays collected in Pitcher (ed.) *Wittgenstein* (1968) and the biography that seeks to connect themes in his work to his life, *Wittgenstein* (Monk 1990).

6 Interesting discussions of Weber's conception of rationalisation are provided by Beetham

1985; Mommsen 1974; and Connolly 1986. See also Brubaker 1984; Lash and Whimster 1987; and Holton and Turner 1990.

7 Attempts to rethink some of Weber's work in relation to the exclusion of women's experience can be found in Sydie 1987 and Bologh 1990.

8 See Sheila Rowbotham's early writings on themes of language and power, 'Women's liberation and the new politics' reprinted in her collected writings *Dreams and Dilemmas* (Rowbotham 1983). Issues of language in relation to women's subordination were opened by Daly 1978; Smith 1992; and Spender 1980. See the responses to this work from Cameron 1985 and Ramazanoglu 1989.

9 Explorations of the historicity of men's relationships to their emotional lives are provided by Roper and Tosh 1990. See also Kimmel 1991. For a sense of how gay men have dealt with these issues see Weeks 1977; Hall Carpenter Archives 1989: and Porter and Weeks 1990. See also Duberman (1991).

10 For a discussion of men's fear of intimacy and disdain of emotional life see Seidler 1989, chapter on 'Intimacy', and 'Rejection, vulnerability and friendship' in Nardi 1992. See also the discussion in Jackson 1990 and Miller 1983.

11 The relationship of respect and self-worth to power is an important theme explored in Blum and Seidler 1984, Ch.7, 'Power', pp. 194–256.

12 The ways our visions of equality and equal relationships are tied in with the capacity to abstract from social relationships of power and subordination is a central theme in Bernard Williams' 'The idea of equality' reprinted in *Problems of the Self* (1973: 230–44). It is also centrally discussed in relation to Kant, Kierkegaard and Simone Weil in Seidler 1991b.

13 Simone Weil's reflections on the moral injuries imposed by the workings of the criminal justice system are in 'Forms of the implicit love of God' (Weil 1959: 94–166).

14 The recognition of the emotional work that has traditionally been left to women to do is a theme in Baker Miller 1976.

4 MORALITY

1 For a useful introduction to Kohlberg's work on moral development and the ways that it grows out of an engagement with both Kant and the psychological work of Piaget see Lawrence Kohlberg *Essays on Moral Development, Vol. 1. The Philosophy of Moral Development* (Kohlberg 1981).

2 Kohlberg's later work on democratic schooling which reports in detail on schools that were being reorganised with more democratic forms of participation is described in terms of the just community approach in Lawrence Kohlberg's *Approach to Moral Education* (Clark Power *et al.* 1989).

3 The case of Hans is reported in Gilligan 1982. She argues that we have tended to diminish the moral experience of women since we have often judged their experience by standards that are drawn directly from the experience of men. It also has to do with the standing of Kant's ethical theory as establishing itself in impartial terms, so making it difficult to explore the relationship of dominant masculinities to particular forms of moral theory.

4 Kant's views about women and marriage are usually dismissed as 'peripheral' and as having little bearing upon the basic structure of his moral theory. This is also said about his racism and anti-Semitism which are all taken to be incidental and only focused upon by those who supposedly have 'an axe to grind'. But this is mistaken, for these views emerge from quite central tenets in his moral theory and the ways its universalism is premissed upon a categorical distinction between reason and nature. For some discussion of these themes see, for instance, Poliakov 1974, 1976; Davis 1989. It seems as if we are only just beginning to come to grips with these issues. Their relationship to modernity is

far more complex than is usually conceived by those who wish to place it safely in the past as we enter a moment of 'postmodernity'.

5 The way that the emotional dependency of men is often hidden within the workings of relationships is a theme in Eichenbaum and Orbach 1983; 1984. It is also a theme in Seidler 1991a.

6 Iris Murdoch talks about the kind of attention that it takes to see a person in this way. It is a theme that recurs in *The Sovereignty of Good* (Murdoch 1970). It is also something that Simone Weil recognises when she talks about 'reading' others. See the section entitled 'Reading' (Weil 1992).

5 FREEDOM

1 For an account of how identities were established within feudal times see Tawney 1926. See also Bloch 1989; Hirschman 1977; and Lovejoy 1936.

2 Conceptions of individualism that emerged with the growth of the capitalist market economy are discussed by Macpherson 1962; MacFarlane 1979; Baechler 1989; and Giddens 1981.

3 Luther's anti-Semitism is a theme explored in Poliakov 1976; and Almog 1988. It has been a significant silence, for it set the terms in which Jews were so often to be treated within modernity. So often they were trapped, echoing the choice Luther had given them and then being blamed for remaining faithful to their own culture and traditions.

4 For some useful discussions of the different forms that tolerance can take within a culture of a capitalist modernity see for instance Moore *et al.*1965; Mendes 1989; Bauman 1991a.

5 The ways Christianity for so long legitimated the slave trade is a theme in Davis 1990.

6 Alice Miller reflects upon the relationship between a protestant tradition and forms of child-rearing that are still very much taken for granted. She alerts us to the injuries we do to the emotional lives of our children while believing that we are acting 'for their own good'. See her discussion of 'Poisonous pedagogy' (Miller 1983a).

7 Gramsci's discussion of the relationships of power to consciousness are to be found in *The Prison Notebooks*, Part 3, 'The philosophy of Praxis' (1) 'The study of philosophy' (Gramsci 1971: 321–77).

8 More sophisticated and complex discussions of religion in the context of expressing material struggles of society are provided by Christopher Hill in, for instance, *The World Turned Upside Down* (1975) and *Milton and the English Revolution* (1977). For an appreciation of this shift within Marxist scholarship see E. P. Thompson's essay, 'An open letter to Leszek Kolakowski' (Thompson 1979: 92–192).

9 For some useful introductory discussions of Althusser and a tradition of structuralist Marxism, see Althusser 1970; Calinicoss 1976: and Benton 1984. For some critical appraisals of this direction of work see, for instance, Clarke *et al.* 1980, and E. P. Thompson's essay 'The poverty of theory' (Thompson 1979).

10 Rawls' account of a just ordering of society is provided in his *A Theory of Justice* (Rawls 1972). For some discussion of this work see Daniels 1975; Walzer 1983; and Sandel 1983; and for a discussion that attempts to relate it to issues of power and subordination see Seidler 1986, Ch.8, 'Liberalism and the autonomy of morality'.

11 Carol Gilligan's abortion study is reported on in *In a Different Voice: Psychological Theory and Women's Development* (Gilligan 1982).

12 This tradition of emotivism has been usefully explored within a cultural and historical context by Alasdair MacIntyre in *After Virtue* (1981, Ch.2 and Ch.3). See also the discussion by Mary Warnock in *Ethics in the Twentieth Century* (1962); Donegan 1977; and Gewirth 1978.

13 There is a useful discussion of these issues of identity between M. Foucault and R. Sennett in 'Sexuality and solitude' in *Anthology 1* (1981). See also the different positions taken

up by Jeffrey Weeks in 'Identities' and Victor J. Seidler in 'Reason, desire and male sexuality' in *The Cultural Construction of Sexuality* (Caplan 1987). Some sense of the development of Foucault's change of heart around the issues is provided in *Technologies of the Self* (Martin *et al.* 1988).

14 Isaiah Berlin in *Against the Current* sets out the terms of discussion between Enlightenment and counter-Enlightenment in illuminating terms (Berlin 1981). See also his essay 'Herder and the Enlightenment' in *Vico and Herder* (1976: 143–216).

6 IDENTITY

1 Richard Rorty's *Philosophy and the Mirror of Nature* can help us reflect upon the ways in which 'modern' philosophy has been characterised (Rorty 1979). See also his introductory essay 'Pragmatism and philosophy' to *Consequences of Pragmatism* (Rorty 1982). For connections with ethical theory see Williams 1985, and MacIntyre 1981.

2 A useful discussion of the historical sources of functionalism within the human sciences is provided by Gouldner (1970). See also helpful discussions in Mary Douglas's *Evans Pritchard* (1982).

3 Durkheim discusses this transition from mechanical to organic solidarity in *The Division of Labour* (1964). See discussions of Durkheim in, for example, Giddens 1978; Lukes 1983; Thompson 1982.

4 Herbert Marcuse's *Reason and Revolution* helps us to think about how positivism as a tradition developed partly as a response to Hegel's sense that oppressive institutions had to be *negated* to be made rational (Marcuse 1986). The fact that institutions existed did not thereby make them rational. This was a powerful impulse in Marx's continuing relationship with Hegel.

5 Introductions to Max Weber and interpretive traditions in sociology are provided by Bauman 1978; Weber 1949; Douglas 1971.

6 Georg Lukács' seminal essay 'Reification and the consciousness of the proletariat' is to be found in *History and Class Consciousness* (1971: 83–222). This element in his thinking has been discussed by Arato and Breines (1979). See also Heller 1983 and Lichtheim 1970.

7 Stuart Hampshire's *Thought and Action* (1959) provides an important contemporary discussion of explanations of human action, especially in their attempts to come to terms with Freud's exploration of unconscious desires. Some of the rationalist assumptions which underpin Hampshire's discussions have been usefully explored by Iris Murdoch in *The Sovereignty of Good* (Murdoch 1970).

8 Helpful introductions to the writings of Alfred Schutz in relation to Weber are provided by his *The Methodology of the Social Sciences* (Weber 1949). See also discussions of Schutz's work provided by Bauman 1978 and Berger and Luckman 1967.

9 Movements towards a phenomenological sociology are usefully sketched in Michael Phillipson's 'Phenomenological philosophy and sociology' and Dave Walsh's 'Sociology and the social world' and 'Varieties of positivism', in Filmer *et al.* 1972. For some critical discussion of this direction of work see, for instance, Giddens 1976; Keat and Urry 1982; Turner 1974; and Bernstein 1978.

10 For studies which question positivist notions of suicide see, for instance, Douglas 1970. For crime see, for instance, Cicourel 1968.

11 A useful and historically sensitive account of phenomenological sociology, as it has emerged from Husserl, is provided by Bauman 1978.

12 Some attempts to learn from Heidegger's critiques of Husserl for social theory are provided by Paci. This is also a significant theme in the development of Derrida's work. For a useful introduction see Derrida 1981.

13 A useful introduction to Garfinkel and the development of ethnomethodology is provided

by his *Studies in Ethnomethodology* (Garfinkel 1984). See also Heritage 1984; Turner 1974; and Sharrock 1982.
14 For a useful introduction to Silverman's work see Silverman 1985.

7 MODERNITY

1 For an understanding of the development of Laing's work see his autobiographical work *Wisdom, Madness and Folly: The Making of a Psychiatrist 1927–1957* (Laing 1985). Some interesting critical discussions are provided by Collier (1977); and Showalter (1987, Ch.9). See also Sedgewick 1982.
2 Some interesting reflections on the history of psychiatry are provided by Porter 1981; Scull 1982; and Jones 1985.
3 An interesting introduction to Foucault's work on the history of madness, *Madness and Civilization*, is provided by Sheridan 1980; and Dreyful and Rabinow 1982. See also the numerous interviews provided by Foucault in which he reflects on his early work in, for instance, Gordon 1980; Kritzman 1990.
4 For a discussion of the relationship between masculinity, madness and modernity, see Seidler's 'Reason, desire and male sexuality' in Caplan (1987: 82–112).
5 A useful text which begins to raise questions about the relationship of an Enlightenment vision of modernity to issues of slavery and witch burnings is *Enlightenment and its Shadows* (Hulme and Jordan 1990). Set in quite different terms, it is also a theme in Griffin 1980.
6 The growth of scientific knowledge in its relationship to the seventeenth-century scientific revolutions is explored in Burtt 1932; Whitehead 1958; Needham 1969; and Mulkay 1984.
7 The marginalisation of women as their knowledge was devalued in the face of the new science of medicine is a central theme in Ehrenreich and English (1979). It is also explored in Merchant 1980; and Easlea 1981.
8 The central notions of an empiricist tradition developed in the philosophical writings on Locke, Berkeley and Hume is introduced by Berlin 1979; Doyal and Harris 1990; and Hollis 1977.
9 Kant's vision of moral agency is discussed in Seidler (1986), where some of the implications of the separation of reason from nature are explored. For a discussion of the place of altruistic emotions within Kant's moral framework see Blum 1980, and the special issue of *Ethics* Vol. 101 No.4, July 1991, with the *Symposium on Impartiality and Ethical Theory*.
10 The relationship of work, success and masculine identities within a Protestant culture is a theme explored in Seidler 1991a, Chs.2 and 3.
11 Stanley Cavell has mentioned these themes about the relationship of our knowledge of objects to persons in the introductory essay *Must We Mean What We Say?* (Cavell 1969). See also his essays 'The availability of Wittgenstein's later philosophy', pp. 44–72, and 'Austin at criticism', pp. 97–114.
12 Martin Bernal's *Black Athena* raises important questions about the construction of the west in its relationship to classical Greece (Bernal 1987). He shows how this Aryan model was constructed in the nineteenth century with the effect of denying the connections between Greece and Egypt which the Greeks were very much aware of themselves. It is part of a denial of the contributions of Semitic, Black and Phoenician heritages and it aids in the construction of Europe as a predominantly white and Christian inheritance having its source in classical Greece alone.
13 Elaine Pagels' *The Gnostic Gospels* provides an insightful introduction to these lost traditions within Christianity (Pagels 1982). It also helps us to rethink the relationship between Christianity and Judaism and the historical sources of a Christian anti-Semitism

with its source in the denial of the Jewishness of Jesus. This is somehow connected to crucial issues of the relationship of authority to knowledge.

14 A helpful introduction to Wittgenstein's work is provided by Norman Malcolm *Nothing is Hidden* (1986). For some interesting discussions of Wittgenstein's arguments about private language, see the papers 'On Wittgenstein's use of the term "criterion"' by Roger Albritton, pp. 231–50; 'Can there be private language?' by R. Rhees, pp. 267–85; 'Wittgenstein on privacy' by John W. Cook, pp. 268–323 in Pitcher 1968.

15 Michael Löwy *Georg Lukács – from Romanticism to Bolshevism* provides a helpful account of Lukács' intellectual and political development (Löwy 1979). See also Lukács *Political Writings 1914–1929* (1972).

16 Some sense of the intellectual and moral development of Wittgenstein's work is provided by Malcolm 1986. See also Drury 1973; and Rhees 1981.

17 The West was able to formulate modernity in its own image partly through the antagonism between reason and nature. It was the threat provided by nature that legitimated its domination and so provided justifications for slavery and colonial oppression. See, for instance, Williams 1964; McLuhan 1971; West 1982; Said 1991; and Wolf 1986.

18 There seems to be some resonance here between Wittgenstein and some of the ways Walter Benjamin was struggling to enrich the conception of experience and so provide a new impulse for philosophical reflection. This seems to be a theme in Benjamin's two essays entitled 'N Theoretic of knowledge, theory of progress', and 'Program of the coming philosophy' in Benjamin 1983: 1–40 and 41–51.

19 For Wittgenstein's remarks on the nature of remembering see *The Philosophical Investigations* (Wittgenstein 1958).

20 It seems possible to think that Wittgenstein's later writings, particularly *On Certainty*, were written as some kind of response and challenge to a Cartesian tradition that has been powerful in shaping our conceptions of modernity and the character of what we have taken to be 'modern philosophy'.

21 Kant was very clear that women and children could only guide their lives by reason if they accepted subordinating themselves to the authority of man's reason. This was a central aspect of the inequality between the sexes that was embodied in reason as essentially a masculine quality. See Kant's discussion of relations between the sexes in *Anthropology from a Pragmatic Point of View* (Kant 1974). Some discussion of this theme is provided by Fink 1981; Mendus, 'Kant: an honest but narrow-minded burgeois?' in Kennedy and Mendus 1987: 21–43; and Lloyd 1984.

22 Some of the clearest formulations of a structuralist challenge to the 'essentialism' of a humanist tradition of classical social and political theory are to be found in Althusser's essays collected in *For Marx* (Althusser 1970). See, for instance, 'Marxism and humanism', pp. 219–47 and 'On the young Marx', pp. 49–86. Some of the frameworks continue to inform poststructuralist ways of thinking and feeling, long after the adherence to Althusserian Marxism has been forsaken. The tradition lives on in some of the influence Foucault has had on contemporary forms of social theory.

23 Wittgenstein extended exploration of the language around pain behaviour in the *Philosophical Investigations* (Wittgenstein 1958).

24 Richard Rorty explores some of these themes, though he moves in quite a different direction, in *Philosophy and the Mirror of Nature* (Rorty 1979). See also his essays collected in *Consequences of Pragmatism* (Rorty 1982).

8 EXPERIENCE

1 The historical emergence of a positivist and functionalist tradition within sociology is explored by Alvin Gouldner in *The Coming Crisis of Western Sociology*, Part 3 (Gouldner 1970). See also Benton 1984 Part 2; Giddens 1974; and 1977, Ch.1.

2 Useful introductions to Hegel's social and political theory are provided by Marcuse 1986; and Taylor 1979. See also Avineri 1972.

3 Some interesting reflections on the relationship between Hegel and Marx are provided by Marcuse 1986; Hyppolite 1969; and Kojeve 1969.

4 Some initial reflections on resonances between Hegel and Wittgenstein can be found in a paper by Karen Feifer entitled 'Hegel's Wittgenstein' (unpublished Ms.).

5 See Vaclav Havel's early essays, 'The power of the powerless' and 'An anatomy of reticence' (Havel 1987: 36–122, 164–95).

6 Sheila Rowbotham's early essay 'Women's liberation and the new politics' sets out some of the themes which inspired the early years of the women's liberation movement. It is reprinted in *Dreams and Dilemmas* (Rowbotham 1983).

7 Useful introductions to Habermas' discussions of language and communication can be found in the interview edited by Peter Dews (Dews 1986, Chs.6, 7, 8 and 12). See also the comprehensive introduction to Habermas' early writings in McCarthy 1978; and Bernstein 1985.

8 Some of the difficulties in abstracting from relations of power and subordination within the liberal theories of Rawls, Dworkin and others are explored in the concluding chapter to Seidler 1986 entitled 'Liberalism and the autonomy of morality'.

9 Discussions of the way that feminist theories have worked to rethink relations between public and private life are explored in Benhabib and Cornell 1987: Elshtain 1981; Young 1990.

10 Useful introductions to this tendency within feminism are provided by Dora Russell.

11 Some interesting issues for feminist method are raised in *Doing Feminist Research* (Roberts 1981). See also Harding 1986; 1989; Fox Keller's 'Feminism and science' in Keonane and Rosaldo 1982; Harding 1987; Bleier 1986.

12 Simone Weil's treatment of power in the capacity to crush and deform human lives is discussed in Ch.7 'Power' in Blum and Seidler 1984: 194–256.

13 The stresses that can be built into relationships between women are explored by Eichenbaum and Orbach in *Bittersweet* (1990).

14 Mannheim's sociology of knowledge was criticised by Adorno in 'The sociology of knowledge and its consciousness' in *Prisons* (1967: 35–50). It has also been usefully discussed by Simmonds 1978.

9 FEMINISM

1 A useful historical sense of the development of the women's liberation movement is provided by Sheila Rowbotham in *Dreams and Dilemmas* (1983). See in particular the essay 'Women's liberation and the new politics' (originally reprinted in Wandor 1972: 5–31). See also the section entitled 'Women, power and consciousness: Discussions in the women's liberation movement in Britain 1964–1981', pp. 136–60.

2 A sense of the difficulties that women faced in discovering feminist values within a man's world is provided by Sheila Rowbotham's *Woman's Consciousness, Man's World* (1973). See also Coote and Campbell 1982; and Firestone 1970.

3 Liberal conceptions of equality and freedom are explored in Seidler 1986. Their links to feminist theory are investigated by Jagger 1983, Chs.3 and 7, and Moller Okin 1980.

4 A discussion of the market is provided in Elshtain 1981. See also 'Desire, consent and liberal theory' by Lenore Coltheart, in Pattman and Gross 1986: 112–22.

5 Equality and the public realm is discussed in Mitchell and Oakley (1979). See, for instance, 'Women and equality' by Juliet Mitchell. See also Iris Young, 'Impartiality and the civil public' in Benhabib and Cornell 1987: 57–76; and Siltanen and Stanworth 1984.

6 A discussion of women's rights and equality is provided by Mary Midgley and Judith Hughes in *Women's Choices: Philosophical Problems Facing Feminism* (1983). For a

critical discussion of the language of rights and the difficulties it has illuminating women's oppression, see Blum and Seidler 1984, Chs.5 and 7.

7 Some record of men's responses to feminism is given in Victor J. Seidler, 'Men and Feminism' in *Achilles' Heel* No. 2. This is collected, along with other pieces from *Achilles' Heel* in *The Achilles' Heel Reader: Men, Sexual Politics and Socialism*, ed. Seidler (1991c).

8 See 'Liberalism and the autonomy of morality' which is the concluding chapter of Seidler 1986.

9 Some discussion of the relationship of Marxism to masculinity is provided by Hearn 1987; and Connell 1987.

10 Some of the difficulties of consciousness-raising as they were experienced by men are explored and situated historically in Seidler 1989, Ch.4, 'Control', pp. 44–71.

11 Juliet Mitchell's *Psychoanalysis and Feminism* very much sets the terms for the introduction of a structuralist reading of Freud, influenced by Lacan (Mitchell 1975). Its vision of the historical relationship of psychoanalysis to feminism is challenged by Baker Miller 1976. The different traditions of work still need to be critically related to each other. Some attempt to provide a broad overview of the issues is attempted by Sayers 1986.

12 An introduction to issues raised by feminist psychotherapy is provided by Ernst and Maguire 1987. See also Eichenbaum and Orbach 1983.

13 Some of the implications of the Enlightenment identification of masculinity with reason are explored in Seidler 1989, Ch.2: and 1991a, Chs.2 and 3.

14 Some discussion of feminist challenges to a positivist methodology is provided by Harding 1986; Roberts 1981; Ramazanoglu 1989; Smith 1988; and Stanley and Wise 1983.

15 In *Rediscovering Masculinity: Reason, Language and Sexuality* (Seidler 1989) I share a particular history and experience of these times. This period in the 1960s and early 1970s is too often rejected rather than investigated for what it can still teach us.

16 The place of emotions and feelings in Kant's rationalistic ethics is explored by Blum 1980. It is also a theme in Seidler 1986.

17 Jeffrey Weeks helps to set out the significance of Freud's work to grasp the precarious character of sexual identities (Weeks 1984, 1985). I have explored some of the difficulties with the structuralist framework within which it is set in a review in *Sociological Review*, May 1988. See also some of the discussions in Connell 1987.

18 The connection between will, determination and jealousy is explored further in Seidler 1989, Ch.3, 'Sexuality'.

19 See discussions of sexualities and sexual identities in Seidler 1992.

20 For useful discussions about the relationship of masculinity to power, see Connell 1987 and Brittan 1989.

21 See Cynthia Cockburn's paper, 'Men's power in organizations: "Equal opportunities" intervenes' in Hearn and Morgan (1990: 72–89).

22 For a sense of how identity and power are related in a way that usefully questions that power is a commodity see Coward 1984. For some critical discussion see Cameron 1985.

23 For a critical discussion of Foucault's work on sexuality in its relation to gender and power, see Seidler, 'Reason, desire and male sexuality' in Caplan 1987.

24 See the interesting round table discussions on 'Feminist consciousness today' and the responses that follow in *Tikkun* July/August 1987, pp. 40–63.

25 An exploration of the connections between identity, experience and language which is often lost within both a structuralist account and discourse theory is given in Seidler 1989, Chs.6 and 7.

26 Laing's critical work on the ways that identities can be invalidated within the family is in Laing and Esterson 1970. See also the presentation of objectification in Laing 1970. In conversation with Dennis Scott I learned of ways Laing was still sometimes trapped

in his work in failing to bring out the person's active involvement in sustaining the situation, so that they are not rendered exclusively as passive victims.

27 A discussion of Foucault's treatment of repression in his *A History of Sexuality* is provided in Seidler's 'Reason, desire and male sexuality' in Caplan 1987.

28 A discussion of feminist morality in relation to sexuality is found in Sue Cartledge, 'Bringing it all back home: lesbian feminist morality' in Gay Left Collective 1980. See also 'Duty and desire: creating a feminist morality' in Cartledge and Ryan 1983.

10 MASCULINITY

1 The relationship of masculinity to Enlightenment conceptions of reason is discussed in Seidler 1989, Ch.2. See also the discussion in Gilligan 1982, where the failure of a rationalist conception of morality to illuminate women's moral experience is explored.

2 Susan Griffin's *Pornography and Silence* explores some of the implications of the particular denial of nature that goes hand in hand with an identification of masculinity with reason (Griffin 1980). Whilst there are difficulties with the notion of 'the pornographic mind', it draws some striking and illuminating connections. See also Cixous and Clement 1987.

3 Some of the difficulties in assuming a radical feminist vision of men and masculinity come out in Rowan 1987. It brings interesting connections to myth and ritual which, until the publication of Robert Bly's *Iron John*, had been largely ignored in discussions of masculinity.

4 Some connections between fathering and masculinity are explored in Victor J. Seidler 'Fathering, authority and masculinity' in Chapman and Rutherford 1988.

5 Questions about the appeal for men of a morality that is organised around principles legislated by reason alone are raised by Gilligan 1982. See also the discussion in Grimshaw 1986 and Kittay and Meyers 1987.

6 A discussion of the links between masculinity, strength and vulnerability is to be found in Seidler 1989, Ch.8.

7 For a sense of the useful work being done about men and masculinity within this kind of framework, see Kimmel 1991; and Brod 1987.

11 HISTORIES

1 Lukács' reading of Marx in *History and Class Consciousness* finds it hard to break with a rationalist tradition. This makes it difficult to escape from prioritising epistemological concerns while paradoxically at the same time providing crucial insights into their weakness for fully appreciating Marx's inheritance. Some useful discussion of Lukács is provided by Löwy 1979; Arato and Breines 1979; and Heller 1983.

2 For useful discussions of analytical Marxism see Cohen 1978; Miller 1984; Elster 1985; Rader 1979; and Wood 1981.

3 Isaiah Berlin's essay 'Herder and the Enlightenment' in *Vico and Herder* pp. 143–216 provides an illuminating introduction to Herder (Berlin 1976).

4 An insightful critique of traditions of orthodox Marxism is provided by Antonio Gramsci, 'Problems of Marxism: some problems in the study of the philosophy of praxis' in *The Prison Notebooks* pp. 381–472 (Gramsci 1971).

5 Charles Taylor talks about Kant and Herder as formative influences on Hegel in Part 1 'The claims of speculative reason' in *Hegel*, especially Ch.1, 'Aims of a new epoch', pp. 3–50 (Taylor 1978).

6 Althusser loses critical insights into the relationship between theory and praxis in Marx in the way that he makes epistemological concerns central to his accounts of ideology

and science. See 'On the materialist dialectic', pp. 161–218 (Althusser 1970); and the interview 'Philosophy as a revolutionary weapon', pp. 13–25 (Althusser 1971). For some sense of how Althusser responded to his critics, see 'Elements of self-criticism' (Althusser 1972: 101–50).

7 Libertarian capitalist positions are defended by, amongst others, Robert Nozick in *Anarchy, State and Utopia* (1974).

8 For an exploration of Marx's conception of the labour process see *Capital Vol. 1*, 1968, Ch. VII 'The labour process', pp. 173–92. See also the ways the labour process has been conceptualised in Braverman 1974, and the rich discussion it provoked in such writing as Nichols 1980; and Walker 1979.

9 Althusser's accounts of the development of Marx's writings are most clearly presented in *For Marx* (1970). See, in particular, 'Marxism and humanism' pp. 219–47.

10 Karl Korsch's essay 'Marxism and philosophy' gives an insightful historical account of the development of Marx's writings in *Marxism and Philosophy*, pp. 28–88 (Korsch 1970). He also wrote a thoughtful biographical account of Marx's theory in *Karl Marx* (Korsch 1938). For a useful introduction to the context of Korsch's life and writings see Goode 1979.

11 Gramsci's account of working-class consciousness and self-activity is explored in 'The study of philosophy' in *The Prison Notebooks*, pp. 323–77 (Gramsci 1971). For useful introductions to Gramsci's writings see Boggs 1976; Davidson 1977; and Fiori 1980.

12 Gramsci explores the tension between a logic of thinking and a logic for action in his essay 'The study of philosophy: problems of philosophy and history' (Gramsci 1971: 343–77).

13 For reflection on the way that consciousness-raising was invoked by the Black Movements in the United States in the 1960s see, for instance, *The Autobiography of Malcolm X* (1968) and Carmichael and Hamilton 1968. For an appreciation of the Black Consciousness Movement in South Africa see, for instance, Biko 1979.

14 For explorations of what 'coming out' has meant in the context of the Gay and Lesbian Movements, see, for instance, Weeks 1977; Hall Carpenter Archives 1989a and 1989b; Cartledge and Ryan 1983; Plummer 1992; and Porter and Weeks 1990.

15 Useful discussions of the development of Durkheim's conceptions of method are to be found in Lukes 1983; Thompson 1982; Gane 1988.

16 Kant's reliance on institutional rules and practices, so freeing individuals from the burdens of constantly having to work moral rules out for themselves from first principles, is a theme in Onora O'Neil's vision of Kant in *Constructions of Reason* (O'Neil 1990).

17 Wittgenstein has numerous discussions of what is involved in following a rule. It is an important theme in *The Philosophical Investigations* (1958). For some helpful discussions see Winch 1980; and Rhees 1970.

18 Marx's conception of justice has been explored in Buchanan 1982; Heller 1986; Cohen 1980; Miller 1984; Young 1990.

19 For the reflections of Emma Goldman and Alexander Berkman on the early years of the Russian Revolution see Goldman 1984; and Berkman 1970. See also Reich 1974; and Serge 1972.

20 Simone Weil's investigations into the labour process are discussed in Blum and Seidler 1984, Ch.6, 'Work', pp. 143–93. See also the 'Journal d'Usine' published in *Simone Weil: Formative Writings 1929–41* (McFarland and Van Ness 1988).

21 Gramsci's account of Taylorism is provided in 'Americanism and Fordism' (Gramsci 1971: 277–318).

22 Useful introductions to Wilheim Reich's life and work are provided by Boadella 1988; and Sharaf 1985.

23 Some interesting reflections upon how the body is conceived within western culture are provided by Griffin 1980; Dychwald 1978; Turner 1984; and Foucault 1990.

24 Early work on introducing the emotions within empirical sociology was done by Arlie Russell Hochschild. See for instance Hochschild and Maclung 1990.

12 RELATIONSHIPS

1 Introductions to Freud and psychoanalysis are provided by Freud 1922; Mannoni 1991; Rieff 1965; Gay 1988; and Isbister 1985.
2 Some interesting reflections upon men's relationships to the public sphere are provided by Hearn 1992; Morgan 1992; Roper and Tosh 1990.
3 Some interesting observations on the difficulties that men and women have in communicating with each other – though in a way less sensitive to issues of power and subordination – are provided by Tannen 1991. See also Cameron 1985 and Spender 1980.
4 How the body is treated within medical knowledge is a theme in Armstrong 1983; Turner 1982; and Showalter 1987.
5 Foucault's *The Birth of the Clinic* (1976) helps us reflect upon the sources of the medical gaze in orthodox medicine by placing it in historical and cultural context.
6 Feminism has helped question women's relationships to their bodies and has worked to foster a more informed and embodied relationship. See, for instance, *Our Bodies Our Selves* (Rakusen and Phillips 1989). See also Smith-Rosenberg 1986.
7 For some interesting reflections upon the relationship of gender to the construction of medical knowledge see, for instance, O'Brien 1981; and Smith 1992.
8 Priscilla Alderson. This was originally a London University thesis. It contains many detailed transcripts which could not find their way into the book, which had a different audience in mind.
9 For some useful reflections upon more holistic conceptions of medicine see, for instance Kidel 1988; and Segal 1986.
10 J-. P. Sartre's *Anti-Semite and Jew* (1960) investigates the conditions of citizenship and the ways in which certain aspects of our being have to be forbidden if we are to be accepted as equal and free citizens. This is something that is less regrettable if, for instance, you see Jewishness as something imposed by others. There is some evidence that Sartre revised his earlier views and sought more positive conceptions of Jewish identity and culture. See, for instance, Friedlander 1990.
11 Reflections on the growth of medical professional knowledge are provided by Freidson 1970; Foucault 1976; Ehrenreich and English 1979; Armstrong 1983; and Turner 1987.
12 For some discussion of the relationship of modernity to notions of identity and the self see, for instance, Taylor 1990; Bernstein 1985; Rutherford 1990; Nicholson 1990.
13 Paolo Freire discusses the objectification of knowledge and the passivity it helps to produce in *The Pedagogy of the Oppressed* (1974, Ch.2).
14 An understanding of the relationship of medicine to inner healing powers is provided by Segal (1986). See also useful discussions in such journals as *Cadeceus*.
15 Georg Simmel writes about issues which bear upon the relationship of masculinity and objectification in *The Philosophy of Money*, Ch.4, 'Individual freedom' pp. 283–354, and Ch.5, 'The money equivalent of personal values' p. 355 (Simmel 1980). For useful introductions to Simmel see Frisby 1981 and 1992.
16 The 'Emotional anatomy of the body' is a title used by Stanley Kellerman to provide a different vision of anatomy and the body.
17 For some challenging discussions of the nature of medical orthodoxies see, for instance, Kidel 1988.
18 For an understanding of Elizabeth Kübler-Ross' pioneering work with those who are terminally ill, see Kübler-Ross 1970.
19 The weakness in Kant's notion of respect being able to acknowledge a need to respect different aspects of our being, is a theme in Seidler 1986.

20 Useful discussions on the difficulties that men can confront in sustaining heterosexual relationships are provided in Seidler 1992. See also Humphries and Metcalf 1985.
21 For work in moral philosophy that was sensitive to the neglect of emotional life, see, for instance, Lawrence Blum 1980; Williams 1973, in particular the papers 'Morality and the emotions', pp. 207–24, and 'Egoism and altruism', pp. 250–266; and Rorty 1980.
22 For examples of recent concern with qualitative methods, see for instance, Silverman 1985; Hammersley 1990; Atkinson 1970; and Pawson 1989.
23 Interesting discussions of fathering within psychoanalytic theory are provided by Samuel 1983. See also Smith, 'The crisis of fatherhood', *Free Associations* No.9, 1987; and Jackson 1982. In a different vein see Hoyland 1991.
24 Carol Gilligan has discussed this move from dependency to independence as a masculine assumption within psychoanalytic theory in *In a Different Voice: Psychological Theory and Women's Development* (Gilligan 1982). It is also a theme in Miller 1976.
25 Interesting discussions of the place of transference within the psychoanalytic situation are provided by Edgar Levenson in *The Ambiguity of Change: An Inquiry into the Nature of Psychoanalytic Reality* (1983).
26 Freud's analysis of the wolf man and its aftermath has been explored in *The Wolf Man: Sixty Years Later* by Karin Obholzer (1982).
27 Questions of fathering and changing conceptions of authority have been discussed in 'Fathering, authority and masculinity' in Chapman and Rutherford 1988: 272–302. This was partly based on an exploration of Max Horkeimer, 'Authority and the family' (Horkheimer 1972) and the illuminating paper by Jessica Benjamin, 'Authority and family revisited: or, a world without fathers?' *New German Critique*, winter issue 1978. Some of these themes are explored further in Benjamin 1990.
28 Issues of the relationship of Marxism to the evaluation of human relationships are explored in Burke *et al.* 1981; Nielsen and Patten 1981; and Lukes 1985.

13 LANGUAGE

1 Norman Malcolm has written thoughtfully about the natural expression of pain in 'Wittgenstein: the relation of language to instinctive behaviour' in *The Philosophical Investigations* (pp. 3–22). It is also a theme in his work on Wittgenstein's philosophical development, *Nothing is Hidden* (Malcolm 1986).
2 A useful account of Weber's description of social action is provided by Max Weber's 'The fundamental concepts of sociology' Part 1–7, in *The Theory of Social and Economic Organisations* (1964).
3 Helpful discussions of Descartes' part in defining the character of 'modern' philosophy are provided by Kenny 1968; and Williams 1978. See also Rorty 1979, Ch.1, 'The invention of the mind', pp.17–69.
4 G. E. Moore remained a powerful influence on Wittgenstein, both personally and philosophically. See, for instance, Moore's papers, 'Proof of the external world' and 'Defence of common sense' both in Moore's *Philosophical Papers* (1959), central texts with which Wittgenstein was concerned in *On Certainty* (1975). For some sense of the intellectual background and influence of Moore's work, see, for instance, Levy 1981.
5 This idea that 'in the beginning was the deed' is mentioned by Wittgenstein as a remark in *Culture and Value* (Wittgenstein 1980). It is a theme that was also taken up by Goethe. It would help Wittgenstein's remark to Drury that 'your religious ideas have always seemed to me to be more Greek than Biblical. Whereas my thoughts are one hundred per cent Hebraic.' See M. O'C. Drury, 'Conversations with Wittgenstein' in Rhees 1981.
6 Some discussion of Wittgenstein as a conventionalist that links to a particular misinterpretation of the philosophy of language is explored by Stanley Cavell's 'The availability of the later Wittgenstein' in Cavell 1969.

7 Useful introductions to Saussure's writings on language are provided by J. Culler *Saussure* (1985); Hawkes 1977; Eagleton 1983. Some attempt to contrast the view of Wittgenstein and Saussure is made by Harris 1990.

8 Phenomenological sociology is helpfully introduced by Douglas 1971; Berger and Luckman 1967. See also 'On Alfred Schutz' and 'Phenomenology' by M. Natandow (1965) in *Social Research* Vol. 32.

9 For a sense of the development of Husserl's writings see the insightful *The Crisis of European Sciences and Transcendental Philosophy* (Husserl 1970). This text is helpfully situated by Bauman in *Hermeneutics and the Social Sciences* (1978).

10 Foucault discusses this 'hydraulic' conception of sexuality which he sees at work in the writings of Freud and Reich in his *History of Sexuality Vol. 1* (1979).

11 Interesting discussions of Reich's work are provided by Boadella (1976). See also Boadella *Life Streams* (1987) which also draws upon Reich's influence.

12 For insights into the development of Foucault's work see, for instance, Gordon 1980; Rabinow 1988; Dreyfus and Rabinow 1982.

13 Lenin's political and intellectual development is thought about usefully in Besancon 1974; and Claudin-Urondo 1977.

14 For a sense of the development of Foucault's thought about the relationship of truth to politics, see interviews collected in *Michel Foucault: Politics, Philosophy, Culture: Interviews and Other Writings*, ed. L. Kritzman (1990).

15 Introductions to the Frankfurt School and critical theory are provided by Jay 1973 which tells the story from the position of Max Horkheimer; and Susan Bucks-Morss 1977, who focuses more on the relationship between T. W. Adorno and Walter Benjamin.

16 See Max Horkheimer's *The Eclipse of Reason* (1974) for a discussion of different conceptions of reason and the relationship of modernity to instrumental reason.

17 Lukács writes critically about Weber's sociology in 'Max Weber and German sociology' collected in G. Lukács 1982.

18 Critical discussions of Lukács' work and the ways it remains trapped within the epistemological concerns that he did so much to illuminate are provided by Arato and Breines 1979; and Löwy 1979.

19 Max Horkheimer's seminal essay that set the terms for critical theory entitled 'Traditional and critical theory' is reprinted in Horkheimer 1972.

20 Weber's conception of bureaucracy is explored in Mommsen 1974; Beetham 1985; and Giddens 1974.

21 Marcuse's 'On Hedonism' is collected in his early essays *Negations* (1970: 154–200). See also his essay 'Philosophy and critical theory' in the same collection, pp. 134–58.

22 Some sense of the development of Marcuse's work is provided by Kellner 1984; and Schoolman 1970.

23 An introduction to Adorno is provided by Gillian Rose in *The Melancholy Science* (1981); and Bucks-Morss 1977.

24 Useful collections of writings of the Frankfurt School are provided by *The Essential Frankfurt School Reader* (Arato and Gebhardt 1982) and *Critical Theory and Society: A Reader* (Kellner and Bronner 1989).

25 See the discussion between Richard Sennett and Michel Foucault (1981), 'Sexuality and solitude' in Anthology 1, *London Review of Books*. Some of the implications of this discussion for issues of identity, sexuality and power are explored in Seidler's 'Reason, desire and male sexuality' in Caplan 1987: 82–112.

26 The relationship of language to the curbing of particular emotions and feelings for men is a theme in Seidler 1989, Ch.7, 'Language', pp. 123–43.

27 Some attempt to link Simone Weil's writings with Wittgenstein, showing a similar philosophical sensitivity at work, is made by Peter Winch. See his introduction to Simone Weil's *Lectures in Philosophy* (Weil 1978). See also Winch 1989.

28 Freud's discussion of modernity in its relationship to sexual repression is found in *Civilization and its Discontents* (Freud 1961). Some useful discussion on this work is provided by Reich 1974; Foucault 1979 and Elias 1983.

29 Questions of what it is intelligible to doubt are explored by Wittgenstein in *On Certainty* (1975).

14 SEXUALITY

1 Some of these connections are made in Freud's early writings. See, for instance, the *Studies on Hysteria* which he wrote with Josef Breuer (1964).

2 The notion of self-control as involving the domination of our natures as men is a theme in Chapter 4, 'Control' in Seidler 1987: 44–71.

3 Jeffrey Masson's discussion of the Dora case is found in 'Dora and Freud', Chapter 2 (Masson 1989: 84–114). For a description of Freud's account, see Rieff 1963.

4 For some discussion around the claims that Masson makes about the seduction see, for instance, Jane Malcolm *In Freud's Archive* (1984). See also some of the various responses Masson has made in *Against Therapy (1989)*.

5 For discussions of the impact of sexual abuse see, for instance, Alice Miller 1984.

6 For some useful discussions of Freud's relationship to morality, see, for instance, Rieff 1965; Bettelheim 1991.

7 For a variety of responses to the predicament Dora finds herself in, see Bernheimer and Kahane 1985.

8 Freud's relationship to female sexuality has been explored in quite diverse ways by Millet 1969; Mitchell 1975; Sayers 1986; Luce Irigaray 1983; and Whitford 1991.

15 DEPENDENCY

1 To help understand the development of Juliet Mitchell's thinking about psychoanalysis and feminism see her *Psychoanalysis and Feminism* (1975) and *Women: the Longest Revolution* (1984).

2 Useful introductions to Lacan's psychoanalytic work are provided by Laplanche and Pontalis 1967; Benevenuto and Kennedy 1987; and Macey 1988. To context Lacan's work historically and culturally, see Turkle 1979.

3 Some of the differences that have characterised feminist appropriation of Freud and psychoanalysis are usefully explored in Irigaray 1985; Benjamin 1990; Sayers 1991; and Whitford 1991.

4 Some of these predicaments that suggest different forms of social theory are helpfully explored by Bauman 1991b; and Giddens 1990 and 1991.

5 For some interesting reflections on the nature of care and concern see Noddings 1984; Ruddick 1990; Gilligan 1982; Trebilcot 1984; and Grimshaw 1986.

6 A useful introduction to Alice Miller's work is provided by her *For Your Own Good: Hidden Cruelty in Child Rearing and the Roots of Violence* (1983a). She has become gradually disillusioned with the more orthodox psychoanalytic assumptions of her earlier work, such as *The Drama of the Gifted Child* (1981). She explains some of these changes in *Thou Shalt Not Be Aware: Society's Betrayal of the Child* (1984).

7 For a sense of Dorothy Rowe's work see, for instance, Rowe 1987 and 1989. For a similar sensitivity see Snail 1987.

8 The way in which different sciences have colluded in the subordination of women is a theme in Showalter 1987. See also Fox Keller 1984.

9 Some interesting reflections upon the ways in which women within the psychoanalytic movement have reflected upon issues of female sexuality are provided by Sayers 1982.

10 Useful discussions of Gilligan's work are provided by Kittay and Meyers 1987; and Belensky *et al.* 1987.
11 For a sense of the development of Kohlberg's work see his *Essays on Moral Development Vol. 1* (1981). His later work is reported in *Lawrence Kohlberg's Approach to Moral Education* (Clark Power *et al.* 1989). A useful discussion is provided by Marilyn Freedman's 'Care and context in moral reasoning' in *Women in Moral Theory* (Kittay and Mayers 1987: 190–204).
12 Gilligan draws upon some of this work on child development to establish certain of her claims. She mentions, for instance, work by Jane Loevinger and Ruth Wessler, *Measuring Ego Development* (1970), and Janet Lever (1978) 'Sex differences in the complexity of children's play and games', *American Sociological Review* 43, pp. 471–83.
13 Some of the ways in which women of colour have challenged the assumptions of white feminism are explored in Lorde 1989; and Hooks 1984.
14 The relationship of feminism to theories of postmodernity is explored in *Feminism/Postmodernism* (Nicholson 1990). See, in particular, the helpful introductory piece 'Social criticism without philosophy: an encounter between feminism and postmodernism' by Nancy Fraser and Linda J. Nicholson.

16 CONCLUSION

1 Weber discusses questions of legitimacy and authority in the modern state in Connolly 1986, Ch.2 (selections from Weber). See also useful discussion of Weber's work in Beetham 1985, especially Chs.3 and 5; and Mommsen 1974.
2 Weber's seminal essay 'Class, status and party' in *Economy and Society* Ch.9 is reprinted in Runciman 1978, Ch.3; and Gerth and Mills 1946, Ch.1. It is discussed by Parkin 1982, Ch.4; and A. Giddens 1973, Ch.2.
3 Durkheim's sense of the dual nature of individuals is a theme in his essay 'The dualism of human nature and its social consequences', reprinted in Woolfe 1964: 325–40.
4 Mill explored the ambivalences of individuality within a liberal democratic society in *On Liberty* (1964, Ch.3). Useful discussions of these themes in Mill's writings are provided by Berlin 'John Stuart Mill and the ends of life' (1969: 173–206). See also Ryan 1974, Ch.5, 'Liberty and the subjection of women'.
5 The difficulties of acknowledging different aspects of our being within modernity and its conception of individuals as rational selves is a theme in Seidler 1991b.
6 Interesting reflections on the nature of Jewish emancipation are provided by Hertzberg 1970.
7 Marx's essay 'On the Jewish question' takes up themes of emancipation which established its universal form. This has been helpfully discussed by Isaiah Berlin in 'Benjamin Disraeli, Karl Marx and the search for identity' in Berlin 1981: 252–86.
8 Useful discussions of Marx's conception of labour are provided by Gould 1974 and Miles 1987.
9 Some interesting reflections upon the ways in which conceptions of modernity have embodied secularised forms of Christian anti-Semitism is a theme in *The Crucifixion of the Jews* (Littell 1973). See also Libowitz 1987.
10 Gramsci talks about how a sense of class consciousness can emerge out of a sense of difference in *The Prison Notebooks* 'The study of philosophy' (Gramsci 1971: 323–42).
11 For some of Gramsci's writings on issues of ethnicity and culture see, for instance, Antonio Gramsci's *Selections from Cultural Writings IV: People, Nation and Culture* (1985: 196–286).
12 Illuminating biographies of Gramsci are provided by Cammett 1977; and Davidson 1977.
13 For a sense of this anti-colonialist tradition of writing see, for instance, Fanon 1967a,

1967b; Memmi 1967; Nizan 1960; Cézaire 1970. For some helpful critical discussions see, for instance, Memmi 1968; Said 1991; and Gendzier 1973.

14 Simone Weil explores notions of exploitation embodied within an orthodox Marxist tradition, while generally staying within the anti-Hegelian framework it provides, in her essay *Reflections Concerning the Causes of Liberty and Social Oppression* (Weil 1958). This work is centrally discussed by Blum and Seidler (1984).

15 Jean Baker Miller talks of the need for women and other powerless groups to operate within two realms, for the reality they are forced to live is at odds with the reality that is presented to them, in *Toward a New Psychology of Women* (1976). This is related to what has been discussed as taking a feminist standpoint, but exactly in what ways calls for careful exploration.

16 For interesting reflections upon the nature of racism within white society see, for instance, Gilroy 1987; Miles and Phizacklea 1984; Ramazanoglu 1989; and Brittan and Maynard 1984.

17 For discussion of the Holocaust that attempts to situate it within western culture, see Bauman 1990. See also the concluding chapter to Seidler 1991b, Ch.10, 'Love, dignity and oppression', pp. 165–204.

18 The way that power can reduce people to matter is a crucial idea in Simone Weil's conception of power. I have explored some of the implications of this conception of power in the chapter 'Power' in Blum and Seidler 1984: 194–256.

19 Foucault's later reflections on the relationship of morality to politics is a theme in 'The return to morality' and 'The concern for truth' in Kritzman 1990: 242–54 and 255–67.

20 For useful introductions to theorists of postmodernity, such as Derrida, Rorty and Lyotard, see, for instance, Bauman 1991b. See also the discussion of David Harvey, *The Condition of Postmodernity* which reminds us that 'the meta-narratives that the post-modernists decry (Marx, Freud, and even later figures like Althusser) were much more open, nuanced, and sophisticated than the critics admit' (Harvey 1990:115).

21 The theme of how frustration can be 'passed down the line' is a theme that is further explored in Seidler 1991a: 111–30.

22 Moller Okin (1980) provides an interesting discussion of how Rousseau's visions of equality and freedom are governed by his conceptions of gender. See Part 3, 'Rousseau', pp. 149–94.

23 Useful introductions to the development of Laing's work are provided by Laing 1985; Sedgewick 1982; Boyers and Orrill 1972.

24 For interesting discussions of Laing's work within families, see for instance Laing 1972, and Laing and Esterson 1970. For a different view of some of this work see Esterson 1972. See also some critical insights into Laing's relationships to women and the heroic and masculine ways that he often conceived his own work in Showalter 1987, Ch.9.

Bibliography

Adorno, T. H. (1967) *Prisons*, London: Neville Speakman.

—— (1986) *The Jargon of Authenticity*, London: Routledge & Kegan Paul.

Adorno, T. H. and Horkheimer, M. (1973) *Dialect of Enlightenment*, trans, J. Cumming, London: Allen Lane.

Almog, S. S. (1988) *Anti-Semitism Through The Ages*, Oxford: Pergamon Press.

Althusser, L. (1970) *For Marx* (trans. Ben Brewster), London: Verso Books.

—— (1971) *Lenin and Philosophy and Other Essays*, London: Verso Books.

—— (1972) *Essays on Self-Criticism*, London: New Left Books.

Arato, A. and Breines, P. (1979) *The Young Lukács and the Origins of Western Marxism*, London: Pluto Books.

Arato, A. and Gebhardt, E. (eds) (1989) *The Essential Frankfurt School Reader*, Oxford: Blackwell.

Armstrong, D. (1983) *Political Anatomy of the Body*, Cambridge: Cambridge University Press.

Atkinson, H. (1970) *The Ethnographical Imagination*, London: Routledge.

Avineri, S. (1972) *Hegel's Theory of the Modern State*, Cambridge: Cambridge University Press.

Baechler, J. (1989) *Europe and the Rise of Capitalism*, Oxford: Blackwell.

Balbus, I. (1982) *Marxism and Domination*, Princeton: Princeton University Press.

Bateson, G. (1979) *Mind and Nature*, London: Windwood House.

Bauman, Z. (1978) *Hermeneutics and the Social Sciences*, London: Hutchinson.

—— (1990) *Modernity and the Holocaust*, Cambridge: Polity Press.

—— (1991a) *Modernity and Ambivalence*, Cambridge: Polity Press.

—— (1991b) *Initimations of Postmodernism*, London: Routledge.

Beetham, D. (1985) *Max Weber and the Theory of Modern Politics*, Oxford: Polity Press.

Belensky, M., Clichy, B., Goldberger, N. and Tarule, J. (1986) *Women's Way of Knowing*, New York: Basic Books.

Bellah, R. (1984) *On Morality and Society, Sociology in France in the Nineteenth Century*, Chicago: Chicago University Press.

Benevenuto, B. and Kennedy, R. (1987) *The Works of Jacques Lacan: An Introduction*, London: Free Association Press.

Benhabib, S. and Cornell, D. (1987) *Feminism as Critique*, Cambridge: Polity Press.

Benjamin, J. (1990) *Bonds of Love*, London: Virago.

Benjamin, W. (1983) 'Philosophy, history and aesthetics' in *The Philosophical Forum*, xv, 1–2.

Benton, T. (1984) *The Rise and Fall of Structuralist Marxism*, London: Routledge.

—— (1977) *Philosophical Foundations of the Three Sociologies*, London: Routledge.

Berger, P. and Luckman, T. (1967) *The Social Construction of Reality*, London: Allen Lane.

Berkman, A. (1970) *Prison Letters of an Anarchist*, New York: Schochen Books.
Berlin, I. (1969) *Four Essays on Liberty*, Oxford: Oxford University Press.
—— (1976) *Vico and Herder*, New York: Random House.
—— (1979) *The Age of Enlightenment*, Oxford: Oxford University Press.
—— (1981) *Against the Current*, Oxford: Oxford University Press.
Berman, M. (1982) *All That is Solid Melts into Air*, London: Verso Books.
Bernal, M. (1987) *Black Athena*, London: Free Association Books.
Bernheimer, C. and Kahane, C. (1985) *In Dora's Case: Freud–Hysteria–Feminism*, London: Virago, New York: Columbia University Press.
Bernstein, K. (1978) *The Restructuring of Social and Political Theory*, Philadelphia: University of Pennsylvania Press.
Bernstein, R. J. (1985) *Habermas and Modernity*, Cambridge: Polity Press.
Besancon, S. (1974) *The Intellectual Origins of Leninism*, Oxford: Blackwell.
Bettelheim, B. (1991) *Freud and Man's Soul*, London: Fontana Books.
Biko, S. (1979) *I Write What I Like*, London: Heinneman.
Bleier, R. (ed.) (1986) *Feminist Approaches to Science*, Oxford: Pergamon Press.
Bloch, M. (1989) *Freudalism*, 2 vols, London, Routledge.
Blum, L.(1980) *Friendship, Altruism and Morality*, London: Routledge & Kegan Paul.
Blum, L. and Seidler, V. J. (1984) *A Truer Liberty: Simone Weil and Marxism*, London: Routledge & Kegan Paul.
Boadella, D. (ed.) (1976) *In the Wake of Reich*, London: Coven.
—— (1987) *Life Streams*, London: Routledge & Kegan Paul.
—— (1988) *Wilheim Reinh: The Evolution of his Work*, London: Routledge & Kegan Paul.
Boggs, C. (1976) *Gramsci's Marxism*, London: Pluto Press.
Bohm, D. (1980) *Wholeness and the Immaculate Order*, London: Routledge & Kegan Paul.
Bologh, R. W. (1990) *Love or Greatness: Max Weber and Masculine Thinking*, London: Unwin Hyman.
Bordo, S. (1986) *The Cartesian Masculinization of Thought, Signs 2, 3, Spring.
Boyers, R. and Orril, R. (eds) (1972) *Laing and Anti-Psychiatry*, Harmondsworth: Penguin.
Braverman, H. (1974) *Labour and Monopoly Capitalism*, New York: Monthly Review Press.
Breuer, J. and Freud, S. (1964) *Studies on Hysteria*, Boston: Beacon Press (35th printing).
Brittan, A. (1989) *Masculinity and Power*, Oxford: Blackwell.
Brittan, A. and Maynard, M. (1984) *Sexism, Racism and Oppression*, Oxford: Blackwell.
Brod, H. (ed.) (1987) *The Making of Masculinities: The New Man's Studies*, Boston: Allen & Unwin.
Brubaker, R. (1984) *The Limits of Rationality*, London: Allen & Unwin.
Buchanan, A. (1982) *Marx and Justice*, London: Methuen.
Buck-Morss, S. (1977) *The Origin of Negative Dialectics*, Brighton: Harvester Press.
Burke J., Crocker, L. and Legters, J. (1981) *Marxism and the Good Society*, Cambridge: Cambridge University Press.
Burtt, E. D. (1932) *The Metaphysical Foundation of Modern Physical Science*, London: Routledge.
Calinicoss, A. (1976) *Althusser's Marxism*, London: Pluto Press.
Cameron, D. (1985) *Feminism and Linguistic Theory*, London: Macmillan.
Cammett, J. H. (1977) *Antonio Gramsci and the Origins of Italian Communism*, Stanford: Stanford University Press.
Caplan, P. (1987) *The Cultural Construction of Sexuality*, London: Tavistock.
Capra, F. (1975) *The Turning Point*, London: Wildwood House.
Carmichael, S. and Hamilton, C. (1968) *Black Power*, Harmondsworth: Penguin.
Cartledge, S. and Ryan, J. (1983) *Sex and Love, New Thoughts on Old Contradictions*, London: The Women's Press.

Cavell, S. (1969) *Must We Mean What We Say?*, New York: Scribner.

Cézaire, A. (1970) *Notes of a Native Son*, Harmondsworth: Penguin.

Chapman, K. and Rutherford, J. (1988) *Male Order: Unwrapping Masculinity*, London: Lawrence and Wishart.

Chodorow, N. (1978) *The Reproduction of Mothering*, California: University of California Press.

Cicourel, A. (1968) *The Social Organisation of Juvenile Crime*, New York: John Wiley.

Cixous, H. and Clement, C. (1987) *The Newly Born Woman*, Manchester: Manchester University Press.

Clark Power, F., Higgins, L. and Kohlberg, L. (eds) (1989) *Approach to Moral Education*, New York: Columbia University Press.

Clarke, S. (1977) *The Moral Status of Animals*, Oxford: Clarendon Press.

—— (1982) *The Nature of the Beast*, Oxford: Oxford University Press.

Clarke, S., Lovell, T., McDonnell, K., Robins, K. and Seidler, V. J. (1980) *One Dimensional Marxism: Althusser and the Politics of Culture*, London: Allison & Busby.

Claudin-Urondo. C. (1977) *Lenin and the Cultural Revolution*, Brighton: Harvester.

Cohen, G. A. (1978) *Karl Marx's Theory of History: A Defence*, Oxford: Oxford University Press.

Cohen, M. (ed.) (1980) *Marx, Justice and History*, Princeton: Princeton University Press.

Collier, A. (1977) *R. D. Laing: The Philosophy and Politics of Psychotherapy*, Brighton: Harvester Books.

Connell, R. W. (1987) *Gender and Power*, Cambridge: Polity Press.

Connolly, W. (ed.) (1986) *Legitimacy and the State*, Oxford: Blackwell.

Coote, A. and Campbell, B. (1982) *Sweet Freedom*, London: Picador.

Coward, R. (1983) *Patriarch Precedents: Sexuality and Social Relations*, London: Routledge & Kegan Paul.

—— (1984) *Female Desire*, London: Routledge.

Culler, J. (1985) *Saussure*, London: Fontana.

Daly, M. (1973) *God The Father*, Boston: Beacon Press.

—— (1978) *Gyn\Ecology: The Meta-ethics of Radical Feminism*, London: The Women's Press.

—— (1984) *Pure Lust*, London: The Women's Press.

Daniels, N. (ed.) (1975) *Reading Rawls*, Oxford: Blackwell.

Davidson, A. (1977) *Antonio Gramsci: Towards an Intellectual Biography*, London: Merlin Books.

Davis, D. B. (1989) *The Problem of Slavery in Western Culture*, Oxford: Oxford University Press.

—— (1990) *Revolutions: Reflections on American Federalism and Foreign Liberation*, Cambridge, MA: Harvard University Press.

Dennison, G. (1971) *The Lives of Children*, Harmondsworth: Penguin Education.

Derrida, J. (1981) *Writing and Difference*, London: Routledge & Kegan Paul.

Descombes, V. (1980) *Modern French Philosophy*, Cambridge: Cambridge University Press.

Dews, P. (ed.) (1986) *Habermas: Autonomy and Solidarity*, London: Verso.

Donegan, A. (1977) *The Theory of Morality*, Chicago: Chicago University Press.

Douglas, J. D. (1970) *The Social Meaning of Suicide*, Princeton: Princeton University Press.

—— (ed.) (1971) *The Understanding of Everyday Life*, London: Routledge & Kegan Paul.

Douglas, M. (1982) *Evans Pritchard*, London: Fontana.

Doyal, L. and Harris, K. (1990) *Empiricism, Explanation and Rationality*, London: Routledge.

Dreyfus, H. and Rabinow, P. (1982) *Michel Foucault: Beyond Structuralism and Hermeneutics*, Brighton: Harvester Press.

Drury, M. O. C. (1973) *The Danger of Words*, London: Routledge & Kegan Paul.
Duberman, M. (ed.) (1991) *Hidden from History*, Harmondsworth: Penguin.
Du Bois, W. E. B. (1969) *The Souls of Black Folk*, York: New American Library.
Durkheim, E. (1950) *The Rules of Sociological Method*, New York: The Free Press.
—— (1961) *The Elementary Forms of Religious Life*, London: Allen and Unwin.
—— (1964) *The Division of Labour in Society*, New York: The Free Press.
—— (1974) *Sociology and Philosophy*, New York: The Free Press.
Dychwald, K. (ed.) (1978) *Bodymind*, London: Wildwood House.
Eagleton, T. (1983) *Literary Theory: An Introduction*, Oxford: Blackwell.
Easlea, B. (1981) *Science and Sexual Oppression*, London: Weidenfeld & Nicolson.
Ehrenreich, B. and English, D. (1979) *For Her Own Good*, London: Pluto.
Eichenbaum, L. and Orbach, S. (1983) *Understanding Women*, Harmondsworth: Penguin.
—— (1984) *What Do Women Want?*, London, Fontana Books.
—— (1990) *Bittersweet*, London: Faber & Faber.
Eisenstein, Z. (ed.) (1979) *Capitalist Patriarchy and the Case for Socialist Feminism*, New York: Monthly Review Press.
Elias, N. (1983) *The Civilising Process*, Oxford: Blackwell.
Elshtain, J. B. (1981) *Private Women in Social and Political Thought*, Princeton: Princeton University Press.
Elster, J. (1985) *Making Sense of Marx*, Cambridge: Cambridge University Press.
Engels, F. (1972) *The Origin of the Family, Private Property and the State*, New York: Pathfinder Press.
Ernst, S. and Maguire, M. (1987) *Living With the Sphinx*, London: The Women's Press.
Esterson, A. (1972) *The Leaves of Spring*, Harmondsworth: Penguin.
Fanon, F. (1967a) *Black Skin, White Masks*, London: Pluto Press.
—— (1967b) *A Dying Colonialism*, Harmondsworth: Penguin Books.
Farrington, B. (1969) *The Philosophy of Francis Bacon*, Liverpool: Liverpool University Press.
Fay, B. (1978) *Social Theory and Political Practice*, London: Allen & Unwin.
Featherstone, M. (ed.) (1988) *Postmodernism*, London: Sage.
Ferenczi, S. (1985) *Journal Clinique, January to October 1932*, trans. Le Group de Traduction du Coq-Héron. Paris: Payot.
Filmer, P., Phillipson, M., Silverman, D. and Walsh, J. (1972) *New Directions in Sociological Theory*, London: Macmillan.
Fink, H. (1981) *Social Philosophy*, London: Methuen.
Fiori, G. (1980) *Antonio Gramsci: Life of a Revolutionary*, London: New Left Books.
Firestone, S. (1970) *The Dialectic of Sex*, New York: Bantam Books.
Foster, H. (1985) *Postmodern Culture, Postmodernism: A Special Issue of Theory, Culture and Society*, London: Pluto Press.
Foucault, M. (1971) *Madness and Civilisation*, London: Tavistock.
—— (1975) *Discipline and Punishment*, Harmondsworth: Penguin.
—— (1976) *The Birth of the Clinic*, London: Tavistock.
—— (1979) *A History of Sexuality*, London: Allen Lane.
—— (1980) *Power/Knowledge*, ed. C. Gordon, Brighton, Sussex: Harvester.
—— (1990) *The Care of the Self*, Harmondsworth: Penguin.
Freidson, E. (1970) *Profession of Medicine*, New York: Dodds Mead.
Freud, E. L. (1961) *Letters of Sigmund Freud 1873–1939*, trans, T. and J. Stern, London: The Hogarth Press.
Freud, S. (1922) *Introductory Lectures on Psychoanalysis*, London: Allen & Unwin.
—— (1961) *Civilisation and its Discontent*, New York: Norton.
—— (1977) *On Sexuality*, Harmondsworth: Penguin.

—— (1974) *The Standard Edition of the Complete Psychological Works of Sigmund Freud*, London: Hogarth Press.

Friedlander, J. H. (1990) *Vilna on the Sein*, New Haven: Yale University Press.

Friere, P. (1974) *Pedagogy of the Oppressed*, Harmondsworth: Penguin.

Frisby, D. (1981) *Sociological Impressionism*, London: Routledge.

—— (1992) *Simmel and Since*, London: Routledge.

Fromm, E. (1991) *The Fear of Freedom*, London: Routledge.

Gane, M. (1988) *On Durkheim's Rules of Sociological Method*, London: Routledge & Kegan Paul.

Garfinkel, H. (1984) *Studies in Ethnomethodology*, Oxford: Polity.

Gay Left Collective (ed.) (1980) *Homosexuality: Power and Politics*, London: Allison and Busby.

Gay, P. (1988) *Freud: A Life in Our Time*, London: Dent.

Gendzier, I. (1973) *Franz Fanon: A Critical Study*, London: Wildwood House.

Gerth, H. H. and Mills, C. W. (1946) *From Max Weber: Essays in Sociology*, London: Methuen.

Gewirth, A. (1978) *Reason and Morality*, Chicago: University of Chicago Press.

Giddens, A. (1971) *Capitalism and Modern Social Theory*, Cambridge: Cambridge University Press.

—— (1973) *Class Structure of Advanced Industrialised Societies*, London: Hutchinson.

—— (ed.) (1974) *Positivism and Sociology*, London: Heinemann.

—— (1976) *New Rules of Sociological Method*, London: Heinemann.

—— (1977) *Studies in Social and Political Theory*, London: Heinemann.

—— (1978) *Durkheim*, London: Fontana.

—— (1981) *The Nation-State and Violence*, Cambridge: Polity Press.

—— (1990) *Consequences of Modernity*, Cambridge: Polity Press.

—— (1991) *Modernity and Self-Identity*, Cambridge: Polity Press.

Gilligan, C. (1982) *In a Different Voice: Psychological Theory and Women's Development*, Cambridge: Harvard University Press.

Gilroy, P. (1987) *There Ain't No Black In The Union Jack*, London: Unwin Hyman.

Goldman, E. (1984) *Living My Life*, London: Pluto.

Goldman, N. L. (1968) *The Human Societies and Philosophy*, London: Jonathan Cape.

—— (1971) *Immanuel Kant* (trans. R. Black), London: New Left Books.

—— (1979) *Lukács and Heiddegar*, London: Routledge & Kegan Paul.

Goode, P. (1979) *Karl Korsch: A Study In Western Marxism*, London: Macmillan.

Gorz, A. (1967) *Strategy for Labour*, Boston: Beacon Books.

Gould, C. (ed. (1974) *Marx's Ontology of Labour*, Boston: MIT Press.

—— (ed.) (1983) *Beyond Domination*, Totowa, NJ: Rowman & Allenheld.

Gouldner, A. (1970) *The Coming Crisis of Western Sociology*, London: Heineman.

—— (1972) *For Sociology*, Harmondsworth: Penguin.

Gramsci, A. (1971) *The Prison Notebooks*, London: Lawrence & Wishart.

—— (1975) *Letters from Prison*, trans. L. Lawner, London: Jonathan Cape.

—— (1985) *Selections From Cultural Writings*, London: Lawrence & Wishart.

Graubard, A. (1972) *Free the Children*, New York: Vintage.

Griffin, C. (1989) *Feminist Review*, 33, pp.103–5.

Griffin, S. (1980) *Pornography and Silence*, London: The Women's Press.

—— (1982) *Made From The Earth*, London: The Women's Press.

Grimshaw, J. (1986) *Feminist Philosophers*, Brighton: Harvester.

Hacker, P. M. S. (1972) *Insight And Illusion*, Oxford: Oxford Univeristy Press.

Hall Carpenter Archives (1989a) *Inventing Ourselves*, London: Routledge.

—— (1989b) *Walking After Midnight*, London: Routledge.

Hall, J. (1980) *Powers and Liberties*, Harmondsworth: Penguin Books.

Hammersley, M. (1990) *The Dilemma of Qualitative Method*, London: Routledge.

Hampshire, S. (1959) *Thought and Action*, London: Chatto & Windus.

Harding, J. (ed.) (1987) *Perspectives on Gender and Science*, Headington: Pergamon Press.

Harding, S. (1986) *The Science Question In Feminism*, Milton Keynes: Open University Press.

—— (1989) *Feminism and Methodology*, Bloomington: Indiana University Press.

Harding, S. and Hintikka, M. (1983) *Discovering Reality: Feminist Perspectives*, Dordrecht: D. Reidel.

Harris, R. (1990) *Language, Saussure and Wittgenstein*, London: Routledge.

Harvey, D. (1990) *The Condition of Post-Modernity*, Oxford: Blackwell.

Havel, V. (1987) *Living In Truth*, London: Faber.

Hawkes, T. (1977) *Structuralism and Semiotics*, London: Methuen.

Hawthorne, G. (1976) *Enlightenment and Despair*, Cambridge: Cambridge University Press.

Hearn, J. (1987) *The Gender of Oppression: Man, Masculinity and the Critique of Marxism*, Sussex: Harvester.

—— (1992) *Man In The Public Eye*, London: Routledge.

Hearn, J. and Morgan, D. (eds) (1990) *Men, Masculinities and Social Theory*, London: Unwin Hyman.

Heller, A. (1983) *Lukács Revisited*, Oxford: Blackwell.

—— (ed.) (1986) *Beyond Justice*, Oxford: Blackwell.

Hennis, W. (1987) *Max Weber: Essays in Reconstruction*, London: Routledge & Kegan Paul.

Heritage, J. (1984) *Garfinkel and Ethnomethodology*, Cambridge: Polity Press.

Hertzberg, A. (1970) *The French Enlightenment and the Jews: The Origins of Modern Anti-Semitism*, New York: Schochen Books.

Hill, C. (1977) *Milton and the English Revolution*, London: Faber & Faber.

—— (1975) *The World Turned Upside Down*, Harmondsworth: Penguin.

Hirschman, A. O. (1977) *The Passions and the Interests*, Princeton: Princeton University Press.

Hochschild, R. and Maclung, A. (1990) *Second Shift: Working Parents and the Revolution in the Home*, London: Piatkus.

Hollis, M. (1977) *Models of Men: Philosophical Thoughts on Social Action*, Cambridge: Cambridge University Press.

Holt, J. (1969) *How Children Fail*, Harmondsworth: Penguin.

—— (1970) *How Children Learn*, Harmondsworth: Penguin.

Holton, R. and Turner, B. (1990) *Max Weber on Economy and Society*, London: Routledge.

Hooks, B. (1984) *Feminist Theory: From Margin To Centre*, Boston: South End Press.

Horkheimer, M. (1972) *Critical Theory: Selected Essays*, New York: Seabury Press.

—— (1974), *The Eclipse of Reason*, New York: Seabury Press.

Hoyland, J. (1991) *Fathers and Sons*, London: Serpents Tail.

Hulme, P. and Jordanova, L. (eds.) (1990) *The Enlightenment and its Shadows*, London: Routledge.

Husserl, E. (1970) *The Crisis of European Sciences and Transcendental Philosophy*, Chicago: Northwestern University Press.

Huyssen, A. (1986) *After the Great Divide*, Bloomington: Indiana University Press.

Hyppolite, J. (1969) *Studies on Marx and Hegel*, London: Heinemann.

Irigaray, L. (1983) *Speculum Of The Other Woman*, Ithaca: Cornell University Press.

—— (1985) *The Sex Which Is Not One*, Ithaca: Cornell University Press.

Isbister, J. N. (1985) *Freud: An Introduction to His Theory*, Cambridge: Polity Press.

Jackson, B. (1982) *Fatherhood*, London: Routledge & Kegan Paul.

Jackson, D. (1990) *Unmasking Masculinity*, London: Unwin Hyman.

Jagger, A. (1983) *Feminist Politics and Human Nature*, Brighton: Harvester.

Jameson, F. (1972) *The Prison House of Language*, Princeton: Princeton University Press.

Jay, M. (1973) *The Dialectical Imagination*, London: Heinemann.

Jones, E. (1958) *Sigmund Freud: Life and Work, Vol. 2, Years of Maturity 1901–1919*. London: The Hogarth Press.

Jones, K. (1955) *Lunacy, Law and Conscience*, London: Routledge & Kegan Paul.

Jordan, W. (1980) *White Over Black*, New York: W. W. Norton.

Kant, I. (1948) *Groundwork to the Metaphysics of Morals* (trans. H. J. Paton), London: Hutchinson.

—— (1974) *Anthropology from A Pragmentic Point of View*, The Hague: Martin Nijhhof.

Keat, R. and Urry, J. (1982) *Social Theory as Science*, London: Routledge & Kegan Paul.

Keller Fox, E. (1984) *Reflections on Gender and Science*, New Haven: Yale University Press.

Kellerman, S. (1975) *The Body Speaks its Mind*, New York: Simon & Schuster.

—— (1979) *Living Your Dying*, New York: Random House.

Kellner, D. (1984) *Herbert Marcuse and the Crisis of Marxism*, London: Macmillan.

Kellner, D. and Bronner, S. (1989) *Critical Theory and Society*, New York: Routledge.

Kennedy, E. and Mendus, S. (1987) *Women in Western Political Philosophy*, Brighton: Harvester.

Kenny, A. (1968) *Descartes: A Study of His Philosophy*, New York: Random House.

—— (1973) *Wittgenstein*, Harmondsworth: Penguin.

—— (1984) *The Legacy of Wittgenstein*, Oxford: Blackwell.

Keohane, N. O., Rosaldo, M. Z. and Gelpi, B. (1982) *Feminist Theory*, Brighton: Harvester.

Kidel, M. (1988) *The Meaning of Illness*, London: Routledge.

Kimmel, M. (ed.) (1991) *Changing Men: New Directions in Research on Men and Morality*, New York: Sage.

Kittay, E. and Meyers, D. T. (1987) *Women and Moral Theory*, Totola, NJ: Rowman & Littlefield.

Kohlberg, L. (1981) *Essays on Moral Development*, New York: Harper & Row.

Kojeve, A. (1969) *Introduction to the Reading of Hegel*, New York: Basic Books.

Korsch, K. (1938) *Karl Marx*, London: Chapman Hall.

—— (1970) *Marxism and Philosophy*, London: New Left Books.

Kritzman, L. (1990) *Michel Foucault: Politics, Philosophy, Culture: Interviews and Other Writings*, New York: Routledge.

Kübler-Ross, E. (1970) *On Death And Dying*, London: Tavistock.

Laing, R. D. (1970) *The Divided Self*, Harmondsworth: Penguin.

—— (1972) *The Politics of the Family*, New York: Vintage.

—— (1985) *Wisdom, Madness and Folly: The Making of a Psychiatrist 1927–1957*, London: Macmillan.

Laing, R. D. and Esterson, R. (1970) *Sanity, Madness and the Family*, Harmondsworth: Penguin.

Laplanche, J. and Pontalis, J-B. (1967) *The Language Of Psycho-Analysis* (trans. J. D. Nicholson-Smith 1973), London: Hogarth.

Lash, S. (1990) *The Sociology of Postmodernism*, London: Routledge.

Lash, S. and Whimster, S. (eds) (1987) *Max Weber, Rationality and Modernity*, London: Unwin Hyman.

Levenson, E. (1983) *The Ambiguity Of Change: An Inquiry into the Nature of Psychoanalytic Reality*, New York: Basic Books.

Levy, P. (1981) *Moore: B. E. Moore And The Cambridge Apostles*, Oxford: Oxford University Press.

Libowitz, R. (1987) *Faith and Freedom: A Tribute to Franklin Littell*, Oxford: Pergamon Press.

Lichtheim, G. (1970) *Lukács*, New York: Random House.
Littell, F. (1973) *The Crucifixion of the Jews*, New York: Harper & Row.
Lloyd, G. (1984) *The Man Of Reason: 'Male' and 'Female' in Western Philosophy*, London: Methuen.
Loevinger, J. and Wessler, R. (1970) *Measuring Ego Development*, San Francisco: Jossey-Bass.
Lorde, A. (1989) *Sister Outsider: Essays and Sketches*, Trumansburg, NY, Crossing Press.
Lovejoy, E. O. (1936) *The Great Chain Of Being*, New York: Harper & Row.
Lowen, A. (1963) *Bioenergetics*, Harmondsworth: Penguin.
—— (1972) *The Betrayal of the Body*, New York: Collier Books.
Löwy, M. (1979) *Georg Lukács: From Romanticism to Bolshevism*, London: New Left Books.
Lukács, G. (1971) *History and Class Consciousness*, London: Merlin Books.
—— (1972) *Political Writings 1914–1929*, London, New Left Books.
—— (1982) *The Destruction Of Reason*, London: Merlin Books.
Lukes, S. (1983) *Emile Durkheim: His Life and Work*, London: Allen & Unwin.
—— (1985) *Marxism and Morality*, Oxford: Oxford University Press.
McCarthy, T. (1978) *The Critical Theory Of Jurgen Habermas*, Boston: MIT Press.
MacCormack, C. and Strathern, M. (1980) *Nature Culture and Gender*, Cambridge: Cambridge University Press.
McFarland, D. and Van Ness, W. (1988) *Simone Weil: Formative Writings 1924–41*, London: Routledge.
MacFarlane, A. (1979) *The Origins of English Individualism*, Oxford: Blackwell.
MacIntyre, A. (1981) *After Virtue*, London: Duckworth.
McLellan, D. (1980) *The Thought of Karl Marx*, London: Macmillan.
McLuhan, T. C. (1971) *Touch the Earth*, New York: Simon & Schuster.
MacPherson, C. B. (1962) *The Political Theory of Possessive Individualism*, Oxford: Oxford University Press.
Macey, D. (1988) *Lacan in Context*, London: Verso.
Macrae, D. (1977) *Max Weber*, London: Fontana.
Malcolm, J. (1984) *Freud's Archive*, London: Jonathan Cape.
Malcolm, N. (1958) *Ludwig Wittgenstein: A Memoir*, Oxford: Oxford University Press.
—— (1986) *Nothing Is Hidden*, Oxford: Blackwell.
Malcolm X (1968) *Autobiography*, Harmondsworth: Penguin.
Mannoni, O. (1991) *Freud*, New York: Random House.
Marcuse, H. (1970) *Negations*, London: Allen Lane.
—— (1986) *Reason and Revolution*, London: Routledge & Kegan Paul.
Martin, L., Gutman, H. and Hutton, P. (1988) *Technologies of the Self*, London: Tavistock.
Marx, K. (1968) *Capital*, London: Lawrence & Wishart.
Masson, J. (1984) *Freud: The Assault on Truth*, London: Faber & Faber.
—— (1986) *A Dark Science: Women, Sexuality and Psychiatry in the Nineteenth Century*, New York: Farra, Straus & Giroux.
—— (1989) *Against Therapy*, London: Fontana.
Memmi, A. (1967) *The Colonizers and the Colonized*, New York: Orion Press.
—— (1968) *Dominated Man*, Boston: Beacon Press.
Mendes, S. (1989) *Tolerance and the Limits of Liberalism*, London: Macmillan.
Merchant, C. (1980) *The Death of Nature: Women and the Scientific Revolution*, London: Wildwood.
Midgeley, M. (1983) *Animals and Why They Matter*, Harmondsworth: Penguin.
—— (1989) *Wisdom, Information and Wonder*, London: Routledge.
Midgeley, M. and Hughes, J. (1983) *Women's Choices: Philosophical Problems Facing Feminism*, London: Weidenfeld & Nicolson.

Miles, R. (1987) *Capitalism and Unfree Labour*, London: Tavistock.
Miles, R. and Phizacklea, A. (1984) *White Man's Country*, London: Pluto Press.
Mill, J. S. (1964) *On Liberty*, London: Everyman Library.
Miller, A. (1981) *The Drama of the Gifted Child*, New York: Basic Books.
—— (1983a) *For Your Own Good: Hidden Cruelty in Child-Rearing and the Roots of Violence*, London: Faber & Faber.
—— (1983b) *Prisoners of Childhood*, New York: Basic Books.
—— (1984) *Thou Shalt Not Be Aware: Society's Betrayal of the Child*, New York: Farmer, Straus & Giroux.
Miller, J. Baker (ed.) (1973) *Psychoanalysis and Women*, Harmondsworth: Penguin.
—— (1976) *Towards a New Psychology of Women*, Harmondsworth: Penguin.
Miller, R. (1984) *Analysing Marx Power and History*, Princeton: Princeton University Press.
Miller, S. (1983) *Men and Friendship*, London: Gateway.
Millet, K. (1969) *Sexual Politics*, London: Virago.
Mitchell, J. (1975) *Psychoanalysis and Feminism*, Harmondsworth: Penguin.
—— (1984) *Woman: The Longest Revolution*, London: Virago.
Mitchell, J. and Oakley, A. (eds) (1979) *The Rights and Wrongs of Women*, Harmondsworth: Penguin.
Moller Okin, S. (1980) *Women In Western Political Thought*, London: Virago.
Mommsen, W. (1974) *The Age Of Bureaucracy*, Oxford: Blackwell.
Monk, R. (1980) *Wittgenstein, London: Vintage Books.*
Moore B. (1959) *Philosophical Papers*, London: Allen & Unwin.
—— (1970) *A Critique of Pure Tolerance*, London: Jonathan Cape.
Morgan, D. (1992) *Discovering Men: Sociology and Masculinities*, London: Routledge.
Mulkay, M. (1984) *Science and the Sociology of Knowledge*, London: Allen & Unwin.
Murdoch, I. (1970) *The Sovereignty of Good*, London: Routledge.
Nardi, P. (ed.) (1992) *Men's Friendships*, New York: Sage.
Needham, J. (1969) *The Great Titration*, London: Unwin & Allen.
Nicholson, L. (1990) *Feminism/Postmodernism*, New York: Routledge.
Nicols, T. (ed.) (1980) *Capital and Labour*, London: Fontana.
Nielsen, K. and Patten, S. (1981) 'Marxism and Morality', *Canadian Journal of Philosophy*, Special issue, Vol. VII.
Nisbet, R. (1967) *The Sociological Tradition*, New York: Basic Books.
Nizan, P. (1960) *Aden Arabie*, Paris: Editions Maspero.
Noddings, N. (1984) *Caring: A Feminist Approach to Ethics and Moral Education*, Berkeley: University College Press.
Noonan, H. (1991) *Personal Identity*, London: Routledge.
Nozick, R. (1974) *Anarchy, States and Utopia*, New York: Basic Books.
Obholzer, K. (1982) *The Wolf-Man: Sixty Years Later*, London: Routledge & Kegan Paul.
O'Brien, M. (1981) *The Politics of Reproduction*, London: Routledge & Kegan Paul.
O'Neil, O. (1990) *Constructions of Reason*, Cambridge: Cambridge University Press.
Pagels, E. (1982) *The Gnostic Gospels*, Harmondsworth: Penguin.
Parkin, F. (1982) *Max Weber*, London: Tavistock.
Pattman, C. (1988) *The Sexual Contract*, Cambridge: Polity Press.
Pattman, C. and Gross, E. (1986) *Feminist Challenges*, Sydney: Allen & Unwin.
Pawson, R. (1989) *Measure For Measure*, London: Tavistock.
Pearce, F. (1989) *The Radical Durkheim*, London: Routledge.
Pitcher, G. (ed.) (1968) *Wittgenstein: The Philosophical Investigations*, London: Macmillan.
Plant, S. (1992) *The Most Radical Gesture*, London: Routledge.
Plummer, K. (1990) *Documents Of Life*, London: Routledge.
—— (1992) *Modern Homosexualities*, London: Routledge.
Poliakov, L. (1974) *The Aryan Myth*, London: Heinemann.

—— (1976) *History of Anti-Semitism, Vol. 3*, London: Routledge & Kegan Paul.
Porter, K. and Weeks, J. (1990) *Between The Acts*, London: Routledge.
Porter, R. (1981) *A History of Madness*, London: Routledge & Kegan Paul.
Poster, M. (1975) *Existential Marxism In Postwar France*, Princeton: Princeton University Press.
Rabinow, P. (ed.) (1988) *The Foucault Reader*, Harmondsworth: Penguin.
Rader, M. (1979) *Marx's Interpretation of History*, New York: Oxford University Press.
Rakusen, J. and Phillips, A. (eds) (1989) *The New Our Bodies Our Selves*, Harmondsworth: Penguin.
Ramazanoglu, C. (1989) *Feminism and the Contradictions of Oppression*, London: Routledge.
Rawls, J. (1972) *A Theory of Justice*, Oxford: Oxford University Press.
Rée, J. (1974) *Descartes*, London: Allen Lane.
Regan, T. (1988) *The Case For Animal Rights*, London: Routledge.
Reich, W. (1967) *Reich Speaks Of Freud*, New York: Farrar, Strauss & Giroux.
—— (1974a) *The Function Of The Orgasm*, Harmondsworth: Penguin.
—— (1974b) *The Sexual Revolution*, New York: Farrar, Strauss & Giroux.
Reiter, R. (ed.) (1975) *Towards An Anthropology of Women*, New York: MRP.
Rhees, R. (1970) *Discussions of Wittgenstein*, London: Routledge.
—— (1981) *Ludwig Wittgenstein: Personal Recollections*, Oxford: Blackwell.
Rieff, P. (ed.) (1963) *Dora: An Analysis of a Case of Hysteria*, New York: Collier Books.
—— (1965) *Freud: The Mind Of The Moralist*, London: Methuen.
Roberts, H. (ed.) (1981) *Doing Feminist Research*, London: Routledge.
—— (1991) *Women's Health Matters*, London: Tavistock.
Roper, M. and Tosh, J. (1990) *Manful Assertions*, London, Routledge.
Rorty, A. O. (1980) *Explaining Emotions*, Berkeley: University College Press.
Rorty, R. (1979) *Philosophy and the Mirror of Nature*, Princeton: Princeton University Press.
—— (1982) *Consequences of Pragmatism*, Brighton: Harvester.
—— (1988) *Contingency, Irony and Solidarity*, Cambridge: Cambridge University Press.
Rosaldo M. Z. and Lamphere, L. (eds) (1974) *Women, Culture, and Society*, Stanford: Stanford University Press.
Rose, G. (1981) *The Melancholy Science: An Introduction to the Thought of Theodor W. Adorno*, London: Macmillan.
Rose, N. (1991) *Governing the Soul*, London: Routledge.
Rowan, J. (1987) *The Horned God*, London: Routledge & Kegan Paul.
Rowbotham, S. (1973) *Woman's Consciousness, Man's World*, Harmondsworth: Penguin.
—— (1983) *Dreams and Dilemmas*, London: Virago.
Rowe, D. (1987) *Beyond Fear*, London: Fontana.
—— (1989) *The Constitution of Life and Death*, London: Fontana.
Rubin, L. (1976) *Worlds of Pain: Life in the Working-class Family*, New York: Basic Books.
Ruddick, S. (1990) *Maternal Thinking: Towards a New Politics of Peace*, London: The Women's Press.
Runciman, W. G. (1978) *Weber: Selections in Translation*, Oxford: Oxford University Press.
Russell, D. (1988) *The Machine Civilisation*, London: Pandora.
Rutherford, J. (ed.) (1990) *Identity: Community, Culture, Difference*, London: Lawrence & Wishart.
—— (1992) *Men's Silences*, London; Routledge.
Ryan, A. (1974) *J. S. Mill*, London: Routledge & Kegan Paul.
Said, E. (1991) *Orientalism: Western Conditions of the Orient*, Harmondsworth: Penguin.
Samuel, A. (1983) *The Father: Contemporary Jungian Perspectives*, London: Free Association Press.

Sandel, M. (1983) *Liberalism and the Limits of Justice*, Cambridge: Cambridge University Press.
Sartre, J-P. (1960) *Anti-Semite and Jew*, New York: Free Press.
Sayers, J. (1982) *Biological Politics*, London: Tavistock.
—— (1986) *Sexual Contradictions*, London: Tavistock.
—— (1991) *Mothering Psychoanalysis*, Harmondsworth: Penguin.
Schoolman, M. (1970) *The Imaginary Witness*, New York: Free Press.
School of Barbiana (1970) *Letter to a Teacher*, Harmondsworth: Penguin.
Scull, A. (1982) *Museum of Madness: The Social Organisation of Insanity in Nineteenth-Century England*, Harmondsworth: Penguin.
Sedgewick, P. (1982) *Psycho Politics*, London: Pluto Press.
Segal, B. (1986) *Love, Medicine and Miracles*, London: Arrow Books.
Segal, L. (1990) *Slow Motion: Changing Masculinities, Changing Men*, London: Virago.
Seidler, V. (1986) *Kant, Respect and Injustice: The Limits of Liberal Moral Theory*, London: Routledge.
—— (1989) *Rediscovering Masculinity, Reason, Language and Sexuality*, London: Routledge.
—— (1991a) *Recreating Sexual Politics: Men, Feminism and Politics*, London: Routledge.
—— (1991b) *The Moral Limits of Modernity: Love, Inequality and Oppression*, London: Macmillan.
—— (1991c) (ed.) *The Achilles Heel Reader*, London: Routledge.
—— (1992) (ed.) *Men, Sex and Relationships: Writings from Achilles Heel*, London: Routledge.
Sennett, R. and Cobb, J. (1970) *The Hidden Injuries of Class*, New York: Vintage Books.
Serge, V. (1972) *Year One of the Russian Revolution*, London: Allen Lane.
Sharaf, M. (1985) *Fury On Earth: A Biography Of Wilheim Reich*, London: Macmillan.
Sharrock, W. (1982) *The Ethnomethodologists*, Cambridge: Polity Press.
Sheldrake, R. (1981) *A New Science of Life*, London: Blond & Briggs.
—— (1988) *The Presence of the Past*, London: Collins.
Sheridan, A. (1980) *The Will to Truth*, London: Tavistock.
Sherman, J. and Beck, T. (eds) (1979) *The Prism of Sex: Essays in The Sociology of Knowledge*, Madison: University of Wisconsin Press.
Showalter, E. (1987) *The Female Malady; Women, Madness and English Culture 1830–1980*, London: Virago.
Shutz, A. (1972) *The Phenomenology of the Social World*, London: Heinemann.
Siltanen, J. and Stanworth, M. (1984) *Women in the Public Sphere*, London: Hutchinson.
Silverman, C. (1964) *Crisis in Black and White*, New York: Oxford University Press.
Silverman, D. (1985) *Qualitative Methodology in Sociology*, Aldershot, Hants: Gower.
Silverman, H. (1989) *Derrida and Deconstruction*, London: Routledge.
Simmel, G. (1980) *The Philosophy of Money*, London: Routledge.
Simmonds, A. P. (1978) *Karl Mannheim and the Sociology of Knowledge*, Oxford: Oxford University Press.
Smart, B. (1983) *Sociology, Phenomenology and Marxian Analysis*, London: Routledge & Kegan Paul.
—— (1991) *Modern Conditions, Postmodern Contradictions*, London: Routledge.
Smith, D. (1978) 'A peculiar eclipsing: woman's exclusion from man's culture, *Women's Studies International Quarterly*, 1, (4).
—— (1988) *The Everyday World as Problematic*, London: Routledge.
—— (ed.) (1992a) *Doing it the Hard Way*, London: Routledge.
—— (1992b) *Texts, Facts and Femininity*, London: Routledge.
Smith-Rosenberg, C. (1986) *Disorderly Conduct: Visions of Gender in Victorian America*, New York: Oxford University Press.

Bibliography 247

Snail, D. (1987) *Taking Care: An Alternative to Therapy*, London: Dent.
Spender, D. (1980) *Man Made Language*, London: Routledge & Kegan Paul.
Stammer, O. (ed.) (1971) *Max Weber and Sociology Today*, New York: Harper & Row.
Stanley, L. and Wise, S. (1983) *Breaking Out: Feminist Consciousness and Feminist Research*, London: Routledge & Kegan Paul.
Stephens, Ernest (1967) *The Black University in America Today: A Student Viewpoint*, Freedomways.
Sturrock, J. (1979) *Structuralism Since 1945*, Oxford: Oxford University Press.
Sydie, K. A. (1987) *Natural Women, Cultured Men*, Milton Keynes: Open University Press.
Tannen, D. (1991) *You Just Don't Understand*, London: Virago.
Tawney, R. (1926) *Religion and the Rise of Capitalism*, Harmondsworth: Penguin.
Taylor, C. (1978) *Hegel*, Cambridge: Cambridge University Press.
—— (1979) *Hegel and Modern Society*, Cambridge: Cambridge University Press.
—— (1985) *Philosophy and the Human Sciences*, Cambridge: Cambridge University Press.
—— (1990) *Sources of the Self*, Cambridge: Cambridge University Press.
Thomas, K. (1971) *Religion and the Decline of Magic*, Harmondsworth: Penguin.
Thompson, E. P. (1979) *The Poverty of Theory and Other Essays*, London: Merlin.
Thompson, K. (1982) *Emile Durkheim*, London: Tavistock.
Trebilcot, J. (1984) *Mothering: Essays in Feminist Theory*, Totowa: NJ: Romanman.
Turkle, S. (1979) *Psychoanalytic Politics: Freud's French Revolution*, London: Burnett/Andre Deutsch.
Turner, B. (1982) *Regulating Bodies*, London: Routledge & Kegan Paul.
—— (1984) *The Body and Society*, London: Routledge & Kegan Paul.
—— (1987) *Medical Power and Social Knowledge*, London: Routledge & Kegan Paul.
Turner, R. (1974) *Ethnomethodology*, Harmondsworth: Penguin.
Walker, P. (ed.) (1979) *Between Labour and Capital*, Brighton: Harvester.
Walzer, M. (1983) *Spheres of Justice*, New York: Basic Books.
Wandor, S. (1972) *The Body Politic*, London: Stage 1.
Warnock, M. (1960) *Ethics Since 1900*, Oxford: Oxford University Press.
Weber, M. (1930) *The Protestant Ethic and the Spirit of Capitalism*, London: Allen & Unwin.
—— (1949) *The Methodology of the Social Sciences*, New York: The Free Press.
—— (1964)*Theory of Social and Economic Organisations*, New York: The Free Press of Glencoe.
Weeks, J. (1977) *Coming Out: Homosexual Politics in Britain*, London: Quartet.
—— (1984) *Sexuality*, London: Horwood/Tavistock.
—— (1985) *Sexuality and its Discontents*, London: Routledge & Kegan Paul.
Weil, S. (1952) *Gravity and Grace*, London: Routledge & Kegan Paul.
—— (1958) *Oppression and Liberty*, London: Routledge & Kegan Paul.
—— (1959) *Waiting on God*, London: Fontana.
—— (1962) *Selected Essays 1934–1943* (ed.) R. Rees, Oxford: Oxford University Press.
—— (1978) *Lectures in Philosophy* (trans. H. Price), Cambridge: Cambridge University Press.
—— (1988) *The Need for Roots*, London: Routledge.
West, C. (1982) *Prophesy Deliverance*, Philadelphia: Westminster.
Whitehead, A. N. (1958) *Science and the Modern World*, Cambridge: Cambridge University Press.
Whitford, M. (ed.) (1991) *Between Feminism and Psychoanalysis*, London: Routledge.
Williams, B. (1978) *Descartes: The Project of Pure Enquiry*, Harmondsworth, Penguin.
—— (1973) *Problems of the Self*, Cambridge: Cambridge University Press.
—— (1981) *Moral Luck*, Cambridge: Cambridge University Press.
—— (1985) *Ethics and the Limits of Philosophy*, London: Fontana.

Williams, E. (1964) *Capitalism and Slavery*, London: Deutsch.

Winch, P. (1980) *Studies in the Philosophy of Wittgenstein*, London: Routledge & Kegan Paul.

—— (1989) *A Just Balance: Reflections on the Philosophy of Simone Weil*, Cambridge: Cambridge University Press.

Wittgenstein, L. (1958) *The Philosophical Investigations*, Oxford: Blackwell.

—— (1975) *On Certainty*, Oxford: Blackwell.

—— (1980) *Culture and Value*, Oxford: Blackwell.

Wolf, E. (1986) *Europe and the People Without History*, London: Faber.

Wood, A. (1981) *Karl Marx*, London: Routledge & Kegan Paul.

Woolfe, K. (1964) (ed.) *Essays on Sociology and Philosophy of Emile Durkheim*, New York: Harper & Row.

Young, I. (1990) *Justice and the Politics of Difference*, Princeton: Princeton University Press.

Young, R. (1990) *White Mythologies*, London: Routledge.

Zeitlin, I. (1968) *Ideology and the Development of Sociological Theory*, Englewood Cliffs, NJ: Prentice Hall.

Name index

Subject index

DATE DUE

NOV 29 '96			
MAR 1 '97			
JA 3 '00			
JY 15 '00			
NO 27 '00			
2-2-01			
2-52-01			
NO 24 '03			

GAYLORD   PRINTED IN U.S.A.